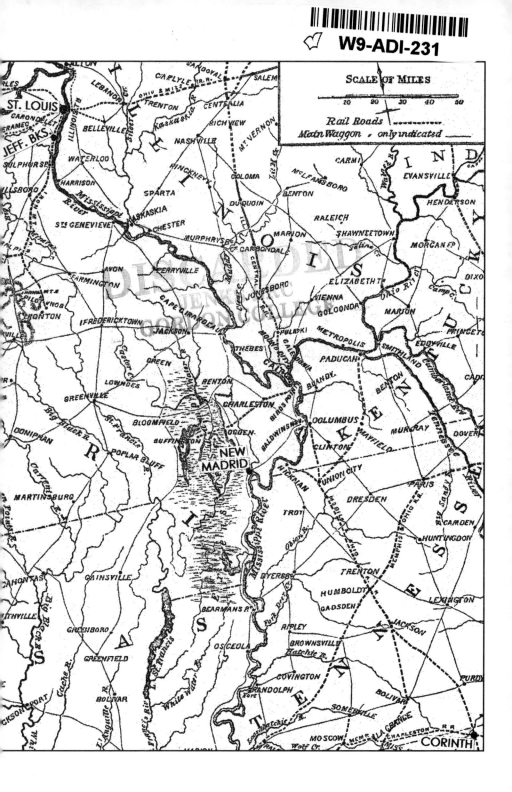

SCALE OF MILES

10 20 30 40 50

Rail Roads ....
Main Waggon - only indicated ____

— ABOUT THE AUTHOR —

Michael N. Ingrisano, Jr., a World War II combat veteran, spent his professional life in public affairs and research. Five years prior to his retirement, he served as the unofficial historian for the U.S. Customs Service's bicentennial producing numerous documents for internal distribution. He also served as technical advisor for the official bicentennial history written by Dr. Carl Prince. This is his first full-length publication. He is presently working on his WWII memoirs.

An Artilleryman's War

An Artilleryman's War

Gus Dey and the 2nd United States Artillery

by

Michael N. Ingrisano, Jr.

 WHITE MANE BOOKS

This White Mane Books publication
was printed by
Beidel Printing House, Inc.
63 West Burd Street
Shippensburg, PA 17257-0152 USA

In respect for the scholarship contained herein, the acid-free paper used in this book meets the guidelines for permanence and durability of the Committee on Production Guidelines for Book Longevity of the Council on Library Resources.

For a complete list of available publications
please write
White Mane Books
Division of White Mane Publishing Company, Inc.
P.O. Box 152
Shippensburg, PA 17257-0152 USA

Library of Congress Cataloging-in-Publication Data

Ingrisano, Michael N.
      An artilleryman's war : Gus Dey and the 2nd United States
   artillery / by Michael N. Ingrisano, Jr.
         p.   cm.
      Includes bibliographical references and index.
      ISBN 1-57249-101-9 (alk. paper)
      1. Dey, Gustavus Adolphus, 1828-1882. 2. United States. Army.
   Artillery, 2nd--Biography. 3. United States--History, Military--To
   1900. I. Title.
   U53.D48I54   1998
   358'.123'0973--dc21   98-13011
                                                                    CIP

Dedication

To Nancy Helen Day Ingrisano for her devotion to and love of family, and for her continuing search for family members and their roots. Her great grandfather, Gus Dey, would have been very proud of her.
I know I am.

Michael

Contents

Illustrations

Maps

Preface

●

The life of Gustavus Adolphus (Gus) Dey gives up its secrets grudg-ingly. Undoubtedly, his military exploits were discussed in his family circle. What little that was passed down through family oral history is a mingling of fact, fiction and presumption. As far as can be determined, Elmer Day, Gus' grandson, was the first member of the family to seek documented history of his grandfather's military service. In his March 30, 1938 letter to the War Department, Elmer expressed his desire to "acquire complete data of the war records of my grandfather who I un-derstand was in the Union Army during the Rebellion 1861–1865." The letter continued with Elmer detailing what he knew or had heard about Gus Dey. He noted that his grandfather was interred in the cemetery in Fredonia, New York, and that the headstone was marked with the in-scription "Lt. G. A. DEY, CO F U. S. ART." And according to the cem-etery records, the person buried in that plot was "Augustus D. Dey, Born Dec. 24, 1828—Died Feb. 14, 1882."

On April 8, 1938, the Adjutant General's Office (AGO), Washing-ton, D.C. notified Elmer that nothing "has been found to indicate that G. A. Dey or Augustus D. Dey rendered any military service. However, the records do show a <u>Gustav</u> Dey, who was born in Koenigsberg [sic], Prussia served as a private, sergeant, corporal, and 1st sergeant, Bat-teries I and F, 2nd Artillery from December 18, 1854 to November 26, 1863. He was appointed 2nd Lieutenant, 2nd Artillery October 31, 1863; accepted November 29, 1863; was promoted to 1st Lieutenant, June 15, 1864; and was dismissed October 6, 1865." The record did not indicate "parentage or the correct date of birth of Lieutenant Dey, however at the time of original enlistment...he gave his age as 27."

Some thirty-odd years later at a family meeting on Thanksgiving Day, 1971, Nancy Day, Gus' great-granddaughter, taped comments by her aunt, Edna Day Patty, Elmer's sister. Most of this data is again a mixture of fact, fiction or presumption. For example, it was a fact that the "1880 census showed that he [Gus] suffered from a disease of the lungs." But Edna falsely assumed that Gus' middle name was David, "as that was his son's middle name." And he "was said to have his own horse while in the Army." As a high-ranking, non-commissioned officer and then as a commissioned officer he would have been issued a mount. In the taping, however, it was suggested that Gus had served in the cavalry. "It was also said that he was 'busted' frequently while in the Army as he went out and celebrated a lot." The AGO's answer to Elmer did not include enough details to lead one to conclude that Dey was "busted frequently." It infers the possibility that he was "busted" once in listing his grade from sergeant to corporal.

It was not until 1973 that Nancy Day researched Dey's records at the National Archives in Washington, D.C. while preparing a genealogical history of the family. Knowing that Gus had immigrated from Prussia, she viewed the microfilms of ship arrivals in the 1850s. This proved to be a fruitless search, and this information still remains one of the secrets of Gus' life. When Nancy requested Gus' pension files, she feared that it would disclose little about him. To her surprise the file was quite bulky; and to her dismay, she discovered that First Lieutenant Gustav Dey had never been honorably discharged from the army but had been dismissed and dropped from the rolls for being absent without leave. In one document, she found that he had been charged with desertion. This information had never been part of the family lore. But then in viewing Dey's A. C. P. file (Appointment, Commission, & Personal), she found his application for appointment as a second lieutenant and the accompanying affidavits by his immediate commanding officer and others up the chain of command of the XVI Army Corps, and his subsequent appointment and promotion to first lieutenant. She read of his bravery at the battles of Wilson's Creek, and Corinth, about the wounds he suffered at Corinth, and again about his ignominious dismissal from the service. She discontinued this line of research simply because she had little or no interest in or knowledge of the military.

Using Nancy's findings as a springboard, I continued the research in 1990, redirecting the effort more toward Dey's military career. At the Archives, I viewed a wealth of information both on microfilm and in original documents. I traced his military record from his first enlistment through to his dismissal. The search took me into muster rolls, returns, special and general orders, regimental histories, descriptive books of recruits and recruiting returns, letters received and sent, pension files and many other like documents which referenced Companies I, F, E, and C of the 2nd Artillery regiment in which he served. I also recorded the histories of many of the men with whom he served during his eleven-year military career. The more I read of his exploits, the more I came to admire this immigrant who honorably served his adopted country in both peace and war.

Then in late November 1992, I underwent a quadruple heart bypass. The experience of this life-saving, life-threatening operation enabled me to view my research from that critical perspective. I had seen combat in World War II as an air crew member in the troop carrier command. We dropped paratroopers and carried gliders into Normandy, Holland, and Germany. I came out of the conflict physically unscathed. But the heart operation pushed me closer to the brink than had all my combat hours.

During recovery, I experienced an unforgettable fantasy in which I saw myself standing at a grave site in Forest Hill Cemetery in Fredonia, New York. It was a cold, overcast February 16, 1882, the day that Lieutenant Gustav Dey was buried. He had died on February 14 in Dunkirk, New York, after suffering, almost since his return from the army in September 1865, from a life-draining hemorrhaging of his left lung.

His fatal illness may have been caused by the wound on his left side from a shell fragment during the battle of Corinth, Mississippi on October 4, 1862. That wound and one to his left hand had been treated by a surgeon from a volunteer unit, and had never been officially recorded except in Battery F records. The wounds were so painful that Gus was unable to mount his horse, and rode in the battery ambulance during the pursuit of the Confederate forces. Or his physical condition may have resulted from the poor food, severe exposure, excessive heat, and cold and just plain hard work during eleven years of campaigning in Florida, Virginia, Kansas, and Arkansas in the pre-Civil War period, and in Missouri, Mississippi, Tennessee, Alabama, and Virginia during the war.

On that afternoon in February, I watched as the solemn cortege wound its way toward the open grave. I thought it odd that Gus was being buried without military honors. I was still there when I noticed that a government issue tombstone, like those at the National Cemetery in Arlington, Virginia, had been placed at the head of the grave. It bore the inscription in two lines: "1st LT. G. A. DEY/ CO F, 2D US ART." Implanted just to the right of the stone was a metal plate, approximately two and one-half feet long, topped with a five-pointed star, which bore the legend in an inner wreath: GAR Post 393, NY." [I later learned that Lt. Day was carried on the rolls of the Williams O. Stevens Post, Dunkirk, New York.]

The fantasy changed to realism when I visited the cemetery in September 1993, almost a year after my operation. Sometime during the previous one hundred years, a fertile seed had fallen near the headstone. It was now a fully grown evergreen tree. The headstone was imbedded in the root system, half-buried, slightly tilted to the left with the inscription still fully legible. The GAR spike too was so deeply caught in the root system that it was impossible to pry it loose or even to wriggle it slightly.

Having fantasized Gus' last moments, and having myself been to the brink of joining him, I became more resolute in my efforts to complete this memorial to him. His story needs to be told because so little has been written about Gus and those other regulars who served so gallantly in that critical period of our country's history. And Gustavus Adolphus Dey, an almost ideally physically dimensioned prototype of the artilleryman (and incidentally also of the average soldier, North or South, in the war), was also the perfect example of how a soldier should serve his battery, regiment, and country. From Florida in 1855 to Camp Barry, Washington, D.C. in 1865, from private to first lieutenant, he personified the spirit of the military forces in his "coolness, bravery and good judgment."

But again Dey's life does indeed give up its secrets reluctantly, making this study both rewarding and frustrating. It was rewarding in that so much official material was available or made available from many sources. It was also frustrating for several reasons, the first of which was the inability to uncover every written word pertinent to his life and times from the letters, diaries, and other personal experiences of the men who knew and served with him and others who were in the same battles as Battery F. The second frustration stems from Gus himself for the secrets he did not leave behind for those who believe in him, who want to understand him, and want to flesh him out of the coldly reported official files.

Although he occasionally misstated or provided meager factual data about himself, he was not totally to blame. The Dey family lore has it that much of his memorabilia and personal papers were packed into a trunk and subsequently lost somewhere in Buffalo, New York. His sword can well be rusting in the wall of a house at 181 Keystone Street. His grandson, Edward, Nancy's father, lived there as a youth, and it is said was forbidden to play with his grandfather's sword.

Be that as it may, many of the answers which he took to the grave rest with him now and forever. But the same can be said about the many officers and enlisted men who were responsible for recording information on muster rolls, returns, and other official documents, both in the field and at regimental headquarters. What remains are those facts which can be overlain with speculation in reconstructing a reasonably intelligent picture of who this individual really was, what he was like, and how he fit into the military environment which was so much a part of his life.

When he came from Prussia, he settled in Dunkirk, New York. One person viewed him as an intelligent, literate individual who was educated in Europe, and served as an officer in the Prussian Army. This has never been verified. He boarded in the home of another German immigrant and supposedly worked on the suspension bridge which was built in the 1850s at Niagara Falls as a link for the Canadian and United States Railways. The two-level bridge, designed by John A. Roebling, was completed in 1856.

Then sometime in late 1854, Dey went to Whitehall Street in New York City to enlist in the United States Army, even though the army regularly held recruitment rendezvous in the Buffalo area. Why did he not enlist in Buffalo, which was approximately fifty miles northeast of Dunkirk? Possibly, recruitment in that area was not the type he preferred, that is, infantry versus artillery. Speculation has it that he had family in New York, but his subsequent actions negate that theory. There is no evidence that he again visited New York City, unless he stopped there en route to Dunkirk after he left the service in June–July 1865. Another possibility is that he heard that the army was recruiting for artillerymen in New York, and that that branch was more compatible with his former military background. (This assumes that Gus had been an artilleryman in the Prussian Army!) That theory, too, does not carry weight since the recruiting officer was First Lieutenant Richard Brooke Garnett of the 6th Infantry.

Dey's enlistment papers reveal other puzzles. He gave his age as being 27. He was born on December 24, 1828, and he enlisted on December 18, 1854, making him just under 26 years old. He listed his occupation as "Farmer." There is no evidence to substantiate that claim. Again, it can be supposed that as a former officer in the Prussian Army, he may have left his country to escape the revolutions which were ravaging Europe in the late1840s, and would want to disguise his former occupation as a soldier by declaring himself a farmer.

The theory of former military service may have some credence. Dey moved up relatively fast in the ranks. By December 1856, he was made a corporal; and by June 1857, he had his sergeant's stripes. Promotions in the regular army did not come easily or quickly for either enlisted men or for officers. The individual who held a rank previously had either to move up, be discharged, be demoted for cause or step down voluntarily, or die, thereby creating a vacancy which could be filled.

Dey's early record with Company I on station in southern Florida indicated that he was a good soldier who never reported for sick call, even though, at one time, almost fifty percent of the enlisted men in the company were absent from duty because of illness or disease. Yet in April 1857, when the company moved from Florida to Virginia, Dey went on sick call twice for "contusio[ns]." Did he get too close to a recoiling artillery piece, or was he in a barracks brawl? There is one puzzling notation in the records that he was "in arrest." But there is no explanation for that or why it was put into his records. Nor is there any evidence that he was disciplined or placed under arrest. He still had his stripes.

Sergeant Dey joined Company F in September 1857. In late November, he was stripped of his stripes and bucked down to private. Here again the record reveals nothing of the reason for his demotion. He and twelve privates were subjected to a General Garrison Court-martial. But a comprehensive search of the records revealed no details, again denying us some insight into the man's character and actions. Then in June 1859, while still on station in Kansas, Dey reported to sick call for "furunculus" (or boils, sometimes caused by anemia, undernourishment, or overtiredness). He remained in the post hospital for a week. But it was the last time that he ever reported for sick call.

There are two possibilities for this latter attitude. He may not have liked army hospitals; or he did not want to be termed a "beat on the government." (A term derived from Josh Billings, *Hardtack and Coffee*, Bowie: Heritage Press, a facsimile copy, 1990, p. 174. In World War II, the term was "goldbricking.") Whatever his attitude, his reluctance to seek official military care cost him dearly when he applied for a disability pension for his wounds.

His arithmetic again failed him when he reenlisted for five years in October 1859. He stated his age as 32, again over one year off the mark. But, again, he was consistent!

Another series of unanswered questions crop up during the Civil War, particularly after the battle of Corinth, Mississippi in October 1862. In one action, Gus was wounded twice, in his left hand and left side. By his own account, he was treated in the field by a medical officer from a volunteer unit. The treatment was never officially recorded. Was he again disdainful of medical treatment or was he afraid that he might suffer the fate of so many soldiers who had limbs amputated? Amputation was a common solution because of the fear of gangrene in an open wound. Or was Gus being a good soldier by not leaving his battery? He later recalled that he was unable to mount his horse because of his wounds, yet, he rode (ironically) in the company ambulance during the pursuit of the retreating Confederates.

Shortly after suffering these wounds, Gus stepped down as the company's first sergeant. Neither he nor the company's records offer any answers for this action. Was he incapable, because of his wounds, of fulfilling his duties as first sergeant? Or was it because the company's command had just been assumed by an officer under whom Dey served in Florida and at Fort Monroe, Virginia, while he was with Company I? Why had he transferred or been transferred out of Company I then? And why had the record shown him as "in arrest" then? Was the disciplinary action cause for the transfer to Company F, which was heading for duty in the West where the Kansas border wars were heating up, and where the army was moving against the Mormons in Salt Lake City, while Company I remained in the relative safety of Fort Monroe? Or did he seek the change as a chance for advancement? Or were his talents as an artilleryman more useful for duty in the field?

After he received his commission, his fortunes seemed to go downhill. Company F's commanding officer wanted him to stay with the company because there were no other officers present and because Dey certainly knew the men in the command. But he was ordered to Company E, which soon joined the Army of the Potomac. Ironically, again, this decision may have saved his life. First Sergeant John Pratt, who succeeded Dey in Company F, was killed by lightning on the Chattahoochee River, Georgia, during the Atlanta campaign in 1864. Lieutenant Albert Murray, who wanted Dey to stay with the company, was captured at Atlanta on July 22, 1864, and died in a prison camp. First Lieutenant Joseph Cabell Breckinridge, second in command (and Dey's replacement), and many of Dey's former comrades were also taken prisoner, were wounded, or killed in this same action.

Incidentally, when Second Lieutenant Dey acknowledged the receipt of his wall commission, he now misstated his age by almost five years! So much for consistency!

But the next action is truly puzzling. First Lieutenant Dey was court-martialed for failing to appear as a member of the board trying two of his people for AWOL (Absent Without Leave). Dey was commanding Company C at that time. For his punishment, he was denied any promotions for six months. He surely must have known the regulations. His action cannot be documented and is unexplainable. He simply absented himself. Did he think that because he commanded the company, he did not need approval to leave his unit and the post? Or was he reluctant to sit in judgment of his enlisted men since he was also a ranker, that is, came up through the ranks?

Then on June 6, 1865, Dey was arrested for riding his horse in Washington, D.C. while intoxicated. He resisted arrest, possibly because of his drunken state. But the arresting officer, a cavalry sergeant in a volunteer unit, also attested that Dey refused to accept arrest or to show his pass to a non-commissioned officer because he, Dey, was an officer in the regular army. This was a very strange attitude, again by a ranker, who should have known that doing one's duty was neither insubordination nor impertinence. And Dey may have been reflecting the friction which sometimes existed between regular army men and volunteers. Yet, Dey may have by then developed a none-too-uncommon attitude that his rating placed him in the elite officer hierarchy. As an enlisted man, he had watched his own officers acting in a similar fashion.

Three weeks after this last incident, First Lieutenant Dey walked out of Camp Barry, and simply disappeared. He was reported as "absent without leave." Then on October 6, 1865, by presidential order, he was dropped from the rolls of the United States Army.

Why did he leave his command without authorization and throw away eleven years of hard work? He may have sensed the aura around Washington of troops being demobilized and wanting to go home. After all, he had not seen his adopted home town since 1854 when he enlisted. Or was he following the tradition that officers were free to absent themselves without orders and without reprisal for their actions? Had not Gibson, Totten, Darling, and Molinard, his former commanding officers, done the same thing? Was he bitter about the court-martial which denied him promotion for six months? But those six months were almost over. His sentence was effective as of January 19, 1865. Did he know that there were no vacancies on the horizon and that he was still junior in rank? Or was he just worn out and reluctant to face the rigors of another campaign in posts unknown? He was stationed near regimental headquarters, which were at Fort McHenry, Maryland. Surely word had already been received of the regiment's orders for its transfer to California. Perhaps he was just tired of army life and did not want to face the trauma of being declared "too old for the field" as he had seen happen with some of his comrades. Perhaps, he still felt the wounds from Corinth. For whatever unknown reason, First Lieutenant Dey walked away from a career that had spanned eleven years in the prime of his life.

Nothing is known of his whereabouts from June 30, 1865 until he appeared in Dunkirk, New York some time in mid-September. It does not seem possible that it would take him almost three months to travel from Washington to his final destination, unless he stopped somewhere in between. But there is no evidence to verify that assumption.

From mid-September until his death in February 1882 some of the pieces of his life come together. Most of the information, from affidavits given by friends while his wife attempted to get a pension, reflects what Dey told his testifiers and friends. They believed that he had been discharged from the army, possibly by an order issued by the president mustering out all the volunteer Union Army veterans. There is no evidence that this was true in Dey's case. Nor is there any evidence that he requested a discharge for personal reasons or because of his illness.

All his friends believed that Dey came home a very sick person. He alleged that his illness began a year before he left the service. Possibly it began during the Wilderness campaign in May 1864 when torrential rains temporarily halted all operations. Dey was exposed to those climatic conditions. Or he could have had a latent lung condition from exposure in Florida or in any of the hard campaigns in the west. Or the wound to his chest may have done more damage than he was willing to admit. Or was it a combination of both? Unfortunately, he could not prove that his illness was service connected. Again his disdain for official medical treatment was self-defeating. He told his wife that he had paid a civilian doctor in Washington for treatment. But he never supplied proof of that treatment.

Some of his testifiers mentioned his wounds at Corinth. But Dey himself had trouble authenticating a fact that physically showed on his hand and chest. He could not remember the names of comrades who might have corroborated his story. Only two, William Wrightenburg and Robert Belt mention him by name. And as far as can be determined from the pension files which have been reviewed, none of his comrades sought him out for testimony. They probably did not know how to contact him. He did mention Lieutenant Murray, whom he knew died in Georgia, and Lieutenant Charles Green, who commanded the company for a short time but who had not been with the company at Corinth. It is strange that he could not remember Captain Thomas Maurice, who commanded the company during that battle. As a matter of fact, Maurice had written Dey's citation for bravery, a citation which stated that although he was wounded, Sergeant Dey stood by his guns for an hour until the Confederates retreated. And Maurice after the war joined and served with the 2nd U.S. Artillery until his death in 1885.

As an old soldier, Dey must have surely known that his inquiries should have gone to the regiment's headquarters where all official records were kept. Perhaps, he was too ill to remember. Or was he afraid to disclose his location for fear of apprehension? He received a pension of $2.00 per month for his two wounds from the pension office in Syracuse, New York. Significantly, that pension had an effective date of October 7, 1865, one day after Dey was dropped from the rolls. The documentation for this action is so flimsy that it is impossible to imagine how or why he received a pension without supplying proof of an honorable discharge. He continued to receive that pension until his death. Perhaps the error resulted from a bureaucratic snarl.

Finally, there was Gus' almost fetish-like loyalty to his old company. He must have spoken about the company to his friends in Dunkirk. Some alluded erroneously in their testimonies that he had enlisted in Company F in 1854. Perhaps, Gus thought it was not necessary to bother with minute details when he spoke with civilians about his military life. They probably never knew that he had served with I, F, E, and C, and that he had been commanding officer of Company C. Regardless, the symbol of that loyalty is embedded on his tombstone.

This search for answers is not meant in any way to demean the image of Gus Dey. He was a good soldier, and his record, needing no embellishments, stands by itself. Had he had the physical well-being and stamina to pursue the truth of his status with the army late in his career, he would have been able to exonerate himself of the charges against him. Failing that he could also have been able to appeal to Congress for relief. Some of his comrades who deserted did appeal successfully. Gus Dey died before he could fire this final salvo. So it remains for us, the living, to dedicate this memorial to a soldier who deserves to be given a posthumous honorable discharge, and to be "released from Arrest and Resume his Sword."

****

Many people helped and offered encouragement during the preparation of this study. Most important was and is Nancy Day Ingrisano, who not only was the initial investigator but who continues to add thoughts and support to the effort.

Nancy's cousin, Christine Day, also worked diligently and contributed much information on the family's genealogy.

Hugh Horton, retired postman and local historian at Corinth, Mississippi, was extremely helpful. Nancy and I visited Corinth in May 1990. Hugh was prepared for our visit. Not only did he walk with us over the battlefield and the entire battle area, he pinpointed the exact location where Sergeant Dey planted his section of guns. From his studies of the battle, Hugh was convinced that Gus suffered his wounds where his guns were firing just to the left or west of Battery Robinett during the final charge by the Confederates on that position. He also showed us where Company F's other two sections were positioned on the field near Battery Williams.

During this same odyssey, we visited the site of the battle of Wilson's Creek, near Springfield, Missouri. There, Richard Hatcher, then the National Park Service historian, spent hours with us walking that battlefield. On "Bloody Hill," we stood where Company F (Totten's Battery, commanded by Captain James Totten) repelled charge after charge by the Confederates before retiring from the field on August 10, 1861. The National Park Service staff there generously allowed us the use of their extensive library for the few days we were in Springfield.

Major Scott Price, U.S. Army, a Civil War scholar, author and reenactor, kindly lent a hand in this continuing search for data. In addition to encouraging me in my task, he sent me the official reports of the surrender and evacuation of Little Rock Arsenal by Captain Totten and his command in February 1861.

The personnel at the Missouri State Historical Society in Columbia, Missouri not only outdid themselves trying to find material, but they continued to be a ready source of other information which they sent promptly. And the local staff at the Fairfax County, Virginia Public Library, Dolley Madison Branch in McLean responded admirably to all my requests.

Glenn Longacre, Ohio Historical Society, Columbus, Ohio, supplied copious amounts of material on Major General John Wallace Fuller and his Ohio brigade. Gus and Company F were brigaded with the Fuller's command for much of the Trans-Mississippi campaign. It was General, then Colonel, Fuller who wrote an outstanding recommendation when Gus applied for a commission in 1863. It was also Fuller who continued to support the company as if it were one of his own volunteer units.

My unqualified thanks to the staff at the National Archives in Washington, D.C., particularly Mike Musick, Bill Lind, now retired, and Mike Meier. Without their personal attention, guidance, advice, and the wealth of material preserved in their files, both hard copy and microfilms, this study would have been impossible to complete. Mike Musick dug out a previously unpublished paper by Major General William Rosecrans wherein the general cited many individuals for meritorious service during the battles of Iuka and Corinth in September and October 1862. Gus was commended in that paper as First Sergeant, Company F, 2nd U.S. Artillery, "for gallantry and coolness...though wounded by a shell." The special paper is reproduced in its entirety as an appendix to this study. Bill Lind also took me into the stacks when we tried to find, unsuccessfully, the papers on Gus' garrison court-martial in 1858.

To the historians at Fort Leavenworth, and the Leavenworth and Lecompton, Kansas, historical societies, my special thanks for their help and wealth of material they supplied. These organizations provided history for the pre-war period when Gus and the company acted as a *posse comitatus* to protect the civil authorities during the struggle for "bloody Kansas" in the late 1850s.

John H. Johnston III kindly loaned me a photo of the Planters Hotel in Leavenworth, Kansas, for use in this study. And the staff of the Kansas State Historical Society responded rapidly to the request for the use of one of its controlled illustrations. The staff at the Fort Scott, Kansas, Historical site also provided some insightful material from this same historical era.

Fran Isbell, David Mycue, Bill Forrester, and Maria O. Leach from three different entities, the Hidalgo County Historical Society, the Hidalgo County Historical Museum, and the Hidalgo County Historical Commission of Edinburg, Texas, responded enthusiastically when I sought information about Richard A. Marsh, alias Robert Belt, who served with Gus and may have been one of his gun crew. Each contributed information or photos which are also part of this study.

Through Jeff Patrick, National Park Service, Wilson's Creek, I was able to contact Michael MacNamara from County Limerick, Ireland. Michael was seeking information about his great-grandfather, Peter Cavanagh. We exchanged much information which has found its way into this text. I am grateful for his help. I hope I likewise have satisfied some of his curiosity about Company F.

Ann and Bill Prosser, our neighbors, spent their free time digging out material on the Wisconsin volunteers, while Bill served on the faculty at the University at Madison. Not only did they find some data for me, but Bill who is more than just an amateur photographer, used his expertise to enhance some of the photos for the study. Good neighbors! Thanks!

My brother, Dr. Louis Ingrisano, helped to decipher some of the medical terms relative to Gus' illnesses in his pre-war service.

Ben Maryniak, president of the Civil War Round Table, Buffalo, New York, reenactor and scholar of the war, read my first manuscript. He was kind in his criticism. Then he suggested that I look into some pension files of Gus' comrades. The task required reeling through countless microfilm indices at the National Archives, until I realized that there were other indices broken down by organization. I was fortunate to uncover and view about one hundred files. I concentrated on those which were pertinent to their war experiences. I found only two references to *Day*, but I also found other material which fleshed out some of the skeletal scenes I had described in the first manuscript. I also found a photo of Albert Wachsman, and surprised the archivists when I requested a copy for the book. Normally, I was told, such items just disappear. What I have not included are the many stories which I culled from the widows' claims, and the stories about some of these women. But that is a tale for another day. I thank Ben for his insight and for what he has added to my knowledge.

The bibliography, from which much of the background was digested, is indicative of my thanks to the many scholars who devoted their time to this entire era.

Bill Birdseye has done a remarkable job editing my scruffy manuscript. He has given me guidance which has allowed me to focus on the real subject of this study. I am most grateful for that assistance.

Although this is a memorial to Gus Dey, it is also a reminder that he did not succeed or fail on his own. He was a member of that unique body of regular soldiers, enlisted men and officers, of the 2nd U.S. Artillery Regiment, who for whatever their personal reasons served our country, as did Gus, when it needed them most. Short biographical sketches of Gus' comrades in Company I and Company F are included in a separate appendix. The more comprehensive descriptions, of the men from Company F, reflect the wealth of material found in their pension files.

I hope all of them will consider this a job well done, and that these names will be read by others who are yet curious about their own dead but still remembered heroes.

Michael N. Ingrisano, Jr.

Chapter 1

Florida: A Troubled Land

The struggle between the Indians and white men in Florida over land for settlement and agricultural development lasted for almost three and one-half centuries. During this long-lasting conflict, the Indian population, which originally may have numbered 100,000, was decimated by annihilation, slavery, and sickness from disease introduced by the white.

As early as 1513, Indians, claiming the land by right of occupancy, tried violently to discourage Ponce de Leon, the Spanish discoverer of Florida, from landing on their shores. Then in 1523, when he returned to colonize the land with people, animals, and farm equipment, he was attacked by Indians, and fatally wounded, and the Spaniards were forced to abandon the project.

Indian tribes continued their warfare over the years against the Spanish, French, and English invaders, and the Seminoles' first encounter with the American military occurred in late 1812, early 1813, when federal troops with support from Georgia and Tennessee militiamen invaded Florida. In a three-week campaign, these troops burned houses, destroyed or consumed many bushels of corn, captured horses and herds of cattle, destroyed deerskins (the Seminoles' trading material), killed twenty of their number, and captured nine Seminoles and their black slaves. (Certain aspects of this initial encounter would characterize the conflict between the two races until the end of the third Seminole war in 1858. The tribesmen quickly detected the approach of their white adversaries. They would then abandon their homes, herds, and crops and seek safety in the nearby swamps and hummocks. The whites would destroy the Indians' properties, but because of their unfamiliarity with the terrain, they seldom found any Seminoles, unless other captured Indians or blacks led them to the Seminoles' hiding places.)

1

When the United States acquired Florida from Spain in 1821, it also acquired the guardianship of an estimated 5,000 Seminoles. From the very outset, federal authorities considered the Seminoles, living near white settlements, a problem. As a solution the federal government planned to relocate the Seminoles either in Alabama or west of the Mississippi River. In 1824, President James Monroe, under pressure from white settlers, recommended that the Seminoles be removed from Florida or placed on a reservation in the state. Because tribal relocation to the West had not been fully explored by the government, the latter option was adopted. The planned reservation was to be located in an area between present-day Fort Myers and Sarasota. In return for accepting this decision and for turning over twenty-four million acres of land which the government planned to sell for $1.25 per acre, the Seminoles were given moving expenses, an annuity of $5,000 for five years, food for a year, payment for improvements left behind in northern Florida, and several other recompenses. The government also established Fort Brooke, a military post, near Tampa Bay. The post was manned by four companies of the 4th U.S. Infantry, which served as a sub-agency for various needs of the Seminoles. The reservation system was not a satisfactory solution, however.

Soon after his succession to the presidency, Andrew Jackson was determined to relocate all the Indians from the East to west of the Mississippi River into the present-day areas of Kansas, Arkansas, and Oklahoma. Through the passage of the Indian Removal Act of 1830, he managed to accomplish almost total relocation, except for those Indians who eluded their captors. Among those who escaped were many Seminoles who hid themselves in familiar haunts. These escapees eventually forced the government into a war which lasted from 1835 to 1842. Known as the Second Seminole War, it cost the government and white settlers an estimated 30 to 40 million dollars, and the deaths of some 1,500 regular soldiers, 55 militiamen, and nearly 100 civilians from battle, disease, and accidents.

As they had done in 1812–1813, the Seminoles used their hit-and-run strategy, disappearing into swamps, hummocks, forests, and lowlands, where they evaded the roving search-and-destroy patrols. Not only were the regulars unfamiliar with the terrain, but they had had virtually no field training on how to react to the Seminoles' guerrilla-like tactics. As a result, 800 warriors were able to stymie the efforts of some 5,000 regulars and militiamen. During this period, the average aggregate strength of the regular army was 8,800, which means that over half of the regular army was engaged in this war. Futilely engaged, even an army experiment using bloodhounds as trackers proved to be a total failure.

After seven years of war against overwhelming odds, some bands of the Seminoles who suffered from lack of food and clothing were forced to surrender. Other bands were so persistent in their refusal to relocate that President John Tyler realized that total removal was impossible. Of its total population of 5,000 in 1835, 4,020 were sent west to Indian territory. In 1842 among the 600 who still survived in Florida was Halpatter Mico, known as Billy Bowlegs, a member of the so-called Seminole ruling class and leader of a large band which had not been aggressively active during the war. By 1849, four years after Florida achieved statehood, he and most of the Seminoles lived within a 6,700-square mile reserve in the Big Cypress Swamp, and south of the Caloosahatchee River.

The military force, which had decreased considerably during this relatively quiet period, was again increased to 1,400 regulars because of isolated incidents by a few Seminoles. The strong military presence was one part of a threefold plan to remove all the Seminoles. The other parts included large financial payouts to tribe members and the use of a delegation of Seminoles who were brought east to persuade the remaining Seminoles to relocate. Despite this latter effort, the Seminoles, under Billy Bowlegs, refused to leave Florida. In August 1854, Secretary of War Jefferson Davis decided on a program which would force the Seminoles to resist, to thereby force a final encounter. His plan included the imposition of a trade embargo, the survey and sale of lands in southern Florida, and again an increased military presence to protect white settlers. He also stipulated that if the Seminoles did not voluntarily present themselves for removal, he would order the military to use force.

The strength of the army had steadily decreased from a high of 47,000 in 1847 because of the war with Mexico to just under 10,000 in 1854. Secretary Davis persuaded Congress to increase the army to 18,000 in 1855 because the new territorial accessions in the west and southwest required more military patrols. To implement the secretary's plans for resolving the Seminole problem and for manning more patrols in the west, the army conducted recruiting rendezvous in Boston, Buffalo, Albany, and New York City. One of the men who enlisted at Whitehall Street in New York was Gustavus Adolphus (Gus) Dey. He was recruited by First Lieutenant Richard Brooke Garnett, 6th Infantry Regiment, into the United States Army on December 18, 1854.[1]

Private Dey—gray eyes, brown hair, a fair complexion, standing five feet, eight and one-quarter inches tall—was "entirely sober when he enlisted." His enlistment papers also note that he was "27 years old." Actually, he was just shy of his twenty-sixth birthday, having been born on December 24, 1828 in Konigsburg, Prussia. He was one of forty civilians who were brought in from various recruiting stations and placed in a pool (General Department) at Fort Columbus, Governor's Island, New York harbor, where theoretically all infantry and artillery recruits were sent for basic training. All forty were assigned to the artillery for duty in Florida. At five foot-eight-and-a-quarter, Dey was considered an ideal physical representation of an artilleryman. According to specifications found in a return of Company M, 2nd U.S. Artillery, recruits "should be strong, active men from 5'8" to 5'10" in height. The new 12 Pdr [12-pounder cannon] require picked men and horses so far as size and strength are concerned. With such men, it is believed, they can be made as manageable, or nearly so as the 6 Pdrs whilst they will be more powerful and efficient than the smaller caliber."[2]

Less than a month after he enlisted, Dey and the other 39 recruits were crammed into the hold of a seagoing vessel, sailed south along the East Coast, around the Florida Keys to Punta Rassa, and on to Fort Myers, Florida. From there, they either marched or boarded alligator boats or shallow draft steamers which carried them some 35 or 40 miles up the Caloosahatchee River to Fort Thompson, located on the south bank of the river near the mouth of Lake Flirt. They arrived at the fort on January 18, 1855. Fort Thompson had recently been built as part of a chain of forts between Fort Myers and Lake Okeechobee. There, Dey and the other recruits joined Company I, 2nd U.S. Artillery, and became a part of the military force under the command of Colonel John Munroe that Davis hoped would remove all the Seminoles from Florida.[3] This force of regulars, located at various posts throughout the state eventually grew to 801, of which 464 were from the 2nd U.S. Artillery, and 337 were from the 1st U.S. Artillery.[4]

When Dey and the new recruits joined Company I, they came under the command of Captain Augustus Abel Gibson,[5] who at the time was on detached service on a coast survey. He had not physically been with the regiment since March 30, 1850, and had not been with the company since he was given its command and promoted to captain on July 9, 1853, a not-too-infrequent occurrence in the regular army, especially for duty in Florida. It would be more than a year before these recruits saw Gibson. But it was not unusual for officers to be absent for long periods for a variety of reasons, from leaves, with or without orders, to assignments on detached service (as was the case with Gibson), for sitting on courts-martial, or because they absented themselves to conduct personal business. On the other hand, for an enlisted man, AWOL was forbidden and often carried stiff punishment when the individual reported back for duty or was apprehended during the absence. And duty in Florida was especially distasteful to officers. During the Second Seminole War, the "four artillery regiments were particularly hard hit, as they lost 55 Junior Officers. Even those [civilians] friendly to the army and West Point might have suspicions that these men avoided going to Florida."[6]

The company was commanded by Second Lieutenant George L. Hartsuff, with Brevet Second Lieutenant Stephen H. Weed as second in command. The other two officers on the muster roll were First Lieutenants Jefferson Nones and Thomas S. Rhett, who like Captain Gibson were absent from the company.[7]

The recruits were also greeted by 43 enlisted regulars who had just returned from two weeks as a working party in the field. The company, with Companies C and L, 2nd U.S. Artillery, had opened a road between Fort Myers and Fort Thompson because the companies were evacuating Fort Meade, southeast of Tampa, and Fort Brooke, to establish a similar post at Fort Thompson. Fort Thompson was officially occupied on November 23, 1854.[8] It soon proved to be unsatisfactory because of the effect a swollen Caloosahatchee River might have on it. As a precautionary measure, in January 1855 Brevet Lieutenant Weed was ordered up the river from Fort Myers to determine if Fort Deynaud, abandoned since the Second Seminole War, could be re-established as a supply depot for troops operating in the region.

Fort Deynaud had first been established in 1837–1838 by Captain Benjamin Bonneville, 7th U.S. Infantry. It sat some 27 miles from Fort Myers on the south bank of the river. Just one of a series of posts linking the military operations from south of Tampa to the east coast of Florida during that war, the fort then consisted of a wooden combination blockhouse and storehouse surrounded by tents for the troops. It was on a point of high land nearly two miles from the river, reached by walking on a road which was actually a sandy lane. Occupied intermittently from 1838 to the close of the war in 1842, it served primarily as a supply depot for troops operating in the Lake Okeechobee area.[9] The fort was abandoned after the war, but Weed's reconnaissance determined that it would be feasible to reoccupy the fort.[10]

On January 22, 1855, four days after the recruits unpacked their gear, the entire Fort Thompson garrison of Companies I, C, and L, under Brevet Major William Hays, was ordered to re-establish Fort Deynaud as a supply depot to serve much as it had during the last war, and to build blockhouses to secure the safety of public property.[11] Fort Thompson was evacuated on January 24, 1855. But on the same day, before they could settle in at Fort Deynaud, Dey and his comrades, under Lieutenant Hartsuff, marched as a working party to open roads and to establish posts south of Fort Myers to a point known as Depot No. 1. Their first stop was Fort Myers, where Company G joined them. The combined detail, commanded by Captain Henry Clay Pratt, worked its way southeast of Fort Myers, reaching the Big Cypress Swamp, where Depot No. 1 supposedly was located, on January 30.[12]

Map of Florida: Company I's area of operations, 1855–1857
(Map reconstructed from an 1856 military map of the peninsula of Florida, south of Tampa Bay, by Nancy Day Ingrisano.)

On February 3, Pratt reported that he and Hartsuff "had explored the country thoroughly for many miles around but have been unable to find the site of Depot no. 1." They also experienced difficulty finding a suitable replacement site for a new depot. "The site selected and where a blockhouse was immediately built was less than ½ mile from where the trail from Fort Myers to the Big Cypress enters it—the Ok-hol-on-Kochee is the only stream of water in the vicinity and passes the place within the cypress." In his February 5 report, Pratt expressed concerns about the accuracy of the maps he was using. "The Maps represent the shape of Big Cypress so differently in this portion of it and also the course of the creek, Ok-hol-on-Cookee [*sic*] forms what I have found that I felt some doubts if I had reached the same place." His frustrations were somewhat mollified when he noted, almost wistfully, that the "lake, came to my relief and told us that [what] we saw was the Big Cypress and the Creek was Ok-hol-on Cookee. We have explored south some twelve miles but could find no sign of Fort Keas [Keais] or Doane."[13]

With the detail completed on February 13, Dey and his comrades returned to Fort Deynaud, their base of operations. There, they settled into the routine of erecting new buildings and restoring old structures to make the compound a suitable supply depot. During this period, Dey was required "to pay for 1 screw driver, 45 cents." Weed transferred to the 4th U.S. Artillery; Lieutenant Thomas Rhett resigned his commission; and First Lieutenant Julian Stiffan Molinard joined the company from promotion, and from absence without leave. The company was still commanded by Hartsuff.[14]

One of the first casualties among the recruits was Private Urban Stoll, who died at Fort Myers on March 2, 1855, of acute dysentery at the age of thirty-four. Stoll, who had enlisted in New York City during the same recruitment rendezvous as did Dey, was from Strassburg, France.[15] Fort Myers had the facilities for handling severe hospital cases, whereas at Fort Deynaud they were quite primitive. Moreover, movement between the two forts and to other forts along this defense line was done mainly on foot. Recognizing this difficulty and the lack of water transportation at Fort Deynaud, Colonel Munroe wrote from regimental headquarters at Fort Brooke to Major Harvey Brown,[16] commanding at Fort Deynaud, that the steamer *Texas Ranger* would soon be available at the revitalized post.

Five days later, on March 10, Munroe again wrote to Brown expressing his concerns that the immediate use of the steamer might further complicate the garrison's situation. He felt that the use of the steamer without competent guides and pilots would undercut its employment, "that an immediate movement would enable you to attain an advantage which would be defeated by the indicated delay." In the same communication, he reminded Brown that he was to be patient for the obvious reason that from "the instructions of the Secretary of War [Jefferson Davis] (21 Sept., and 27 Oct. 1854) it is obviously intended to keep the troops in the field, so long as the season justifies it, with the view of opening roads to the Indian settlements."[17]

The prospect of water transportation, whether to be used or just available, was of little comfort for some of Dey's comrades. Artificer [Mechanic] George Gill, and Privates John Beckman and William Klein (the latter two were among the 40 recruits who joined the company with Dey in January), deserted on March 22, 1855. And seven privates were listed as being sick at Fort Deynaud or Fort Myers. Molinard noted under instructions that they were "Not good. More than $1/2$ recruits imperfectly drilled."[18]

The devastation within the ranks and the seriousness of the unhealthy conditions at Fort Deynaud, reopened just a few months, were noticed by Colonel William Selby Harney, the new commander of the federal troops in Florida.[19] In a series of orders from May 15 to May 26, Harney ordered Brown to withdraw the garrison from Fort Deynaud "on account of the sickness prevailing" there and make camp near Fort Myers, to set all the tents at Deynaud on stilts protected by palmetto sheds, to send the water tanks to that fort from Fort Myers, and finally to withdraw the garrison from Fort Center on Fisheating Creek on Lake Okeechobee, and to store all public property there in Fort Deynaud.

Brown was then instructed on May 16 to procure a large supply of anti-scorbutics to combat further sickness from dysentery and scurvy. On May 26, he was told to leave a guard at Deynaud which "should consist at first of the number specified in my letter of 15th inst. Should it be found at a future period, that a smaller number is sufficient, the detachment can then be reduced, but not below the number recommended in your letter (25)." The detachment was to consist of one medical and one company officer and 40 non-commissioned officers and privates. They were to be relieved "from time to time as directed." On May 28, Companies I, C, and L, under the command of Brevet Major (Captain) Lewis Golding Arnold, left Fort Deynaud on the *Texas Ranger*, covering the 22 miles to Camp Daniels on the same day. They were to remain at Camp Daniels until conditions at Fort Deynaud permitted return to that outpost.[20]

Camp Daniels does not appear on any maps, today, but Francis B. Heitman, in volume 2 of his *Historical Register and Dictionary of the United States Army*[21], notes that it was near Fort Myers. [There is a Daniels Avenue in present-day Fort Myers which could give some indication of the location of the camp just south of the city of Fort Myers.] Thomas Gonzalez in his book, quoting from the *Reminiscences of General Hancock*, written by Hancock's wife, provided another clue to the possible location of Camp Daniels. She noted that troops for service in the Everglades were encamped about one mile from Fort Myers because there was insufficient quarters for either officers or men at the post.[22] The conditions at Fort Myers differed greatly from those that existed in the makeshift, tent-city fort which Dey and the company had just evacuated. Fort Myers was one of the largest posts in the South. It was established in February 1850, and Major General David Twiggs named it for Brigadier General Abraham Charles Myers, his son-in-law.[23]

Captain Francis Asbury Hendry, a long-time Florida resident, first visited the fort in 1854 with Lieutenant Henry Benson and gave a contemporary account of it. Hendry observed that "there is not a single [civilian] settler nor a trace of civilization in the surrounding country." At the fort, he found the "grounds tastefully laid out with shell walks and dress parade grounds. The officers' and soldiers' quarters were neatly and comfortably constructed, and very near where our present academy stands (now the Andrew D. Gwynne Institute) I beheld the finest vegetable gardens I ever saw." In contrast to the troops who came to the fort from field duty, Hendry commented on the "long lines of uniformed soldiers with white gloves and burnished guns, and their officers with their golden epaulettes and shining side arms were grand and magnificient [sic] to behold."[24] Fort Myers was used both as a health resort, where any officer suffering "from any trouble, organic or functional, might enjoy the advantages of its healthful climate," and as a frontier guard post.[25]

Fort Myers was the ideal retreat for troops suffering from scurvy and dysentery, since its hospital served as a center for treatment of the seriously ill and dying, as in Urban Stoll's case. Moreover, the disciplined regulars at that garrison served as exemplary role models for the "imperfectly drilled recruits" from Company I. At Camp Daniels, Molinard reported that instructions for his men were improving and that their arms were in good service order. But he also reported that their clothing was wearing out, and that which had been requisitioned six months prior had not yet been received. On the same muster (June–August 1855), Lieutenant Thomas Grey joined the company but he was immediately put on detached service with regimental headquarters.[26]

Although Dey continued to stay healthy, the same muster showed that the company's sick list lengthened. Three of the men were in the hospital at Fort Myers, while nine others were sick in quarters. One other was in chains, having been tried by general court-martial.[27] The illness which plagued Company I continued throughout the summer of 1855. Its severity caused the discharge of two more soldiers for disability. Three others joined their comrades in sick bay. Private Alexander Nelson deserted on October 14 from Camp Daniels. On October 23, Dey went to Fort Deynaud on detached service. And before the rest of the company followed in late November, eight more men reported to sick bay.[28]

On November 21, Molinard led the men onto the *Texas Ranger* and reoccupied Fort Deynaud after a six-month hiatus at Camp Daniels. Two new recruits joined the company in November and December. And within two weeks, Private Henry Miller, after a year of military service, deserted from Fort Deynaud, taking with him his accoutrements, musket and bayonet, worth $16.66—$14.63 for the musket and bayonet, and $2.03 for the bayonet scabbard, waist belt, waist belt plate, cap pouch, screw drive, wiper and gun sling.[29]

Dey and his comrades settled in at Fort Deynaud. Hartsuff, with orders to find Seminole fields and towns but not to provoke any Seminoles he might encounter, set out with a patrol of ten men (six mounted, two foot soldiers, and two teamsters) from Fort Myers on December 7 and moved through the center of southwestern Florida. This area was occupied by Halpatter Mico, Billy Bowlegs, and his band of warriors. On December 17, the patrol encamped on a pine island approximately three miles from a camp that Billy Bowlegs had used the previous year. The next morning, Hartsuff and his men entered the deserted village and helped themselves to a bunch of bananas. The next day, December 19, the detail visited other deserted villages. Hartsuff's orders called for his return to Fort Myers on the twentieth. To prepare for the long march back, the men retired early in the evening of the nineteenth. Under cover of darkness, a party of Seminoles, wearing traditional black and white plumes in their hair, moved toward the camp. At approximately five o'clock on the morning of the twentieth, while the soldiers were saddling up their mounts and packing their wagons, the Seminoles attacked. After killing four soldiers and wounding four others, including Hartsuff, the attackers withdrew.[30]

With this unfortunate action what was to be known as the Third Seminole War began. The official commentary included in the final report of activities for 1855 simply stated that on "the 20th December 1855, Lieutenant Hartsuff, 2d Arty, with a party of ten men from Fort Myers was attacked by Indians and hostilities again resumed... This closes the reconnaissance for 1855." (Since there had been no other recent encounters with the Seminoles, the comment "again resumed" apparently alluded to the last action of the second war which ended in 1842.[31]) The attack on Hartsuff signaled the federal government that Colonel Munroe's attempts to execute the provisions of the earlier treaties with the Seminoles had failed.[32] They failed primarily because the Seminoles were becoming increasingly alarmed at the surveying and scouting parties moving through their temporary reserve and disrupting their way of life.[33]

There were approximately 400 Seminoles, including women and children, still living in Florida. The one most influential Seminole, who had the greatest authority among them and who had approximately one hundred warriors, was Billy Bowlegs. Hence the Third Seminole War is often called the "Billy Bowlegs' War."[34] He was described in *Harpers Weekly* (June 12, 1858) as: "a rather good-looking Indian of about fifty years. He has a fine forehead; a keen black eye; is somewhat about medium height and weighs about 160 pounds. His name of Bowlegs is a family appellation, and does not imply any parenthetical curvature of his lower limbs. When he is sober, which I am sorry to say, is by no means his normal state, his legs are as straight as yours or mine. He has two wives, one son, five daughters, fifty slaves and one hundred thousand dollars in hard cash. He wears his native costume; two medals on his breast, of which he is not a little proud bear the likeness of Presidents Van Buren and Fillmore."

Two days after the attack on Hartsuff and his men, Company I, with Molinard in command, scouted the Caloosahatchee up to Fisheating Creek near Lake Okeechobee and Fort Center, a distance of 26 miles. On Christmas Day (years before it would be treated as a universal holiday), Dey and the company left Fisheating Creek under Lieutenant Frank Hunt Larned, and arrived at Fort Deynaud on the same day, closing its "reconnaissance for 1855."[35] Early in January 1856, Lieutenant Henry Benson left Fort Myers with a patrol of 20 men to scout the area bordering the Big Cypress Swamp, just as Captain Pratt had done a year earlier. This time, however, the Seminoles ambushed the patrol, killing two men and wounding eight. Benson himself was shot in the shoulder and almost bled to death.[36]

Around Fort Deynaud, the Seminoles kept a close watch over that garrison. Major Lewis Arnold had aroused them by burning one of their villages. On January 18, 1856, a party of five privates and a corporal was returning to the fort with a load of firewood to be used for cooking and for repelling mosquitoes when it was attacked by a force of 15 to 20 Seminoles. Five soldiers and 12 mules were killed. The lone survivor made his way back to the fort where he identified Oscen Tustenuggee, another important Seminole leader, as the leader of the ambush.[37] The incident at Fort Deynaud occurred while Dey and Company I were in the field scouting again near Fort Center, Fisheating Creek, and around Lake Okeechobee, and north to the mouth of the Kissimmee River, from January 2 to February 23.[38]

While in the field, the company made itself more mobile by using the boats which were now kept at re-occupied Fort Center near Lake Okeechobee. These boats allowed scouting parties to move constantly between Fort Center, re-occupied Fort Thompson and Fort Deynaud. In all of these scouts, the company never had any encounters with the Seminoles who continued to strike at other settlements in the area. Despite the increased activity the health of individual soldiers did not improve. Munroe again lamented the condition of his command when he reported that there "has been a good deal of sickness among the troops during the past summer and autumn, and although not of a very agravated [sic] character has influenced unfavorably the physical condition of the whole command—at Fort Deynaud since the return of the troops to the post about the middle of December the sick list has been very heavy as reported by the commanding officer and Surgeon at the post."[39] A day later, on January 24, 1856, Arnold, commanding at Fort Deynaud, not only confirmed the colonel's comments but he added an interesting description of the garrison's work and military routines:

> Every soldier under my command in addition to the misfortune of being stationed at an unhealthy Post, has been employed without intermission, when not on guard, mostly with axe or spade in hand, performing active labor, and when the necessities of service required that work should be suspended, to perform the legitimate duty of the soldier: long marches, scouting through mud and water and escorting wagons to Forts Center and Myers were the alternatives presented, till in many cases, exhausted nature calls aloud for relief, and the obedient soldier sickened by debilitating climate, added to new fatigues & exposure, seeks his best friend The Doctor,—who breaks his fever, or stops his diarrhea for a time, but the first extraordinary exposure or fatigue causes a relapse—in short a lot of men are completely broken down.[40]

As both of these officers penned their words, the men in Company I continued to feel the debilitating effects of the environment. When Molinard took the company out on scout from January 2 to February 25, he left behind 23 out of 75 enlisted men (almost 33 percent) who were either sick in quarters or in the hospital.[41] Captain Gibson, who still had not physically taken over command of the company, was finally relieved from detached service with the Coast Survey on January 3, 1856. But he was again placed on detached service mustering state troops to assist the regulars, and helped to press 260 into federal service.[42]

The Florida state authorities also recruited six companies from nearby counties and ordered them to protect settlers, because the governor did not believe that the number of men mustered into federal service was sufficient to meet the state's defensive and offensive needs. These units were armed, equipped and rationed with the assistance of private funds. The force was offered to Jefferson Davis, Secretary of War, who accepted three mounted and two infantry companies. The entire force, including regulars, men mustered into the federal service, and state volunteers, now totaled approximately 1,500, giving it the advantage of 15 whites for every Seminole warrior.[43] The volunteers were described as "a very sorry looking bunch of ragamuffins alongside Uncle Sam's troops. Nearly all shook with ague, were raw-boned, had yellow, emaciated faces and were clad in butternut suits. Their hair was long, thin and straight. [They were] mounted on wretched looking beasts, both men and animals appeared as though they were in the last stages of consumption...they resembled a ragged funeral procession."[44]

As further inducement for the volunteers, the federal Indian agent on March 28, 1856, offered the "following premiums for every living Indian Warrior, Woman, or boy, over ten years of age, who may be captured or induced to come in for emigration to the West: For each Warrior—$250 to $500; for each Woman—$150 to $300; for each boy over ten years—$100 to $200. The maximum rate or highest rate will be paid for all except the infirm, bedridden and helpless in which case the rates will be decided by a Board." On October 9, 1856, the agent extended the premium to include "all under as well as over ten years of age."[45]

In Company I, on March 3, Private Charles Falk, from Bern, Switzerland, who had been recruited in Buffalo, New York, died of acute dysentery at Fort Deynaud. Sergeant James Smith reenlisted and Corporal James McCabe was discharged after five years' service. Lieutenant Jefferson Nones resigned his commission. Seven men continued on the sick list, and Molinard reported that the men's accoutrements were "nearly worn out." Company I continued its patrols and escort duties while the volunteers pursued the Seminoles. On March 26, the company was reinforced with nine recruits from the General Department at Fort Columbus, New York. These men had also been recruited in the New York and Philadelphia areas. The company strength now stood at three officers and 86 enlisted men.

On April 6–7, a detachment of 108 men from the 1st and 2nd Artillery, commanded by Brevet Major (Captain) Lewis Arnold, was attacked by a large force of Seminoles in the Big Cypress Swamp. The Indians were repeatedly charged by the regulars and driven from their positions in the swamps and hummocks. One enlisted men was killed and six wounded. It was not known how many Seminoles were killed.[46]

On April 30, still-a-Private Gus Dey was sent on detached service with an unspecified unit, escorting a train to Fort Center. On May 6, Company I resumed its scouting activities covering the area south of Fort Myers through the Big Cypress Swamp, where the detachment had battled the Seminoles in early April. On May 8, it linked up with Arnold at his camp at Depot No. 2. Arnold reported that his command continued operations in the Big Cypress Swamp and that it "had scouted the wet and dense hummocks around Bowlegs' town, [and that] the Big Cypress [was] wet and the Indians had all left it."[47] The scout lasted until June 9. The company returned to Fort Deynaud commanded by Gibson, who finally had joined his outfit in the field on May 29, 1856. That scout again proved devastating to 21 of the men, who went into sick bay, either in quarters at Deynaud or into the hospital at Fort Myers.

Ten others were sent on detached service with other units; three worked in the Quartermaster Department; and four, who completed their enlistments, were discharged. Forty-eight men, or 59 percent of the company, were on station available for duty and training.[48]

Each artillery company had to establish a thorough system of theoretical and practical instructions in the essential elements of artillery and infantry sciences. The company requested and received numbers of copies of the then standard textbooks and regulations governing instructions in *Bayonet Exercises*; *Heavy Artillery Tactics*; *Mounted Tactics*; and *Sword Exercise*. But there is no evidence that the company actually engaged in such practical exercises as live firings. As a matter of fact, rarely did it have enough healthy personnel available for any extensive training during the Florida campaign.[49]

On August 11, Dey was again sent out on detached service with Lieutenant Henry Benson's mounted detachment to scout along the Caloosahatchee. Dey remained with the unit until well into October. Privates Joseph Koch and Frederick Kroppe went to Fort Myers on detached service with the regimental band. Both would transfer permanently in November 1856 to the band at regimental headquarters at Fort Brooke. Privates John Ginger and Charles Kell were in confinement awaiting a garrison court-martial. Since the medical facilities in Florida were not that capable of handling the very sick, Sergeant David Donnon, Corporal Patrick Flynn, and five privates were sent to the General Hospital at Fort Columbus, New York. Private Frederick Schudt, not up to the rigors of such a long voyage, died of acute dysentery at Fort Myers on July 19, four days before the others were sent to New York. Schudt had been sick since June 1855. Three people remained in sick quarters, and Private Lawrence Walsh pulled extra duty as a hospital cook. Corporal Andrew McKeon, who had enlisted in New York in July 1851, was discharged at Fort Myers. Privates Ignatius Everett and Charles Chambers were promoted to corporal to fill vacancies created by the discharges. Most of these actions occurred while the company was at Fort Myers from June 13 to July 28. The company then returned to Fort Deynaud.[50]

The company reported on September 1, 1856, that First Lieutenant Judson D. Bingham, who had been mustered on the rolls on March 12, 1856, had not joined the company and had not been "heard from since promotion [on March 12]." Lieutenant Grey never returned to the company. He had been appointed adjutant of the Caloosahatchee District (eventually, he would become adjutant of the 2nd Artillery and remain in that post until late in the Civil War).[51]

On November 12, shortly after Dey returned from detached service, he and the company left for Fort Myers. They remained there through December 25, returning to Fort Deynaud on December 26. On

Lieutenant Colonel Augustus Abel Gibson. Captain Gibson commanded Company I, 2nd U.S. Artillery, Dey's first assignment in Florida, 1854–1857.

December 23, Private Dey was promoted to corporal, effective December 1, almost two years from the date of his enlistment. He also learned that Private John Berklanth, who had joined with him, was discharged at Fort Columbus, New York. Berklanth, originally from Uri, Switzerland, and an upholsterer by trade, was given a disability discharge on November 16. He had been with the group which had been sent previously on July 23 to the General Hospital at Fort Columbus.[52]

For the period from October 1856 through February 1857, Gibson reported that instructions for the men were "indifferent: the mixed duties of the Company do not allow for [not legible] military instructions." Moreover, the unsettled environment around Fort Deynaud, which had forced the company to abandon the fort in May 1855, again caused it to shift bases. On orders from Brigadier General William Harney, the company evacuated Fort Deynaud on February 28 and moved "to a more convenient position two miles below and opposite old Fort Simmons on the Caloosahatchee." Since many of the men were sick or on detached service Gibson had to use the remaining men to evacuate Deynaud and to build shelters at the new camp. He formed a mini-quartermaster department with Sergeant Gilbert Robinson as quartermaster sergeant. Robinson used Private John Bacheman, a shoemaker in civilian life, as a harness maker. Private Isaac Watkins worked as a blacksmith, his former occupation. And Privates Max Boll (painter), Charles Jordan (cloth maker), Martin Gilroy (tailor), Michael Dillon, Henry Meir [Meier] (laborers), and Henry McAnally were used as teamsters.

To erect shelters, Gibson used Private Charles Chambers, a carpenter, assisted by Privates Henry Howell (laborer) and John Luz (ropemaker) as laborers. When the men on escort duty returned, they were given extra duty gathering material. For commissary duty, Gibson made Private John Carroll, a former clerk, acting commissary sergeant. Working with Carroll were Privates William Neuman[n], a butcher, and Peter Strous, a baker, practicing their former trades during the move. To attend the sick and anyone who might be injured during the move, Gibson made Corporal Ignatius Everett (laborer) acting hospital steward. Private Almon Johnson (machinist) was hospital attendant, and Private Henry Stiller was hospital cook.[53]

In a report to Fort Brooke, Gibson described this entire operation, and the other tasks which were undertaken by his command during the evacuation of Fort Deynaud:

> The [supply] train, almost uniformly, has made its trips to Fort Center and Fisheating Creek once in four days, with an escort ranging from ten to fifteen men...the establishment of a new depot; being preliminary to the abandonment of Fort Deynaud. In the mean-time a party of fifteen men, under Lieut. Molinard, was employed in opening the road from Camp [Simmons] to the terminus

of the Fort Center road, opposite Fort Deynaud and in bridging Five-mile Creek. The party has since been on extra duty in erecting buildings for the use of the Post. The materials for a defensive Guardhouse, with a cell, used for a storehouse have been nearly all collected. A bakery with shed, a cattle pen and a Sutler's shanty have all been completed... I remained at Fort Deynaud to direct the transfer of the property at the latter post. The property was moved by water and the boat (a large float) was employed about 2 weeks making two trips a day in the accomplishment of this work. I mustered the Command at this Camp, and left a detachment of eleven men, at Fort Deynaud to protect the Commissary building until it could be moved. The Sutler was moved on the 4th of March, and on the 9th of March, a party of 50 men was sent down to the Commissary to remove it, if possible in one day.

Orders from HdQrs were also received on this day to send Company "M" 4th Art to Big Cypress. This leaves me without the means to finish the forage house, and the shed for the Hospital and Stable. With the whole command I could, in ten days, have put this post in condition to answer the purposes requisite for so important a depot. The paulins [tarpaulins] with one exception, and large tents are old, and inadequate to the protecting of the stores.

The site of this post is in a hummock, so threaded with such palmetto as to absorb two weeks of labor of our Company, to open a walk around the post and a miniature parade ground with a place for tents. I estimate the area of the post at about twelve acres. No command had ever worked more faithfully and apparently to such result. The hours of fatigue have been from three quarters of an hour after "Reveille" to eleven Oclock, and from one Oclock, to half an hour before Retreat. The extra duty party worked an hour longer.

The constant interruptions from unforeseen contingencies have been a great drawback to the Work generally; but the health of the Command has been remarkably good.[54]

Gibson stated that with his whole command at Fort Deynaud he could have made the new depot fully operational in ten days. By March 27, 1857, however, Company I left camp opposite Fort Simmons, boarded the steamer *Tampa,* and headed for Fort Myers, which it reached the same day. On April 10, the company boarded the schooner *Col. Washington,* which set sail from Fort Myers for Punta Rassa (old Fort Dulany), arriving there on April 11. On the next day, Corporal Dey and Company I left Punta Rassa on the schooner *Storm Cloud,* reaching Key West one day later. And on April 14, still aboard the same schooner, they sailed for Fort Monroe, Virginia, where they landed on April 25. Their participation in the Third Seminole War had ended.[55]

In fact, general orders from regimental headquarters and the War Department had already set in motion the withdrawal of the troops from Florida. An advance cadre with regimental property was sent to Fort Hamilton, New York. The sick from various companies went to Fort Monroe, as did Companies I and F. Companies C and L went to Fort Independence in Boston harbor, Massachusetts; Company E to Fort Mackinac, Michigan; Company G to Fort Brady, Michigan; and Companies H and K to Fort Hamilton. Regimental headquarters, under Colonel Matthew Payne, stopped briefly at Fort Monroe before moving on to Fort Hamilton.[56]

In March 1858, the Seminoles, assured by the federal government that they would be granted a separate reservation in Arkansas, agreed to leave their traditional homeland. On the day of their departure, May 4, 1858, Colonel Gustavus Loomis declared that the Third Seminole War was over. Some 160 Seminoles left Florida. Some 300 chose to stay, not as part of the Seminole nation but as individual, non-propertied natives of Florida.[57]

After almost 350 years, the struggle over land in Florida ended. Federal troops had served there for almost 40 of those years; various companies of the 2nd Artillery had played prominent roles in both the Second and Third Seminole Wars. During the final phases of this struggle in a troubled land, Corporal Gus Dey had spent half of a five-year enlistment in that battleground, serving with 102 enlisted men. Of these, 50, including himself, remained relatively healthy, 52 had reported sick, four died from disease, five were discharged after serving their enlistments, two of these reenlisted, two transferred to the regimental band, five deserted, and 11 new recruits joined in Florida.

The ethnic makeup in Dey's first military assignment was quite representative of the regular army at that time. Dey, a German [Prussian], was joined by 23 of his countrymen. There were 35 Irishmen, four Englishmen, three Frenchmen, two Swiss, and one each from Italy, Poland and Scotland. There were also 24 native-born Americans.[58]

At the company command level, Dey never served under a full roster of officers. The standard then for an artillery company included a captain, two first lieutenants, and two second lieutenants. When he joined Company I in January 1855, Dey served under two junior officers, Second Lieutenant Hartsuff and Brevet Second Lieutenant Weed. He had already served 16 months in Florida before he met Captain Gibson, who returned to his command on May 29, 1858. At the final muster in Florida, the rolls showed an aggregate of 81, four officers and 77 enlisted men. In actuality, only two officers, Gibson and Molinard, stood muster. The number of enlisted men on duty was quite below the muster number because of those on the sick list and others who were on detached service.

Even the company's military designation as a unit in the 2nd U.S. Artillery was almost farcical. Major Lewis Golding, reporting in 1856, provided an interesting perspective of how artillerymen functioned in Florida. He lamented that his artillerymen labored mostly with "axe and spade in hand [like engineers or pioneers]." Even when they were soldiering, their "legitimate duty" consisted of long marches, scouting through mud and water and escorting trains, much in the manner of infantry or cavalry.

When Molinard found in June 1855 that more than half of the recruits were imperfectly drilled, he could do little to change their status considering the health of the company and its assigned duties. The records indicate that even when the company was at Camp Daniels, near Fort Myers, that quintessence of military posts where conditions seemed ideal for training and instruction, it still did not fulfill its designated role. As late as February 1857, two months before its departure from Florida's hostile environment, Gibson ruefully stated that instructions for his men were "Indifferent: the mixed duties of the Company do not allow for [not legible] military instructions."

So Corporal Gus Dey and his comrades finished their tour. They watched from aboard the *Storm Cloud* as the coast of Florida faded into the horizon. They must have been happy to shed the memories of a campaign that seemed to go nowhere, cost some lives, disabled some bodies and added little to their knowledge of artillery practices. They soldiered on foot, wielded non-military implements, never fired a shot, and must have wondered if that was what war was all about.

Chapter 2

Virginia: A Brief Stopover

The *Storm Cloud* sailed up the East Coast toward Fort Monroe, Virginia, carrying men of many different intentions, some determined to pursue life after enlistment. And some, like Dey, determined to make a career in the regular army. On another frontier in the Kansas Territory, John Brown, a militant abolitionist, brutally massacred five pro-slave settlers in their cabins in Pottawatomie; the Supreme Court outraged abolitionists by ruling in the Dred Scott case that Congress had no right to exclude slavery from any territory; and the panic of 1857 had closed every bank in New York City, ruining thousands of businesses and causing widespread unemployment among industrial workers. Meanwhile, some 17,000 army regulars remained gainfully employed at many outposts throughout the country.

Historic Fort Monroe is at the tip of a peninsula in southeastern Virginia between the York and James Rivers and due west of the mouth of the Chesapeake Bay. Readily accessible by land or water, the site was deemed by the English colonists an ideal defensive position against seaward invasion and maintained that reputation with succeeding military planners. In 1819, after two years of study by the United States Army, the basic foundations were laid for a fort. Almost simultaneously, another study by a board of officers looked into the feasibility of establishing a school of application or instruction for young officers, particularly recent West Point graduates of the artillery, engineering, and topographic corps, since this study had also shown that the graduates were prepared only to begin their professional duties. Fort Monroe, although even under construction, was the largest fort at that time and had the advantages of good location, climate, and access to transportation. It was most feasible that it be designated a school for instruction of artillery officers, making it the first of what would become a network of professional service schools under the army's jurisdiction.

20

Fort Monroe, Virginia: aerial view from color lithograph, 1861

Casemate Museum, Fort Monroe, Va.

Baltimore Wharf and Hygeia Restaurant, Fort Monroe, Virginia, 1864
Casemate Museum, Fort Monroe, Va.

The first class began assembling in February 1824, when three companies from the 4th Artillery arrived. They were joined by three companies from the 2nd U.S. Artillery, and two companies each from the 1st and 3rd Artillery, with the entire complement on post by late May 1824. These companies joined Company G, 3rd Artillery, which was the first garrison to occupy the fort, having arrived in July 1823, but which did not partake in the training.

It is interesting to note at this point that a unit was then designated as "company," as opposed to the present day usage of "battery." (The term "battery", technically the assembly of artillery pieces themselves, would not officially supplant "company" as the unit identifier for the artillerymen themselves until after the Civil War, despite the common practice of using "battery" together with a commander's name to designate a unit, i.e., "Totten's Battery.") Similar designations of companies (A, B, C, etc.) in different regiments (1st, 2nd, 3rd, and 4th) caused some confusion. The custom which had been used prior to 1816, wherein each company was identified by its commander's name, was restored. Even though the commanding officer might be absent for many years, as was the case with Captain Gibson, he still commanded the company and fixed his name to its identity. This practice continued when the term "battery" became more widely used. For example, during the Civil War, official reports cited "Totten's Battery" rather than the letter and number designation, which were worn on the soldiers' caps as F/2, i.e., Battery F, 2nd U.S. Artillery. Today, the military has gone to shoulder and breast patches for unit identities.

In the artillery school at Fort Monroe, both officers and enlisted men were rigorously and thoroughly trained and disciplined in police duties of roll call, mustering, guard, cooking, messing, washing, and cleaning quarters and grounds. (In World War II, "GIs," or "Government Issue," the common label for enlisted men, were constantly "policing" an area, picking up cigarette butts and other debris. This activity was prevalent particularly during basic or non-professional training.) Infantry and cavalry exercises, parades, reviews, and inspections were other training routines. Artillery drills included the manual and service of field and garrison pieces, seacoast guns, mortars and howitzers, mechanical maneuvers, and exercises of horse and foot artillery, and the evolution of batteries. These dry runs were followed with practical gunnery and target practice with hotshot, grape, canister, and shell. In the laboratory, students learned to prepare every type of ammunition, making fuzes, and loading shells, rockets, and other military fireworks; packing caissons, ammunition boxes, and wagons; and inspecting and proofing gunpowder, shot, and shell. The students were also trained in arsenal construction, the service of artillery in the field, in garrison, and in sieges; crossing rivers, marshes, and other water barriers; in reconnoitering, convoys, topographical surveys; construction of field works, and attack and defense of fortified places. The final phase of the training cycle was in field duties and in practical gunnery. For this exercise, the entire garrison moved into "Camp Experiment" or "Buck Roe Farm" for the entire month of May. (There is a Buckroe Beach just northeast of the present day fort.)

In practice this program covered four periods of daily instruction, beginning at sunrise and ending at 9:00 p.m. when "Tattoo" was sounded. Breakfast was served at 9:00 a.m., and dinner at 3:00 p.m. At 4:00 p.m., there was a dress parade, in gray woolen overalls ("fatigues"), followed by infantry drill until retreat. A review and inspection of troops was held at 11:30 a.m. every Sunday morning. Except for breakfast occurring at 8:00 a.m., this schedule would not change until after the Civil War. But infantry instructions predominated the schedule because the artillery, since the Revolutionary War, had generally been equipped as infantry.

Although there were plenty of troops at the fort, the amount of materiel available for practice was small. Nevertheless, a second class arrived in 1826, and a third in 1828 for the two-year course. Unfortunately, since the fort held one of the largest garrisons in an army whose total strength barely reached six thousand, different companies from time to time were ordered out on detached service, interfering with the school's curriculum, so that the school virtually stopped functioning by 1834. These extraordinary duties involved suppressing slave uprisings, fighting Indians in Alabama and Florida, fighting in the Mexican War, returning to Florida for a third Seminole war, and manning outposts in Oregon, California, and across the United States.

In 1855, Jefferson Davis proposed reactivating the artillery school at Fort Monroe. In October 1856, the War Department directed Companies M, 2nd U.S. Artillery; C, 3rd Artillery; and G, 4th Artillery to be discontinued as light artillery, and with Company I, 1st Artillery designated as garrison, seacoast, and siege artillery, concentrated at Fort Monroe to form a school of practice for service with heavy guns. Company G arrived in December 1856, and would remain until May 1860. Companies M and C arrived late in January 1857. But Company M left for Fort Leavenworth, Kansas Territory, in September 1857, and Company C left for the same post in April 1858. Company I never did arrive for its assignment.[1] It was not immediately clear at this point if the school would be used for training for service with heavy guns or with both heavy and light guns. In November 1856, right after the October order, the 2nd U.S. Artillery, which was slated for duty at Fort Monroe, began its pullout of Florida by moving property out of Fort Brooke. The regimental sergeant major was sent to Fort Hamilton, New York,[2] while some personnel and the sick from Companies I, C, and G were sent to Fort Monroe as an advance cadre.[3]

Corporal Gustav Dey and his company arrived at the fort from Florida on April 28, 1857, where they met up with their comrades. Evidently, Company I was ordered to Fort Monroe for training, pending the reactivation of the artillery school. In May 1857, the Department of the Army ordered that the 2nd U.S. Artillery Regimental Headquarters transfer from Fort Hamilton to Fort Monroe.[4] The change of station from Florida, where discipline was rather haphazard because of the climate and type of duty assigned to Company I, to the more structured environment at Fort Monroe, seemed to have its effect upon some of Dey's comrades. Privates Henry Barry, Charles Chambers, Amos J. Collins, John A. Forney, John Ginger, Patrick Goldrick, Thomas Harney, Martin Kilroy, William Mahoney, James Smith, and Cornelius Sullivan were all placed "in confinement" for misconduct.

Private Charles Dohn was still under general court-martial. Private Michael Hennessey had been reduced in rank from corporal just before Company I left Fort Myers in April. Private Bernard McKenna, who had deserted from Fort Columbus, New York, while convalescing from illness sustained in Florida, rejoined Company I under guard of a non-commissioned officer from Fort Hamilton. Private Michael Hughes, who had been court-martialed in June 1855, remained in custody. He had been sent to Fort Monroe early in March 1857. On March 6, he was reported as having deserted. Then on March 30,1857, his body was found in Mill Creek, near the fort, where he had drowned. Private Joseph Diez had died in Fort Myers on April 9 from some unspecified disease which had claimed the lives of other company members. Private Charles Kell deserted from Fort Monroe just two days after the company arrived on post. And Gibson himself went on a seven-day leave of absence on the same day that the company landed, leaving Molinard, the only company officer present, in command.

Molinard, who signed the company muster, reported that its discipline, instruction and military appearance were improving (although he did not state over what, and he ignored the number of men in confinement), but that its arms and accoutrements were old. He also reported that new clothing had been requisitioned for the seventy-eight men reported on the rolls.[5] For the first time in almost two and one-half years of military service, Dey reported for sick call. He was admitted into the post hospital with "contusio" on May 4, and returned to duty on May 5.[6] Private Frederick Schmidt, who never recovered from his Florida illness, was given a discharge on a surgeon's certificate of pension on May 24, suggesting that he still suffered some incapacitating physical damage. A week later, on May 31, Herman Meir (or Meier) deserted. John Ginger, who had been in confinement, deserted on June 9.

In this same muster, Company I's non-commissioned officer structure changed. After six months in grade, Corporal Dey was given his

sergeant's stripes, effective June 1. Privates John Bacheman and James
Smith moved back up to corporal. Smith, working on his second enlistment, regained the rating he had held in 1854 (when he reenlisted in
1856, he held the rank of sergeant). Company strength, which had
dropped to seventy-four through desertions and discharges, increased
by one with the transfer of Private James Ellett from Company G, 2nd
U.S. Artillery. Gibson returned from his short leave. But then on May
20, 1857, Molinard was ordered to Troy, New York, to serve as aide-de-
camp to aging Brigadier General John Ellis Wool, who then commanded
the Departments of the East and of the Pacific. General Wool, a hero in
the war of 1812, had also received a sword from Congress for heroism
during the Mexican War. In 1862, he would be promoted to the full rank
of major general after succeeding in keeping Fort Monroe from falling
into Confederate hands.[7]

By the next muster, the enlisted men's totals dropped to 63. Six
men deserted: Privates Charles Dohn, who had enlisted on the same
day as had Sergeant Dey, David Prinzing, John Rossler, Frederick Kemp,
James Pender, and Michael Hennessey, who had lost his corporal stripes
in April. Sergeant Dey again reported to the post hospital with contu-
sions on July 21. He was returned to duty on July 23. The muster also
notes that he was "in arrest," but does not specify any charges, nor is
there any evidence of his having received any punishment. In addition
to the desertions and other company problems, Sergeant David Donnon
and Private James M. Gillon, both of whom had been ill in Florida
(Donnon had been sent to Fort Columbus for treatment), were discharged
on a surgeon's certificate of disability, Donnon on July 20 and Gillon on
July 31.

The non-commissioned ranks were again reshuffled. Patrick Flynn,
who was sick in the post hospital, was reduced from corporal to private.
James Smith, who made corporal on June 1, was promoted to sergeant
on June 20, replacing the discharged Donnon. But he was again reduced to private by August 10. He was also shown sick in quarters.
David Williams was appointed corporal from artificer; and Matteo
Bianchi, after four years in service, was promoted to corporal.[8]

While Company I was going through a series of personnel changes,
the rest of the garrison at Fort Monroe was also having problems. Brevet
Lieutenant Colonel Harvey Brown, 2nd U.S. Artillery, who commanded
the garrison, exchanged a series of memoranda with Colonel Samuel
Cooper, Adjutant General, Department of the Army, in which Brown discussed critical shortages in his command. He noted that Company C, 3rd
U.S. Artillery could only muster 24 enlisted men; and Company F, 2nd
U.S. Artillery, just 26, present and absent, making it impossible "to man
a single gun for drill." The appeal did not fall on deaf ears, but Cooper
advised Brown that "the service in Utah and New Mexico will absorb all

the General Service Recruits for some months to come." He did not include the Kansas-Missouri border war which was also heating up at this time. Nevertheless, he suggested that if "there is prospect sufficient to justify the expense, a [recruitment] rendezvous may be opened in Norfolk or a moving recruiting party might be sent to Hampton or both adopted." Both cities mentioned by the Adjutant General were almost within sight distance of Fort Monroe.

Brown then suggested that "the chance of success either at Norfolk or Hampton will hardly warrant the expense of opening a Rendezvous, but that Richmond, Petersburg, and Harper's Ferry and other towns in Western Virginia & North Carolina will offer a fair chance of filling up those companies." He was then given authority to send out two parties, one for each regiment. The 2nd U.S. Artillery was assigned to recruit North Carolina. Sergeant Gilbert Robinson of Company I went on detached service with the recruiting party to Charlotte, North Carolina. The success of this rendezvous shortly became evident as the new recruits entered the service with the 2nd U.S. Artillery.[9]

Company I received 11 new recruits from the North Carolina rendezvous. A twelfth man was added to the roster when Charles Dohn, who had deserted in July, rejoined in late September, only to be discharged in November 1857 as a result of a general court-martial. Privates Patrick Flynn, who had given up his corporal stripes because of illness, and William Brady, who had joined Company I at the same time as did Dey, were discharged for disability.[10]

Dey again reported for sick call at the post hospital suffering from "phlegmon" [an inflammatory tumor, boil, or carbuncle tending to secrete pus]. This time he spent a full month, from July 30 to September 1, in the hospital.[11] On the day he was released, he and twelve privates were transferred to the understaffed Company F. He replaced Sergeant John Chambers of Company F, who, in his fifth enlistment, was considered too old for service in the field. The 12 privates were transferred because Company I had gotten the 11 recruits. Company F, alerted for movement to Fort Leavenworth, Kansas Territory, had better use for these seasoned soldiers; while Company I, which was to stay at Fort Monroe until May 1860, provided a garrison environment for training recruits. In the same order, it was stated that "the enlisted men having less than three months to serve, will be left at this Post, with all other men of said companies [F and M, 2nd U.S. Artillery] left behind will be attached to Company I, 2d Artillery."[12] Also remaining at the fort from Company F were Privates Robert B. Morse and Charles Tappler, who were serving extended sentences for desertion.[13]

After 33 months with Company I, which included service in Florida during the Third Seminole War, and a brief stopover at Fort Monroe, Virginia, Sergeant Dey and 12 privates joined Company F, were ordered to another frontier in the west. Months after Dey and his comrades left Fort Monroe for Kansas, Brown was ordered to organize an artillery school of practice. In January 1858, he formed a board of officers to arrange a two-year schedule of instruction. One of the members of this board was Captain Augustus A. Gibson of Company I, Dey's former commanding officer.[14]

Chapter 3

Kansas: A Troubled Frontier

When Dey and the 12 privates, Patrick Goldrick, Andrew Hochstadter, Francis Kellett, Edward Koppe, Matthew Long, John Luz, Michael Nulty, Henry C. Stiller, John G. Stroh, Albert Wachsman, Robert Warriner, and Isaac Watkins, marched across the compound at Fort Monroe with their personal gear to join Company F, 2nd U.S. Artillery, they found little to distinguish that command structure from that of Company I. The four officers assigned to Company F were absent on other duties. Captain James Totten, commanding since Captain and Brevet Major Francis Woodbridge died suddenly on October 20, 1855 at Barrancas Barracks, Florida, was on detached service sitting on a general court-martial at Fort Monroe. First Lieutenant Anderson Merchant was also sitting on that general court-martial. First Lieutenant Marcus De Lafayette Simpson had been appointed commissary and subsistence officer on March 26, 1855, but he had not been with the company since March 8, 1848! At least Second Lieutenant Joseph Peck Jones was still serving his company. Assisted on a recruiting rendezvous in North Carolina by Sergeant Daniel R. Hudson and Private William A. Bingham, he successfully recruited 12 new enlistees for the company: James W. Abernathy, Julius A. Baker, William Belcher, Raleigh Brewer, Vardry Camp, James H. Crosby, Joseph A. Hendricks, Milton Hill, William C. Huggins, John Russ, Hiram C. Sherrill, and William J. Williams.

Within days of his transfer to Company F, Dey and the entire company along with Company M were ordered to embark on a steamer at Fort Monroe to sail to Baltimore. From there they were to travel on the Baltimore and Ohio Railroad to Fort Leavenworth for service in Kansas. The order also specified that all officers and enlisted men of both companies were relieved from duty at Fort Monroe to prepare immediately for their march.[1] These orders were followed almost immediately by one specifying that Lieutenant Armistead Lindsay Long was to be "temporarily assigned to duty with Company F (The Captain [Totten] & Lt. [Merchant] being detained at the Fort on a General Court Martial) and will assume command of, and conduct it to Fort Leavenworth; on being relieved by an Officer of the Co. he will rejoin his own [Company E]."[2]

At its last muster in Fort Monroe, Company F numbered only 68 (four officers, and 64 enlisted men), giving it a shortfall of 13. But when it came time to board the steamer for Baltimore, only 57 of the enlisted men answered the call. Some were on detached service, some sick or in confinement. In the 1850s, the authorized enlisted strength for a light artillery company was 76 (four sergeants, four corporals, two artificers, two musicians, and 64 privates). Although none of the company's officers were in this initial move, at the command level, each company was authorized a captain, two first lieutenants, and two second lieutenants, one of which could be a brevet, for a company total of 81.[3]

After Dey and the other enlisted men from Company F debarked from the steamer at Baltimore, and boarded the train, they rode a multiplicity of lines west: the Baltimore and Ohio to Marietta, Ohio; the Marietta and Cincinnati Railroad to Cincinnati; the Ohio and Mississippi to St. Louis, Missouri; and the Northern Missouri to Macon; then the Hannibal and St. Joseph to St. Joseph, Missouri and on to Weston, Missouri, which was just four or five miles above Fort Leavenworth on the Missouri River. From Weston, they could have marched the distance or taken ferries down to the fort.[4] They were part of a contingent of 245 men which arrived at Fort Leavenworth on September 13, 1857, just nine days after leaving Fort Monroe, Virginia. Company F was billeted temporarily in a camp near the fort because it could not accommodate more troops in its overcrowded facilities.[5]

What the newly arrived troops found at Fort Leavenworth (established in 1827 and still active) was a center for assembling large numbers of troops and a supply depot for posts on the Plains and along the

Albert Wachsman served with Dey in Companies I and F, 2nd U.S. Artillery, from 1854–1862. In 1862, he accepted a commission with the 2nd Missouri Light Artillery Regiment.

National Archives

Missouri River.[6] Readily accessible by land and by water, the fort stood
on the threshold of the still untamed western frontier where the Plains
tribes and Indians who had been relocated west of the Mississippi River
by the Indian Relocation Act of 1830 continued to protect their lands
against incoming settlers, who were invading the midlands in vast numbers. In turn, some of these settlers, especially in the Kansas and Utah
territories, were intent upon changing the political complexions of their
respective areas. In the Kansas territory, many of the immigrants from
Pennsylvania, Ohio, Kentucky, the District of Columbia, and the New
England states flooded into the territory, desirous of making Kansas a
free state. Farther west, in the Utah Valley, the Mormons, there since
1847, wanted to establish the State of Deseret, independent of any federal ties. In every case, from Indians resisting encroachment to Americans intent on their own aims, the military was called upon to act as a
police force to control attempts by any factions to ignore or overthrow
the authority of the federal government. Following their old Seminole
enemies west, Dey and his comrades began a campaign far more dangerous than Florida had been.

In 1857, the Mormons renewed their threat to establish an independent state. President James Buchanan, at the behest of Congress,
appointed a governor and three federal judges to enforce the laws of the
United States in Utah territory, and ordered 2,500 troops and supply
trains west from Fort Leavenworth to protect and support them. Meanwhile, the ideological and social struggle between free-staters and slave-
staters in Kansas territory had overflowed into the state of Missouri,
where the population was also widely divided on this issue. The slave-
staters from Missouri claimed land in Kansas to propagate their cause
for slavery. Beginning in 1854, after the enactment of the Kansas-Ne-
braska Bill, which ignited this potential conflict, sporadic fighting between the two factions grew into what could eventually lead to a civil
war. As with Utah, in 1857 the military was offered as a police force to
the federally appointed territorial governor while differences were settled
lawfully.[7]

With little time to adjust to their new environment in the camp
near Fort Leavenworth, Sergeant Dey and Company F were ordered to
join Light Company E, 3rd U.S. Artillery, under the command of Major
Thomas West Sherman[8] for their first police action in the territory. On
September 28, 1857, the two companies marched to Lawrence because
the governor wanted a show of force to discourage any violence or other
disturbances during the upcoming election on October 5. Carrying a two
weeks' supply of subsistence and forage, they were sent to serve as a
posse comitatus to ensure that the laws were obeyed and the public peace
preserved.[9] Brigadier General William A. Harney, under whom Dey had
served in Florida, issued the order which was signed by Captain Alfred

Bird's-eye view of Fort Leavenworth, Kansas, 1881, showing many the same features as when Dey served there in 1858–1860.
National Archives

Brigadier General James Totten. Captain Totten commanded Company
F, 2nd U.S. Artillery from 1857–1861—Dey's second assignment.

Pleasonton[10] of the 2nd Dragoons, serving as the assistant adjutant general on Harney's staff. Company F arrived at Camp Walker[11] near Lawrence and stayed there until October 20, when it moved into camp near Lecompton, the capital of the territory, about ten miles northwest of Lawrence. On the next day, after a four-hour march, the company camped at eight o'clock in the evening at Tecumseh, another polling district, about 15 miles west of Lecompton, just on the northeast fringe of the present-day boundary of Topeka. At daylight on October 22, the company moved into Topeka "in search of a fugitive slave." There is no record of who ordered the search or of its success or failure.[12]

At noon the next day, the company camped near Lecompton, where it mustered and remained until November 8. Dey and the company were kept in the field around Lecompton because of the constitutional convention which assembled there on October 19 and remained in session until November 7.[13] When Company F returned to Fort Leavenworth on November 8, after six weeks in the field, it settled into its former camp near the fort. The day before, however, Harney had issued orders about winter quarters in Cincinnati, a hamlet just west of the city of Leavenworth. Before the soldiers could move into the area, Dey and his comrades had to build their own huts, mess rooms, and kitchens. These tasks were completed by November 18.[14]

Shortly after moving into winter quarters, Sergeant Dey, for some unknown reason, was reduced to private through the judgment passed down from a general garrison court-martial. Corporal Peter Socin, a three-year veteran and native of Switzerland, succeeded him on December 2. In addition to the loss of his stripes, Private Dey owed the government $11.15 for overdrawing his clothing account and seven cents for losing his "No. 4 Letter."[15] Privates Thomas Darby, Patrick Goldrick, Matthew Long, Bernard O'Donnell, James Reynolds, George Rooke, Michael Russell, John Ryan, Luke Smith, and William J. Williams were also cited in the same court-martial for "conduct prejudicial to good order and military discipline" and for being AWOL. Some of these men served with Dey in the Florida campaign. Privates Milton Hill, Edward Koppe, George Reilly, John Russ and John W. Sedgwick deserted during the period from December 4 through December 16, each taking his haversack, canteen, and "3 great coat straps," and owing the government $3.42 for various unpaid bills. Sedgwick also owed Mrs. Lawless, the company laundress, one dollar. Two others, who deserted from the company while it was at Barrancas Barracks, Florida, returned. Private John Rush had deserted on September 21, 1855, and Private William Nelson, five days later. Both returned to the company on December 20, 1857, after an absence of two years! Both forfeited their pay up to January 1, 1858, and had to "make good all the time lost by desertion." No reason was found for their actions.

Company F at Constitution Hall, Lecompton, Kansas Territory, October–November 1857
John Drury, *Midwest Heritage*, A. A. Wyn, Inc., 1948

Yet, Lieutenant Merchant, in command while Captain Totten was on a sixty-day leave of absence, reported that discipline was improving. Captain Totten was not only granted a two-month leave, but he applied for an extension until April 1, 1858, which was granted, providing he left two officers on duty with the company.[16]

While the troops were in winter quarters, Harney ordered commanders of regiments and corps to "commence a regular system of instruction with their commands, according to tactics of their respective arm of service. Daily drill will be instituted whenever the weather permits, and schools of instructions for the officers and non-commissioned officers will be established in each command," and to submit monthly progress reports on this training. He issued another order detailing the markings and punishment for serious offenses against military conduct. For desertion, a soldier was to have the letter "D" indelibly marked on his right hip. For mutinous conduct, the letter "M," one and one-half inch long, was to be indelibly marked on the left hip. In addition, the guilty party was to serve a year at hard labor, wearing a "ball & chain weighing 12 lbs. Attached to his leg— After serving time to have his head shaved and then drummed out of the service."[17]

At the beginning of 1858, the new territorial governor, James Denver, calling for military support in his efforts to conduct orderly and non-violent elections, requested that Harney send troops to Delaware, Kickapoo, Topeka, Lawrence, Oxford, and Leavenworth City for the election scheduled for January 4. Company F, with Private Dey, was one of the units which drew duty in Leavenworth. On January 2, 1858, the troops were alerted to standby. The 2nd U.S. Artillery, under the command of now Colonel Munroe (another of Dey's commanders in Florida), waited at Cincinnati throughout the day to act "at a moments warning as a *posse comitatus.*" Rations were prepared beforehand to be taken with each company. Each man, armed as infantry, was issued forty rounds of ammunition for his cartridge box. The command then moved into Leavenworth City, where Company F was positioned near the Planters Hotel. The election took place without incident, and without intervention by the military.[18]

But that same evening, Lieutenant Merchant was charged with and placed under arrest for violating the 44th Article of War for his conduct during the duty in Leavenworth. The incident, involving Merchant, occurred at the Planters Hotel, a social center (a New Year's Eve Ball had just been held there, and attended by many of the officers from the fort) and also the main arena for murders, kidnapping fugitive slaves and election rows. It provided housing for visiting national figures and was, upon demand, "the gathering ground for diplomatic encounters between Pro-slavery and Abolitionist sympathizers." In effect, the hotel's patrons often reflected, in microcosm, the political and social essence of the entire territory. The first owners opened the Planters as a pro-slavery establishment. "It was a splendid hotel offering the best furniture of the period with 'silverware and plate from the finest New York masters.'" They sold the hotel in 1857. The new owners modified the previous policy by allowing both abolitionists and pro-slavers to use the facilities provided they paid their bills and acted as "gentlemen." To keep peace, they provided two kinds of political bartenders who served night and day. "When a Pro-slavery man came in and shouted, 'I can lick any man north of the Mason-Dixon line,' the [pro-slavery] drink dispenser told him that was the talk and encouraged him. A Northern radical, who could whip any man south of the dividing line, was encouraged likewise by the Abolitionist bartender. Talk was permitted but when shooting started, the offender, regardless of political affiliation, was kicked off the premises." One of the owners once remarked "that no discussion of politics was ever started that it did not end up at the Planters Hotel."[19]

Merchant, who commanded Company F at the Planters' Hotel site on January 4, was charged for dereliction of duty by Captain William Scott Ketchum, 6th U.S. Infantry, who was in overall command of the detail. In the court-martial held at the fort on January 14, 1861, Ketchum charged that Merchant on that night "did leave his command and place of rendezvous, without the consent of his Commanding Officer, Captain Ketchum, and did fail to join his command before it was dismissed." Merchant pleaded not guilty to both the charge and specifications. "The court after mature deliberation of the testimony adduced" found Merchant "not guilty" as charged. He was released from arrest and rejoined his company.[20]

The same court-martial which tried Merchant passed a different sentence on two of Dey's comrades who had been disciplined in the same action in which Dey lost his stripes. This time, Private Bernard O'Donnell was caught drunk on guard duty. He received 60 days at hard labor. Private James Reynolds was charged with disobedience of orders and mutinous conduct, for which he was given 60 days at hard labor, plus the forfeiture of eight dollars a month for the same period.[21]

Harney continued to monitor the condition of his forces by tightening discipline and by discouraging drunkenness. The causes leading to the latter state were the post laundresses who sold liquor on the base. To counter this, Harney ordered that "any Camp woman belonging to the command who is detected in selling whiskey to soldiers or others will be discharged from the service. Any such persons quartered in the garrison will be immediately put off the military reserve."[22] In addition to his administrative problems, Harney received more calls from Governor Denver for military support at Leavenworth City, where a mob was parading up and down the streets "breaking open stores and

Planters Hotel, Leavenworth, Kansas Territory

Private Collection of J. H. Johnson, Leavenworth, Kans.

searching private homes." And at the Kickapoo land office, the U.S. Register and Receiver complained to the governor that they feared an attack by "certain bands of lawless men" and that the public moneys and archives were in danger.[23]

At Cincinnati, Merchant was having his own problems. Private Gilbert Baker, a Pennsylvanian serving in his second enlistment, deserted on January 29. One day later, Private Hiram C. Sherrill, a North Carolinian who had joined the company in August 1857, also deserted. Both left owing the government $3.42 for gear which they took with them. And Sherrill also owed Mrs. Lawless, the laundress, one dollar.[24]

Outside the military compound, Governor Denver's problems moved southward near the city of Fort Scott. In February, he requested that Colonel Munroe, now commanding at Fort Leavenworth (Harney had gone to command the troops in Utah), send two companies of mounted troops to Fort Scott. But Munroe did not honor the request. In late March, the murder of two free-staters near the city triggered retaliation by free-state gangs. The town "had become a haven of intrigue. Settlers who had sold goods here to soldiers now operated stores in the abandoned buildings. Two hotels housed the slave and free factions. At night partisans rode out to plunder settlers belonging to the opposing faction, and returned to make merry in town. Times were never so gay nor so dangerous in the days when the army was stationed here."[25] Fort Scott, the military base, was strategically located between Fort Leavenworth and Fort Gibson (built in 1824), which was 150 miles to the south in what is now Oklahoma. Fort Scott, a frontier post from 1842 to 1853, was used primarily to check upon the surrounding Indian tribes, particularly the Osage, and to control illegal liquor traffic from the settlers on the Kansas Territory-Missouri borders to the tribes. In 1853, as the frontier moved west and Fort Riley was built in the western part of the Kansas Territory, Fort Scott was abandoned. Its garrison was transferred to Leavenworth, and the buildings sold at auction.[26]

While Dey and Company F were waiting for possible duty at Fort Scott, they witnessed the public humiliation of Private George Reilly, who deserted in December 1857 and was apprehended in early 1858. He was dishonorably discharged on March 30, 1858. The company was formed by Merchant to watch as the guards led Reilly, at bayonet point, out of the guard house. His head was shaven, his right hip imprinted with the letter "D," and he was stripped of his military gear. He was then drummed off the post as the musicians played the "Rogue's March."[27]

The first units sent to Fort Scott in early April were the dragoons. They remained for a relatively short time because by mid-April Governor Denver lifted the emergency and suggested that one of the mounted companies could be returned to Fort Leavenworth. But then on April 27, Company F, along with one section of Captain Sherman's battery of

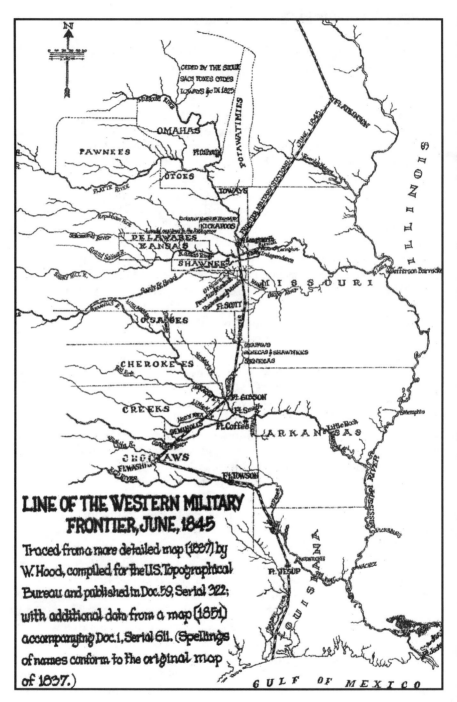

Line of the Western Military Frontier, June 1845
Kansas State Historical Society

the 3rd Artillery, and Company K of the 2nd Dragoons, were ordered to Fort Scott under the command of Captain Thomas John Wood, to act as a *posse comitatus*. Wood was also ordered to turn Company C, 1st Cavalry, which was in transit, back to Fort Scott.[28]

From April 27 to June 22, Dey and Company F made two round trips between Fort Leavenworth and Fort Scott. They covered approximately 300 miles in twenty-eight marching days, while spending the equivalent time on their mission at Fort Scott and refurbishing their supplies at Fort Leavenworth.[29] The company was caught between two sets of orders governing its movements. While at Fort Scott, it was the subject of a set of orders specifying that upon release from detached service at Fort Scott, it was to garrison the post at Fort Riley, Kansas Territory, along with Company H, 2nd U.S. Artillery. Fort Riley needed replacements for troops ordered to Utah Territory.[30] Despite these orders, the company was held at Fort Scott from May 31 to June 16, its longest stay from the repeated movements. It was awaiting the arrival of its relief, Companies B and D, 2nd U.S. Infantry, commanded by Captain Nathaniel Lyon.[31] These troops were delayed en route from Fort Leavenworth because heavy rains slowed their progress, causing them to report on June 11, several days after their scheduled arrival.

During these past two months, Dey lost a tompion from his piece, for which he was docked ten cents by the government. (A tompion was used as a muzzle plug or cover for a 12-pounder, smoothbore, when the piece was not being fired.)[32] Three of his comrades deserted. Private Isaac Watkins left on May 25, a day after the company marched out of Fort Leavenworth on its second trip to Fort Scott. Private Charles Wusshasskeise deserted from the company's first campsite, nine miles out of Fort Leavenworth on May 26. Then Private William Belcher deserted from the Indian Creek encampment (just south of Kansas City) on May 28. Merchant, who had been in command during this entire drill, left on a general recruiting trip on June 25, just three days after the company returned to Fort Leavenworth, and two days after Captain Totten returned from special duty at Fort Monroe.[33]

For the next twenty-six months, from late June 1858 to early September 1860, Dey and Company F became acclimated to garrison duty. They spent three more months at Fort Leavenworth, eight months at Fort Riley, and another fifteen months at Fort Leavenworth. The company actually left to join Company H at Fort Riley on June 29, 1858, but was recalled to Fort Leavenworth on the same day. But it was not until October 2 that Company F again left for Fort Riley. Under the command of Lieutenant Oliver Duff Greene, who transferred into Company F in exchange for Lieutenant Joseph Peck Jones, the company took station at Fort Riley on October 9. It remained there until May 31, 1859.[34]

Life at Fort Riley consisted of training and post routines, except for Private Franz A. Rennick, a native of Sweden and a druggist in his civilian life, who enlisted in Company F at Fort Leavenworth in July 1858. On November 2, he was reported as having died "of disease." But another record explicitly states that he died "by discharge of a pistol in the hands of Sergt. Peter Soukin [Socin] at Fort Riley." Socin, who had succeeded to Dey's sergeant's stripes, was then given a discharge on a surgeon's certificate of disability on November 8, 1858. Dey again moved up the promotion ladder when he received his corporal's stripes on December 1. A week later, the company added nine recruits, bringing its enlisted strength to 72. Captain Totten reported the company's comportment as "Very Good," and the men received their pay from Major James Longstreet, paymaster.[35]

The next six months were quite uneventful. Corporal Dey spent a day in the post hospital in March 1859 with cephulalgia (a fancy name for a "headache"); and while Dey stayed at Fort Riley on detached service, Company F returned to Fort Leavenworth on June 7. On June 18, he again went on sick call with "furunculus" (or boils, sometimes caused by anemia, undernourishment, or fatigue). This was the same physical problem which had plagued him at Fort Monroe in 1857. He then returned to duty on June 24. He rejoined Company F at Fort Leavenworth on September 27.[36]

Two other tragedies occurred while Dey was still at Fort Riley. Private David Stewart, a 34-year-old immigrant from Ireland, already in the fifth year of a five-year enlistment, died at the post hospital at Fort Leavenworth on July 22. And the perennial mischief of the company who was constantly in trouble was "drummed out of the service" on September 23. Private Bernard O'Donnell walked off the post owing Mary Armstrong, the laundress, $12.00 for sixteen months of washing and Hiram Rich, the sutler, $15.50 for various and sundry items. The previous January, O'Donnell had been sentenced to four months at hard labor, and assessed $13.00 for one "Rifle Musket." His continuing misconduct was just cause for a dishonorable discharge from the service.[37]

On October 19, just three days after John Brown captured the arsenal at Harpers Ferry, Dey enlisted for another five years. He received a $39.00 bonus. Conversely, the company's enlisted strength fell to 76 when seven of Dey's comrades opted to let their five-year enlistments expire. Private George Rooke, who reenlisted, was given a disability discharge after serving only six months of that enlistment.[38] In its year-end summary, the 2nd U.S. Artillery Regiment reported that, in 1859, seven men had died, 123 deserted and 13 were apprehended. Company F's contributions to these statistics were one death, eight desertions, and no apprehensions.[39]

In April 1860, Second Lieutenant St. Clair Dearing and 12 recruits joined the company, bringing the enlisted strength to 77. The number increased again when 12 new men enlisted. By the end of June, the enlisted total was 87, with six desertions and one discharge complicating the arithmetic.[40] By the end of August, Dey was pulling duty as provost sergeant; six new recruits joined; six more members deserted; and one, Private John H. Frank, died. From Germany, Frank had first enlisted in 1852 in Syracuse, New York, and reenlisted in Hampton, Virginia, in 1856. He rose to the rank of sergeant, but at the time of his death, he was a private. The company ended 15 months of garrison duty at Fort Leavenworth with orders to go to Fort Smith, Arkansas.[41]

When Company F marched out of Fort Leavenworth for Fort Smith on September 9, it left with 80 enlisted men (four more had deserted).[42] Dey and his comrades had spent just over three years in Kansas Territory. For the first nine months, after their arrival in the territory, they had been engaged in civilian affairs of this troubled territory. Always present, they had not fired a shot.

When that duty was over, the company pulled garrison duty, at Forts Riley and Leavenworth. Although there were many personnel changes, it maintained a hard core of seasoned veterans like Sergeants Hudson, Mahoney, Armstrong, and Connell; Corporals Dey, P. O'Brien, and Wachsman; and privates, some of whom had lost stripes but still practiced good military discipline and gained irreplaceable knowledge of artillery and infantry tactics, all of which was invaluable for the training of new men. At the command level, Captain Totten and Lieutenant Merchant were still assigned to the company. Merchant was with the men for the entire period, while Totten's presence was sporadic because of detached service and leaves of absence. Lieutenant Dearing was added, but he, too, was placed on detached service. Of the 12 privates who joined Company F from Company I with Sergeant Dey in 1857, Goldrick, Hockstadter, Long, Nulty, Stiller, Wachsman, and Warriner still remained. Kellett, Luz, and Stroh were honorably discharged after the expiration of their five-year enlistments. Koppe and Watkins deserted and presumably had disappeared into the Kansas landscape.

Chapter 4

Arkansas: Rumblings

The military road from Fort Leavenworth, Kansas to Fort Smith, Arkansas, ran along the eastern edge of the reservations of the five civilized Indian tribes, Cherokees, Chickasaws, Choctaws, Creeks, and Seminoles, parallel to the eastern borders of present-day Kansas and Oklahoma. Patrols from Fort Smith policed this territory removing squatters and clearing lands for the tribes. West and southwest of Fort Smith, in an area called the Leased District, approximately along the present-day eastern border between the northern border of Texas (Red River) and present-day southern border of Oklahoma, the Comanches and Kiowas ranged. As the military frontier had moved into the southwest, Fort Smith had become the commissary and quartermaster depot for troops controlling any problems caused by these tribes, who similarly resisted encroachment. Periodically, U.S. troops attacked Indian villages in retaliation for an Indian raid on settlers or in an attempt to intimidate the Indians.

In October 1858, Major Earl Van Dorn (later of Civil War fame in the Trans-Mississippi theater) and four companies of cavalry had attacked a Comanche village. Instead of being intimidated, the Comanches threatened to strike back for revenge. During the winter, the menace died down, only to be revived in the spring of 1859, when the warriors resumed their raids on settlements and emigrant trains. The military was sent to protect these people. Then in July 1859, the War Department directed the construction of a new post in the Leased District on or near the Washita River, adjacent to a reserve selected for relocating Texas Indians. After the post, named Fort Cobb (present day Fort Cobb, Oklahoma), was constructed and occupied by some troops from Fort Smith, Companies F and E, 2nd U.S. Artillery garrisoned Fort Smith as replacements.[1] This was the reason that Dey and his comrades had received their orders; the two companies, 140 officers and men, reached

44

their destination on September 29 after marching 330 miles, or an average of sixteen miles a day.[2]

The troops had no sooner arrived when Company F was ordered back to Fort Leavenworth, and Company E to the arsenal in Augusta, Georgia.[3] Company E was ordered east because the Augusta Arsenal was garrisoned by just one company. The artillery posts on the East Coast had all but lost their garrisons as the imminent dangers of the West called for the use of available troops in that part of the country. Of the 198 companies in the U.S. Army, 183 were stationed on the western frontier. In addition, the changing political climate warranted a change in the military thinking, particularly around the facilities which housed military stores. The upcoming election in November pitted the Republican Party, which was primarily Northern and for controlling slavery, against a Democratic Party, which was primarily Southern and desirous of keeping and expanding slavery. Commenting on how Major General Winfield Scott predicted the consequences of the slavery issue, Bruce Catton later concluded that "Neither side believed that the other side was deeply in earnest, and neither side was prepared to face the consequences of its own acts." But these differences could lead to armed conflict.[4]

For some unknown reason, Dey and Company F did not leave for Fort Leavenworth until October 16, almost three weeks after receiving their orders. The company then marched 165 miles to Cow Creek in Kansas Territory, just south of Fort Scott, when it was ordered to countermarch to Fort Smith. It left Cow Creek on October 25 and reached Fort Smith on November 3.[5] Abraham Lincoln was elected president on November 6, and on November 7 at Charleston, South Carolina, the city officials arrested a federal officer who attempted to transfer supplies from Charleston Arsenal to Fort Moultrie.[6] On the same day, the AGO in Washington wired Fort Smith, "Asking if Co. 'F' 2nd U.S. Artillery has left Fort Smith and if not why." A week later, on November 15, the AGO again wired. "Directing Co. 'F' 2nd U.S. Artillery to proceed to Fort Leavenworth." Then on November 20, the AGO told the garrison commander to detain "Co. 'F' 2nd U.S. Artillery until further notice." The very next day, November 21, Company F was ordered to garrison the Little Rock, Arkansas arsenal.[7]

Thus the police duty at Fort Smith ended almost before it began, if in fact the soldiers did any policing. Dey and Company F left for Little Rock, 160 miles east, on November 27, with Lieutenant Merchant in command. Captain Totten took a seven-day leave of absence on the same day so that he could proceed quickly to visit family in Little Rock. He then rejoined his command on December 6 as it marched into Little Rock, with Merchant and 76 enlisted men.[8] There were some personnel changes. Private Charles Clark (deemed at Fort Monroe as "too old for field service" in 1857 but back with the company) and Private James Vaught were left at the post hospital at Fort Leavenworth. The company also added Private Francis Newboldt, who had deserted on September 6, been apprehended on September 10, and was placed in confinement when the company reached Little Rock. He was then released without trial and put back to duty with the conditions that he make good the time lost and that he would reimburse the government for the cost of his apprehension.[9]

As Dey and Company F settled in at the arsenal, their status as garrison was still not settled. On January 11, 1861, the Assistant Adjutant General, Department of the West, inquired of the AGO in Washington if "Captain Totten's Company be considered as detached from Fort Leavenworth or accounted for as the 'regular garrison' of Little Rock Arsenal?" Apparently the commanding officer at Fort Leavenworth claimed that he had "received instructions from the Adjutant General's Office not to drop Captain Totten's Company from his post returns." Eight days later, the AGO responded: "Respectfully returned with the remark, that, as circumstances have greatly changed from what they were at the date of the last endorsement on the subject, made this office, the Company may now be dropped from the return of Fort Leavenworth and for the present be considered as regularly stationed at Little Rock Arsenal."[10]

The AGO's response suited Totten. Though born in Pennsylvania and appointed to the Military Academy from Virginia, he had family ties in Little Rock through his father, Doctor William Totten. The elder Totten was an old soldier who "did service at the Little Rock Arsenal from the laying of its foundation (and was a favorite with every child raised in Little Rock between 1839 and 1860)."[11] As a matter of fact, when the Arkansas State Militia formed a new light artillery battery in 1860, it was named "Totten's Artillery" "in compliment to Dr. Totten and his son, Captain James Totten, the new garrison commander at the Arsenal." Totten's arrival at Little Rock relieved his stepbrother, Captain Richard H. Fatherly, M.S.K. [military storekeeper] of the command of the United States arsenal. Because of these relationships, Totten and his troops were readily accepted by the citizens of Little Rock.[12] W. E. Woodruff, commanding "Totten's Artillery", also noted, "There was no question of his [Totten's] sympathy with the Southern people."[13] The same sentiments might also have applied to Totten's subalterns, Merchant (Virginia) and St. Clair Dearing (Georgia).

The circumstances which caused Company F to be "regularly stationed at Little Rock Arsenal" had indeed changed by January 15, 1861. South Carolina had seceded from the Union in December 1860; Mississippi seceded on January 9; Florida followed on the tenth and Alabama on the eleventh; and Georgia, Louisiana, and Texas would soon join the Confederacy. One of the first acts of secession was the seizure of public property belonging to the federal government, especially of those facilities where the government had stockpiles of military equipment and ordnance. South Carolina seized the arsenal at Charleston. Alabama took over the arsenal at Mount Vernon, and Florida, the arsenal at Apalachicola.[14] The Little Rock Arsenal represented another potential prize for the Confederacy.

Sentiment in Arkansas, like Kansas and Missouri, was divided. Unionists were strong in the northwestern part of the state, if for no other reason than in that sector along the border of the powerful Indian nations, the federal government, through the military, kept those tribes under control. The secessionists prevailed in those sectors of the state where cotton was grown. Late in December 1860, the Arkansas legislature had called for an election to be held on February 18, 1861, to determine if there should be a convention to consider secession, and to elect delegates if such a convention was approved.[15] But secessionists, guided by the strong hand of Governor Henry M. Rector, took matters into their own hands. On January 28, 1861, Rector informed Totten that "the public exigencies require me to make known to you that the U.S. Arsenal at this place will be permitted to remain in the possession of the Federal officers until the State, by authority of the people, shall have determined to sever their connection with the Federal Government, unless, however, it should be thought proper to order additional forces to this point; or, on the other hand, an attempt should be made to remove or destroy the munitions of war deposited in said arsenal." He then asked Totten to assure him that he would observe these conditions and thereby "greatly tend to quiet the public mind, and prevent the collision between the sovereign people of Arkansas and the Government troops now stationed at this point."

Totten's response on the next day was that the troops under his command "were ordered here at the request of some of the members of Congress from this State, and several good citizens also for what reason, if any, I have not been apprised." He also reminded the governor that "as an officer of the Army of the United States, my allegiance is due to that Government in whose [service] I am, and that I act by its *authority* and *permission* and until absolved from that allegiance my honor is concerned in the faithful performance of what I conceive to be my duty." Moreover, he told the governor that he had not been given any instructions nor did he expect the federal government to agree to the governor's two propositions. But while awaiting a response from Washington, Totten concluded, "I most cordially concur with your excellency in the desire to avoid collision between the Federal troops under my command and the citizens of Arkansas, and shall do everything in my power which an honorable man in my position can or dare to do to prevent so deplorable an event."

Almost simultaneously, Totten sent the Adjutant General in Washington a copy of his reply and a copy of the governor's letter. He also requested the AGO to place his information before the secretary of war and the president so that they could provide him with some guidance on policy for this situation. He also informed his commanding officer at the Department of the West in St. Louis of what was happening by forwarding to that office copies of the governor's letter, his own reply and his letter to the AGO. He also requested of the Department "that means and money may be sent to me to carry out the orders which may be given to me in the premises."[16]

While these preliminaries were being considered, early in February, "as suddenly as unexpectedly appeared at Little Rock, several companies of troops under command of Colonel Patrick Cleburne, of Helena, with the avowed design of capturing the United States force of Captain Totten and the arsenal."[17] Totten ordered Dey and the other men of Company F to take a defensive position with their guns in the basement of the main arsenal building in position to repel an assault.[18] Fearing the consequences of a conflict (the arsenal was within a half mile of the business center of the city), the mayor *pro tempore* of Little Rock called an emergency meeting at 3:00 p.m. on February 5. The city council convened another emergency meeting at 4:00 p.m. on February 6. The major concern was that the armed crowd could swell from 400 to "one thousand, or to five thousand, if necessary for the purpose designed." The council called for a peaceful evacuation of the arsenal by Federal troops to avoid the "destruction of much of the property of private citizens, and the probable sacrifice of the officers and their command in charge of the arsenal." Their written resolutions were included in the governor's demands, which were hand carried later in the evening of February 6 by T. D. Merrick, general of the First Division of the Arkansas Militia, that Captain Totten surrender the arsenal.

Totten had not watched the proceeding in Little Rock passively. He wired the AGO early on February 6 about the massing of armed citizens in the city: "Instructions are urgently and immediately asked. Collision seems inevitable if this arsenal is to be held." Then when he received the governor's message, with enclosures, he sent these off immediately to Washington, again requesting guidance: "I am perfectly in the dark as to the wishes of the administration, from the want [of] instructions how to meet such a crisis as at present." That same evening, stalling for time, Totten placed before the governor three points which he wanted resolved before he answered the governor's demands for the surrender of the arsenal:

> 1.   Would the Governor take charge of the arsenal and munitions of war in the name of the U.S. Government, and hold them until legally dissolved of such responsibility?

2.   Would the Governor guarantee safe passage for the forces at that arsenal in whatever direction the commanding officer chose to lead them and would he allow them to take with them all the public and private property they brought with them to the arsenal?

3.   If the arsenal and munitions of war were left intact, would the Governor guarantee the right to march away with all the honor due them as federal officers and soldiers who did not surrender their trust, but simply evacuated a post for want of instructions from their superiors to avoid the bringing on of a civil war?

Totten expected explicit and detailed answers which "will have great influence upon the undersigned in his answer to the communication of the governor of Arkansas, which is promised by 3 o'clock p.m. tomorrow."[19]

Concerned citizens were quite apprehensive of the entire exchange between the governor and Totten. The U.S. senators from Arkansas, R. W. Johnson and W. K. Sebastian, pleaded with the governor, reasoning that "the motives which impelled the capture of forts in other States do not exist in ours. It is all premature. We implore you prevent attack on arsenal if Totten resists." Senator Johnson then repeated his plea to the mayor of Little Rock and the chairman of the city council: "If Totten resists, for God's sake deliberate and go stop the assault."[20]

Johnson's fears were for naught. The governor, who had received Totten's queries at 11:00 a.m. on February 7, answered immediately and affirmatively accepting Totten's three propositions. He then stated that since the company had not brought any cannons with it, "so none are to be taken away." He assured the troops safe passage out of the state, provided "you do not station yourself within the limits of the State of Arkansas or on the borders thereof." At noon on February 8, Captain Totten and Governor Rector signed a memorandum of agreement. Totten reaffirmed in this memorandum that he acted because of the presence of a greatly superior armed force; because any resistance on his part would have resulted in the loss of public and private property, and the lives of innocent people; and because he desired to avoid civil war by "the first instance of a hostile and bloody collision, yet protesting for himself and in the name of his Government against events beyond his control, and which have actuated him to this course."[21] Then Totten ordered Company F and all the enlisted men of the Ordnance Department at the arsenal to move to a camp on the banks of the Arkansas River to await transportation out of the state. The order was signed by Lieutenant St. Clair Dearing, who had resigned his commission the day before to join the Confederate Army.[22]

On February 12, 1861, from the camp at Fletcher's Landing, in the vicinity of Little Rock, Corporal Gus Dey and the men of Captain Totten's command boarded the steamboat *Medora* for St. Louis, Missouri.[23] The people of Little Rock were sorry to see the company leave. Woodruff, who admired Totten greatly, summed up the feeling of Little Rock citizens: "Up to the time of this movement, great hopes had been entertained that Totten would join the Southern cause. He and his officers were personally very popular with the people of the city, who honored him signally on the occasion of his withdrawal, by escorting him and his men to the steamer which took them to St. Louis." The ladies of Little Rock presented Totten with a sword, and a scroll which read, "You feared the danger of a civil war and the consequence to your country." Totten accepted the honor, and to the chagrin of the Little Rock ladies would wear it later leading troops against the Confederate Army.[24]

Chapter 5

●※

Missouri: From St. Louis to Dug Springs

Ten days after sailing from Fletcher's Landing in Little Rock, Arkansas, Corporal Dey and Company F steamed into St. Louis, Missouri. From there they took post at Jefferson Barracks, some twelve miles south of the city, on February 22, 1861.

The last time that Dey had been in Missouri was in September 1857 on his way to duty at Fort Leavenworth, Kansas Territory. Now Kansas had been admitted to the Union as a free state on January 29, three weeks earlier, and now the raging political dramas had shifted to Missouri. When Dey and his compatriots arrived in Missouri, they found the situation different from that in Kansas, and what they had just left in Arkansas. Missouri's position had not yet been decided. Unionists and secessionists were both determined to secure the strategically located state with its great river highway, its railroads and its two arsenals in Liberty and St. Louis.

The United States arsenal at St. Louis was located on approximately fifty-six acres in the southern part of the city, fronting on the Mississippi River on low, sloping ground and enclosed by high stone walls. Much larger than the one at Little Rock, it was considered the key for the control of the state and nearby states. Its stores housed approximately 60,000 muskets, 90,000 pounds of gunpowder, one and one-half million cartridges, forty field pieces, siege guns, and machinery for the manufacture of arms. Although it was the largest arsenal in the south, it was garrisoned by only a handful of men.[1]

Shortly after the beginning of the new year, the War Department had ordered a detachment of 40 men from Newport Barracks, Kentucky, to St. Louis. The arrival of this small detachment was viewed by the Southern sympathizers as an intrusion by the federal government on the affairs of the state, and "insulting to the dignity and patriotism of

51

The arsenal at St. Louis, Missouri, 1861

Harper's *Pictorial History of the Civil War*

the State, and calculated to arouse suspicion and distrust on the part of the people toward the Federal Government." The General Assembly at Jefferson City, capital of Missouri, on January 21, approved the governor's call for a secession convention for the election of delegates on February 18. In addition, the legislators adopted a set of resolutions, declaring that if the federal government should attempt to coerce the South into rejoining the Union, Missouri would aid in the resistance.[2] The pro-Union advocates countered by actively encouraging the city's Union elements to arm themselves, and urgently pleaded with the federal government to send more troops to the arsenal.

On February 6, Captain Nathaniel Lyon and 80 regulars from Co. B, 2nd U.S. Infantry joined the garrison at the arsenal. This was the same unit which had replaced Dey's company at Fort Scott in June 1858. By mid-February, the garrison had grown to nine officers and 484 enlisted men. Two hundred of them were part of a contingent of 250 unassigned recruits from the artillery recruitment depot at Fort Columbus, New York (Gus Dey's old stomping grounds), who were first sent to Jefferson Barracks on February 6, and then ordered to the arsenal on February 16. The other 50 had remained in Jefferson Barracks.[3] Now, a week later, Dey and his company were at Jefferson Barracks.[4]

Company F would stay on post at Jefferson Barracks for two months. Privates Charles Brown, Andrew Sellers, and George Wilson deserted on March 13. They were followed by Privates Bartholomew Tonry, and William H. Sutliff on March 29, by Privates William Doyle and John Russell on April 7, and by Privates Andrew Burns and James Leavitt on April 21. It was not unusual for enlisted men to desert from the regular army. At this time, however, *The Missouri Democrat* editorialized, "There is reason to believe that many soldiers have been tampered with by secessionists and induced to desert, with the view of going South and joining the Southern Confederacy." General Harney, commanding the Department of the West, "could not deny that a significant number of men at the arsenal *were* currently being tried by court-martial for desertion."[5] There is no evidence to substantiate that the men from Company F deserted to the Confederacy, although Tonry, Doyle, Russell and Burns were Irish-born. St. Louis had a large Irish population which lived in the city's worst slum, Kerry Patch. The Irish there opposed freeing slaves who they feared would replace them in their principal labor market as laborers, boatsmen, and railroad workers, and many of these Irishmen did fight for the Confederacy.[6]

After three-plus years, Corporal Dey was again given the three stripes he had lost in November 1857, but he again owed the government ten cents for losing another tompion en route from Little Rock. Earlier Sergeant Daniel Hudson replaced Sergeant John Mahoney as first sergeant. Mahoney just stepped down, and it was Hudson's spot

that Dey filled. Privates William Wrightenburg and Lorenzo Dow Immell
were made corporals. All three promotions were effective as of April 1,
1861.[7] On April 9, Sergeant Dey and Company F were ordered to proceed by train to St. Louis Arsenal. And the detachment of ordnance
troops which had moved from Little Rock with the company was to transfer to the arsenal. The next day, the order was countermanded and Company F was sent to the munitions magazine on the Jefferson Barracks
reservation to secure it against loss to any rebellious forces in the area.
The magazine consisted of two stone buildings, each enclosed within an
outer wall. Each building contained many tons of rifle powder in bar-
rels, fixed ammunition for heavy guns, and a quantity of "composition"
for rockets. A third building, near the gate of the compound, was used
as quarters for the men, while another nearby was used as a barn for
the storage of stores, and as a guard house.

Two days later, a third of a continent away, the nation was on the
brink of a civil war when South Carolina troops fired on Fort Sumter.
The same day, to put seasoned veterans on site, Company F "with all
necessary equipage" was ordered to replace Captain Albert Tracy and
his company of new recruits at St. Louis Arsenal. By April 15, 1861 the
nation was at war. President Lincoln called for 75,000 volunteers.[8]

On the day the war started, Harney received a letter from Colonel
Edward Davis Townsend, Assistant Adjutant General, stating: "It is
reported that Captain Totten, commanding part of the garrison at St.
Louis Arsenal, holds violent secession language in his conversations in
the garrison. The General-in-Chief directs that, if this be so, you immediately send him away from his command for the time being." Harney
was relieved of his command on April 21, and took no action on the
Totten matter.[9]

Townsend's communication should have been directed at Totten's
subaltern, Merchant. Shortly after the company arrived in Missouri,
Merchant went on a leave of absence. He then returned to duty. But on
April 22, 1861, "Having tendered my resignation as an Officer in the
United States, I have respectfully to ask to be relieved from duty at this
post [St. Louis Arsenal]." Lyon forwarded the resignation to the AGO on
the same day.[10] Merchant would serve as a captain of artillery in the
Confederate Army from 1861 to 1865.

Governor Claiborne F. Jackson of Missouri ignored the president's
call for volunteers. Pretending to espouse the abolitionist's cause, Jackson was, in actuality, sympathetic to the pro-slavery factions of Missouri. The War Department, on the other hand, shored up its military
strength in the state. It directed that quasi-military clubs ("Wide-
Awakes") which were unionist be mustered into the regular army. By
April 27, more than 2,700 men were mustered in. Reserve regiments,
which included 5,000 men, were also organized.[11]

The first armed attack had already been struck on April 20, five days after the declaration of war, when armed secessionists from Clay and Johnson counties captured the small arsenal at Liberty, just east of Kansas City, Missouri. They took 1,500 muskets and four small cannons. Jackson made the next aggressive move. On advice from Brigadier General Daniel M. Frost, commanding the state militia in St. Louis, Governor Jackson, as he was empowered to do, called for an encampment for training the militia. The camp was set up at Lindell Grove on the western outskirts of the city, just east of the present-day campus of St. Louis University. It was called Camp Jackson in his honor. On May 6, the first of the militia marched into camp.[12]

Captain Lyon, who had taken over command of both the garrison at the arsenal and the United States forces (he assumed the rank of brigadier general even though he was not yet officially elected to the rank), in the area during Harney's absence, deployed troops to counter any threat made by Jackson's militia. Lyon had already partially neutralized the arsenal by surreptitiously shipping most of the materiel stored there to the arsenal at Springfield, Illinois. He retained only enough supplies for approximately 10,000 troops, which were authorized to be armed. He also sent some 600 men to the Marine Hospital, which was administered by the U.S. Customs Service in St. Louis, and sent three volunteer companies, together with Totten's Company F, to occupy buildings outside the arsenal. These buildings had previously been leased specifically to give troops shelter and to enable them to command strategic positions "which the secessionists had intended to occupy themselves, and which they openly avowed they would plant siege batteries to reduce the place."[13]

Early on the morning of May 10, Captain Lyon ordered his troops to surround Camp Jackson. Since he knew that arms had been sent to the state militia from the Confederate-controlled arsenal at Baton Rouge, Louisiana, Lyon suspected that these troops were ready to make a move against the federal government. He ordered the First Regiment, commanded by his ally, Colonel Frank Blair, to the arsenal to join two companies of infantry under Lieutenant Thomas Sweeny. The Second Regiment, volunteers under Colonel Henry Boerstein, starting from the Marine Hospital, followed Blair's route to Camp Jackson. Colonel Franz Sigel's Third Regiment and the Fourth under Colonel Nicholas Schuettner followed. Lyon also planted his artillery on a hillside overlooking the camp. With approximately 6,000 men surrounding the 1,000 militiamen, the latter surrendered grudgingly. Lyon had not devised a system for handling prisoners, so he offered them parole if they swore allegiance to the constitution of the United States. Only a handful accepted his terms. The others said that they had already sworn allegiance to the United States and to defend the government. A repetition of that pledge would only be an admission that they were in rebellion.[14]

This entire action had drawn a large, curious crowd of citizens and onlookers, and in general, a mob hostile to the Union forces. Inevitably, violence erupted when the mob threw rocks at the Union soldiers, causing indiscriminate shooting. One of the officers of Volunteers, Captain F. C. Blandowski, was killed, and one other soldier was reported killed. Twenty-eight of the mob, including children, were killed, and many were wounded.[15]

A day after the Camp Jackson affair, Harney was restored to his command. Totten was also given additional responsibility. In addition to Company F, and Company A, 2nd U.S. Artillery, he now commanded two companies of the 4th U.S. Infantry, and two companies of the 2nd U.S. Infantry. The troops, totaling five officers and 308 enlisted men, were posted on Walnut Street, close to the arsenal.[16] Also in this reorganization, Dey and Company F were "mounted as [a] Battery of Light Artillery," with two sections of two guns each. Totten also ordered that "Company F is hereby detailed for the Service of the two Sections of Artillery and all Chiefs of Pieces, Cannoneers, Drivers, etc., will be selected from his Company. First Lieutenant R. Saxton, 4th U.S. Artillery will assist and superintend the Organization of the Light Artillery and will immediately make all the necessary preparations and Requisitions for the complete and efficient Service of the Artillery."[17] Dey also saw the addition of two new names to the list of company officers. Henry A. Smalley and John W. Barriger had just been promoted to first lieutenant. But neither joined the company. Lieutenant Marcus Simpson was promoted to captain, and then simply disappeared from the company's rolls.[18]

Other changes occurred. Private Joseph Henry Meyer was given a discharge with a surgeon's certificate of disability on May 27. Corporal William McGinniss was discharged on May 30 to join the staff of Colonel Blair's 1st Missouri Volunteers. Blair, who wrote the request, noted that McGinniss' discharge "has been asked by the Hon. John Hickman of Pa and Mr. Hatch, Secy of State of Illinois & other influential friends. He appears to be a man of some education & have influential friends & it seems nothing but right that he should have a chance of advancement." McGinniss, a surveyor in civilian life, who had enlisted at Fort Leavenworth on June 15, 1860, was the first of the company to enlist in a volunteer unit. Private Darius Street received an honorable discharge upon the completion of his five-year enlistment. And Private James Abernathy died on May 29 from disease, type of disease not noted.[19]

Totten continued to whip his new command into military shape. On May 30, he ordered that the regular monthly inspection as prescribed by the army "will take place tomorrow at 9 O'clock A.M." After the inspection, the "Command will hold itself in readiness to move from its present position to the Post called Camp Harney at the Abbey, in the outskirts of the City of St. Louis." The command was to "move in full Uniform if possible & if this cannot be accomplished the Officers commanding Companies will see that the men of their Commands are as uniformly dressed as possible for the movement."[20]

On May 31, 1861, General Harney was officially relieved of his command for the last time and would see no further active service before his retirement from the army in 1863. Lyon had been elected to and accepted the rank of brigadier general of the 1st Brigade, Missouri Volunteers on May 12, and on May 17, to brigadier general of United States Volunteers.[21] Lyon was close to his goal of assuming command of the Department of the West. Since his arrival in Missouri in February, he had managed to succeed Brevet Major Peter Valentine Hagner as commander of the arsenal by Lyon claiming that his captaincy was senior to Hagner's brevet. Then by insisting that the secessionist movement was gaining momentum while Harney placated and mollified those forces, Lyon was able to convince the politically influential Frank Blair that Harney needed to be removed.[22]

Lyon's appointment shocked both Governor Jackson and Major General Sterling Price, ex-governor and now commander of the Missouri State Militia. They did not trust Lyon, especially after witnessing his actions against Camp Jackson in May. They fully expected him to move quickly against their meager forces. Lyon did move quickly to consolidate his position as commander of the Department of the West. On the same day that Harney was relieved, Lyon issued General Orders No. 5 assuming command.[23] He mustered all the troops which had been authorized but not enrolled by Harney. In all, he had some 10,000 soldiers at his call by June. Several of the volunteer regiments he reenlisted to a three-year term of service.[24]

Still stalling for time, Jackson and Price were asked "by some well-meaning gentlemen" to work out a truce with Lyon, hoping that Missouri could hold its neutrality. A conference was arranged and Jackson and Price were safely escorted to St. Louis from Jefferson City. The meeting, held at Planters Hotel, lasted about four hours. Lyon ended the meeting by saying that he would see every man, woman, and child in Missouri buried before he would consent to a state dictating to "his Government" as to the movement of troops within her borders, or for that matter, any other conditions however important. "This," he said, "means war. One of my officers will conduct you out of my lines in an hour." With that, he turned on his heels and stormed out of the room without muttering another word.[25]

Almost immediately, Lyon sent Captain Tom Sweeny and Brigadier General Franz Sigel with about 3,000 soldiers to the southeastern part of the state to cut off any retreat by Jackson and Price, if they chose to move in that direction. Then personally taking command of another force, he left the arsenal and loaded 2,000 men, including Dey and Company F, aboard steamers to sail up the Missouri River to capture Jefferson City, the state capital. The company left Camp Harney on the night of June 12, marched to the arsenal, and there embarked with their battery of four guns and their horses on the steamer *Iatan*. The flotilla also included troops from Blair's 1st Missouri Infantry, made up of volunteers and unassigned regular enlistees. Dey and the other experienced cannoneers of Company F had trained some of these troops. The *Iatan* and the *J. C. Swan* reached Jefferson City on June 15, and the troops took the capital without incident.[26]

After Jackson and Price had left St. Louis, they hurried to Jefferson City, burning bridges and cutting telegraph wires behind them, in anticipation of an overland invasion by Lyon's army. They had not considered the possibility of a cross-state invasion by water. The ease with which Lyon's army took the capital was described in a contemporary newspaper account:

> About 3 o'clock last Saturday evening (June 15, 1861) the Federal troops under the command of Gen. Lyon disembarked from boat at Jefferson City and took possession of the town... The regulars landed first and immediately took possession of the heights near the penitentiary, and part of...the Blair's regiment marched to the Capitol, took possession of the building, and hoisted the national flag. The balance of the troops remained on the boats with the artillery.
>
> Col. Boerstein was placed in command and held the capitol while Lyon and the main force continued in pursuit of Jackson's followers. Lyon's force went up the river to Boonville on the steamers *Iatan, A. McDowell,* and *City of Louisiana*.[27]

Dey and his company stayed with the boats at Jefferson City, but they were not inactive. The steamer, *Augusta McDowell*, had been left unguarded and tied up at a wharf across the river. The men managed to cross over and seize it.

The next day, June 16, Lyon's column sailed out of Jefferson City toward Boonville. Company F's muster report recorded:

> The command including Company "F" proceeded up the River Missouri landing next morning 3 miles above Rockport intending to march thence to Boonville MO Seven miles distant. After a march of some two or three miles the State Troops of Missouri were perceived in force drawn up to oppose our advance. One Section of the battery was [unlimbered and] brought into action supported by Skirmishers from our foot on either flank.

General Nathaniel Lyon's army landing at Jefferson City, Missouri, June 1861
Harper's Weekly, July 6, 1861

The march to Boonville, Missouri, 1861

Harper's *Pictorial History of the Civil War*

The action may have lasted here half an hour at the end of which the enemy gave way & a running fight of a mile or more ensued & the affair ended. The camp of the Missouri Troops was taken & there arms found scattered in every direction. Sergt. Armstrong of Company F 2d Artillery who was in the rear with his Section slightly wounded by a spent ball. One horse killed & two wounded.

The non-Commissioned officers and men behaved admirably. The Command entered Boonville the same day.[28]

In contrast to the low-key tone of the muster report, two other writers provided different views of the battle. Colonel Thomas Snead, aide-de-camp to Governor Jackson, saw the battle as "a very insignificant thing but it did in fact deal a stunning blow to the Southern-rights men of Missouri, and one which weakened the Confederacy during all of its brief existence." William Switzler, writing in 1901, recollected:

Governor Jackson and Colonel John S. Marmaduke [were]in command of an untrained, unorganized and badly armed force, if force it could be called. These troops were marshaled in battle array about six miles below Boonville, on the farm of William M. Adam, near the Missouri River. Learning of this, Lyon and Blair disembarked their troops and marched them into conflict. They opened with Totten's Battery and their infantry on Marmaduke's forces, which soon scattered in every direction and in such haste that the engagement is to this day referred to by participants on both sides as the "Boonville" races...in this engagement, two cannon balls from Totten's battery passed through the east brick wall of Adams' residence and evidence of this penetration can be seen to this day. Adams still lives there.[29]

Company F had fired its first shots in the war. It had been blooded, albeit with minimum loss not directly attributable to the action but to exposure in the field. Private William A. Simpson, a two-year veteran from Caroline County, Maryland, was taken seriously ill with rheumatism, forcing him into the field hospital which had been set up at Boonville. Unable to recuperate, he was then sent to the hospital at Jefferson Barracks. He would be subsequently given a disability discharge in Sedalia, Missouri, in January 1862. On Simpson's discharge, Captain [then Lieutenant Colonel] Totten wrote that "Simpson always done his duty and was a good soldier and never was in the Guard House to my knowledge."[30]

Relentlessly, Lyon's army raced on in pursuit of the governor's forces. He ordered Major Samuel Sturgis, with about 2,500 regulars and Kansas volunteers, from Fort Leavenworth. Sturgis joined Lyon near Clinton, Missouri, on July 7. The combined force pushed on. Lyon did not learn until July 9 that Sigel, who he had earlier proposed to attack the Confederates from the southeast with 1,200 men while Lyon hit their left flank, was defeated at Carthage by Missourians and Texas and Arkansas troops, led by Brigadier General Ben McCulloch. Lyon hurried to Springfield, Missouri, where he set up headquarters. He had some 7,000 to 8,000 men, almost half of whom were three-month volunteers.[31]

Lyon's rapid move into the Springfield area with so many troops caused a shortages in supplies, especially of essential food and water for this marching and fighting army. Private Patrick Meehan, an unassigned regular attached to Lieutenant Warren Lothrop's 4th U.S. Artillery and 1st Missouri Light Artillery, Company M, serving as infantry, complained how he and his comrades "suffered from poor water and from very poor rations. The beef being poor & not fit to eat, in my opinion this was the first cause of my having scurvy." Another private in the same command spoke of the "insufficient and unwholesome food, viz.: one (1) pint of cornmeal in 24 hours without either coffee, sugar, or vegetables of any kind, said cornmeal had to be cooked in the ashes as we had no cooking utensils and no commissary stores."[32]

On this same headlong march, Sergeant Dey and his comrades witnessed another tragedy to one of their numbers, Henry Roller: "On the 7th day of July 1861 on the march from Boonville to Springfield, Missouri, about twenty miles from the latter place, he was run over by a Caisson and his left arm and leg were broken and by reason of said injury his left arm has been amputated and his legs permanently injured." Totten commented on Roller's disability discharge that he "has always been a good faithful soldier." Totten then signed the document as "Commanding Company at the [time] of Roller's Misfortune." Roller, German-born, was into his second five-year enlistment. He had enlisted in the company after having served five years with Company L, 7th U.S. Infantry.[33] Roller was sent to the hospital in St. Louis, where he would be discharged in December.

On the day that Roller was hurt, the company bivouacked at Camp Sigel, about twelve miles from Springfield. Totten assessed his company's fitness for the upcoming campaign and wrote to General Lyon about his immediate needs to get his company combat ready:

Major [John Schofield, Actg. Asst. Adj. Gen. to Lyon]

I have the honor to call the attention of the General Commanding the United States Troops near Springfield to the reduced condition of my company as regards numbers. It is absolutely necessary that the Company should be increased to the Effective force of 84 Privates present for duty in order that it may prove efficient to the action which is doubtless ahead. I therefore have to ask respectfully that the General commanding will cause to be transferred to my Company 32 Privates from the 4th Artillery and General Service Recruits now under command of 1st Lieut. Lothrop in this Camp; and moreover, that I may also have authority to select such men as are best adapted and qualified for the Service intended. The present halt at this place will give me an opportunity to instruct the new men placed at my disposal; and, I feel assured the interests of the Service generally as particularly those of General Lyon's command will be advanced by his authorizing my request.

General Lyon's same-day response was that "The within application is approved and orders given accordingly-Col. [Chester] Hardy will cause them to be executed and beside the clothing for Capt. Totten's company that [is] on hand for all the regulars here should be sent to them."[34] At the company's last muster in St. Louis, its enlisted strength was 66. Besides Simpson and Roller, it had lost William Roberts, a musician. He drowned accidentally in St. Louis, the day before the company left there. Moreover, the animals' harnesses were "old as well as rotten"; and the men's clothing was "worn by service in the field."

In its next muster with the immediate transfer of 32 recruits, all regulars, the number of enlisted personnel rose to 92. When Totten asked to be allowed to choose recruits who were "best adapted and qualified," he knew that his veterans had met and instructed possible transferees in the artillery and infantry drill while they all served in St. Louis, prior to beginning this campaign. In addition, he received help when Lieutenant George Oscar Sokalski joined the battery on detached service from the 2nd U.S. Cavalry and when materiel was sent to upgrade the conditions of the men's clothing and the harnesses for his horses.[35]

On July 20, the company marched twelve miles from Camp Sigel to Camp McClellan, just outside Springfield. On that same Saturday evening, Lieutenant Sokalski, with a two-gun section, was ordered to join a task force of about 1,200 men, commanded by now Brigadier General Thomas Sweeny to attack a concentration of Confederates at Forsyth, Missouri. Sweeny's command, in addition to Company F, included companies from the 2nd U.S. Cavalry, 2nd Kansas Infantry, and about 500 Iowa Infantry Volunteers. This small army marched the 45 miles from Springfield to Forsyth in two days.

There they found a small force of some 150 Missourians. The section of Company F unlimbered its 12-pound howitzer and 6-pound cannon and "began to hammer the hillsides where the Missourians were holed up with shell and canister. Unable to cope with the Union Artillery, the State Guards ceased firing and vanished into the surrounding hills." The brief action cost the Union troops two men wounded and four horses killed, one of which was "Prince" belonging to Captain David

Stanley, commanding Company D, 2nd Cavalry. The task force returned to Springfield on July 25, having marched 90 miles, fought a successful skirmish, and fortuitously secured needed blankets, clothing, guns, provisions, horses, and a quantity of lead which had been thrown into a well.[36]

At Camp McClellan, Sergeant Dey and the rest of the company trained the new transferees. On July 26, Private Edward W. Robie, who was on the Forsyth raid, deserted from the battery at Ozark, near Forsyth. Then during one of the artillery drills, Private Josiah Pond, like Roller before him, was run over by a field piece, causing a rupture on his left side and the enlargement of his testicles. He was picked up by his comrade and taken to camp. For the next fifteen months, Pond was treated in the hospital at St. Louis. He would be given a disability discharge in October 1862 from the Military Hospital at Keokuk, Iowa. Pond, a native Virginian, was an eight-year veteran with the company.[37]

On the evening of August 1, the company left Camp McClellan, with the rest of Lyon's army, which now numbered about 6,000 men. They marched for "points south where the enemy was concentrating." The next morning, with Dey and Company F in the lead, the Union Army continued southward toward Dug Springs. At about eleven o'clock, the company encountered Confederate pickets "at a house by the roadside with a wagon partially laden with cooked provisions from which they were driven away by a shell from one of Capt. Totten's guns."[38]

By mid-afternoon, the army, struggling through heat and dust, found that most of the streams and wells were dry. It was said that toward evening a canteen of dirty, rancid water was selling for five dollars! These unbearable conditions affected both armies. In a memoir published in the *Missouri Historical Review* in 1913, Private Joseph Mudd, a member of the Missouri Home Guard, wrote that "the dust was a foot deep, and every man was so thickly coated with it as to be not recognizable by his fellow. Not a drop of water could be had, and the thirst was almost maddening. The spring [Moody's] was a bold stream a dozen feet wide, issuing from the base of the hill, but a strong guard kept the men from approaching, except in their turn. A hundred yards nearer was a stagnant pool packed with cavalrymen. I reached down between the hind legs of a horse, scattered the thick green scum, filled my quart cup, and emptied it at one gulp. From my first perception until now nothing half so delicious has ever passed my lips."[39]

Still later on that hot afternoon, Company F "found the Enemy in force":

> At Dug Springs...at about 5 o'clock in the evening a skirmish took place between [General] Rains secessionists and a battalion of regular infantry under Capt. Fred Steele, a company of U. S. Dragoons under Capt. D. S. Stanley, and two 6-pounders of Capt. Totten's battery. The Southerners were driven away with the loss of one killed, perhaps a dozen wounded and ten prisoners...

The federals pursued the next morning, going as far as Curran or McCullah's store, nearly on the county line between Stone and Barry counties, and twenty-six miles from Springfield. During the day a scouting party of secessionists, which had come across country from Marionville, was encountered at dinner. Totten's artillery was brought up, a few shells fired, and the Southern troops did not wait for desert[sic]! This is a brief but correct account of what is referred to in histories of the civil war as the *"battle"* of Dug Springs.[40]

Joe M. Scott, of the Arkansas Home Guard Mounted Infantry, saw the action quite differently. At Dug Springs, he recalled that he had the closest call he would experience throughout the war. His unit was dismounted with every fourth man holding the horses. After they had advanced about an half a mile, "We found the enemy...the word 'charge' was given and on we went." His unit attacked the Union force only to discover that more "than double our number of Federal cavalry was upon us with drawn sabers, and a hand to hand fight was the result." He found himself and three others surrounded by cavalrymen. One of his number was Hunter, a Negro slave who served as their cook. The federals fired but missed. They then moved toward the four and cut Hunter on the head and arm as he fell trying to escape from the charging cavalrymen. Scott took shelter behind a sapling when a cavalryman rose up in his stirrups and headed for him. Scott warded off the cavalryman with his bayonet when "the negro came to my rescue, shooting him, and he fell before me, the first dead man I ever saw in battle."

Scott claimed that as the skirmish continued, the Confederates unsaddled the federals as "fast as they made their appearance." While he tried to cut his way out of the fight, he heard the Union artillery as it "opened fire on us with a four gun battery [Company F] throwing grape and shell among us." Most of the horses, including his own, were frightened and ran off. He mounted the chaplain's horse, and Hunter boosted Chaplain J. N. Brigance up behind Scott. Hunter then put his master, Horace Beneaux, on his [Hunter's] horse, and got up behind him. The four made their escape, as "bullets and bombshells were falling thick." As they rode back about three miles, they met General McCulloch, the Confederate commander, who advised them to get back out of danger ending Scott's first but not his last war experience.[41]

As Steele and his infantrymen advanced about a mile and a half from Dug Springs, they saw Confederate cavalry crossing and recrossing the road to their front. At this point, Lyon joined Steele and decided not to pursue the attack any longer. The general's decision was based on his analysis of the terrain (it was so configured that he could not gauge the enemy's strength) and on the condition of his troops. There had been many stragglers. For nearly three weeks before this march, they had been on less than half rations. Many suffered from diarrhea, were poorly clothed, and debilitated by the dust, heat and thirst.[42] So Dey with Company F along with the rest of Lyon's army pulled back to Dug Springs, as the general called a council of war to decide the army's next move.

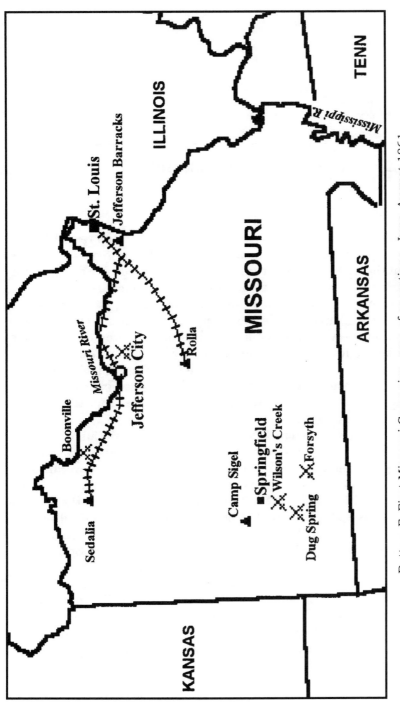

Battery F: First Missouri Campaign, area of operations, June–August 1861

Chapter 6

Missouri: Wilson's Creek, or Oak Hills

On August 4, Dey and Company F, along with the rest of Lyon's army, camped near Dug Springs because the Union scouts could not pinpoint the whereabouts of the main body of Confederate troops. Lyon called a council of war to air out options for advancing or retreating. Totten, who was present, was willing like many of the others to risk an all-out war. But after considering the physical conditions of the troops, the fact that many of the three-month enlistments were running out for some, like the Iowa and Missouri volunteers, and the absence of good scouting reports, it was decided to retire to Springfield. There, hopefully, the army could regroup, receive needed supplies and men from St. Louis, and get better and more current intelligence about the enemy's activities. The army arrived in Springfield on August 7.[1]

While Lyon was engrossed with his problems, McCulloch, whose troops included regiments from Louisiana, Texas, and Arkansas, threatened to pull them back to Arkansas if he were not given overall command of the Confederate Army in Missouri. The problem was resolved when General Price of the Missouri State Guard reluctantly granted McCulloch his wish on August 4.[2] The combined forces numbered slightly more than 10,000 men. In the next few days, McCulloch moved his troops into camp on Wilson's Creek, about ten miles southwest of Springfield, to wait for supplies, and to reconnoiter Springfield. For the next several days, he probed Lyon's position without success. Price, in turn, was exasperated because McCulloch would not attack the Union army. He threatened to resume command of the Missourians and lead an attack himself, with or without McCulloch and his troops. McCulloch acquiesced and gave orders for the troops to move on Springfield at 9:00 p.m. on August 9, for an attack at daybreak on the next morning. Just as the army began to move, however, it began to sprinkle. Fearing that the light rain would become heavier, ruining the ammunition his poorly-equipped army was bearing, McCulloch canceled the attack but kept his troops standing by their arms for immediate movement.[3] Captain W. E. Woodruff, a friend of the Totten family in Little Rock, and commanding the four-gun Pulaski Battery, recalled that that night he and his men kept their horses "harnessed and hitched, and his men at ease or resting near posts, all night. No move was made during the night, and very early the next morning, the 10th, the men got their breakfast, largely green corn which they had gathered during the day before from adjacent fields."[4]

In the meantime at Union headquarters in Springfield, Lyon had learned from one of his patrols that McCulloch and Price had joined forces and were massing for an attack. He called another council of war on Thursday, August 8. He told the principal officers of his command:

> Gentlemen, there is no prospect of our being re-enforced at this point; our supply provisions are running short; there is a superior force in front; and it is reported that [Confederate General William Joseph] Hardee is marching with 9,000 men to cut our line of communication. It is evident that we must retreat. The question arises, what is the best method of doing it. Shall we endeavor to retreat without giving the enemy battle beforehand, and run the risk of having to fight every inch along our line of retreat, or shall we attack him in his position, and endeavor to hurt him so that he cannot follow us. I am decidedly in favor of the latter plan. I propose to march this evening with all our available force, leaving only a small guard to protect the property which will be left behind, and marching by the Fayetteville road, throw our whole force upon his at once, and endeavor to rout him before he can recover from his surprise.

There were no objections, except that a large part of the command had just returned from a long scout. The troops were tired and hungry, since they had not eaten since morning. It was then decided to delay execution of the plan to the evening of August 9.

On that morning, Sigel met with Lyon, advocating that instead of attacking the Confederates with the entire force, it be divided for an assault on two fronts. Sigel proposed that he circle the Confederates and attack from the southeast, while Lyon hit them, as he had proposed, on the left flank.[5] At 6:00 p.m. as scheduled, Lyon ordered his command to pull out. It moved out in two columns. The first, led by Lyon, consisted of three brigades totaling 4,200 men, including Dey, with Totten's Battery, now mounting six guns, with the new section just recently added in Springfield. The second column, led by Sigel, totaled 1,200 men.

Lyon instructed his officers to control all unnecessary noises. Therefore Dey and the other non-commissioned officers of the company, before leaving Springfield, had the men wrap the wheels of their guns,
limbers, and caissons with blankets. The horses' hooves were covered
with burlap which was banded at the fetlocks. Lyon's fear of giving notice to the enemy that he was on the move was almost carried to a fault
when he refused to allow the medical teams to bring their ambulances,
fearing that the rumbling of the teams would alert the Confederates.
Fortunately at the urgings of Major Samuel Davis Sturgis, commanding the 1st Brigade, the general changed his mind and allowed the two
ambulances, large spring wagons drawn by six mules, to accompany
the command.[6]

Despite the order for silence, as the army moved south, the 1st
Iowa Volunteer Infantry burst into its favorite marching song: "So let
the wide world wag as it will,/ We'll be gay and happy still,/ Gay and
happy, gay and happy,/ We'll be gay and happy still." Not to be outdone,
the 1st and 2nd Kansas Infantry Regiments sang "The Happy Land of
Canaan" and "raised the neighborhood with their vocal efforts."[7]

At about midnight, Lyon insisted upon quiet. At about one o'clock,
his column reached a point where he expected to find the enemy's advanced picket. When no picket was found, the column halted and the
men lay on their arms until early dawn. When they resumed march, a
battalion of regular infantry took the lead followed by a battalion of the
2nd Missouri Infantry, and Totten's Battery. At about 4:00 a.m., the
advance units found the enemy pickets, who then fled. With the Confederates alerted, the 2nd Missouri Battalion was sent to the right of
the column as skirmishers; the regular infantry occupied the left and
the 1st Missouri Infantry Regiment was brought forward to support
Totten's Battery. In this formation, the entire column moved forward
for about a mile and a half, when about 5 o'clock a brisk skirmish opened
along the entire Union front against a considerable force of Confederates, occupying the crest of a ridge running almost perpendicular to the
Union line of march and to the valley of Wilson's Creek where the main
Confederate camp was located.

The 1st Missouri moved forward, deployed in line of battle, and
immediately advanced toward the ridge under a brisk fire. The 1st Kansas engaged the enemy, to the left of the 1st Missouri, forcing them to
retreat. During this skirmish, as the left section of Company F, under
Lieutenant Sokalski, moved quickly toward the crest of the hill, Private
Stephen Nolan was struck in the eye from a low-hanging limb of one of
the Chinkapin oaks which dotted the hillside. The blow was so severe
that Nolan eventually would lose the use of his right eye.[8] Sokalski's
section was the first to fire against the enemy. Shortly thereafter, the
other four guns were brought forward in battery onto the higher ground,

where their fire helped to drive the enemy back from its first position. Totten then moved his guns up to the crest of the hill where "I soon found a position, where I brought it into battery directly over the northern position of the enemy camp."[9]

The firefight signaled to the Confederates that the Union Army was on the field, in strength, and poised for battle. One Confederate recalled that "the sun rose clear and beautiful on the 10th of August. I had just come off guard duty, tired and sleepy, had thrown myself on the ground to get a little rest before breakfast, when, almost at the first glint of the sun, a cannon shot broke the stillness of the air. Instantly all was activity. Springing to my feet I saw half a mile to the north the woods blue with Federals. It could not have been more than twenty minutes after Totten's first cannon shot before we were moving at quick step in line of battle."[10]

From his vantage point, Totten found that his battery was planted to the left and front of Woodruff's Pulaski Battery, which was in easy range of Totten's guns. Since these guns were in a wooded area, Totten instructed Dey and the other gunners to direct their fire to the flash and smoke of the enemy's artillery. At one point, while a section of Company F was supporting the 1st Missouri Infantry, Totten spotted a Confederate regiment, some 200 yards from his position in a thick wood and underbrush, displaying both a federal flag and a secession flag. For a moment, he hesitated, not sure if they were Union troops who had advanced. But when these troops opened fire on his battery, he blasted them with canister from both guns.

As the battle continued to intensify and the firing increased to a continuous roar, the action centered around Totten's Battery. "The enemy appearing in front often in three or four ranks, lying down, kneeling, and standing, the lines often approaching to within 30 or 40 yards of each other, as the enemy would charge upon Totten's battery and be driven back."[11] The battle raged for almost an hour, with each side gaining a little ground, and then giving away to rally again. The hill where the fighting was most intense around Totten's Battery became known as "Bloody Hill," an appellation attributed to Confederate Colonel John T. Hughes of the Missouri State Guard.[12] And bloody it proved to be for some of Dey's comrades. Private Joseph Keyes was standing sideways to the enemy loading his gun. His arm was raised and a bullet entered his right breast, hit his right lung and passed through his right arm breaking the bone. Almost immediately he was again hit by a buckshot under his right arm. He went down, seemingly dead. Three others were left for dead during this exchange. There were no records left about the seemingly fatal wounds sustained by Privates Jacob [John] Miller, John Pratt, and James Wallace who received a gunshot wound in the left side near the seventh rib. The ball entered and pierced the cavity of his chest. Corporal Lorenzo Dow Immell also received the first of two wounds, a buckshot in his right shoulder from the gun of a charging Confederate.[13]

There was a short lull in the battle. At about 9:30 a.m., Totten's men saw Lyon for the last time. Early in the battle, the general was leading his horse along the line to the left of Company F when he was wounded in the head and leg. His horse was killed at the same time, forcing him to take another horse from one of his orderlies. Totten later recalled: "...I observed blood trickling from his head. I offered him some brandy, of which I had a small supply in my canteen, but he declined, and rode slowly to the right and front."[14]

Immediately after that meeting, Lyon ordered Totten to support the Kansas regiments on his right. Totten "ordered Lieutenant Sokalski to move forward with his section immediately, which he did and most gallantly, too, relieving the Kansas from being overthrown and driven back."[15] One fourteen-year-old Kansan recalled that support: "The grim and heated Artillerymen (Regulars) were standing near. One old gunner—hatless –bantered our boys on what we might expect and cheered us up with expressions like this: 'Ah, boys, its a divil of a hot place yo's are goin in, and it's many a one you kids that'll never come out o' that.' "[16] While leading these Kansans, General Lyon was killed, just moments after he left Totten's position.

At about the same time, more of Dey's company mates were hurt. Privates William Porter, Henry C. Stiller, and James C. Vaught were wounded. No details survived regarding the seriousness of their wounds. Private James H. Crosby was hit by a minie ball which entered the inner side of his right leg. The ball passed obliquely through the lower third of the tibia, and embedded itself in the inner side of the fibula. Private Richard Dooling was struck in the left arm, and Corporal Immell received his second wound when he was struck on the shin bone of his left leg by a spent ball. Immell was in the act of saving a caisson which had been left on the field by Corporal William Wrightenburg's crew. Wrightenburg claimed to have been hit but no details were found about his wound. Private Cyrus Young was standing immediately behind the battery guarding the horses when he was hit in the left leg about an inch and a half above the knee, fracturing the bone.[17]

Shortly after Lyon's death, the Union Army's advance stalled. Some 800 Confederate cavalrymen, unobserved, had formed below the crests of the hills to the right and rear of the Union lines. Fortunately, Totten reported, "some of our infantry companies and a few pieces of artillery from my battery were in position to meet this demonstration." The cavalrymen were handily repulsed. To Totten, "This was the only demonstration made by their cavalry, and it was so *effete* and ineffectual in its force and character as to deserve only the appellation of child's play. Their cavalry is utterly worthless on the battlefield."[18]

Battery F in action at Wilson's Creek

Borderland Rebellion, The Ozarks Mountaineer

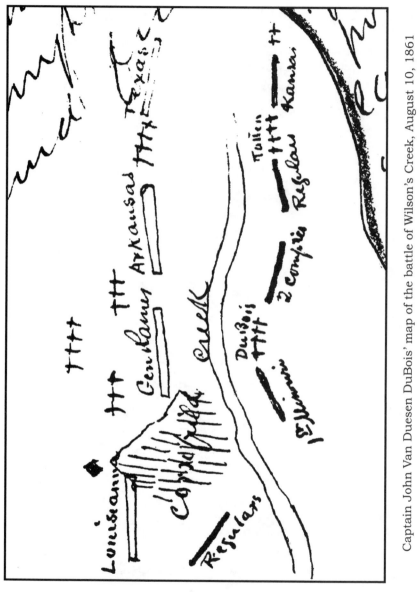

Captain John Van Duesen DuBois' map of the battle of Wilson's Creek, August 10, 1861
Yale University Collection of Western Americana,
Beinecke Rare Book and Manuscript Library

After battling for six hours, the next and last point where Dey and the battery were engaged was on the right of the left wing of the Iowa regiments. Totten recounted how "the battle was then and had been for some time, very doubtful as to its results. General Lyon was killed, and all our forces had been all day engaged, and several regiments broken and had retired. The enemy, also sadly dispirited, were merely making a demonstration to cover their retreat. At this time the left wing of the Iowa regiment was brought up to support our brave men still in action, while two pieces of my battery were in advance on their right. The last effort was short and decisive, the enemy leaving the field and retiring down through the valley, covered by thick underbrush, to the right of the center of the field of battle toward their camp on Wilson's Creek."[19] Sturgis, who took over when Lyon was killed, recalled about the closing moments of the battle that "Captain Totten's battery in the center, supported by the Iowas and regulars, was the main point of attack. The enemy could frequently be seen within 20 feet of Totten's guns, and the smoke of the opposing lines was often so confounded as to seem but one."[20]

Shortly thereafter, the Confederate Army left the field toward its camp on Wilson's Creek. For the Union Army, this withdrawal came at an opportune time. The 2nd Kansas Infantry found its ammunition exhausted. Sturgis directed it "to withdraw slowly and in good order," leaving the right flank exposed to a last desperate lunge by the enemy. This was quickly repulsed by Steele's battalion of regulars. Sturgis then reported, "thus closed, at about 11:30 o'clock, an almost uninterrupted conflict of six hours. The order to retreat was soon given after the enemy gave way from our front and center. Captain Totten's battery, as soon as his disabled horses could be replaced, retired slowly with the main body of the infantry...[with] no enemy in sight, the whole column moved slowly to the high open prairie about 2 miles from the battle ground. Meanwhile our ambulances passed to and from, carrying off our wounded. After making a short halt on the prairie, we continued our march to Springfield."[21]

During the battle, the wounded had been taken away from the battlefield to a ravine behind the Union lines, where there was an adequate supply of water. They were transported to the site on baggage wagons, caissons and six-mule wagons. Since there was a shortage of supplies, each surgeon used his personal instruments. There was no medical director, "and there was no drilled ambulance corps, and the wounded were not systematically carried from the field." The treatment they received was trifling. Assistant Surgeon S. H. Melcher, 5th Missouri Volunteers, reported that "The flies were exceedingly troublesome after the battle, maggots formed in the wounds less than an hour after dressing them, and also upon any clothing or bedding soiled with blood

Death of General Nathaniel Lyon at the battle of Wilson's Creek, August 10, 1861
Steel Engraving from Author's Collection

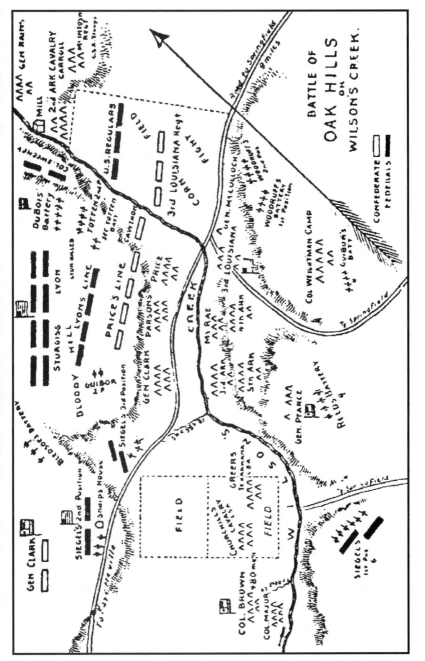

Confederate battle map, August 10, 1861

Borderland Rebellion, The Ozarks Mountaineer

or pus. The wounded left on the field in the enemy's hands were swarming with maggots when brought in." These wounded were brought in under a flag of truce from "half-past eleven a. m. of the day of the fight, and midnight." Most of the wounded brought back by the Union Army and later by the Confederates were placed in churches, hotels, the court house, and private dwellings in Springfield. Very few were carried along with the retreating army.[22]

Of Dey's comrades, Immell, twice wounded, was one of the last men to leave the field, disdaining any medical treatment. Crosby, Dooling and Young were taken along with the company and because of the seriousness of their wounds eventually given disability discharges; Young would be discharged on September 17, Dooling, on September 19, and Crosby on January 7, 1862. Stiller and Vaught, the company saddler, returned to duty after treatment. Of the four men left on the field assumedly dead, Miller and John were eventually released by the Confederates and returned to duty with the battery. Wallace, upon release by the Confederates on September 9, was sent to St. Louis. He returned to duty on November 28. Joseph Keyes was picked up by the Confederates on the next day after the battle and placed in the court house in Springfield. He would remain there until the Union Army recaptured Springfield in September 1861.[23]

On the Confederate side, "the next morning in the camp [one saw]— a scene of desolation, torn tents, wreck-wagons and dead horses, the effect of the enemy's cannonading."[24] The Confederate Army buried its dead. The Union dead were left unburied. Members of the 3rd Louisiana who visited the battlefield two weeks after the battle found the "dead of the enemy were strewn all over the field unburied. They found 150 of them. Dead horses, old clothes, broken wagons, canteens, haversacks were strewn over the field. They noticed particularly the hill that Woodruff's battery had been playing on [Bloody Hill]. Oak trees a foot in diameter were cut into by canon-balls [sic]. More dead men were scattered here than at any other point of the field. Here fell General Lyon. Here the last of the battle was fought. Some of the wounded crawled into the shade of the trees and died there, while others died in the ranks where they fell. The whole scene was a mournful picture of war's desolation."[25] The remains of the Union dead were finally interred by members of Fuller's Ohio Brigade, which had just come into the Missouri area late in September 1861: "While here the regiment was sent on a march of twelve miles to Wilson's Creek to bury the dead left after the battle. The work of internment was done as humanly as possible, but it was difficult on account of the rocky and irregular surface of the battlefield."[26]

The Confederate Army lost 1,222 out of a total of 10,125 soldiers; 277 were killed, and 945 wounded, or approximately 12 percent of their total force. The Union Army lost 1,317 out of a total 5,400, for 24.5 percent. There were 254 killed, 873 wounded and 186 missing. The number of killed was four less than the official records show because the four men from Dey's company were erroneously reported as killed in action in the official reports. The muster roll for Company F (June–August 1861) recorded that at "the time that Muster Roll was made out it was believed that Privates Joseph Keyes, John Miller, John Pratt, and James Wallace of Company F 2d Artillery were killed in battle as stated in the remarks but from unofficial reports it is probable that these Soldiers are still living although seriously wounded, in Hospital in Springfield, Mo. They were left for dead, where wounded and the wounded on the field were not all brought into Springfield until after the army retired on Rolla. The next morning their fate was not known. The correction will be made on the next Muster Roll." It was corrected.[27]

In the after-action reports, Sturgis paid Totten the ultimate compliment when he stated that the "services of Captain Totten are so emphatically interwoven with the various operations of the day as to appear in many, if not all the subreports, and his name deserves to become a 'household name.' "[28] Woodruff of the Pulaski Battery, who traded salvos with Totten's Battery, felt obligated to correct any misinformation about that battery's performance: "All the reports of the Pulaski battery 'whipping Totten' are foundationless. He manifested himself a courageous and capable officer. He was in the fight from 'end to end' and in the very forefront…Totten's guns were abandoned at one stage, Colonel De Rosey Carroll's regiment (he told) went over his, Totten's ground, and found them abandoned. They were recovered, however, and drawn away, I freely say that while our post was dangerous enough, I am glad the conditions were not reversed."[29]

In his after-action report, Totten spread praise among his men. About Sokalski, he wrote that "it gives me the liveliest satisfaction to bear witness to his coolness and bravery throughout the entire day." Sokalski was with the company for just a brief period before fading from its history. Totten also cited Captain Gordon Granger, acting adjutant general, and Lieutenant David Murphy, First Missouri Volunteers, both of whom helped sight guns, momentarily, during the height of the battle. For the non-commissioned officers and other enlisted men, "to a man [they] behaved admirably and it is hard to distinguish between them in this particular; but I am constrained to mention Sergeants Robert Armstrong and Gustavus Deyand [should have read "Dey and"], Corporals Albert Watchman [Wachsman] and Lorenzo D. Trummel [Immell], who were on several occasions during the day greatly exposed and severely tried, and bore themselves with great credit." The other non-commissioned officers and privates also received high praise. But, he continued, "those mentioned were constantly engaged nearly, and

Cadet George Oscar Sokalski, USMA, 1861. Lieutenant Sokalski, detached from the 2nd U.S. Cavalry, commanded a section of Totten's Battery (Company F) at the battle of Wilson's Creek, August 10, 1861.

deserve particular notice, because they were always equal to the duties imposed upon them."[30]

The final honor bestowed upon Dey and the men who fought at the battle of Wilson's Creek was a resolution approved by the Congress of the United States wherein it recognized the "eminent and patriotic services of the late Brigadier General Nathaniel Lyon. The country to whose service he devoted his life will guard and preserve his fame as part of its own glory." For the brave officers and men who served under him, Congress authorized that each regiment bear upon its colors the word "Springfield" embroidered in gold letters.[31]

Lieutenant Lorenzo Dow Immell, with Totten's Battery, cited for bravery, was one of five who were awarded the Medal of Honor for their actions at the battle of Wilson's Creek. In 1862, he accepted a commission with the 1st Missouri Artillery Regiment.

Copy provided by R. A. Collins,
Medal of Honor Historical Society

St Louis Arsenal Oct 12th 1861.

Col. J.C. Woods D.O.S.
    Head Quarters in the Field

Colonel:

The time is now about arrived when you directed me to notify you of the progress of Marshall & Co. Contract for 5 batteries of Brass Guns.

The first battery of Guns is now here: the Guns of the second battery, will be ready in a week, and a battery per week afterwards. The carriages will be delayed somewhat, at least a week behind the guns, but fortunately having carriages from Cincinnati without guns, this delay is of no real moment.

Marshall & Co. are required by their Contract to make 4 more similar batteries, if so ordered.

The present seems a proper time to make a new contract if more guns be needed – Marshall & Co. have secured another shop & without interference with their present work can finish another gun daily. — The carriages can be procured partly in the arsenals, & of good work in short time & at reasonable prices in Cincinnati, besides such as can be built here.

Since Major Schofields return from the East, I have learned from him, that experience has shown that Rifled Brass guns, swell at the chamber so that in 200 rounds, they barely take the rifling till near the muzzle. – Rifled guns are therefore recommended by Gen'l Barry to be made of Iron & steel – using the smooth bore only in Brass Guns — Predicated on this opinion, we have suspended the rifling of the brass guns of Marshall & Co. until further orders – which I now respectfully apply for.

Gen'l Barry advocates the Napoleonic 12 pdr as a very efficient smooth bore gun – its weight is about 1220 lbs & can be drawn by 6 horses on good roads –

Capts McKeever, Callender, & Granger, speak in high terms of their knowledge of such guns & of their efficiency. —

Awaiting your reply I am

Very Respectfully
Your obed Serv't
John Hoskin
Capt & A.O.S.

The status of artillery manufacture, 1861

National Archives

Chapter 7

Missouri: Rolla to New Madrid

In the last short and decisive action of the battle of Wilson's Creek, one of Dey's people, Private Robert J. Black, sustained a minor wound, the nature of which was not recorded although it was evidently severe enough to keep him from doing his duty.[1] This left Dey one man shy as he and the other artillerymen of Totten's company replaced their dead horses and prepared to roll their guns toward Springfield. The company would move in the middle of the day, and Dey, like the rest of the Union Army, had had no water since early in the evening before, "and could hope for none short of Springfield, 12 miles distant."[2] As the company moved toward the rear, the enemy having already left the field, it passed through the rear guard manned by Captain John V. D. DuBois and his four-gun company, with support from the 2nd Missouri Volunteer Infantry. The rear guard was poised on the crest of the hill immediately behind Dey's last position. When DuBois received his orders from Sturgis that he was to provide cover for the retreating army, he was amazed that the commander was calling for retreat. Ten days after the battle, he expressed his dissatisfaction with Sturgis' decision even though he was not thoroughly knowledgeable of the total condition of the Union troops: "Half an hour after all had left I examined the field with my glass, and as far as I could see to the enemy's rear, the road was a line of dust moving in retreat. The enemy set fire to his camp and wagons. When we reached the prairie and found how good a condition our troops were in, we again proposed to attack, but Sturgis (I think on Totten's representation) refused."[3]

The Union retreat cheered the Confederates that the battle was over and that the enemy was defeated. But there was also consternation that they did not pursue and finish off the enemy. Generals McCulloch and Pearce of the Arkansas militia and their staff officers

83

watched through their field glasses, as the Union Army left the field, *"and we were glad to see them go."* The reluctance to pursue was logistically sound: "Our ammunition was exhausted, our men undisciplined." Their scouts had also informed them "that reinforcements were coming to the federal army by forced marches." Yet Pearce like Dubois but better informed of the condition of his army harbored some doubts about not delivering a knockout blow: "It was found on the next day that the disaster of the retreating army was greater than we had supposed, and a few fresh cavalry troops could doubtless have followed and captured many stragglers and army stores."[4] Pearce had no idea where the "few fresh cavalry troops" would be found, nor did he mention that a few days after the battle his brigade of Arkansas militia was disbanded, having served its term under arms, and many of his men headed for home.[5]

Joseph Mudd with the Missouri State Guard disputed DuBois' contention that the Confederates burned their camp and destroyed their wagons. "If we retreated one step, burned or destroyed a wagon, or an article of value, I neither saw nor heard of it, and I was on the scene through it all."[6] While Mudd did not deny that the Union Army had inflicted severe damage on the Confederates, he did report how his commanding officer, Brigadier General John B. Clark, was remarkably upbeat about his troop's performance: "General Clark was sitting before his tent nursing his wounded leg and talking to Colonel Casper W. Bell, his assistant adjutant general, when he suddenly broke from his subject with the exclamation, 'But didn't my men fight, though? Didn't they fight like devils?' "[7]

Dey and Company F were among the last of the Union forces to return to Springfield, after roughly 16 hours of almost uninterrupted movement and fighting. Fearful that the Confederate Army might follow quickly, the command was fed, rested, and ordered to resume marching at 2:00 a.m. on August 11 from Springfield to the railhead and depot at Rolla, Missouri, approximately 120 miles to the northeast. The main body's baggage and supply train contained 370 wagons, many of which were non-standard military conveyances hired from local sources. The train also included many Union sympathizers who fled Springfield under the protection of the army. The caravan stretched for many miles and moved slowly. It was not until after daylight that DuBois' rear guard left Springfield. The Confederate forces arrived there late in the afternoon, capturing the wounded and sick and any supplies which the Union Army could not carry in its retreat. The warm weather taxed both men and animals, forcing the Union train to stop often to repair or remove broken down wagons from the road. The waiting was particularly wearying on the troops who remained standing in column in the hot sun when the train halted. The civilians, who kept a better pace, arrived at

Rolla on August 16. The army after a six-day march reached there on August 17.[8]

Charles Monroe Chase, a bandsman who was with the 13th Illinois Infantry, was stationed at Rolla. He wrote about the arrival of the civilians and the subsequent arrival of the army. Of the first, he noted that the men, women and children came with all their movable effects, "leaving well stocked farms and everything save what they could conveniently bring with them. They flee before the approach of their enemy, leaving their property to supply their enemies wants." On Sunday, August 19, Chase and a comrade walked west from their camp, where they came across Major Sturgis' troops at "the first real stopping place they have made since the battle of Springfield on the 10th inst." Chase described the scene in reasonably literate language: "The men presented a fair specimine of soldiers who had seen service. They looked exhausted; were ragged, poor and as dirty as if they had just been dug out of the ground. Horses, harness, wagons, guns, swords, and the clothing of the men were in the worst possible condition. Everything seemed to be mix up and in confusion. The worst sight however was the wounded men who were lying around the fence and in open wagons waiting for cure or death. Allmost every discription of bruises were to be seen among the soldiers. Legs, arms, heads &c were bandaged in every way or any way to cover their wounds. Eight or ten wagon loads of wounded ready for the depot to take cars for St. Louis, where they could have proper treatment."

With the curiosity of a non-combatant, Chase talked with many members of the 1st Kansas Regiment, which had formed the line just to the left of the 1st Iowa and Dey's Company F on "Bloody Hill." They told him how they were in the "thickest of the fight and suffered much." They also told Chase that they had no idea how many were killed. "It is put between 250 and 450 [the 1st Kansas lost 284, killed, wounded and missing]...many showed me minor wounds where balls just took off the skin, others could show ball-holes in their clothes but no wounds. *I* should be satisfied with the *holes*, though I should object to a slight *flesh wound*, but this loosing an arm, leg or a head: *excuse me!*"

Then on Friday, August 23, Chase again watched as Sturgis' troops passed his camp to encamp two miles from his regiment. "I could not help noticing the contrast between these haggard, ragged, war torn soldiers and our own fresh, well dressed and inexperienced regiment...Their warlike bearing—though they appeared exhausted, was interesting to me. They have done their country much service, and may yet be called upon to sacrifice more of their number in her defense. As they passed we played several tunes for them; the sight of these men experienced in war inspired our boys so that they played their best."[9] Chase, the bandsman, rightly reported the troops' condition. Dey and Company F in the report of its comportment noted that discipline, instruction and military appearance were "excellent." But for its arms, accoutrements, and clothing, all were not only worn but much lost during the battle. Dey owed the government eighteen cents for one canteen, and ten cents for another tompion. As a matter of fact, every enlisted man in the company owed the government for one or more of these lost items. Eventually, these debts would be overlooked as losses resulting from accidents of war.[10] The muster also showed that Totten was again on detached service and that Sokalski commanded the company. Although the company would be identified, for a period of time, with Totten's name, it saw him as its leader for the last time. He had commanded the unit since 1855. Dey had served under him since 1857, longer than he would serve under any other regimental officer.

On August 19, the Western Department in St. Louis (it had ceased to be the Department of the West on July 1, 1861) reorganized the 1st Regiment of Missouri Volunteers into a regiment of artillery, consisting of twelve companies. The order further stated that Company F, DuBois' Company, and the general service recruits, the regulars, under Lieutenant Warren F. Lothrop would return to St. Louis and be attached to the 1st Regiment. Totten was made senior major, Schofield, junior major, Lothrop, first captain, and DuBois, second captain of the regiment.[11]

On the heels of Totten's departure, the company lost another of its designated regular officers. Captain H. A. Smalley, who never did report to the company, was separated entirely. On August 27, Smalley, a Vermont native, was authorized by the War Department to organize and command a regiment of Vermont volunteers. Smalley was replaced by Lieutenant John A. Darling, who assumed command of the company.[12]

The reorganization had a long-lasting effect on the company. Since 1857, when Dey had joined the company prior to its move to Kansas Territory, it had acted independently of its own regiment, having been physically separated from it by half a continent. During the campaign climaxed by the battle of Wilson's Creek, it had acted almost like an independent arm in Lyon's army, being one of three artillery companies at that battle. Now it was detached to a volunteer regiment which, until the reorganization, had served as infantry. On September 10, the new command was ordered from Camp Lyon in Rolla to St. Louis. There Dey and Company F prepared for their next assignment. "The 1st Missouri Light Artillery will at once commence preparation for active service in the field and will follow the movement now ordered as soon as they can be equipped under the order of Lieut. Colonel Totten. The regiment will serve as Infantry only whilst their Batteries are being prepared."[13]

During this lull, three of the wounded, Young, Cooling, and Porter, received disability discharges. Then Privates George Coons, Charles Evert, Christian Ebeychien, John Hauser, William Mooser, Jacob Roth, and Eugene Stumpf deserted. All had joined the company as general

Major John Augustus Darling. Lieutenant Darling commanded Company F during the siege of New Madrid, Missouri, and at the battle for Island No. 10, in February–March 1862.

USAMHI

service recruits on July 7, a month prior to the battle at Wilson's Creek. Two old soldiers also deserted at the same time; Private Dennis Connell had enlisted in 1849, and Private John Wares, in 1855.[14]

The company's stopover in St. Louis was rather short-lived. On September 26, the fully-equipped company with a four-gun battery boarded the *William E. Ewing* from St. Louis en route to Jefferson City. Three days later Dey and Company F joined Brigadier General John Pope's second division of Major General John Fremont's newly-organized Western Department.[15] Fremont's mission was to gain "firm possession of the State of Missouri, freed and protected from the secession forces within and around it." The basic plan had been discussed with President Lincoln early in July 1861. According to Fremont, the president had given him a free hand to do what was necessary to fulfill his mission in the Western Department. Fremont soon learned, after the Union defeat at Bull Run in late July, that Lincoln's strategy shifted to protecting the capital above all other military considerations. Fremont recognized that there "was a wide difference between the situation here and at Washington. The army of the East was organized under the eyes of the President and Congress in the midst of loyal surroundings and loyal advisors where there was no need to go outside of prescribed military usage, or to assume responsibilities. But in Missouri all operations had to be initiated in the midst of upturned and revolutionary conditions and a rebellious people, where all laws were set by defiance."[16]

Moreover, Fremont was convinced that in addition to armed men swarming over the state, that a Confederate force of nearly 50,000 men was already on the state's southern border. Because of these convictions, and his overestimation of the enemy force, Fremont had not supported Lyon's and his meager force at Wilson's Creek. But now, almost a month and a half later, he took the field on September 27 personally to lead a force of some 38,000 men.

By the end of October, Fremont reached Springfield with some 21,000 effectives.[17] (In September, other troops had freed Private Keyes of Company F and other Union wounded who had been brought in by the Confederates after that army occupied the city in August.) Fremont sent cavalry to scout in all directions to determine the position of the Confederates. These scouts reported that Price and McCulloch (both of whom had been at Wilson's Creek) had joined forces again to attack his army. Fremont dispatched orders to Major General David Hunter and Brigadier General John Pope to bring their divisions to Springfield as quickly as possible. Pope, believing that Fremont's intelligence was faulty, sent just one regiment, including Dey and Company F. The company, which had been camped at Quincy, Missouri, slightly northwest, arrived in Springfield on November 2. On that same day, Fremont was relieved of command by Hunter on orders from President Lincoln, who had issued the order on October 24 but directed that it was not to be served if Fremont fought a battle or was about to fight one. Hunter "assumed that there was no enemy near and no battle possible, and withdrew the army" to Sedalia, Missouri. Dey and Company F left Springfield on November 13, and arrived at Sedalia on November 19.

Fremont did not accept his relief of command lightly, and claimed that he had conducted his command correctly. But Franc Wilkie, war correspondent for the Dubuque [Iowa] *Herald* saw it differently: "In every essential respect the campaign of Fremont is the greatest humbug and farce in history. Weeks were taken up in preparation to meet an enemy at a certain point many miles distance who had no existence. The entire operation was a gigantic picnic, whose main qualities were display, vanity, ostentation, demoralization and all sorts of rascally developments."[18]

On the other hand, when the president sent the order relieving Fremont, he also sent Hunter a note, in which he, Lincoln, appeared to be more knowledgeable of the affairs in that area than was Fremont. The president believed that the Confederates had retreated from Missouri into Arkansas. He, therefore, felt it imprudent for Hunter to pursue the enemy and thereby needlessly lengthen dangerously his supply lines and reinforcements. Lincoln then suggested that Hunter divide his army into "two corps of observation, one occupying Sedalia and the other Rolla, the present termini of the railroad." (Sedalia was the western terminus for the Pacific Railroad and Rolla the southwestern terminal.) Lincoln advised Hunter to go into winter quarters to reestablish and improve discipline and instruction, refurbish his soldiers' clothes and equipment, and provide less uncomfortable quarters. He also felt that with the approach of cold weather, the Confederate Army would be reluctant to return to Missouri. Further, with an eye toward the attitude of the civilians there, Lincoln felt that before "spring the people of Missouri will probably be in no favorable mood to renew next year the trouble which afflicted them during this."[19] Acting on the president's advice, Hunter ordered Pope to Sedalia and Sigel to Rolla.

There were no major operations ongoing at this time in Pope's sector. His scouts reported no organized forces in the area, although there were rumors that Price was preparing to move north of the Missouri River and eventually occupy St. Louis. There was considerable activity by guerrillas operating free lance through the western part of the state and into eastern Kansas, attacking or harassing anyone who came within their sights. There was also considerable movement by small unorganized Confederate troops, and also action by sympathizers to the southern cause. To counter these threats, Pope sent his command out in small detachments on scout and reconnaissance missions to search out, destroy, or otherwise contain any pockets of resistance and to keep any large organized Confederate force from initiating a large-scale operation in the middle of winter, despite the president's feeling that nothing would stir in the area before spring. There were skirmishes at Butler and Little Santa Fe on November 20. On November 21, Union stores were destroyed at Warsaw. These incidents were within easy riding distances of Pope's headquarters at Sedalia.

On November 22, a section of one 12-pound howitzer and one 6-pound gun was sent on detached service, "where not known" but "is supposed to be at Leavenworth, KT." The section, under the command of Captain Francis Howard, 1st Missouri Light Artillery, included the two chiefs of pieces, Sergeants Dey and Armstrong, Corporals Wrightenburg and Francis McGinnis, and Privates Robert Belt, Robert Black, Michael Bourke, Richard Burke, James Carney, Samuel Davis, Lewis Dewey, James Garry, Henry Halteman, Randolph Hand, Joseph Hendricks, Thomas Leahy, John Lowry, Christian Mendenez, John Miller, George Moose, Patrick Murphy, George Myrick, Stephen Nolan, Patrick O'Brien, John Pratt, Thomas Smith, James Vaught, John Wares, and James Woods.[20] Despite the muster comment by Darling about not knowing where his men were, or why they were sent on detail, they were evidently part of a scout in areas where skirmishing was taking place. One of the men, Belt, would recall 27 years later in his application for a veteran's pension that the section was on the line of march between West Point and Independence, Missouri, just outside Kansas City. (West Point is not shown on modern-day maps but it was about fifty miles south of Independence.) He did not recall why the section was on this detail but he named Howard ("but...does not remember what organization he belonged to."), Sergeants Dey and Armstrong, and twelve of the men. He also remembered that the "the full strength of the section was only 26 enlisted men" for only one section (2 guns). Belt recalled that the "day was excessively cold; the thermometer being several degrees below zero, and while crossing a small stream [possibly part of the Osage River then, but now a tributary of the Lake of the Ozarks], which was frozen over, the weight of the gun carriages broke the ice, and deponent who was marching immediately behind at the time stepped through into the water filling his left boot, and not having any means to immediately change his stockings or dry his boot, he was compelled to wear his wet foot coverings until he reached camp a distance of ten or twelve miles, when it was found that his left foot was frozen."[21] Vaught was also victimized by the severe cold weather. He was hospitalized in Kansas City in December 1861 with a "disease of the lungs." The attending physician also declared that Vaught would never be "fit for service again" and that he was "without clothes or money." Nevertheless, he would return to the company in June 1862, and serve until his discharge in 1865.[22]

Richard A. Marsh, county judge, Hidalgo County, Texas. Marsh served with Company F from 1860 to 1865 under the alias, Robert Belt.

The company's records are not clear at this point. The return for December states that "Company F, 2d Arty left Sedalia, MO Dec. 15th on an expedition under command of General Pope, marched about 100 miles & returned to this place on Dec. 22, 1861."[23] There is no mention of where the section with Dey and his people, under Howard, was during this exercise. Fragmentary evidence indicates that it was still on scout along the Kansas-Missouri border around Papinsville, Morristown, and north toward Independence.

The Pope expedition resulted from intelligence that Price was again moving north to link up with a large body of recruits, escorts and supplies moving south from the Missouri River. Once joined, this body would represent from 4,000 to 6,000 troops and a large train of supplies. Pope's intention was to wedge his troops between Price, moving north from the Osage River, and Confederate trains moving south off the Missouri River. On Sunday, December 15, Pope sent 4,000 men just south of Sedalia to lead the Confederates into thinking that he was actually moving in force in a southwesterly direction to attack Price. By December 18, he actually posted most of his command between Warrensburg and Knobnoster, thereby essentially closing all roads to the south. Then at Milford on Blackwater Creek, Pope's troops overwhelmed a body of Confederates moving from the north, who surrendered with minimum opposition. The Union forces captured 1,500 prisoners, 1,200 stands of arms, nearly 100 wagons, and a large quantity of supplies.

The section of Company F is only listed as part of the artillery train that participated in the expedition, but Pope's efforts received "valuable journalistic coverage overplaying the victory, as usual, in hopes of driving from memory the earlier Missouri disasters at Wilson's Creek and Lexington. The little battle had the practical effect of breaking up the Confederate forces and making them withdraw to Missouri's southern border." And it showered Pope, Major General Henry Halleck, then commander of the Department of the Missouri, and Colonel Jefferson C. Davis, Indiana Volunteers, who commanded the First Brigade, with honors. Davis was promoted to brigadier general of volunteers, assuming his grade on December 18. On December 20, Halleck sent Pope a letter congratulating him "on the brilliant success of your expedition." Then on January 27, 1862, Halleck wrote to Pope, "You will certainly have a suitable command if I can give it to you."[24]

After the Blackwater expedition, Company F went into winter quarters. Darling with one section was at Sedalia with the main body of Pope's army, and Dey and one section remained around the Kansas-Missouri border. Pope constantly kept elements of his command on scout in a continuing effort to disarm any threat against the Union forces. Halleck advised Pope that a new operation was being planned, and that Pope was to have it "generally understood that your troops are going into winter quarters." There were minor clashes along the areas where both sections of Company F were quartered but there is no evidence that either actively participated in any of them.[25]

The new year opened with Dey and his section at Morristown (which no longer exists) and the other section at Sedalia weathering the cold and snow of a typical Missouri winter. Private William Simpson was discharged at St. Louis on January 19 for rheumatism contracted earlier in June at Boonville, Missouri. Private William Bingham completed his five-year enlistment, on January 1, and was discharged at Sedalia. Henry Brown, a musician into his seventh enlistment, was discharged, "by order." He was probably too old for service in the field.[26]

Meanwhile, Dey's old Company I was stationed at Fort McHenry, Maryland, where it would remain on duty as a heavy artillery company and see no combat, staying at that post practically the entire war. Perhaps because of its closeness to Washington and the political hysteria over the capital's security, and its non-combat status, the company's regular army soldiers were required to sign a pledge of allegiance to "maintain and defend the sovereignty of the United States paramount to any and all allegiance, sovereignty, or fealty we may owe to any State, county, or country whatsoever; and that we will at all times obey the legal orders of our superior officers and the rules and articles governing the armies of the United States. So help us God." This pledge was signed by the non-commissioned officers and privates on January 19, 1862, ten months after the declaration of war. Many of the men signed with their mark, "x", which was verified by an officer and a sergeant.[27]

Private William F. Casper, a native of Rowan, North Carolina, was not present at that signing. He was on detached service with the Ordnance Department at the fort. Unfortunately, he was accused, by person or persons unknown, of disloyalty. In a letter sent on January 22, 1862, to Colonel W. W. Morris, commanding the 2nd U.S. Artillery, Casper swore "that I have ever been loyal in my heart, and that [I] have never made remarks that could injure the service and the Government." His testimony was corroborated by two members of the 3rd Regiment of New York Volunteers, who worked with him in ordnance, and by three members of his own company, who had previously signed the pledge of allegiance. Their statement was then countersigned by Ordnance Sergeant T. H. Dailey, who stated, "I have no hesitation in saying that I firmly believe that Casper would turn his face to the enemy as willingly as nine tenths of the Soldiers at Fort McHenry."[28] Colonel Morris accepted Casper's appeal. Casper reenlisted in Company I on June 22, 1862, and transferred to Company F on the next day.

Winter quarters at Sedalia, Missouri proved unhealthy for some members of the section. Private George Nash was stricken with chronic diarrhea, resulting from exposure to the elements and from drinking bad water. He was sent to the City General Hospital in St. Louis also suffering from pneumonia and rheumatism, and would return to duty some six months later. Private William J. Williams, teamster, was "hauling wood and water for the Company [when] the team scared off without any fault of his [Williams] own throwing him off the saddle causing kidney and bladder disease,—as to render him unable to do any kind of duty for several months." Williams was left in the hospital at Sedalia, and would not rejoin the company until it had moved southeast toward New Madrid. And Private Owen Donnelly, while leading his horse to water, was kicked by the animal, fracturing his kneecap. Donnelly was given a disability discharge in May 1862.[29]

Winter quarters were about to end for Pope's army, Dey, and the rest of Company F. Lincoln was getting increasingly anxious about the inactivity of his commanders in the west. As early as the first of the year, he had problems "trying to get Gen. Halleck from St. Louis to Cairo [Illinois] and Gen. Buell from Louisville [Kentucky] to cooperate 'in concert' in drives on Nashville, Tenn., and Columbus, Ky." Then on January 9, he informed Major General George B. McClellan, who had just recovered from an illness and was back in command of the army, that both Halleck and Buell refused to name a day when they would be ready to take the offensive.[30] Finally, after weeks of frustration, the president issued General Orders No. 1 in which he "ordered that the 22nd of February, [Washington's Birthday, and the day that Jefferson Davis was inaugurated as president of the Confederate States] be the day for a general movement of the Land and Naval forces of the United States against the insurgent forces."[31] This general order applied to all Union forces, including Halleck's Department of the Missouri.

Halleck, in correspondence with McClellan on January 22, had discussed a broad plan of operations, which included among other possibilities the occupation of New Madrid, Missouri, "so as to cut off [the Mississippi] river communications from the south with Columbus [Kentucky]."[32] But as the president had complained, Halleck set no timetable for his proposal. The president's order forced Halleck into action. He ordered Pope to set up a base for marshaling troops and supplies at Commerce, Missouri, just north of New Madrid on the Mississippi. Pope arrived there on February 23 with an advance cadre of 140 men. Halleck wanted Pope to have at least 10,000 men with "the infantry, artillery, and cavalry being in due proportions,"[33] for the siege of New Madrid and the subsequent capture of Island No. 10. Both of these sites were keys to controlling traffic on the Mississippi.

Company F began its movements for this campaign as early as February 3, when the right section of two guns, under Lieutenant Darling, left Sedalia and marched approximately 190 miles to St. Louis, arriving there on February 20. The left section of two guns, with Dey's

and Armstrong's crews, left Morristown on February 12, and reached
Sedalia the next day. This section had been on scout and in winter quarters since November 22. From there it went by rail to St. Louis, arriving
on February 19. The company, together for the first time in almost four
months, and now mounting six guns, two of which were added from the
St. Louis arsenal, boarded the steamer *Edward Walsh* and joined Pope's
gathering force at Commerce on February 27.[34] Before the company left
St. Louis, Corporal Lorenzo Dow Immell was discharged so that he could
receive a commission as a second lieutenant with the 1st Missouri Light
Artillery. As a member of this volunteer unit, he would continue to serve
in or near the same command with Company F.[35]

On its arrival at Commerce, the company found that Pope, who
had arrived there just a few days before, was reorganizing his army
into five divisions, plus a cavalry division and an artillery division, which
included Company F, under Major Warren Lothrop. The aggregate
present for duty operating against New Madrid would be more than
20,000 men.[36] The march from Commerce to New Madrid (a distance
of approximately 50 miles) began on February 28 and was made under adverse weather conditions, in a mixture of "drizzling snow and
rain" over a corduroy road which had not been repaired for years. To
Pope's surprise, the Confederates did not attack his army. He attributed this to the fact that a march over that "country at that season of
overflow [from the Mississippi River] was entirely impracticable." But
after "incredible labor and exposure, wading through the swamps, and
in many places dragging wagons and artillery by hand, we appeared
before New Madrid on the 3d of March, and at once drove in the pickets
and outposts of the enemy and closely invested the place."[37]

Pope's initial strategy was to blanket the area with troops from
New Madrid to Point Pleasant, about 12 miles below New Madrid and
the terminus of the plank road from the interior of Arkansas, in such a
manner as to blockade the river and cut off reinforcements to the Confederate troops from the south. His intent was to take New Madrid,
which he considered a weak point in the Confederate defense system in
this section of the Mississippi.

Company M, 1st Missouri Light Artillery, which was part of
Lothrop's division, was sent to Point Pleasant along with other elements
of Brigadier General Joseph B. Plummer's Fifth Division. The march
from New Madrid was made under extremely difficult conditions of inclement weather and over bad roads. Many of the men became extremely
fatigued, and in wishing to reach their objective before nighttime, the
commanders pushed their people, causing mistakes and accidents. One,
Private Joseph Zimmer, a regular on detached service with Company
M, was driving the wheel team of three teams pulling a 10-pound Parrott
gun. As the piece turned into a lane and passed through two fence bars

into an open field, the lieutenant in charge ordered the lead driver to make a sudden move to the left. The abrupt turn caused Zimmer's leg to be jammed between the left horse and the post, severely bruising his ankle. Fortunately, the painful injury was not permanently disabling.

Another regular in the same company, Private John Vallender, in his application for a veteran's pension in 1880, described the climatic conditions which he claimed caused rheumatism which plagued him for the remainder of his life: "About 2 o'clock p. m. 10th day of March 1862, our command became engaged with the enemy. Said engagement lasting about 2 hours. There was a snow upon the ground at this time and weather very cold. Snow 4 inches in depth at this time." On March 11, sometime during the night, "my Company M 1st Regiment Artillery Vols together with General Plymouth's [Plummer] Brigade recieved [sic] orders and started immediately South arrived at Point Pleasant by a circuitous route traveling a distance of 25 miles." On the next day, the troops found the enemy aboard gunboats. "We immediately became engaged with the enemy upon our arrival and were persistently [engaged]." The exchange of fire "continued with little or no cessation for four long weeks. Each party stubbornly contesting for victory with a persistence rarely known in the annals of war. Our men were under fire night as well as by day." Vallender also recalled the night of March 15 (actually the thirteenth) when "to add to the misery ...after having been fighting for days and nights continuously A Terrible rain storm setting in and the weather being cold this rain storm continued for three weeks raising the water of the Mississippi to overflow and our little army was here subjected to incredible hardships."[38]

The siege of New Madrid began on March 3, 1862. The Confederates occupied the town with five regiments of infantry and several companies of artillery. Also anchored offshore were six gunboats, each equipped with from four to eight heavy guns. As the Union forces, now the Army of the Mississippi since February 23, entrenched themselves, the Confederates continued to be reinforced with troops from Island No. 10. The Union forces were enhanced by the arrival of siege guns which had been sent through Sikeston, Missouri from Cairo, Illinois. These guns, placed within 800 yards of the Confederate main works, were able to overlook that work and the river above New Madrid.

The Confederate main works consisted of Forts Thompson and Bankhead. Fort Thompson was garrisoned with the 11th and 12th Arkansas Infantry Regiments and two batteries of artillery, under Brigadier General Edward W. Gantt. Dey and Company F's guns were planted opposite Fort Thompson. Fort Bankhead, newly constructed at the mouth of Bayou St. John at New Madrid, was manned by three infantry regiments and two field batteries.[39]

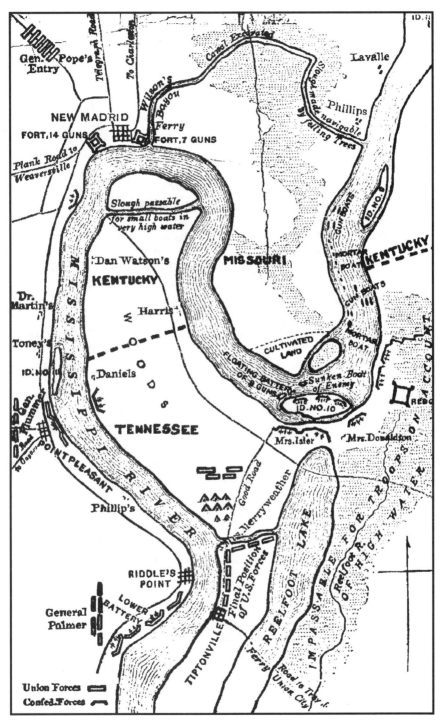

New Madrid, Missouri and Island No. 10
Borderland Rebellion, The Ozarks Mountaineer

The Union siege guns opened fire at daylight on March 13, just 24 hours after they arrived from Cairo. The Confederates responded in kind both from their land and water batteries. During that same night, beginning at about 11:00 p.m., a violent thunderstorm (Vallender's "Terrible rain storm") raged throughout the night. Pope then reported that at dawn of the next day, "a flag of truce approached our batteries with information that the enemy evacuated his works." The small parties of Union troops which were sent into the area found that the Confederates had departed hastily, leaving their dead unburied and all their personal belongings behind. Pope further noted: "Nothing except the men escaped, and they only with what they wore."[40]

Gantt explained in his report the difficulties he had evacuating Fort Thompson. His first objective was to get the guns on the transports which were available for the retreat. The extremely violent storm, however, made it impossible to save but two guns. The mud from the rain and the high water also made it difficult to board the boats, thereby forcing the troops to save only what they could carry. The presence of more transports to carry off other materiel would have alerted the Union army that the Confederates were evacuating the fort. Because of the loss of so much gear and the disarray of the seemingly disorderly evacuation, Gantt was accused of drunkenness. He denied the charge vehemently, claiming he had never accustomed himself to liquor.[41]

Company F's participation in the siege of New Madrid was quite understated in its muster roll. "The Company was stationed March 2nd to April 13 at New Madrid, Mo. [and] was engaged in the bombardment of Fort Thompson."[42] Actually its role in the siege was much greater. In his after-action report, Lothrop noted that at "daylight in the morning [of March 12] the enemy's forts and gunboats opened on our Company and kept up a constant cannonading until about 12 o'clock m [meridian/noon]. After this they continued to fire at intervals until sundown." And, moreover, during the entire "investment of New Madrid, Capt. A. M. Powell, First Missouri Light Artillery; Capt. Henry Hescock, same regiment; Capt. N. T. Spoor, Second Iowa Light Artillery; Captain Sands, Eleventh Ohio Light Artillery; and Lieutenant Darling's Company F, Second Artillery, U.S. Army, were frequently under the enemy's fire, and all behaved in a very creditable manner."[43]

Immediately after the Confederates evacuated New Madrid, the second phase of Pope's campaign, to neutralize Island No. 10, began. The heavy guns captured at New Madrid were "dragged by hand and established in battery at several prominent points along the river, the lower battery being placed immediately opposite the lowest point of dry ground below Tiptonville [Tennessee]. This extended my lines 17 miles along the river."[44] Pope's next move was to build a canal across the peninsula just north of Island No. 10. The canal, which was begun on

March 17 and completed April 4, was 12 miles long and 50 feet wide. Six miles of the canal were through heavy timber. The engineers had to saw these trees to four feet below the waterline, thereby providing enough depth to allow shallow transports to transverse the canal with troops and artillery. The intent was to float batteries opposite the island where Confederates could not establish their batteries.[45]

Pope also enlisted the U.S. Navy to allow its gunboats to run the Confederate batteries on Island No. 10. The first of these gunboats, the *Carondelet,* passed through on the night of April 4. The boat was not hit by any of the shots fired at it. By April 8, the combined pounding by the gunboats and land batteries and the advance of the Union infantry caused the Confederates to surrender at Island No. 10 and at Tiptonville. The campaign cost the Union one officer and seven enlisted men killed, 21 enlisted men wounded, and three captured or missing, out of an aggregate of 20,808 present for duty.[46]

None from Company F was a casualty from this last campaign in Missouri. The company did lose Private Joseph Rush, who received his honorable discharge after two enlistments, on March 2 at New Madrid. Private Victor Buschelberg had deserted on March 1, before the campaign really started, and Private Christian Mendenez deserted on April 13, just as the campaign ended. Private William Ratchford died on April 4 of acute diarrhea at St. Louis' New House of Refuge. His mother claimed, without substantiation, that her son died from gunshot wounds received at Wilson's Creek.[47] Darling had left the company on March 23 for 40 days of sick leave granted by the brigade surgeon, and never returned to it. The muster was signed by Captain Thomas D. Maurice on detached service from the 1st Missouri Light Artillery.[48] Private Vallender undoubtedly summarized every veteran's experience of the New Madrid campaign when he wrote: "We were continuously on duty, continuously soaked in water that was falling and wading and standing in water varying from ankle to knee cap. There was no place to rest or sleep as the entire country was flooded by the overflow from the river and rain was continuously falling. No pen can realize our misery and suffering in this campaign."[49]

After leaving Little Rock and landing at St. Louis on February 22, 1861, Dey and Company F had spent just over a year in Missouri. They engaged the enemy at Camp Jackson, Jefferson City, Boonville, Dug Springs, Forysth, Wilson's Creek, in Fremont's campaign in southwest Missouri near their old battlegrounds around Springfield, in Pope's winter campaign around Sedalia and points west, and at Blackwater Creek or Milford, and finally at the siege of New Madrid and the fall of Island No. 10. They had marched countless miles dragging their guns over all types of terrain, in heat, drought, ice, snow, sleet, and rain.

The highlight of their Missouri service was their heroic stand on "Bloody Hill" at the battle of Wilson's Creek. There Dey and his comrades received richly deserved accolades for a job well done. There they had been blooded, and had flourished under Totten, who would go on to his own glory. And there they received the honor of sewing "Springfield" on their battle flag. Under Darling, they performed their duties. The low point of the Missouri outing was the Fremont campaign against an invisible enemy which never did materialize.

With Darling's departure, and Maurice's arrival, Dey and Company F would gain a very capable officer who never reached the stature of Captain Totten, but who would lead them competently through their next encounters with the Confederate Army.

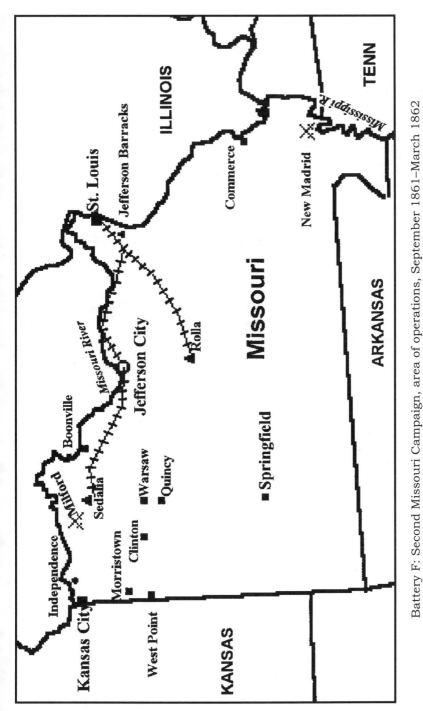

Battery F: Second Missouri Campaign, area of operations, September 1861–March 1862
Created by American History Atlas for Windows 1.0,
Copyright 1993 by Parsons Technology, Inc.,
Used by permission

Chapter 8

Mississippi: Hit and Unhorsed

On April 13, 1862, Captain Thomas D. Maurice,[1] commanding, led Dey and Company F, with its six guns and horses, on to the deck of the transport *Metropolitan*.[2] It was one of 30 steamers which were embarked at Fort Thompson, one mile south of New Madrid. The entire fleet, which carried approximately 20,000 men of the Army of the Mississippi under Pope, was accompanied by the entire Mississippi naval fleet, consisting of 12 mortar boats and seven gunboats, under Commodore Andrew Hull Foote. The flotilla was under sail to attack Fort Pillow, Tennessee, the next fortified point below Island No. 10, just 40 miles north of Memphis. With this fort neutralized, the Mississippi would be opened completely to the Union Army. The run toward Fort Pillow had an air of picnic about it. Brigadier General David Sloan Stanley, commanding the 2nd Division of Pope's army, was awe-stricken by the view: "When all this array of craft was stretched out in one of those very long bends or curves in which this big river flows, the sight was grand. Then the occasional roar of a big cannon added excitement to the spectacle."[3]

Movement was quite slow. Foote feared that some of the Confederate gunboats operating just ahead of the Union fleet might run past the Union gunboats and attack the transports. And because of the slowness, the big troop transports would tie up on the banks of the river several times a day. During these pauses, the soldiers were allowed to go ashore to cook.[4] For some of these men the frequent stops meant more than just cooking a meal. At a stop at Oceola, Arkansas, a low swampy spot on the bend of the river just above Fort Pillow, Dey and every other soldier "had an opportunity to wash themselves and their clothing and to fight to a finish, for the time being at least, the great army plague, an insect known as the grayback [lice], which infested clothing. These insects became so numerous, vicious, ravenous that they almost ate the shirts from the soldiers' backs. Millions were destroyed by boiling the clothing in the camp kettle, the same utensils used for cooking. The crowded conditions of the transports gave no opportunity for the soldiers to change their clothing, was the direct cause of this infection." Once on land, however, the soldiers then came under the "scourge of swamp mosquitoes, locally known as 'galnippers.' They bit the soldiers and even killed horses and mules."[5]

The four-day, 120-mile mission was aborted on April 17. Fort Pillow was a very strong fortification sitting on a high bluff of the river. The Confederate batteries on the bluffs could cascade shells down on the Union gunboats, which could not respond. The mortar boats in the Union fleet were totally ineffective. So bombardment by the Navy was ruled out. Landing an assault force of infantry and artillery was also impractical. Trying to find a suitable landing zone, Stanley reported that he tried "to enter the Forked Deer River but the current of the Mississippi running into the Forked Deer, apparently running upstream, was so violent that we came near wrecking our steamboat, which was caught in the fierce current and carried crashing through the timber overhanging the river." When he returned to the transports, he reported that no landing "could be found at the present stage of water."[6]

News of the battle of Shiloh, or Pittsburg Landing, which had been fought on April 6–7, was the other reason for aborting the campaign against Fort Pillow. The Army of the Mississippi was directed to Hamburg Landing, just south of Pittsburg Landing, and due east of the Mississippi River and Fort Pillow. The convoy left the Fort Pillow area on April 17, traveling up the Mississippi to the Ohio and then the Tennessee Rivers. The 350-mile voyage was completed by April 22 when the army disembarked at Hamburg Landing after passing the "battlefield of Pittsburg Landing, where were seen the long rows of newly made graves of the heroes who fell at Shiloh."[7] The Confederate Army, defeated at Shiloh, retreated south to take a defensive position at Corinth, Mississippi. Corinth was located at the intersection of the Mobile and Ohio Railroad, and the Memphis and Charleston Railroad. At this junction, movement could be controlled to the four points of the compass. At Hamburg Landing and at Pittsburg Landing, Tennessee, and at Eastport, Mississippi, on the Tennessee River, freight steamers could travel even at the lowest stage of water depth. Moreover, Memphis, on the Mississippi River, was just ninety miles away.

Both armies recognized the strategic advantages of controlling Corinth. The Confederates, commanded by General Pierre Gustave Toutant Beauregard, had been decimated from losses at Shiloh and from disease. Of the 80,000 officers and men at Corinth, 15,000 were hospitalized. Only 53,000 were present for duty.[8] His army had retreated in good order, but because of its weakened condition, and the numerical superiority of the Union Army, Beauregard called for help. President Jefferson Davis wired the governors of South Carolina, Georgia, Alabama, Mississippi, and Louisiana on April 10: "Beauregard must have reinforcements to meet the vast accumulation of the enemy before him. The necessity is imminent, the case of vital importance. Send forward to Corinth all the armed men that you can furnish." On April 22, the Confederate Congress enacted legislation calling for the conscription of all white males between the ages of eighteen and thirty-five.[9]

The Union force, 100,000 strong, in a three-pronged front, advanced on Corinth, with Pope's Army of the Mississippi, including Dey and Company F on the left, Major General George H. Thomas' Army of the Tennessee on the right, and Major General Don Carlos Buell's Army of the Ohio in the center. Halleck assumed field command, and named Major General Ulysses S. Grant his second in command. The entire command moved at a snail's pace. Halleck's army was not near the Tennessee River, had no north-south railroad running south, and had to depend solely on ground transportation. The roads were almost impassable because of the heavy rains which had fallen over the past five months. With the need to move large amounts of supplies to support his army, Halleck was forced to build corduroy roads, and to retrench constantly to protect his troops against a powerful army that was on the defensive. The advance consumed nearly seven weeks, moving at a rate of less than a mile a day.[10]

During the siege of Corinth, which lasted from April 27 to May 30, Company F had some personnel changes. First Sergeant Daniel R. Hudson, who had erroneously been reported as AWOL, and charged with desertion, had, in fact, been discharged to allow him to accept a commission with the 18th Missouri Infantry Volunteers. Lieutenant Hudson had been taken prisoner on April 6 just as he joined his new command at Shiloh. He had been sent to prison camp at Macon, Georgia, and would not be released until October. Sergeant Dey was promoted to first sergeant, replacing Hudson, effective May 1, 1862, although Captain Maurice did not request approval for the promotion until May 22. He was then advised by 2nd U.S. Artillery Regimental Headquarters that "the 1st Sgt of a Co is selected from the Sgts by the Capt and that such selection does not require the approval of the Commander of the Rgt. Thus leaving the Capt the sole control of the appointment." Wrightenburg, Frank S. McGinnis, and Francis McIntyre moved up to sergeant. And Raleigh Brewer, Thomas Grant, Bernard Dunnigan, John Pratt, and David Kirkland filled the corporal slots. In addition to the regulars, the company also had attached to it privates from the 34th Indiana, 47th Indiana, and 43rd Ohio volunteers.[11]

Beginning a month of being periodically under fire, First Sergeant Dey and the company, with the rest of Stanley's division, moved into

Mississippi. On May 2, the division was within twelve miles of Corinth. From May 4 to May 8, the division was employed in moving supplies forward. Then on May 8, the division, together with Brigadier General Eleazer A. Paine's division, made a reconnaissance in force. Stanley's division took the left-hand road through Farmington, Mississippi, toward Corinth. Paine's took the right-hand road. Company F shelled the enemy's pickets driving them out of their positions twice. The division then followed the Confederates until it was immediately "under the guns of the enemy's battery in their principal entrenchment. We remained there from 3 p. m. until sundown and returned to camp on the Farmington Road."[12]

During this action, two of Dey's people were injured. Private Stephen Nolan, who had been accidentally hurt at Wilson's Creek, again suffered a temporarily disabling accident. While the company was going into action at the double quick, the caisson on which Nolan was riding struck a stump and overturned. He was thrown to the ground and fractured his right arm. He was hospitalized in the field before being sent to St. Louis. He returned to duty in less than two months. Private James Brennan was not so fortunate. Although he escaped untouched during the action, he accidentally shot himself in the hand while cleaning his revolver. The ball passed through his left hand between the wrist and fingers, fracturing the metacarpal bone of the middle finger, and tearing some of the tendons. He could not close his hand, thereby rendering him unfit for further service. He would be given a disability discharge in October 1862.[13]

Nothing consequential happened then until May 15 when preparations for a move were made. The men stood on their arms all day, but did not move. Then on May 17, with two days' cooked rations, the division moved to Farmington. There, keeping with Halleck's tactics, the troops entrenched within two miles of the enemy's works, "and picket firing was constant." The entrenchments consisted of a single ditch and parapet in the form of a parallel constructed to cover the infantry from the enemy's artillery.[14] Because of this constant firing, on May 24, Stanley dispatched five companies of the 11th Missouri, five companies of the 39th Ohio, a company from the 3rd Michigan Artillery, and a detachment of one howitzer from Company F to silence and scatter the Confederates. Once achieved, he had the 3rd Michigan lob a dozen shells from its Parrott guns into the enemy's works to quell their "annoying and insolent" harassment.[15]

On May 28, the division moved, "presenting a diagonal double line toward Corinth, the right flank nearest the enemy's main work and the front facing the large earthwork battery erected by the enemy south of the Memphis and Charleston railroad. This company was silent for several hours until about noon."[16] Stanley then ordered the 3rd Michigan and Company F to fire. Dey and the company "engaged a rebel company and a large infantry force of the enemy for four hours." Four of the men, Privates Black, Peter Campbell, Vardry Camp and John Tippett, were wounded; six horses were killed and three wounded. One man from a section of the 10th Wisconsin, attached to Company F, was killed and three wounded. The 10th Wisconsin also had three horses killed and two wounded.

It was about 3:00 p.m., after a few hours of firing, Stanley later reported, that "when the enemy appeared in force on our front and right flank. Maurice's battery fired one round, but the men and horses were being rapidly shot down. One section was limbered up by Capt. Maurice and carried off, but two pieces and a caisson being left on the field." The first man to go down was Black, who was struck in the right shoulder by a minie ball which exited through his back. As he fell, he was kicked in the left breast by a dying horse. Maurice saw Black go down, ordered him carried to the rear, and sent to the hospital. Tippet, who was acting as number 4 cannoneer on his gun, was hit in the left forearm. The shell was so shaped as to make "four very bad wounds, causing the loss of the left hand." Campbell had his tongue shot out. And Camp was also severely wounded, but left no description of his wounds. During this same action Private William J. Williams, riding the swing saddle horse, had his horse shot out from under him. As the horse reared, it threw Williams between the tongue and the horse and then fell on him. Williams' right hand was smashed, two teeth were knocked out, his nose was broken, and his face badly disfigured. Maurice saw the horse shot out from under Williams, thought him badly injured, and had him sent to a hospital in the rear.

When Stanley saw that Company F had lost some of its guns, he went "in person to Capt. Spore's [Spoor] battery (2 Iowa) and directed him to ply the advancing enemy, rushing to the abandoned guns of Maurice's battery, with canister and shot." The fire from Spoor's company drove the Confederates off. Lieutenant Daniel P. Walling, 2nd Iowa, and Dey and McGinnis "borrowed horses and gallantly brought off the two guns, and the caisson (Totten's old battery) of Maurice's battery, during the engagement."[17] The resilient Black, who had also been wounded at Wilson's Creek, rejoined the company in October. Tippet would be given a disability discharge at Danville, Mississippi, a month after the battle at Farmington. Campbell would receive a disability discharge in November 1862, and Camp would receive his honorable discharge in August 1862, after completing his five-year enlistment.

As early as May 25, Beauregard in consultation with his subordinate commanders had decided to evacuate Corinth as early as May 30. The withdrawal was so cleverly conceived and secretive that the Union forces actually believed that the Confederates were receiving reinforcements for a counterattack. The rebel troops were instructed to cheer "as though re-enforcements had been received," whenever a railroad engine whistled during the night in their vicinity.[18] Before daybreak on May 30, all of the forces except cavalry had been withdrawn from Corinth.[19] A correspondent from the Cincinnati *Commercial* who entered the town soon after the evacuation wrote that "Corinth was evacuated and Beauregard had achieved another triumph. I do not know how the matter strikes abler military men, but I think we have been fooled. The works are far from being vulnerable and the old joke of quaker guns has been played on us. They were real wooden guns, with stuffed 'paddies' for gunners…The place is entirely deserted, except by one or two families."[20] While the other Union troops settled in Corinth, Dey and Company F, with other units in Stanley's 2nd Division, continued the pursuit of the Confederates. They followed the enemy from May 30 to June 12 as far south as Booneville, Mississippi, before returning to make camp at Clear Creek, near Iuka.[21]

During this period, many changes took place for the Army of the Mississippi. Fort Pillow, evacuated on June 3–4, and Memphis, evacuated on June 6, were occupied by the Union Army. Halleck limited the pursuit of the Confederate Army. As he explained to Secretary of War Edwin M. Stanton, "General Pope, with 50,000 men is following him. I do not, however, propose to follow him far into Mississippi. Having no baggage trains, except railroad trains, he can move faster than we can pursue."[22] And Halleck did not want to further disable his troops with disease by following the Confederates into the Mississippi swamps.[23] He then sent Buell with his Army of the Ohio to open communications along the Memphis and Charleston Railroad, thereby to reinforce troops in Tennessee preparatory to confronting the Confederates at Chattanooga. Pope was called east to command the Army of the Potomac. Halleck himself was ordered to Washington to take command of all the Union troops. Grant was given command of the Department of West Tennessee, and Major General William Starke Rosecrans given the Army of the Mississippi.[24]

Changes also occurred on the Southern side. General Braxton Bragg replaced Beauregard, who moved the main body of troops to Chattanooga, leaving Van Dorn and Price in Mississippi. Van Dorn moved south near Vicksburg, and Price, Company F's old adversary from the Missouri campaign, especially the battle of Wilson's Creek, remained at Tupelo to "keep and eye on Grant."[25]

Changes also took place in Dey's company. Pratt, who had been wounded at Wilson's Creek, was named sergeant to replace Albert Wachsman. Wachsman, who had served with Dey since 1854, received a commission with the 2nd Missouri Artillery Regiment. Private William Kelly replaced Pratt as corporal. Private Francis Newboldt transferred

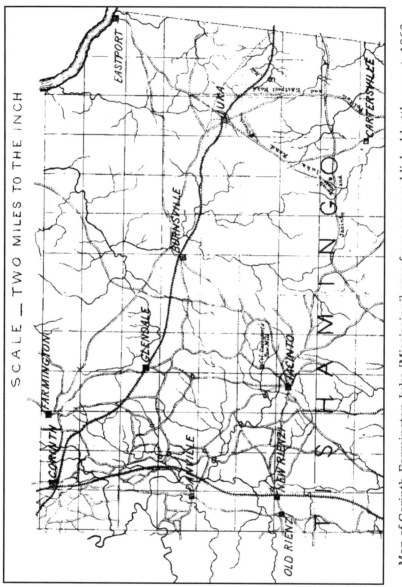

Map of Corinth-Farmington-Iuka [Mississippi] area from an unpublished battle report, 1863
National Archives

in from Company A, 2nd U.S. Artillery. And Baker, Brewer, Hendricks, and Williams completed their five-year enlistments. Baker, Brewer, and Hendricks eventually reenlisted in volunteer units. Henry Simon, a Mexican War veteran, who had been seriously injured in October 1861, would be given a disability discharge in September 1862. Company F also had 27 privates attached from the 34th and 47th Indiana, 43rd Ohio, and 11th Missouri volunteers. The company's paper strength was five officers and 65 enlisted men. Yet none of the five officers (Captain Molinard, the nominal commander, Lieutenants Smalley, Barriger, Darling, and Arnold) was present for duty. Captain Maurice, of the 1st Missouri Light Artillery, was still in command, although he had received a letter from regimental headquarters at Fort McHenry, Maryland, indicating that Molinard had left there on July 14 to take command of the company.[26] Molinard's non-appearance and seeming disappearance was of little or no concern to Dey and the men in the company who were preparing for the upcoming campaign. During these summer months, temperatures soared; wells and streams ran dry; the graybacks and galnippers plagued the men and animals. Dysentery, which had debilitated so many Confederates, became a curse as well for the Union men at or near Corinth.

About six miles from Corinth, Rosecrans, the new army commander, found a level spot, "a beautiful location on rolling land partially timbered and near large springs of pure water which gushed from the ground in such quantities that a large creek was formed."[27] Here beside the appropriately named Clear Creek, the general established a convalescent hospital and also made every effort to improve the men's diets. Private Patrick Meehan, another of the regulars attached to Company M, 1st Missouri Light Artillery, had complained of scurvy during the Missouri campaign and was one of the patients at the hospital. He recalled that his gums were in such "a bad condition and the flesh dropped from my teeth and my legs became swollen & sore. I was on the sick report on and off during the spring and summer of '62 and received from the post hospital a wash for my gums and I used linament [sic] for my legs." Meehan was also stricken with "moon blindness" which affected him so badly that he was excused from night guard duty. When he needed to go out at night, after he left the light of the tent, he was assisted by one of his comrades. Another regular in the same company was the victim of chronic diarrhea and a severe case of rheumatism. Private James E. Twiname also complained of such pains from piles from the constant and hard riding while chasing the retreating Confederates that he was excused from riding and marching until the affliction cleared up.[28]

Dey and his company mates enjoyed the benefits of clear water and recuperation. They "encamped on Clear Creek, Miss. Mooving [sic]

camp twice a short distance. On August 21, 1862 the company marched
14 miles and camped. On the twenty-second marched 6 miles and encamped at Iuka on the Memphis and Charleston Railroad where it at
present remains." And the company, like the rest of the army, was constantly drilling. During one of these drills, McGinnis, one of the heroes
at Farmington, was riding his horse when it tripped, fell on him, and
dislocated McGinnis' wrist. Lowry caught the runaway horse, unsaddled
him and tied him to the picket line. McGinnis went off to the post hospital for treatment.[29] While Rosecrans' army was healing itself, it also
witnessed the revitalization of Corinth. The town filled with sutlers
and merchants "who sold goods at very high prices to both soldiers and
native inhabitants. Butter was $1.60 a pound and a quart can of peaches
$1.50." At least two newspapers were published: *The Corinth War Eagle*,
a weekly, and *The Corinth Chanticleer*, edited and published by C. W.
Hildreth of the 2nd Iowa Infantry.[30]

Rosecrans, who had assumed command on June 15, spent the next
two months "in guarding our front lines, securing the prestige of our
cavalry, and in introducing the system of preparing photograph 'information maps' for the Army under my command." He also sent on "August 2d two Divisions of my command to Middle Tennessee to reinforce
Gen'l Buell."[31]

While Rosecrans was shoring up his defenses around Corinth, Price
wanted more than to just keep an eye on Grant. On July 31, he suggested to Van Dorn that they combine forces and move "toward Grand
Junction or some other point on or near the Tennessee line." There, he
suggested that Van Dorn take over "command of the combined armies
and move thence through Western or Central Tennessee into Kentucky."[32] When Van Dorn did not respond, Price again wrote to him. On
August 24, Van Dorn notified Price that he would be ready to join Price
with 10,000 men in about 20 days. On September 2, Price received a
wire from Bragg informing him that Union General Buell was "in full
retreat upon Nashville; watch Rosecrans and prevent a junction, or if
he escapes, follow him closely." Van Dorn then advised Price that he
would move on September 12.

In the meantime, Price, learning that Rosecrans had set up headquarters at Iuka, Mississippi, with 10,000 men, was convinced that the
Union Army was moving toward Tennessee to support Buell. Price
quickly dispatched his cavalry, under Brigadier General Frank C.
Armstrong, hoping to keep Rosecrans in check. It arrived in Iuka on
September 13. His infantry and artillery got there a day later, only to
find that the Union troops had departed during the night of September 12, marching 20 miles back to Clear Creek.[33] Rosecrans had left
Colonel Robert C. Murphy, commanding the 8th Wisconsin Infantry,
as rear guard to save or destroy commissary stores. Instead, Murphy,

finding himself outnumbered, withdrew his command and marched toward Farmington. For abandoning Iuka, he was reprimanded by Grant; his withdrawal "caused a considerable amount of commissary stores to fall into the hands of the enemy which properly should have been destroyed."[34]

On September 13, Rosecrans reported to Grant that Price occupied Iuka with from 13,000 to 20,000 thousand men. Rosecrans "reconnoitered his position and reported it to Gen'l Grant who decided to attack him." While Price watched Rosecrans, he urged Van Dorn to unite with him and to attack Corinth. Rosecrans, in the meantime, proposed that he march his whole force "via Jacinto and surprise their rear, while he [Grant] should attack the rebels in front which he approved." On September 18, Rosecrans marched to Jacinto, while Grant went to Burnsville, seven or eight miles west of Iuka.[35] Price was informed by his cavalry that a strong Union force was on its way to Iuka. Late the same night, he was informed by Van Dorn that President Davis had authorized him to assume command of Price's army, and for Price to link up with him at Rienzi for a campaign into Tennessee. Price ordered his army to pull out of Iuka immediately.

On the morning of September 19, while his men were loading their wagons, Price received a communication from Brigadier General E. O. C. Ord, calling for surrender because Robert E. Lee's Army of Northern Virginia had been routed at Antietam, Maryland, and the war would soon be over. Appended to the order was a telegram from Cairo, Illinois, describing Lee's defeat and stating that Lee's army was surrounded. Price did not believe the news and countered that his army would not lay down its arms until the South's independence was recognized by the United States.[36] Rosecrans' army was elated when it heard the rumor of Lee's defeat. "During the day [19th] the troops were halted, and by order of General Rosecrans a dispatch was read at the head of every regiment as follows: 'General Lee of the Confederate Army is killed! Longstreet is taken prisoner. Both commands are captured and destroyed.' "[37] The jubilation was short-lived as the men returned to the reality of their own war.

Because a dense wood, with swamps and without a road of any kind lay between Grant and Rosecrans, the two could only communicate by sending couriers on a circuitous 20-mile route. Grant decided not to move on his front until Rosecrans arrived at Iuka, or until he, Grant, heard firing from the south of town indicating that Rosecrans had engaged the enemy. Grant never heard the guns. Sergeant S. H. M. Byers, 5th Iowa Infantry, which had many of the casualties as part of Brigadier General Charles Hamilton's 3rd Division, later recalled, "An unlucky wind kept him and Ord and his whole army resting in complete ignorance of a severe battle raging within a dozen miles of them—a battle in which their comrades were being slaughtered for want of help so near—a battle where was wasted one of the opportunities of the war."[38]

The battle of Iuka was primarily an infantry engagement. At 10:30 p.m., Rosecrans messaged Grant that he "had met the enemy in force just above this point [two miles south of Iuka]. The engagement lasted several hours. We have lost two or three pieces of artillery. Firing was very heavy. You must attack in the morning *in force*. The ground is horrid, unknown to us, and no room for development. Could not use our artillery at all. Fired but a few shots. Push into them until we have time to do something. We will try to get a position on our right which will take Iuka."[39]

Grant did not receive the message until 8:35 a.m. the next day. He assumed that the battle had resumed when he heard artillery fire. But the Confederates had retreated during the night, leaving their dead and wounded on the field. The firing Grant heard was from Union soldiers pursuing the retreating army.

The majority of Stanley's division, with Dey and Company F, which was now brigaded with Colonel John Wallace Fuller's 1st Ohio, saw little or no action. From September 16 to September 21, the company moved out of Camp Clear Creek; reached Iuka on the nineteenth, and was within hearing distance of the shooting. It was then ordered to within one mile of the battlefield, remained in position during the night, and moved up to the front in sight of the town, but the enemy had already retreated. Company F had "no loss or casualties to report."[40]

Union casualties, primarily from Hamilton's 3rd Division, were 141 dead, 613 wounded, and 36 missing or captured. The Confederate count was 86 killed and 408 wounded. They left 286 wounded and 129 sick in Iuka; and 79 on the road out. Brigadier General Lewis Henry Little, considered one of the South's better commanders, was killed.[41]

On September 20, Rosecrans received notice of his appointment as major general of volunteers, effective September 16. Byers, 5th Iowa, which suffered the most casualties (217), commented bitterly about Rosecrans' strategy: "Note—Rosecrans got a star for Iuka, but Gen. Grant reported officially that a part of Hamilton's division, including Iowa regiments, did all the fighting, directed wholly by Hamilton in person...Rosecrans had twenty regiments and thirty cannons near the field, and yet allowed three or four regiments to do all the fighting, and left open the only single road by which Price could escape. Stars were easily earned in those days."[42] Byers was wrong on both counts. Rosecrans received his star before the battle. And the issue of allowing Price to escape on the only road (Fulton Road) out of Iuka was not really resolved.[43]

Price retreated to Baldwyn, approximately thirty miles south of Corinth. He remained there until he joined Van Dorn at Ripley to plan their next move against the Union Army. Grant moved his headquarters to Jackson, Tennessee. Rosecrans returned to Corinth. He posted elements of his command on an outside perimeter at Jacinto, Rienzi, Burnsville, Iuka, and at strategic bridges along the Mobile and Ohio Railroad. Dey and Company F and other units of Fuller's brigade encamped at Jacinto from September 21 to 29, and then at Rienzi from September 29 until October 2. Rosecrans, using a "Battalion of Colored Engineer Troops, which I had organized a few weeks previously; the first I believe in the service," set about putting Corinth in a defensible position "to meet emergencies."[44]

Van Dorn and Price in preparing their attack plan considered several alternatives, such as Memphis, Bolivar, and Jackson, all in western Tennessee, and Corinth. They ruled out all except Corinth. To Van Dorn surveying all the possibilities, "the conclusion forced itself irresistibly in my mind that the taking of Corinth was a condition precedent to the accomplishment of anything of importance in West Tennessee....It was clear to my mind that if a successful attack could be made upon Corinth from the west and northwest, the forces there driven back on the Tennessee and cut off, Bolivar and Jackson would easily fall....West Tennessee would be in our possession and communications with General Bragg effected through Middle Tennessee."[45] Moreover, if he struck quickly, he could catch Rosecrans before his outposted troops could be recalled, giving him a three to two (22,000 versus 15,000) numerical advantage.

On October 2, Rosecrans was informed that "the Rebel's Price and Van Dorn, with all the troops they could gather together in Mississippi, had reached Pocahontas advancing to attack us, or to feint on us and attack Bolivar."[46] Rosecrans had already begun to recall his outposted troops. At 1:30 a.m. on October 3, he dispersed them in his first line of battle: "General [Thomas Jefferson] McKean, with his division will occupy his present position [on the left of Davies]; General [Thomas A.] Davies will occupy the line between the Memphis and Columbus Roads; General [Charles Smith] Hamilton with his division will take position between the rebel works on the Purdy and the Hamburg Roads, and General Stanley will hold his division in reserve at or near the old headquarters of Major-General Grant. The respective divisions will be formed in two lines, the second line being either in line of battle or close column by division, as circumstances may require."[47]

The Confederates attacked on the morning of October 3. The battle lasted all day with neither side gaining any significant advantage. On this first day, Dey and Company F formed in line of battle south of Corinth. Toward evening they were positioned to the left of a company of siege guns commanded by Captain George A. Williams and manned by regulars of the 1st U.S. Infantry near the Memphis and Charleston

Railroad, and covering the wagon road to the southwest. At about 5:30 p.m., Stanley's division was ordered to support Davies' division, which was being pressed by the enemy. But Stanley decided first to provide for his people, who were "almost famished for water," before committing them. By then, "the action had ended for the day, the enemy retiring beyond cannon-shot."[48] Maurice, with Company F, subsequently reported that firing "had now ceased on the right and front, and I remained in position during the night."[49] Van Dorn and Rosecrans both believed that each should have been successful on that first day. Van Dorn wanted "one hour more of daylight and victory would have soothed our grief for the loss of the gallant dead who sleep on that lost but not dishonored field." Rosecrans "bewailed that lack of daylight, which would have brought Hamilton's fresh and gallant division on the Confederate left and rear. That hour of daylight was not to be had."[50]

Both sides, resting on their arms within six hundred yards of each other, were harshly reminded of the hot day's work to come when the Confederate artillery opened fire at 4:00 a.m. on October 4. "The enemy's guns in front of our position sounded the reveille, which instantly aroused the entire command."[51] And "Fuller's Brigade lay flat on the ground, listening to the roar of flying missiles, which passed over them, but the regulars in the Second United States Battery [F], replying with their guns, soon silenced the enemy" in less than thirty minutes and "they retired, leaving one gun and caisson on the field."[52]

The heaviest fighting centered on Battery Robinett, a small three-gun redan. It sat slightly north and west of the town, just above the junction where the Mobile and Ohio and the Memphis and Charleston railroads crossed. The company was commanded by Lieutenant Henry C. Robinett, and manned, like Battery Williams, by regulars from the 1st U.S. Infantry. Dey and the other veterans of Company F likened the fierceness of the successive assaults on Battery Robinett to what they had lived through on "Bloody Hill" at Wilson's Creek in August 1861. There the company had faced the fury of repeated attacks on an open hill without the protection of any earthwork, or of a field littered with felled trees, and stumps, which provided a decided defensive advantage for Battery Robinett. The Confederates stormed Battery Robinett in three separate thrusts. At one point, the regulars manning the 20-pound Parrotts abandoned the guns to defend their position with muskets. Each enemy thrust was beaten back by elements of Fuller's Ohio Brigade, with help from Colonel Joseph A. Mower, commanding the 2nd Brigade. Before the third attack, which came at about 1:00 p.m. when the rebels again showed themselves in force, Fuller ordered Maurice to dispatch a section of guns and plant the two 12-pound howitzers outside and to the left or west of Battery Robinett.

Dey was the chief of piece of this section. He unlimbered his guns just before the third charge by the Confederates. Soon after he got into position, he was struck in the left hand by a bursting shell and in his left side by a fragment of that shell. Private Randolph Hand, one of his gunners, was mortally wounded. And Private John Mitchell, another member of the crews, was hit by a shell on the knuckle of the second forefinger of his left hand. Although he was severely wounded, Dey remained with his guns throughout this attack, which also cost three horses killed and four wounded.[53] The Union defenders' resistance broke the Confederate spine in this last attack. Colonel William Rogers, leading his 2nd Texas Legion, was killed as he stuck his regimental flag on the parapet of Battery Robinett. He was struck by numerous bullets, and was dead as he hit the ground.[54]

Although the Confederates withdrew their forces shortly after the last setback, their rear guard was still active. At about 8:00 p.m., some members of the 63rd Ohio Volunteers went out about 20 yards in front of Battery Robinett to retrieve a gun and caisson which had been abandoned early in the morning of August 4. They were forced to leave the piece on the field because enemy sharpshooters opened fire on them. A second contingent of four men from the 1st U.S. Infantry succeeded, and when they were "about half way in, they were met by and assisted by Private Strange, of Company F, Second Artillery."[55]

The Confederates lost 505 killed, 2,140 wounded and 1,812 missing or taken prisoners. The Union's losses were half that of the Confederates, with 345 killed, 1,841 wounded, and 324 missing or taken prisoners.[56] Each army singled out its heroes. Many accounts of the battle highlight the valiant but unsuccessful charge by Colonel Rogers and his 2nd Texas Brigade, which is still memorialized by some of the citizens of Corinth: "Be that as it may [the number of bullets it took to fell the Colonel] Colonel Rogers is Corinth's Civil War Hero: we have his grave, a monument, a statue dedicated to his memory. We will remain synonymous with Battery Robinett, where he is buried."[57] His feat and that of the entire Confederate Army were praised also by the men who fought against them. One Union soldier from the 8th Wisconsin "Eagle" Regiment verbalized his feeling poetically:

> Ah! Well—you know how it ended—
> We did for them, there and then;
> But their pluck throughout was splendid.
> (As I said before, I could love them!)
> They stood, to the last, like men—
> Only a handful of them
> Found their way back again;
> Sad enough I must say
> No mother to mourn and search

No priest to bless or pray—
We buried them as they lay.
Without rite of the church—
But our eagle all that day
Stood solemn and on his perch.[58]

Two days before he was ordered to his new command with the
Army of the Cumberland, Rosecrans mentioned those men in his army
who were to be singled out. In his official report of October 25, he alluded to a special paper in which were listed officers and enlisted men
to receive "Honorable Mentions for Meritorious and Distinguished Service during the 'Battle of Corinth' on the 3d and 4th Days of October
A. D. 1862." (The list also includes names of individuals who distinguished themselves in the battle of Iuka.)[59] Five men, including Company F's commanding officer, made the list. Maurice's earlier sub-re-
port of October 9 made special mention of the gallantry of "Sergts. Dey,
McGinnis, Wrightenburg, and McIntyre; Corpls. Kirkland, and Kelly,
and Privates Garvey [Garry], Hennessey, Newboldt, Black, and Walsh."[60]
A few days later, Maurice further refined his remarks in a report to
Colonel Fuller: "And [I] would further mention 1st Sergt. Gustave Dey,
for coolness, bravery, and his good judgment, during the battle of the
4th inst, he was wounded by a shell from the Enemy, but continued to
do his duty at his gun for one hour after being struck, I can heartily
recommend him for honorable notice in the General's report."[61]

The pursuit of the Confederate Army into southern Mississippi by
units of the Union Army, including Company F, was a very painful experience for Dey. The wound on the left index finger was not as incapacitating as the wound to his left side, just below the left lung. In his
application for a veteran's pension, he would affirm that "I was the Orderly Sergt of Batty F, 2nd US Artillery the time I received the wounds,
which were dressed by a Volunteer Surgeon on the field of battle, but
his name I never learned—On the next day after the battle, in following
up the rebel's retreating army, on account of not being able to mount my
horse, I had to follow in our Company Ambulance."[62] Fortunately for
Dey, the chase after the Confederates ended a week later on October 12,
and the company returned to Corinth. In mid-November, the company
would finally meet Captain Albert J. S. Molinard. For some of the veterans, like Dey, the meeting would conjure memories of the days in Florida
in 1857, when Molinard was second in command of Company I.

Chapter 9

Mississippi: Failed Command

Ten days after the battle of Corinth and two days after the Union Army discontinued its pursuit of the retreating Confederates, Maurice sent an appraisal of the fitness of his command to regimental headquarters at Fort McHenry, Maryland. Writing on October 14, Maurice first apologized for not responding sooner to reports from headquarters: "The very rapid movement of our army recently has been a great hinderance [*sic*] in sending returns promptly, by order, I was obligated to leave behind the company papers and even the blankets of the Company, only one wagon being allowed, to carry rations." He then again pleaded for some word about the whereabouts of Captain Albert Molinard, who was supposed to be commanding Company F: "I am anxious to join my own Battery" [1st Missouri Light Artillery]. He then praised the company's demeanor in its "most excellent condition for the field, and in the recent Battle of Corinth, Oct. 4/62 the Company behaved nobly and was highly complimented by the Generals. Our loss was slight [three wounded, one mortally]. The Company is now composed of 2 10 pdr Parrotts and 2 12 pdr How." The other two guns (6 pounders) were turned over to the 1st U.S. Infantry commanded by Captain George A. Williams. The reason for the transfer was that "we could not procure horses and men sufficient to man a 6-gun Company on the pursuit after Price." At Corinth, the company "expended 900 rounds of ammunition." Maurice also observed, "We shall have another fight near here." And "The men are being discharged—expiration of service—are not enlisting. They will go to Ft. Leavenworth & soon find employment in the QM Dept. or receive comms. [commissions] in the Vol. Service."[1]

Six veterans, Gilbert Baker, John A. Baker, Vardry Camp, Joseph Hendricks, George Myrick, and William J. Williams, had already been discharged prior to the battle. Sergeant Albert Wachsman accepted a

117

commission with the 2nd Missouri Artillery, and Sergeant Robert Armstrong went as a second lieutenant to the 1st Missouri Militia regiment. Owen Donnelly, Josiah Pond, Henry Simon, and Mahlon Smith went out on disability discharges. After the battle, William Wrightenburg, Frank McGinnis, and Franklin Myrick were given their discharges for expiration of service. They were soon followed by James Strange. Word was also received that Private James Brennan, who had suffered from the cold weather in the campaign in Missouri, had been given a disability discharge on October 4 from Newport Barracks, Kentucky. By December, the company's enlisted total numbered just 51.[2]

Shortly after Maurice wrote his report, he was appointed chief of artillery of the 2nd Division, Army of the Mississippi, commanded by General Stanley.[3] First Lieutenant John D. McLean, who had served as second in command to Maurice, assumed command of Company F. McLean, from Stevens Point, Wisconsin, was on temporary detail from the Wisconsin 8th Independent Light Artillery.[4] Sometime between October 12 and November 2, Captain Albert Molinard took command of the company. At about the same time, Dey, still convalescing from his wounds, stepped down to sergeant. Sergeant Francis McIntyre, a four-year veteran and native of Tyrone, Ireland, who had not previously served under Molinard, replaced Dey as first sergeant. After having been without a regular officer from its own regiment since March 1862, when Lieutenant Darling left the company after the siege of New Madrid, Missouri, Company F now had one of its own. Molinard joined, but did not lead, the company as it was readying for a campaign along the Mississippi Central Railroad, in company with approximately 80,000 men. As part of that vast army, Company F was still attached to Fuller's Ohio Brigade. The brigade, still in the 2nd Division, came under Major General James B. McPherson, commanding the right wing of Grant's Department of the Tennessee.

On Sunday, November 2, Fuller's Brigade, with three days' rations in its haversacks and three in its wagons, marched out of Corinth on the Chewalla Road and trekked "over a hilly country, passed fields of white with unpicked cotton, crossed the Hatchie River, and on the 3rd passed through Grand Junction [Tennessee] twenty miles distant."[5] On the next day, Grant personally took command as he went south to complete railroad and telegraph lines for transporting supplies and for establishing communications. His plan, approved by Halleck, was to begin an active campaign along the Mississippi, attack Vicksburg, and shut off the entire river from further access by the Confederates.[6]

For most of the next two months, Dey's Company F and the Ohio Brigade would be almost constantly on the move. On the first day, they marched 14 miles before camping on the Tuscambia River, south of Corinth. On the next day, 15 miles later on the Memphis road, they camped on the Little Hatchie River within sight of the battlefield where elements of the Union Army had caught and fought the Confederates retreating from Corinth. On November 5, four pieces under McLean were sent out on reconnaissance and drove off Confederate pickets. Company F and the Ohioans set up camp at Grand Junction, near Davis' Mills. Since rations were becoming scarce "the troops had to grind corn at the mills and use the cornmeal for baking bread." They also noted that wagon trains loaded with cotton were guarded at the railroad. They remained at this camp for 12 days. Then on November 17, they marched four miles to Davis' Mills, and camped there until November 28. One of the Ohioans recorded that during the marches in extremely dry weather, the "clothes of the soldiers took on the color of the earth upon which they slept, while the dust stirred up by the large numbers of teams and thousands of men marching over the roads, made the soldiers very uncomfortable, getting into their rations and filling their eyes and nostrils." He also noted that under such trying conditions where men sought relief wherever they could find it, the command issued "stringent orders against plundering and very little was done."

The march was resumed on November 28. The troops passed through Holly Springs, about eight miles from their last camp at Davis' Mills. As they passed through the streets of the town, "a few of the citizens stood on the corners and many ladies appeared at the doors of homes. A few of them cheered, others seemed spell-bound at the sight of the old flag and the great army." Seven miles beyond Holly Springs, the company set up camp near Waterford, Mississippi, and remained there until December 10. On that morning the company marched from Waterford for nine miles, and camped across the Tallahatchie River, one mile north of Abbeville. There members of the company and Fuller's Brigade "washed their clothes in the river, water and wood had to be carried about a mile back to camp." They were also near "the rebel lines of heavy earthworks, fort and rifle pits upon which the enemy had spent ten months of labor." They were so close that on the next morning they watched as "about ten thousand of the Union cavalry swam over on their horses and pursued the enemy."

But there was no resting in Abbeville. Soon after watching the cavalry pursue the Confederates, the company and brigade marched toward Oxford. After covering 15 miles, through very beautiful country, they camped two miles south of Oxford. As they passed through the town, they heard that many of the "citizens took the oath of allegiance to the United States Government." They rested in this camp for the next nine days. During that time, Major Charles H. Smith, 27th Ohio Regiment, Fuller's Brigade recalled in his 1909 history of the brigade, "the soldiers enjoyed the beautiful starlight nights by the camp fires, around which they would gather in knots and rehearse the marches and brave deeds of their army, how they stood together and cheered each other upon many battlefields. Their eyes were bright, their cheeks were sunburned and weather beaten, some looked toil worn, their clothes were ragged, but they were self-reliant."

Then on December 17, Dey, the company, and members of the brigade were ordered to brush up their clothes, blacken their shoes, and polish their guns and accoutrements for a grand review scheduled for the next day. Generals Grant, Hamilton and Leonard Fulton Ross reviewed the troops. "The General [Grant] rode down the front and up the rear lines on a cream colored horse. He was dressed in a frock coat, black hat, and a rich silk sash and belt. He was saluted at the head of each regiment by dipping flags, fife and drums, and by 'present arms.' He raised his hat and when he passed the colors, he saluted them." The review marked a reorganization of Grant's Army of the Tennessee into four corps: the XIII, XV, XVI and XVII. The Ohio Brigade with Company F became a part of the XVI Corps, under Major General Stephen A. Hurlbut.

On December 20, the company and brigade moved nearer to Oxford.[7] When the troops encamped, they heard that Confederate General Van Dorn had attacked the garrison at Holly Springs, Grant's major supply depot. Van Dorn reported that he "surprised the enemy at this place at daylight this morning; burned up all the quartermaster's stores, cotton, &c.—an immense amount; burned up many trains; took a great many arms and about 1,500 prisoners. I presume the value of the stores would amount to $1,500,000. I move on to Davis' mills at once."[8] The attack on Holly Springs and the destruction of the vast stores of supplies virtually wiped out, for the time being, Grant's strategy for his attack on Vicksburg. Colonel Murphy, 8th Wisconsin Infantry, who had earlier abandoned his post at Iuka with similar devastating results, was in command of this garrison. He was dismissed from the service for his "cowardly and disgraceful conduct."[9]

From December 21 to January 13, 1863, Company F and the brigade retraced their steps from Oxford through Abbeville, Cold Water, LaGrange, and Grand Junction. On January 13, the company went into camp at Corinth. During the entire Mississippi Central campaign, McLean commanded the company while Molinard had remained on sick leave in Corinth since he had taken over command sometime near the end of October.

On March 24, 1863, Fuller ordered Molinard to turn over two of his ten-pounders, together with the caissons and ammunition, to Captain Benjamin Tannarath of the 1st Missouri Light Artillery. He also ordered that "the horses required for the other four guns together with the proper number of spare horses will be selected from those in Captain Molinard's hands and retained and the remainder with harness not required will be turned over to Capt. Wing A QM." Molinard was not pleased with Fuller's order. He sent a request to regimental headquarters (and to XVI Corps] that his company be sent to Carlisle, Pennsylvania for reorganization and refitting. He painted a bleak picture of the company's condition for field duty: "The Company of your Regiment which I have the honor to command has been doing duty in and about the Department untill [*sic*] is destitute of men and Horses to carry on the duty of the Company properly. The Horses are in such condition as to make them nearly unable to draw the pieces for any distance. The men for duty as per last morning report with the exception of Volunteers attached are marked 18, whereas by law and regulations I am entitled to 150."

He further stated that even the volunteers attached to the company were being recalled to their own commands by application of their commanding officers to Grant and Rosecrans. He continued by again alluding to Fuller's order relative to the transfer of his guns: "My Battery at present is becoming rapidly disorganized for want of men and horses. The last order which accompanies this communication show [*sic*] you that not only men and horses have been taken from my command, but also 2 Ten Pound Parrot Guns, which were the best and only long range pieces." Molinard's request passed quickly through the hands of Major George H. Stone, chief of artillery, District of Corinth, to Brigadier General Grenville M. Dodge. The general approved Stone's endorsement of Molinard's request and ordered the issuance of Special Orders No. 62, authorizing the company's move to Carlisle. Fuller was totally ignorant of Molinard's communication, and was not consulted about its contents or veracity. When Colonel Fuller learned of the special order, which was dated March 28, he immediately acted to have it rescinded. He also called for a board of inquiry into the entire affair. Although several of Molinard's past commanders knew about his alcoholism, Fuller had no idea of it when he ordered the investigation of Molinard's behavior.[10]

Early in October 1860, Lieutenant Colonel William W. Morris, commanding at the field artillery school in Fort Ridgeley, Minnesota, had reported Molinard to Major Irvin McDowell, then acting inspector general, "as one [officer] of habitual drunkenness without any prospect of reformation—and on the 23rd of the same month arrested him for utter inability to perform his duty." On October 25, Molinard had offered, while under arrest, to resign unconditionally "date and rank left blank, to be supplied by my commanding officer whoever he may be, should I at any future time be found by him or known to him, to be under the influence of intoxicating liquor or to be unfit for duty from the same cause. This resignation the date and rank being filled up by him to be forwarded to the Secretary of War, in the above case." Morris accepted

Molinard's word. On November 22, 1860, he released Molinard from arrest, assured that Molinard would abstain from intoxicating liquor while serving "under my command." But on May 25, 1861, at Fort McHenry, where Morris had been transferred, he was compelled to "arrest him again for neglect of duty in consequence of intemperance." Morris kept Molinard in "close arrest until 6th June, when he tendered me a renewed written assurance with closer restrictions, [and] I again released him." Then on July 10, 1861, Morris again arrested Molinard on the same charge. Molinard was released on July 31, when he was ordered to go to Fort Delaware to serve under Captain Augustus Gibson, his old commander.

He was at that post for just three days. But in those three days, he was charged by Gibson with "conduct in the prejudice of good order and military discipline." The specific of Gibson's charge was that Molinard "was so much under the influence of intoxicating liquor, as to be incapable of performing military duty properly." The charge was issued by Gibson on August 6, but was withdrawn on the next day, August 7. Perhaps it was because Gibson felt that Molinard's talents could be used. Gibson saw Lieutenant Molinard as "a thorough soldier—at home in the field. But for the unfortunate propensity to indulge in the too free use of liquor, he would be invaluable. Under the instructions of the Depart. of Washington, and the activity and excitement of duty (as a sight artillerist) with that Army, he would, in my opinion exercise a due self-restraint, and become a highly efficient officer. Therefore I urge that this disposition be made of him, and under it the withdrawal of the charge here presented."

On August 17, 1861, just two weeks after Gibson withdrew his charge, a surgeon with the 3rd New York, stationed at Fort McHenry reported to Morris that Molinard had been on "a spree" for four or five days "and that there was a danger of his having delirium tremens unless he could be restrained." Morris' treatment was again to place Molinard under arrest and to confine him to his quarters. Morris closed his report about Molinard with an apology for not having brought him to trial sooner, but he had believed that Molinard was in earnest about reforming. Unfortunately, that had not been the case. Morris was now convinced that "this is beyond hope. I would respectfully suggest that this case be presented for the consideration of the 'Retiring Board.' "[11] Major General John Adams Dix passed the report on to the AGO. The reply from Major Julius Peter Garesche was emphatic in its denial: "This is not a case with which the Retiring Board can have anything to do."[12] Since the Retiring Board denied his request, Morris dropped any further disciplinary action against Molinard. Molinard was placed in command of his and Dey's old company, I, 2nd Artillery, remained at Fort McHenry, and was promoted to captain in November 1861.

In September 1862, Morris reported to the AGO in Washington that Company F had not had a regular officer since March 1862, when Darling left after the siege of New Madrid, Missouri. Then the colonel noted that he "would respectfully command Captain Molinard be ordered to join [Company F] without delay and that he be directed to report to these Head Quarters [2nd Artillery] the cause of his unaccountable absence therefrom."[13] The same communication from Morris indicated that Molinard left Fort McHenry on July 14, but still had not reported to Company F. The comment in the muster roll for the period June–August 1862 was that Molinard was absent "on det. Service, comdg company "I". SO No. 115 Hqrs., Middle Dept. April 30, 1862." In another communication from regimental headquarters, the commanding officer reported to the Adjutant General that "the want of officers for this company [F] was respectfully brought to the notice of the Adjutant General on May 4, July 25, and Sept. 23d 1862."[14] Other communications from Rosecrans' and Grant's headquarters, dated respectively October 2 and 16, 1862, indicate that nothing had ever been heard of Captain Molinard, or that he had ever reported for duty in the District of West Tennessee.[15]

In one muster roll, Molinard is listed as being on "Special Duty, Chief of Artillery, 8th Div. Army of the Tennessee."[16] Molinard tried to explain his absence from Company F. While requesting a sixty-day leave of absence for illness, he stated that he first contracted his disease while serving in Florida in the 1850s. He then contended that "after having been taken prisoner on the 13th August last [1862], I was so much exposed and suffered so largely that ever since the 29th October last, when exchanged, I was never able to perform my duties properly." In his statement before the Retiring Board, Molinard would recount his capture and release by Confederate guerrillas:

> I left my company on the 1st of July 1862, and proceeded from St. Louis on the Steamer Sky Lark towards Corinth where my Company was supposed to be. The Steamer ran aground on the Tennessee River at a place called Rocky Mound, and was aground three days. The third day she was lightened by the Callie and was getting up stream to back off the bank when we were attacked by Capt. Napier's Company of Guerrillas. There were neither troops nor arms on board, and no resistance was offered. All on board were ordered ashore dressed as we were, and on account of the intense heat of the weather almost every one was in his shirt sleeves. All I had on was a white shirt, white pants, drawers, and a pair of thin dress boots. After helping themselves to what they wanted, the Guerrillas set fire to the boat, and I lost everything I possessed, besides wearing apparel, there being some valuable manuscripts burnt up with all my retained papers since my first

entry in the Service. I was marched by the Guerrillas through Middle Tennessee, without another stitch of clothes being given me. I was forced to bivouac without a blanket, or other covering, and was drenched through with a dew night after night. There was nothing to eat but horribly fat bacon, and corn, with no salt, coffee, or any thing else. My boots were soon worn out on the horrible roads of this country and my feet were on the ground. The Guerrillas would not turn me over to the regular troops, as they wished to exchange me for some of their company which had been captured by Gen" Thomas then in command at Nashville. It has been a wonder to <u>all</u> to whom I related the details of my imprisonment how I came out of it <u>alive</u>. I was finally exchanged for Capt. M. T. Polk on the 29th of October, and immediately proceeded to join my company which was serving with Gen" Ross. I was appointed by him Chief of Artillery, and continued serving as such when my health permitted until superseded by Major Stone of the 1st Mo. Arty.[17]

He then joined Company F in Corinth in November 1862. It was not until March 24, 1863, that the problem between Molinard and Fuller really surfaced. On April 8, Molinard left on a sixty-day leave of sickness.

After having the special order rescinded, on April 13 Fuller sent a letter to Lieutenant Colonel Henry Binsmore, Acting Adjutant General, XVI Corps, to correct Molinard's statements and to give his assessment of the efficiency and effectiveness of Company F and the volunteers who served with it. Fuller labeled Molinard's statement that the company only had 18 men and that their time of service had nearly expired as "grossly eroneous [sic]." Actually, Company F had "now for duty one hundred enlisted men; Forty six (46) of whom are regulars, and fifty-four (54) are volunteers attached. The term of service of not a single man will expire before September [1863], and only four (4) within the present year." As to the company's effectiveness, Fuller contended that there "is no company in this Army which has acquitted itself more creditably nor which has rendered more efficient service...At Wilson's Creek, at Farmington, and at Corinth, as well as other places, it has been distinguished." And the "Volunteers now attached have long served with the guns in which they all take pride, and share with the regulars in that <u>esprit de corps</u> so essential in every command."

As for Molinard, Fuller stated that the "only drawback to the discipline and efficiency of the Company has been the temporary want of an officer competent to command." Furthermore, Fuller stated that Molinard, since he joined his company in November 1862, "has been on sick report most of the time, and has had no less than two attacks of <u>delirium tremens</u> since we have occupied our present camp." It was for these reasons that Fuller called for a board of inquiry to look into the entire case of Molinard's behavior.[18] Fuller had been aware of Molinard's condition and its negative effect on Company F. On March 18, he had ordered First Lieutenant Charles Green, 1st Missouri Light Artillery, to take over command of Company F, "Captain Molinard being habitually on sick leave." But Molinard remained in Corinth with the company until he departed on his sixty-day leave in April.

On May 18, from Baltimore, Maryland, where he had gone on sick leave, Molinard sent a letter to regimental headquarters rebutting many of Fuller's allegations. He documented the letter with four exhibits: his original report requesting the transfer of the company to Carlisle, Special Orders No. 62 approving that move, Special Orders No. 106 rescinding the order, and a statement from the company clerk, Private Charles Dulkewitz. Molinard admitted that his original reports "were a little short of the truth, instead of being exaggerated." Special Orders No. 62 came about because Major Stone "was furnished at his own request with a copy of said report, which was duly forwarded by him." Here Molinard offered an excuse for bypassing Fuller, his commanding officer. The fourth enclosure was a copy of Dulkewitz's letter in which he warned Molinard that there was "a commission setting up to investigate the truth of your Report about the Company being unfit for Service." He then informed Molinard that "you made a mistake about the time when the enlistments of the Regulars will expire, but, I think you can correct now –somehow or other." Dulkewitz enclosed a copy of Molinard's original report "to faccillate [sic] you in correcting the mistakes, and getting ahead of your friends at Corinth." The conciliatory tone of Dulkewitz's letter suggests that either he felt some loyalty toward his commanding officer or that he was acting out of some self-interest. [In WW II, we called it "brown nosing."] Dulkewitz deserted on September 1, 1863. One has to wonder, in light of Molinard's actions and ultimate fate, if Dulkewitz's desertion was not encouraged by his comrades.[19] Molinard used this letter as an example of "what machinations are going on during my forced absence from my company to keep the remains of my battery living with an Army composed entirely of Volunteers, and where the Volunteer Artillery of course has precedence over mine in being supplied with everything." Moreover, he justified the claim of only 18 soldiers being fit for duty by contending that many of his men were old soldiers who suffered from various disabilities and who were unable to take the field when the company was sent out on scout. He then ended his appeal by stating that he would have personally traveled to Fort McHenry to place his case before the regimental command "but his health (which even now renders the use of a Secretary necessary to address you), was such that it would not allow him to leave his house."[20]

Fuller sent a copy of his April 13 letter to regimental headquarters. On May 21, 1863, the regimental commander requested that Fuller press charges against Molinard so that he could be brought to trial either at Corinth or at Baltimore, "as he is now in the latter city on 'Sick leave.'"[21] But Fuller had not waited for direction from the regiment. On the same day, May 7, that Dulkewitz had written to Molinard, Fuller issued orders setting up a board of inquiry to look into the truth of Molinard's allegations about his company's fitness for field service, and if his excessive use of liquor had caused him to misperform his military duties. The board called two ranking non-commissioned officers, First Sergeant Bernard Dunnigan, and Sergeant Gustave Dey, as witnesses. Both testified that the company was in as good condition as when it was commanded by Captain, now General Totten, nearly two years before. The company also had the requisite number of horses for a four-gun company, all of which were in good condition. All the necessary harness and trappings were in excellent condition. And there was a full complement of 103 men for duty, of whom 43 belonged to the regular army. According to Dunnigan and Dey, in the two months since the company had returned to Corinth on January 13, and until Green relieved Molinard on March 18, all that changed. All "the horses were poor, and almost unserviceable, from exposure and ill usage; and everything was rapidly becoming or had become dilapidated and useless.—Not from necessity but in consequence of the lack of some officer competent to command the company, and look after their interests and the good of the service." Then under Green everything was put back to proper order. The horses were cared for. The harness repaired; the equipment perfected; and the discipline and drill of the company attended to. And the company, to Colonel Fuller, "is what it has been before, one of the most valuable, effective and usefull [sic] in the service." Being restored to their former effective status, the "guns are just what are needed for close action, and the men are the sort who will fight in close action."[22]

When asked to discuss Molinard's dissipated life style, Dunnigan and Dey both agreed that Molinard was unfit to render effective service. They testified that he complained of rheumatism and much of the time was unable to mount his horse. They also testified that he was a "free drinker, but are unable to say whether his illness was caused by dissipation or not." That judgment was left to the surgeons who were asked for testimony on Molinard's alcohol abuse. The assistant surgeon of the 27th Ohio Infantry had treated Molinard in two attacks of delirium tremens during the month of March 1863. The surgeon from the same outfit testified that "Captain Molinard applied to him at least a half a dozen times for whiskey; that he gave him some the first time but never afterwards; that he was usually unduly under the influence of liquor when he made such applications;--that he was called to Capt. Molinard in Nov. 1862, and found him in a state bordering on <u>delirium tremens</u>. He had all the marks of dissipation."

The board also found that Molinard's claim about the numbers of men fit for duty was false. In fact, he had himself, along with the orderly sergeant, affirmed that the company had almost a full complement of 40 regulars and 54 volunteers on duty. This information was authenticated from the company's morning report book. The board found that, contrary to Molinard's claim, the company was in excellent condition and fit to render effective service. With reference to the condition of the company, Molinard's claims were "false in letter and spirit, and the Board is unable to understand how he could have been honestly mistaken." Finally, it found that his excessive use of liquor rendered him totally incompetent to give proper attention to his duties as the commander of "Light Co. F, 2d U. S. Art." Since its only charge was to investigate the facts of the case, the board made no recommendations regarding Molinard's future.[23]

In a memorandum dated August 1863, to Major General Irvin McDowell, president of the Retiring Board, the commanding officer of the 2nd U.S. Artillery transmitted certain papers "in relation to Capt. A. J. S. Molinard, 2d Arty., who has been ordered to appear before the 'Retiring Board.' "[24] Having heard witnesses in the case, the examining board found Molinard "incapacitated for active service in the field, and that his incapacity does not result from any incident of service." On October 3, 1863, Molinard was wholly retired from the service, with one year's pay and allowance, and his name was removed from the Army Register."[25] After the Molinard affair, Dey and his comrades in Company F, including the volunteers attached to the company, performed their duties as professionally as they had before and during this unfortunate episode.

Chapter 10

Alabama to Tennessee: Foray, Fix, and Farewell (1863)

After returning to Corinth from the Mississippi Central campaign on January 13, Dey and Company F moved into rather shabby but temporary winter quarters. Corinth had been fortified with earthworks. Within these, camps were made and the troops gathered up tents to sleep in. The tents were old and worn, soiled and patched. But by using blankets and overcoats stretched over poles, some protection was afforded from inclement weather. Damaged ends of stovepipes stuck out through the tents, so that when looking down the company streets, one was reminded of a shanty settlement along the railroad. To keep the troops occupied, police squads were formed and camp was thoroughly cleaned each day. Drills, reviews, parades, and inspections of troops were held, while companies were sent out on picket and guard duty.

In the company, First Sergeant Francis McIntyre, stepped down on February 20, 1863, after having completed a six-month stint as Dey's successor. He was replaced by Sergeant Bernard Dunnigan, a nine-year veteran in Company F. Molinard was relieved on March 18 and replaced by Lieutenant Charles Green, on detached service from the 1st Missouri Light Artillery. The company along with Fuller's Brigade was assigned as the Fourth Brigade, 2nd Division, of the left wing of the XVI Corps, under General Grenville Mellen Dodge.[1]

During March, the brigade moved into log houses which the troops had built. Each cabin had a chimney, and one window. The doors had hard leather hinges, and the wooden latches were moved by leather strings. The weather was cold and stormy. But with April, the calmer weather signaled the end of winter quarters. On April 5, Dodge reviewed Fuller's Brigade, their barracks and camp. Then on April 7, a grand review of all the troops in Corinth, infantry, cavalry, and artillery took place: "Arms were burnished bright, clothing brushed up, and all the troops passed headquarters on the south side of the square."[2]

Although Corinth had been in Union hands since the battle in October 1862, Confederate troops under Brigadier General Philip D. Roddy, and his 4th Alabama Cavalry, operating under Brigadier General Nathan B. Forrest, continued to harass Union troops around northern Mississippi, Alabama, and Georgia. To neutralize that and other threats in the area, the Union launched two expeditions. One was led by Colonel Abel D. Streight, 51st Indiana Infantry, who was sent by Rosecrans to "cut the Georgia railroad so as to prevent troops from being sent by that route to re-enforce General Bragg, and to impede the forwarding of ammunition and supplies to his army in our front."[3] To cover and protect this movement, Dodge was ordered to advance "from Corinth to Iuka, thence to Tuscumbia [Alabama], and finally as far as Town Creek, taking Colonel Streight with him."[4]

Dodge, with most of his command, left Corinth on April 15 with the intent of meeting Streight at Eastport on April 16. Streight did not arrive at the appointed time, causing Dodge to delay his schedule.[5] In the meantime, after having been provided with ammunition and supplies, and with three days' rations and other supplies in wagons, Fuller's Brigade and Company F, commanded by Lieutenant Charles Green, moved out of Corinth on April 20. On that day, they marched over such weather-beaten roads that the infantry had to help the artillery by lifting the wheels of guns and caissons out of the mud. After 17 miles, the troops camped near Burnsville, Mississippi. On April 21, they marched another 16 miles, crossed Big Bear Creek on pontoon bridges, and bivouacked on the other side.

After resting a day, they resumed their march on April 23. After covering 13 miles, they camped at Cane [or Caney or Caine] Creek, as the Confederates on their front retreated 13 miles. The next day, they reached Tuscumbia and camped on a hill on the west side of town, near "the magnificent springs, where the pure water boiled up from under the mass of rocks." Tuscumbia, an old village, contained some palatial residences. Even "the negro quarters looked well-kept and clean, with fresh coats of whitewash." They remained there for three days, having the opportunity to refresh and clean themselves and to drink of the fine water in pleasant surroundings.

On April 27, after an 11-mile march away from the Tennessee River, the brigade camped near Leighton. On the next day as they neared Town Creek, the infantry moved in line of battle against the enemy. The Confederates, "dressed in butternut clothing, were formed in line for action three times, then broke and retreated." Company F unlimbered its guns and fired several rounds, driving the enemy cavalry and artillery from the field. The brigade, still following the enemy, "deployed from right to left out of the woods into line in an open field, through tall grass and then steadily advanced proceeded by a long skirmish line."

The Confederates broke again and retreated across Town Creek. The troops camped there for the night. On April 29, the raid having been successfully completed, the forces turned back toward Corinth, arriving there on May 2.

Fuller had some high praise for Company F during this campaign. He wrote to the 2nd Artillery Regimental Headquarters that "this company formed a part of the command which recently marched into Northern Alabama, and though my brigade made the march in less time by two days than other troops, your company was obliged to abandon a less number of horses than any other company in the command."[6] In his after-action reports, Dodge saw the raid in this "garden spot of Alabama" as "rendering desolate one of the best granaries of the South, preventing them from raising another crop this year, and taking from them some 1,500 negroes." He also reported that his command fought in six successful engagements, driving the Confederates, 3,000 strong, from Bear Creek to Decatur. While losing only 100 men, including three officers, his forces destroyed 1,500,000 bushels of corn, and large quantities of oats, rye and fodder, and 500,000 pounds of bacon. They took 150 prisoners, 1,000 head of cattle, hogs, and sheep—enough to keep the entire command in meat for three weeks. They also destroyed the railroad from Tuscumbia to Decatur, 60 flat boats and ferries in the Tennessee River, "thereby preventing [General] Van Dorn from crossing my rear. Also destroyed five tan-yards and six flouring mills."[7]

The expedition led by Colonel Streight, however, ended in disaster when he and his command were captured by Forrest who pursued Streight for five days and nights. Using a ruse to convince Streight that he was outmanned, Forrest got Streight to surrender.[8]

On May 10, Dey, Company F, and Fuller's Brigade took freight cars to Memphis: "The soldiers expressed themselves grateful to the government for the privilege of riding, even if the accommodations were not luxurious." They arrived in Memphis at 6:30 a.m. on May 11. Memphis, on the Mississippi River, was under martial law. Although many of the citizens were Unionists, a large number were secessionists. The soldiers, after having been away from large cities for quite some time, fell prey to the temptations offered. Those who overindulged in alcohol and became unruly ended up in the guardhouse. They were put to work on the fortifications of Fort Pickering [Memphis] near the Mississippi River. But in the main, most of the soldiers, "under the rigid discipline of the army, soon got down to the usual military regulations and the novelty of changed surroundings wore off."[9]

Company F was garrisoned at Memphis for nearly six months. In that time, Colonel Warren Lothrop, chief of artillery, XVI Corps, recommended that First Sergeant Dunnigan be given a commission. Dunnigan was discharged on May 29.[10] On this same day, the troops watched as more than 5,000 Confederate prisoners arrived from Vicksburg on steamboats and were sent to Indiana under a guard detail of 400 men from Fuller's Brigade. On June 1, Dey was reappointed first sergeant of Company F, which in this period mustered five officers and 52 enlisted men. The rumor that Molinard was relieved of his command circulated through the 2nd Regiment. On June 17, Brevet Captain and Second Lieutenant Albert M. Murray applied for a position in the company: "I understand that a company of my regiment ("F" of the 2d) is without a regular officer, and would most respectfully request to be transferred from Comp. 'L' to Comp. 'F' and be assigned duty with it."[11] On July 2, Company F added 38 regular army enlisted men who joined from detached service with Company M, 1st Missouri Light Artillery. The newly added men were actually recruits which the company had trained at the St. Louis Arsenal in 1861. These men had fought side-by-side with Company F throughout the western Missouri campaign and at New Madrid. They had also seen combat at Corinth as part of Brigadier General Napoleon B. Buford's 1st Brigade, 3rd Division, under Major General Charles S. Hamilton, Army of the Mississippi.

During the siege of Vicksburg, May 1 to July 4, Company M had been in the 1st Brigade, 7th Division, XVII Corps, commanded by Major General James B. McPherson, in Grant's Army of the Tennessee. After the surrender of Vicksburg, all the men of the company became ill with malarial fever. The company commander, First Lieutenant Junius MacMurray, was also taken ill and "was sent away soon after and it was expected would die." John Kelly, a member of the company, explained the cause of this wholesale sickness, when he later wrote a testimony on behalf of John Fisher, a comrade:

> On or about the 20th of July 1863 while serving on detached service in Company M, 1st Missouri Light Artillery on the march from Jackson to Vicksburg while in Camp near Baker's Creek, the said Fisher and about 40 men of the Company myself among the number were taken Sick very suddenly on account of useing [sic] the water out of Baker's Creek. The Division Surgeon had the water analyzed and stated that the cause of so many of the men being taken ill so violently and suddenly was on account of the water of Baker's Creek being tainted with the Bodies of Dead Soldiers who fell at the Battle of Champions Hill [May 16] in the month of May previous and were never buried, 6 of our men died afterwards from the effects of this Sickness while in camp near Vicksburg.[12]

Other afflicted soldiers included Owen Dillon, Patrick Meehan (he of the scurvy and moon blindness), Charles Akehurst, Elijah Auld (who also suffered from deafness from the "constant service at the Guns and by the Explosion of Shells" during the siege), John Fisher, Joseph Zimmer, Joseph Englebert, and Louis Emery (who also suffered deafness).

Brevet Major Albert Morse Murray. Lieutenant Murray commanded Company F from July 1863 until his capture during the battle for Atlanta, July 22, 1864. He died in prison camp less than a month later.

On July 28, Murray relieved Green of command of Company F. Murray, who had already seen hard fighting in the East and had been brevetted captain for gallantry and meritorious service at Antietam, Maryland, inherited a company which also had seen its share of hard service. Murray had transferred from the 5th to the 2nd U.S. Artillery in October 1862, and was the fourth regimental officer to lead the company since Dey had joined it in 1857.[13]

With the company relatively assured of continuing duty in Memphis, Dey requested and was approved for a 20-day furlough beginning on August 7, 1863. This apparently was Dey's first furlough since his enlistment in 1854.[14] McIntyre, who had been named first sergeant after Dey was wounded at Corinth, was discharged on September 3, having completed his five-year enlistment. Black, wounded at Wilson's Creek and at Farmington, moved up to sergeant replacing McIntyre.[15]

Then on September 22, the company received six new 12-pounders. Its old four-gun battery was turned over to the ordnance officer at Memphis.[16] On the same day, Confederate troops appeared on the outskirts of Chattanooga, Tennessee, after having defeated the Union Army at Chickamauga, Georgia on September 20.[17] The Union high command, however, was well aware of the precarious position of its army. On September 15, Halleck wired Major General Stephen A. Hurlbut, commanding the force in Memphis, to dispatch "all the troops that can possibly be spared in West Tennessee and the Mississippi River to assist" the Army of the Cumberland on the Tennessee River.[18]

In the meantime, First Sergeant Dey applied for a commission on September 25. In a letter through the chain of command addressed to Brigadier General Lorenzo Thomas, Adjutant General, U.S. Army, Dey requested an appointment "as brevet 2d or 2d Lieutenant in the U.S. Artillery."[19] The transmittal sheet signed by Second Lieutenant Murray affirmed and endorsed Dey's request. Murray stated that he believed "the Sergeant *highly qualified* for the promotion he asks." Murray then apologized for not sending forward many "strong recommendations" because "the loss of company papers" prevented his adding more.[20] When the papers reached brigade headquarters on the same day, Fuller forwarded them with the comment that "Sergeant Dey has served this brigade for more than a year—I have frequently noticed his soldierly qualities & his gallant bearing in action—His personal efforts saved one gun of his company at Farmington May 28th & he was wounded at Corinth Oct. 4th while gallantly commanding the section to which he was assigned—I think he has *earned* promotion & respectfully urge his appointment."[21] Headquarters, XVI Corps, received Dey's request and the endorsements from Murray and Fuller on October 1, 1863.

After several weeks under orders to move, Dey, who had had no reply to his request, the company and Fuller's Brigade marched out of

Memphis on a 400-mile trek toward Chattanooga. Their first stop was at Germantown, Tennessee. Then on successive days, from October 19 to 23, they moved along a route that is the present-day State Highway 57 through Lafayette, Moscow, Saulsbury, Pocahontas, and then south off that road to Chewalia, covering 95 miles in five days. On October 24, after marching 28 miles in one day, they arrived at Corinth. After a night's rest, they moved on four miles to the company's old camp at Clear Creek. There they had a chance to rest and refresh themselves and their animals. On October 26, they marched 18 miles to Barnes Farm, Mississippi, rested overnight, and then covered the eight miles to Iuka, arriving there on October 27. They camped at Iuka for the next six days.

When the company and the brigade left Iuka on November 2, they were in advance of the rest of the XVI Corps. After eight miles, they camped at Eastport, Mississippi, on the Tennessee River. "The river at this point has a rapid current and winds in graceful curves around the hills, and the water so clear and deep gladdened the soldiers who were fatigued by the march. The great waterway furnished them with abundance of water to drink, to put in their canteens, to bathe in, and to wash their clothes in." They remained there for two days. And at night the campfires of 20,000 men "illuminated the sky for miles around." It was a beautiful sight but "Union scouts reported at this time that all of [General Joseph] Wheeler's, [General Stephen D.], Lee's and [General Nathan B.] Forrest's cavalry were between Tuscumbia [Alabama] and Decatur [Georgia]."

On November 4, they boarded transports and ferries, with the gunboat *Lexington* and others assisting, and crossed to the east bank of the river. They camped there for the next two days in rainy weather which caused the troops much discomfort. For the next leg of their march, they covered ten miles on the first day, 12 miles on the next, and 15 on the third, arriving at Otterdale Factory, which was a collection of log houses inhabited by "a large number of Union people." (Otterdale Factory was in northern Alabama, but it and the other small camps along this route are no longer identifiable.) The next stop, after marching 15 miles on November 9, was at Lexington, Alabama, a small town on the Tennessee southern border. From there, the troops swung northeast to Pulaski, Tennessee, reaching the city on November 10 after a 20-mile march. There they camped on Chicken Creek and found barns filled with wheat, fields with ripening corn, and plantations with plenty of livestock. But they were unable to enjoy the largesse of the countryside since they moved on through Pulaski on November 11.

On that same day, Dodge ordered Fuller to move his brigade "to Prospect on the Nashville and Decatur roads, fifteen miles from this place and go into camp and guard the railroad from Elk River to Athens,

Alabama, and set heavy details at work repairing that portion which was burned and destroyed, especially Elk River Bridge. Your division will be unloaded and sent here to go to Columbia for supplies. In the meantime you will seize any mills and set them running. All destruction of property is prohibited." Acting on Dodge's orders, Fuller's Brigade and Company F moved near to Prospect. The town was on a hill "at whose foot ran a stream of pure spring water." The troops built earthworks around their camp, and the "trestle work on the Elk River, which had been destroyed by the enemy was rebuilt."[22]

In the meantime, General Braxton Bragg, who was on Missionary Ridge overlooking Chattanooga, needed information about the location of Dodge's army before he could disperse his army. He dispatched four scouts to ferret out that information. One of these scouts was a young volunteer named Sam Davis. Davis quickly obtained information that the Union Army in middle Tennessee "was likely to move from Nashville to Corinth and reinforce the army at Chattanooga." Davis got "an exact number of regiments, and the whole of the artillery of the 16th Corps" (to which Dodge's wing belonged). He also got complete maps of the fortifications at all the principal points, including Nashville and "an accurate report of the entire Federal Army in the whole of Tennessee." Unfortunately for the Confederates, before he could relay this information to Bragg, Davis was caught by the 7th Kansas Cavalry, a unit in Dodge's command, in Pulaski soon after he visited his fiancee. Although pressed by Dodge, Davis refused to reveal his source or sources from whom he had gathered the information so rapidly. Even after Dodge gave him more opportunities to divulge his sources, Davis stubbornly refused, and was ready to die rather than to betray his word. He was then hanged by a very reluctant general.[23]

In retrospect, the march from Memphis, which occupied 26 days, with the exception of one week of rain, was one of the most pleasant made by the brigade. For the most part, the weather was cool, with many days of sunshine and crisp air. The numerous mountain streams along the way provided an abundance of good water for the troops. "At night communication was kept up between the marching columns by fire rockets."[24]

On November 26, 1863, First Sergeant Dey was discharged from the regular army "by reason of promotion to 2d Lt." His papers were signed by Fuller and Murray, who credited Dey as having an excellent character, and who during "his whole term of service has proved himself a Soldier and a Gentleman." On November 29, Second Lieutenant Gustav Dey acknowledged the receipt of his commission. In his letter to the Adjutant General, he wrote that "I have the honor to accept the appointment tendered to me by the President of a Second Lieutenancy in the Second Regiment of the United States. I am a native of Prussia, a Resident of New York and thirty years of Age.—Please find enclosed the required Oath duly signed and returned."[25] Even during wartime, commissions in the regular army did not come easily. But Dey's came through rather quickly because an opening existed for a second lieutenant in the regiment when William Borrowe was promoted to first lieutenant. Dey's place in the Company F's table of organization was filled by Sergeant John Pratt. Corporal George Myers moved up into the vacancy left by Pratt's promotion. In this same period, the company lost Private Michael Bourke, who died in Memphis on November 28 of chronic diarrhea, and Sergeant Daniel McShane who died in Prospect of apoplexy on November 29.

Dey remained with Company F for the rest of 1863. He actively recruited volunteers for the regular army. He signed Private John Smith from the 11th Missouri Infantry on December 1, and Private Oscar Sisson, a farrier, from the 6th Wisconsin Artillery on December 2.[26] On December 7, Fuller signed an order assigning Dey to Company F.[27] In the December 31, 1863 organization of the troops in the Department of the Tennessee, under the command of Major General William T. Sherman, in the Left Wing of that command, Second Lieutenant Gustave Dey was shown as commanding Company F, 2nd U.S. Artillery.[28] The honor was short-lived. Dodge ordered Dey to join his new company, Company E, 2nd U.S. Artillery, at Knoxville, Tennessee.[29]

So after six-plus years with Company F, which he joined as a sergeant, was demoted to private, and worked his way up to first sergeant, Dey left as a second lieutenant in his regiment. In the first three years of the Civil War, he had seen action in every major skirmish or battle in which the company was engaged. He had been cited for bravery at Wilson's Creek where the company, under Captain Totten, performed heroically on "Bloody Hill." He had been credited by Colonel Fuller as having saved one of his guns at Farmington, Mississippi. And at Corinth, he had sustained two wounds but remained with his guns, and was cited for his coolness, bravery, and good judgment.

Chapter 11

Washington to New York: AWOL to Taps (1864–1882)

Newly commissioned Second Lieutenant Gustav Dey joined Company E, 2nd United States Artillery, on January 28, 1864, in Knoxville, Tennessee.[1] Company E had served with the Army of the Potomac, fighting in the first and second battles of Bull Run, at Malvern Hill, and at Chantilly in Virginia. And it had been in the battles of South Mountain and at Antietam in Maryland before being sent to the west. There it had been at Grant's siege of Vicksburg and at Jackson, Mississippi. Its last engagement before Dey joined had been defending Fort Sanders, during the Confederate siege of Knoxville from November 18 to December 4, 1864. After the Confederates under Lieutenant General James Longstreet were repulsed and subsequently withdrew, Company E remained garrisoned in Knoxville until March 23, 1864.

On that date, Dey and the company left by rail for Annapolis, Maryland. There they joined other elements of the army's IX Corps under Major General Ambrose Burnside. That corps had been brought east by Grant, who had taken over command of the armies, including the Army of the Potomac, for the upcoming spring campaign in Virginia. The IX Corps, over 20,000 strong, was in an excellent position at Annapolis. It "could be brought at the last moment as a reenforcement to the Army of the Potomac, or it could be thrown on the sea-coast, south of Norfolk, to operate against Richmond from that direction. In fact, up to the last moment Burnside and the War Department thought the Ninth Corps was intended for such an expedition."[2]

Dey's company, 83 strong, left Annapolis on April 14 for Washington, D.C. While there, they along with the rest of the IX Corps participated in a grand review. "Burnside stood beside the President on the balcony of Willard's [a landmark hotel on Pennsylvania Avenue and 14th Street, Northwest]" as regiment after regiment of infantry, cavalry, and artillery passed by.[3] On April 27, Company E left Washington, crossed the Potomac River and camped at Fairfax, Virginia. On the next day, the company moved to Manassas Junction, over ground unfamiliar to Dey, but familiar to the veterans in the company who had fought at nearby Bull Run. From there they marched to Warrenton Junction, arriving on April 29. The company, with the rest of the IX Corps, moved along the Orange and Alexandria Railroad, so that, if necessary, they could relieve elements of the Army of the Potomac as it moved south toward the Wilderness.[4]

On May 4, the Army of the Potomac moved across the Rapidan River in Virginia to start what was hoped would be the last campaign against General Robert E. Lee's Army of Virginia in the east. The battle of the Wilderness opened on May 5 and lasted through the next day. Both armies suffered tremendous losses in that battle and at Spotsylvania Court House. In the west, Sherman had simultaneously opened his campaign against the Confederates. Company F, 2nd U.S. Artillery, Dey's former outfit, was in the thick of the fighting throughout that campaign.

During the entire campaign, Dey and Company E were part of the Reserve Artillery. They moved almost constantly for the next three weeks, always on the fringe of the fighting but yet always out of harm's way. In their movements, they passed through Brandy Station, the site of the great cavalry battle of June 9, 1863. On May 5, they crossed the Rapidan at Germanna Ford, slightly southeast of present-day Culpeper. On the next day, they moved to Wilderness Run, where they could see the smoke from the burning woods where many of the wounded perished. Then they marched on to Spotsylvania Court House on May 7, but left there before the two armies again fought bitterly from May 8 to May 19. They then swung a few miles south to Chancellorsville where there had been another great battle just a year before. Moving east, they marched into Salem Church on May 12. Two days later, still on an eastward course, they reached Fredericksburg, where the Union Army had lost over 12,000 men in early December 1862, when then Sergeant Dey and his old company were deep into Grant's Mississippi Central campaign. On May 18, they marched to Belle Plain on Potomac Creek, where Grant had set up a base of supplies for his campaign. Dey and the company remained at Belle Plain for the next six days. On May 24, they left for King George Court House, slightly west of Belle Plain. And on the next day they pushed on to Port Conway, which is southeast of Fredericksburg, on the Rappahannock River, and which was set up as a debarkation point. On this same day, May 25, the IX Corps was made a part of the Army of the Potomac.

But Dey and Company E were no longer to be part of the IX Corps. On May 28, they boarded transports at Port Conway, sailed down the

Rappahannock and up the Potomac River to Washington, D.C. They arrived on May 29, and turned their guns in at the Washington Arsenal, the site of present-day Fort McNair. On May 31, the company marched to Battery Kemble, near the Georgetown section of Washington, D.C. and near Chain Bridge, which is a crossing into northern Virginia. Company E was then assigned to the XXII Army Corps.[5]

On the march through Virginia, and shortly thereafter, the company changed command three times. Captain Charles S. Peirce was in command on April 30, First Lieutenant James S. Dudley on May 5, and First Lieutenant Samuel B. McIntire on May 31. Second Lieutenant Dey was promoted to first lieutenant on June 15, 1864. In this entire campaign, the company never fired one round![6]

Dey and Company E were ordered to move from Battery Kemble to Camp Barry, the light artillery depot and training school. Camp Barry was located near the old tollhouse at the intersection of the Bladensburg (Maryland) Turnpike and Benning Road, District of Columbia, or approximately one mile northeast of the Capitol. There is no trace of the camp today.[7]

After the hard marches and duty in Kansas, Arkansas, Missouri, Mississippi, Alabama and Tennessee, under every climatic condition men can endure, the relatively short excursion through Virginia, except for one torrential rain in mid-May, was child's play for Dey. While he relaxed in the relatively quiet life at the garrison at Camp Barry, he learned as reports drifted in and from newspaper accounts of Sherman's campaign in the west. As this campaign progressed, he started to get traces of information about how some of his former army mates, and his old Company F, which he never left in spirit, suffered devastating losses during Sherman's move toward and to Atlanta. Company F was engaged in the battles at Resaca, Georgia, on May 13 to 15, 1864; at Dallas, Georgia, May 28; at the siege of Kennesaw Mountain, June 14 to July 7; at Ruff's Mill on July 4; at Atlanta on July 22 and July 28, and through the occupation of the city. At Resaca, the company took no casualties, but Lieutenant Lorenzo Immell, an old comrade, commanding a section of the 6th Ohio, ruptured his rectum while helping to place a gun in position under enemy fire (was also hit, fracturing his right instep, in front of Atlanta on July 23). Then during the battle at Dallas, Private George Seckler, who was No. 2 man "in front of the guns," was left quite deaf: "the firing of cannons near us [he and George Nash, No. 1 man] set up such a loud noise that it was enough to make us all deaf." While one section of guns was in action at Kennesaw Mountain, on June 14 and from June 22 to July 4, Private John Lowry, serving as No. 1 cannoneer on his piece, was run over by the gun as it recoiled. The accident broke some bones in his left foot. He was treated in the field, but by orders from Lieutenant Murray, he was relieved of duty as one of the drivers and allowed to ride on one of the caissons.

Bad luck continued to plague the company. On 14 July, it crossed the Chattahoochee River during a violent rain and lightning storm. First Sergeant John Pratt, who had been wounded at Wilson's Creek and had succeeded Dey as first sergeant, was struck and killed by a lightning bolt that also killed Private John Felker, the seventeen-year-old bugler who had been recruited by Molinard in Corinth, and Private Thomas Smith, an Englishman. Also struck were Privates James Twiname and [?] Murphy. Twiname was knocked unconscious for some time. His comrade, Private John Kelly, "examined him and found evidence of the lightning stroke about 3 inches wide and 6 inches long near the small of the back and right side." Private Elijah Auld later recalled that the jolt seemed to affect Twiname's nervous system. And Corporal Lewis Dewey, acting chief of piece, remembered that he detailed Twiname to drive a team but Lieutenant Breckinridge excused Twiname from that detail.

Then on July 22, the company suffered its most devastating losses of the war. On orders to change its position and without infantry support, the company moved at a trot with the guns in the lead through a thick wood when it was suddenly surrounded by Confederate troops. Before the gunners could unlimber and reverse their pieces to fire on the enemy, the Confederates captured the battery. The incident occurred at almost the identical place where Major General James Birdseye McPherson was killed. First Lieutenants Albert Murray, Dey's last commanding officer before he left the company, and Joseph C. Breckinridge were captured along with Sergeant Patrick Hennessy, Corporal Nathaniel Gibbins, Bugler James Wood and Privates Robert Armstrong, John J. Fisher, Luther Havens, John H. Kelly, Joseph Maisch, George Noll, and William Murray. Corporal Josiah Steele and Privates Garrett Barry, Vardy Franklin, and Charles Ritchey were killed. Privates William Race, Jacob Huber, and Henry Beck were severely wounded; Beck died from his wounds six days later. Private Patrick Meehan was one of the men who managed to escape. He later recalled those anxious moments: "I was on a gun carriage and Corporal Miller was alongside me on the gun—one section of our company was captured and the officers told us to run and look out for ourselves. We did so, and jumping off the gun, I ran hard to the rear..." The company lost all its guns on that day; 102 horses were killed or captured. Eventually some of the caissons were recovered. It also lost 352 rounds of ammunition and its ambulance.[8] The enlisted men who were taken prisoners were sent to Andersonville, Georgia, and most were eventually exchanged at Rough and Ready, Georgia.[9] Dey learned from the official reports of this disaster and through those informal channels of information in the regimental grapevine that Murray died of typhoid pneumonia on August 12 in the Macon, Georgia prison where the officers had been sent.

Atlanta, Georgia, July 22, 1864. Site of General James B. McPherson's death near where Company F was overrun by Confederates. Fifty percent of its personnel were wounded, killed or taken prisoner; and its six guns and all of its horses were lost.

Harper's *Pictorial History of the Civil War*

The final tragedy was played at Atlanta on August 11 to 12. The remnants of the company, 28 regulars and 48 volunteers, were temporarily attached to the 14th Ohio Battery, and the 1st Missouri Battery (the old command of some of the regulars). Miller and Meehan, who escaped from the same gun carriage on July 22, were again mounted on the carriage when it was struck by a Confederate shell. Meehan was hit in the right hip, Miller in the right knee. Miller's right leg was then amputated above the knee. He recalled that "I did not see him [Meehan] struck but heard him hollowing [sic] and saw them pull him out from under the piece; I was much the worst but he hollowed [sic] out loud. I think we went to the hospital in the same ambulance, and at any rate he came to my tent the next day...I was lying in bed when he came to see me & of course [I] did not feel like noticing anything...I am sure of the shell wound which looked red & raw about as large as three fingers." Miller, who had also been wounded at Wilson's Creek, would be discharged with total disability in June 1865, and continue to complain for many years of pain from an ill-fitting artificial limb.[10]

In the east, the Army of the Potomac and the Army of Northern Virginia continued their duel in Virginia. Dey's Company E and Company C, 2nd U.S. Artillery were temporarily consolidated and remained at Camp Barry. Dey was placed in command of the reconstituted Company C after he joined it in early November. The muster roll also showed that he was "in arrest."[11] Company C consisted of 49 people: two sergeants, a bugler, artificers and 31 privates on duty. Eight privates were in arrest or in confinement.[12] Two of the soldiers, Privates George DeForest and David Barringer, were charged with deserting on December 12. Dey was ordered to be a member of the court-martial board which was to meet on December 20. For some inexplicable reason, he failed to appear. He was then charged with "1. Neglect of duty; 2. Absence without leave; 3. Disobedience of orders; and 4. Breach of arrest." The specifications in the first charge stated that Dey "did absent himself from said court martial until the 24th day of December. The day the enlisted men's trial was completed." On the second charge, Dey "did absent himself from his command and Post, on or about the 21st day of December; and did remain absent until the 28th day of December 1864." For disobedience of orders, Dey "having been ordered by Major Hamlin, A. A. General, on the 26th day of December, to report to his Commanding Officer at Camp Barry, DC, immediately did fail to so report until on or about the 28th day of December 1864." Finally, on the fourth charge, Dey did fail to report in arrest to his commanding officer until December 28, two days after he was ordered to do so. The court found Dey guilty on the first three charges. On the fourth, it found him not guilty of breach of arrest, but guilty of disobedience of orders.

The court sentenced Dey "to be reprimanded in General Orders and to be suspended for six months from all promotions." Brigadier General Albion Howe, inspector of artillery, commanding, added a final admonition: "The Court has found Lieut. Dey guilty of gross offence. The Commanding General trusts that the mild sentence of the Court will prove a sufficient warning to Lieut. Dey so that the offence of which he had been found guilty shall prove his last as the evidence show it to have been his first. Lieut. Dey will be released from Arrest and resume his Sword." The two enlisted men's charges were reduced from desertion to absence without leave.[13] Dey remained in command of Company C. On March 18, 1865, he charged the same DeForest in a garrison court-martial with being absent without leave from March 12 to 17.[14]

On Palm Sunday, April 9, 1865, the Army of Northern Virginia surrendered at Appomattox Court House, Virginia, effectively ending the war. On Friday, April 14, President Lincoln was assassinated at the Ford's Theater in Washington, D.C., by John Wilkes Booth. On May 23, the Army of the Potomac passed in its last review in Washington, D.C. The next day, Wednesday, Sherman's military division of the Mississippi then passed in its last review in the city. On Tuesday, June 6, Dey was arrested in Washington, D.C. by Sergeant Edward H. Lynch, Company L, 16th New York Cavalry [a detachment from the 16th had assisted in the capture of John Booth]. Lynch's arrest report stated,

that he arrested Lieut. Day [sic] 2d U S Arty in the lane between H and G Streets intoxicated and running his horse up and down the lane, just before he was arrested he fell from his horse he was so drunk he was not able to sit his horse. Except with great difficulty—When I undertook to arrest him he resisted & refuse [sic] to come stating he would not be arrested by a non Commissioned officer as he was an officer in the Regular army—with difficulty I succeeded in getting him up H as far as 10th he then started his horse on full run & turned down 11th Street I then caught him— he used abusive language & damned my soul several times he dismounted & swore he would not come. He finally mounted & after considerable difficulty—I succeeded in bringing him to this office— He stated he had a pass but would show it only to a Commissioned Officer.[15]

On June 7, 1865, Dey was released by Captain Theodore McGowan, Assistant Adjutant General and Acting Judge Advocate, to Colonel F. Ingraham, Provost Marshal General. There were no further charges against Dey.[16]

On Friday, June 30, 1865, the day that the military commission sitting in Washington found all eight alleged Lincoln assassination conspirators guilty, Dey was reported as "being absent without leave."[17] While he was AWOL, he missed the report that the 2nd Regiment of Artillery

was calling its companies to Baltimore, Maryland, for a change of post
to California. Camp Barry was closed on July 12, 1865. Company C
moved from there to Camp Bailey, Maryland. From Camp Bailey it
marched to Bladensburg, Maryland, where it went by rail to Fort
McHenry, arriving at the fort on July 25.[18]

On July 31, First Lieutenant Henry C. Dodge, who assumed command of Company C, recommended that Dey be "dismissed from the
service of the United States," since there was no record of his whereabouts since June 30, 1865. On August 4, the AGO recommended that a
notice be officially published requesting Dey to appear before the military commission in Washington within fifteen days. In that appearance,
he was expected to defend the charge of absent without leave, or "be
recommended for dismissal from the service." The notice was published
on August 14.[19] Two days earlier, on August 12, the regiment had reported that Companies F and I, Dey's old companies, "have arrived from
the West and the Regiment will be ready to embark as soon as the transports arrive."

Not all the men in Company F were ready for duty in California.
Albert Boker deserted en route from Chattanooga, Tennessee, to Fort
McHenry, and John Smith and William Fallbright deserted at Louisville, Kentucky, on August 7. William Masters deserted on August 16;
and James Garry, Henry Halteman, James Fuller and Thomas Seig on
August 18; and Thomas Farrell on August 19. Michael Flynn, alias John
Collins, and his brother, Michael Collins, deserted on August 18, but
were apprehended two weeks later and sent off to the West Coast to
join the rest of the regiment.[20]

On August 18, 1865, with the various batteries assembled, the
regiment embarked at Fort McHenry aboard the steamers *G. R.
Spaulding* and *Ben Deford* and arrived at Aspinwall, Panama, on August 31. There, the commanding officer requested from the superinten-
dent, Panama Railroad, transportation to the west coast of the Isthmus
for 38 officers, 11 officers' wives, 14 officers' children, 534 enlisted men,
41 laundresses, 29 laundresses' children; 22 officers' servants, and 18
female servants, with 6,000 pounds of luggage in bulk, weighing thirty
tons.[21]

On the same day that the regiment docked at Aspinwall, Dey, who
had not appeared before the military commission, was dropped from
the rolls of the United States Army for "absence without leave."[22] On
September 5, the AGO sent Dey the official notice of his promotion to
first lieutenant. He had been promoted in November 1864; his "wall
commission" had already been signed on June 1, 1865, by President
Andrew Johnson and Edwin M. Stanton, Secretary of War. It was deposited subsequently in Dey's Appointment, Commission and Personal
(ACP) file, now stored at the National Archives in Washington, D.C.

Officers and men of Battery C and E, 2nd U.S. Artillery, at Camp Barry, Maryland/District of Columbia, July 1865. Dey's last assignment. The picture was taken in July 1865, shortly after Dey went AWOL.

USAMHI

Since Dey had already left Camp Barry, the unsigned "Oath of Office" was returned to the AGO with the notation "due to absent without leave."[23] October 6, 1865, "By direction of the President, 1st Lieutenant Gustav Dey, 2d U.S. Artillery, is hereby dropped from the rolls of the Army for absence without leave."[24] Dey probably never saw the August 14 notice or the final presidential order declaring his separation from the army.

For the next 17 years, life for private citizen Dey must have been a continuing struggle to maintain his livelihood and his health, which began to deteriorate almost from the moment he left the army. His activities and whereabouts from June 30 to September 1865 are a mystery and will remain thus. He did return to Dunkirk, New York, in mid-September. There he was a boarder in a home owned by Leopold Gunther on Buffalo Street. Dey went to work almost immediately as a clerk in the mercantile firm of Bradley and Isham [or Esham], and stayed with that firm until January 1867.

In January 1867, he married Victoria Gunther Taylor. She was Leopold's sister and the widow of Private Charles Taylor, who died on February 28, 1864, in Elmira, New York, while on his way from Dunkirk to join his unit with the Army of the Potomac. Victoria and Charles had two children. Gustav and Victoria had one child, Gustavus Adolphus, Junior, who was born on October 10, 1869 in Dunkirk.

In 1873–1874, Dey was elected as overseer of the poor. By then he was too ill to do physical labor. He was elected (or appointed) to the position "out of sympathy of his neighbors and a desire to help him by reason of his health & the fact that he was a soldier, in the war of 1861." To supplement his meager earnings, he took in boarders and kept "a small grocery [on Ruggles Street in Dunkirk] which was attended by his wife & her children." On April 14, 1879, through George Lemon, attorney and agent, Washington, D.C., he filed a claim for pension for wounds to his left hand and side suffered during the battle at Corinth, Mississippi, on October 4, 1862. Almost a year later, in March 1880, Dey supplied proof of his service in the army to substantiate his claim. In fact, however, on February 20, 1880, the AGO had affirmed that Dey was slightly wounded at Corinth, 'but the records of this office do not show the nature and location of the wound..." He then did receive $2.00 per month for wounds from October 7, 1865. It is not known if he received the pension for the entire period, which would have amounted to approximately $400. It is also strange that the effective date was the day after Dey received the presidential order dropping him from the rolls. His pension was administered from the Syracuse, New York, pension office as claim number 186876, April 12, 1881. On June 4, 1881, he submitted a "Declaration for the Increase of An Invalid Pension" for the "Total loss of use of left Lung with Hemorrage [sic] from about the time of discharge from the service."

Victoria Gunther Taylor Dey
From a Family Portrait, Christine Day Collection

Dey died of consumption on February 14, 1882. His last claim for an increase of pension was rejected on January 13, 1883, almost a year after his death. The reason for the rejection "for disease of lungs, (newly alleged disability) on the ground that the declaration of said disability being informal, the soldier having died, the widow is not entitled to any accrued pension for disability." Dey had not filed an inclusive claim to include his lung ailment. Evidently he chose initially to file a claim for his hand and side wounds since it was easier to prove that these had been service connected. The later claim for his lung condition was more difficult to prove as having happened while he was in the service. In either case, both claims were difficult to prove since he never was treated by military personnel who would have documented and provided official proof of his disabilities.

The affidavits of contemporaries, without exception, stressed his weakening condition, which was apparent immediately upon his return to Dunkirk in September 1865. In fact, as recorded in an 1886 affidavit, Dey told his wife, Victoria, and a doctor who attended him shortly after their marriage that "one year before he left the Arme, he got a sevire cold and from that time he had a bad cough and spidt blood, he told us at that time, where he was with his company, but I cannot remember now." Dey had seen some hard duty in eleven years of service. If, as he claimed, his condition occurred just a year before he left the army, it may have happened during the Wilderness campaign (May 4 to May 31, 1864). On or about May 12, "Torrents of rain had mired the Virginia Roads, and offensive operations were discontinued for a week."[25] Again, as Victoria testified, at that time Dey did not go on sick call or to a base hospital, choosing instead to be treated by a civilian physician, spending "a great deal of Mony to get well."

He made, in hindsight, a similar mistake after the battle of Corinth. He was treated for his wounds in the field by a physician who was with a volunteer unit. No official records were made. Hence, he had to provide a statement (and hopefully some eyewitnesses) about those wounds when he applied for his initial pension in 1879. By then, he had no records and he could not recall the names of his comrades who could have attested to the truth about his wounds. He mentioned that Lieutenant Murray had died in prison camp in Georgia in 1864. He also mentioned Lieutenant Green, but Green was already dead by then, and he would have been of no use since he was not with the company during that battle. Dey, as a first sergeant, should have recalled that the company was required to furnish muster rolls, which included information on casualties.

Victoria Dey continued her attempts to receive a widow's pension for Dey's wounds and fatal illness. As late as July 19, 1890, she tried through a friend to determine if the charge of desertion against Dey's name was valid, thus keeping her from getting his pension. The quick response from the AGO on July 25, 1890, was that Dey was dismissed from the service from being AWOL, which was not considered desertion.[26] Victoria Dey died two weeks later on August 8, 1890. She never obtained any pension for Dey's lung ailment. But she died with the knowledge that Gustav Dey had not been a deserter.

On the day after Gus Dey died, an editorial appeared in the local newspaper on the subject of veterans' pensions. It read as if it had been written for him. Entitled "Arrears of Pensions," the writer decried the public opposition to such payments to veterans: "A great outcry has been raised in certain quarters against the law granting arrears of pensions to soldiers of the war of the rebellion, because it costs so much to pay these claims. After all these soldiers suffered in defense of their imperiled country. It ill becomes the nation whose preservation, present prosperity and ability to pay these claims is the result of these perils and suffering to be niggardly in their recognition and allowance." The writer went on to cite a passage from President Lincoln's Gettysburg address as an example of how the "martyr President showed his appreciation of what soldiers accomplished." He then continued with examples of the "patriotic soldier who periled his life on the battle field, or suffered untold horrors in rebel prisons or lingered in hospitals, with all the discomfit attendant on camp life, should be deprived of the award of a grateful people because frauds are sometimes perpetrated." Still, "We have known of some cases of soldiers who entered from the highest motives of patriotism and served faithfully during their period of enlistment, and came home with shattered health and have not seen well days since, and have got pension [sic] through this act of which so much complaint had been made of, and we are most heartily glad of it."[27]

Lieutenant G. A. Dey, Co. F, 2nd U.S. Artillery was buried on Thursday, February 16, 1882, in Forest Hill Cemetery, Fredonia, New York. Private Charles P. Taylor, (Victoria's first husband), a member of Company G, 112th Regiment, New York Volunteers, is also buried in the same family plot. Both are joined there by Victoria Gunther Taylor Dey, who is interred in an unmarked grave.[28]

Montage showing details of grave site of Lieutenant G. A. Dey and Charles Taylor, Victoria's first husband, at Forest Hill Cemetery, Fredonia, N.Y. Victoria is also buried there in an unmarked grave.

Courtesy of the Artist, Kristin B. Maher

Chapter 12

The Regulars: Old Soldiers Do Die

The soldiers who served in Company F, 2nd U.S. Artillery were part of that branch of the military which came to be known as the "lost arm" when compared to the infantry and cavalry. Moreover, these men had the misfortune of serving in the Trans-Mississippi theater early in the Civil War, away from the media center of focus, and then later in the western theater of operations. And they were regulars. Each was one of approximately 16,000 thousand officers and enlisted men who were serving in the United States Army when the Civil War broke out. Many were out on the frontiers, far away from the sudden spots of interest. Once the volunteers from the various states came upon the scene, this relative handful of men moved further into obscurity. As the numbers of units under arms increased, the 2nd U.S. Artillery no longer operated independently as it had since 1821. Now like many of the volunteers units, it was detached, brigaded, increased or decreased in manpower within itself as individuals deserted, died, were disabled, or discharged, honorably or dishonorably.

Yet the men who served in Company F had an unique talent, especially those gun crews who drilled many hours and took that expertise into the early battles in Missouri. Trained artillerists were a scarce, sought-after commodity, as were the field-wise veterans who could just plain soldier. When the shooting stopped, these regulars who came from diverse backgrounds could either continue to soldier or drift into civilian life. Many of the men were foreign born; many were from the South which they had helped to defeat. Lorenzo Immell, a native of Ohio, once remarked that when he joined Company F in 1860, half the men were from the South. After all, there had been a very active recruitment rendezvous in North Carolina in 1857, when Gus Dey first joined the company. Immell failed to mention the Irish, Germans, and Prussians, like

151

Gus Dey, and other foreign born. Relatively few chose to go home, especially to the South where their families no longer existed or resided.
William J. Williams, a native of Charlotte, North Carolina, declared
that "I have not seen a Relation since August 12th 1857 [the day he
enlisted]. My Father, Mother, Sisters and Brothers are all Dead since
shortly after the War." He finally settled in Kansas City, Missouri, after
he was discharged in 1862.

Some of the foreign born may have returned to their homeland.
But of the men covered in this study, only one is known to have done so.
Peter Cavanagh [Cavanaugh or Kavanaugh] completed his second enlistment in 1867. He was honorably discharged at Fort Vancouver, Washington Territory, boarded ship on the West Coast, and returned to
Cappancur, Ireland, where he was born. He married, had two daughters, died in 1871, and was buried in the cemetery across the road from
where he was born. His wife continued to collect his pension after his
death.

Most of the other foreign born adopted America as their homeland. Generally they gravitated to places familiar to them during their
soldiering days or to where they would be among people with similar
national origins. Dey returned to Dunkirk, New York, which he had left
in 1854, to be with other German immigrants who had settled in this
small community in western New York. Albert Wachsman, born in
Sonderhausen, Germany, chose to live in Kansas City, Missouri. On his
enlistment, he had been assigned to Company I, just as Dey had been in
1854. Wachsman received a commission in 1862 with the 2nd Missouri
Light Artillery, and served primarily in western Missouri and in eastern and southeastern Kansas, in areas familiar to him during his service with Company F. He was mustered out in August 1865, married
Virginia Bridger, daughter of the famed mountain man, Jim Bridger,
and settled in the Westport section of Kansas City, Missouri.

Those who chose to remain in the military literally marched from
the battlefields onto transports in Baltimore and sailed west to San Francisco. For Company F, its next post was California, and eventually the
newly acquired territory of Alaska. Others finished their enlistments and
went into civilian life, or deserted rather than continue the hard life in
the regular army becoming fugitives in the eyes of the military.

During the war, some of the more talented men translated their talents into positions of command. Only one, Gus Dey, was allowed into the
exclusive fraternity of the regular army officer corps. Robert Armstrong,
Andrew Hockstadter, Daniel Hudson, Lorenzo Immell, William McGinniss,
Albert Wachsman, and William Wrightenburg became commissioned officers, but with volunteer (state) forces. With the exception of Wrightenburg,
who went with the Kansas Cavalry, the rest went with the 1st and 2nd
Missouri Artillery or with the 18th Missouri Infantry.

Others from the company who were honorably discharged or discharged for disability chose not to stay out of the war. Julius Baker,
after driving a team for the government at Fort Leavenworth, joined
the 2nd Missouri Artillery in 1863. Raleigh Brewer also drove a government team before enlisting in the Kansas Cavalry. Joseph Hendricks
and George Myrick joined Brewer in the Kansas Cavalry. Joseph Keyes,
who walked away from Wilson's Creek with a bullet in his body, enlisted in the Veterans' Reserve Corps, 82nd New York Volunteers; and
Cyrus Young, who carried a bullet in his leg from the same battle, joined
the Independent Company of the Pennsylvania Light Artillery.

James Crosby, who received a disability discharge for his wound
at Wilson's Creek, became a mess cook for the government. While working in Little Rock, he and his assistant were taken prisoner by the Confederates, shipped off to Shreveport, Louisiana, and then exchanged
four months later. And Frank McGinnis, who opted for a discharge rather
than a promotion and reenlistment after the battle of Corinth, joined
General Dodge's staff as a civilian scout. McGinnis, from North Carolina, was captured by the Confederates in Mississippi and imprisoned
at Castle Thunder, Richmond, Virginia, as "an alien enemy."

Charles Bussard, after his discharge in 1864, joined the 2nd Missouri Volunteer Cavalry, "Merrill's Horse." Bussard was unique in that
he saw service with both armies. An Ohioan, he was working in Columbia, South Carolina, as a carriage maker when the war broke out. To
escape, he enlisted in the Columbia Flying Artillery. He managed to
work his way "through the lines and reach Cincinnati." He then enlisted in Company F.

Midway through the war, a few men from volunteer units joined
the company. Joseph Fahrenbaker from the 11th Missouri, and William
Payne and Oscar Sisson (recruited by Dey) from the 8th Wisconsin stayed
with the company and were discharged on the West Coast. James Rogers
and John Smith (also recruited by Dey) from the 8th Wisconsin deserted
from the company in 1864. Captain Maurice, who commanded the company from New Madrid through Corinth, accepted a second lieutenancy in 1866 and remained with the 2nd Artillery Regiment until his
death in 1885.

There were other regulars whose life work was the military. Charles
Clark served from 1839 to 1862. Left at Fort Monroe in 1857 when the
company went to Fort Leavenworth because he was too old for service
in the field (this may have been the fate that Gus Dey envisioned when
he went AWOL in 1865), he managed to survive the rigors of army life
in the field for another five years.

Charles Thorp Childs, who served from 1845–1871, was wounded
at Mexico City in 1847 while serving as a private with the 8th U.S. Infantry. The bullet in his thigh was never removed. His second enlistment

under the name of Issacher Thorp was with Company B, 2nd U.S. Artillery. In 1860, he enlisted as Charles Thorp with Company F. In 1898 during an operation to remove the ball, which he had carried for forty years, gangrene set in. Childs died three days later.

William Murray had a very checkered career during his 33 years in service from 1846 to 1879. At one point, he assumed the alias of William Madden, deserted, was restored to duty, and subsequently retired. Murray suffered from scurvy during the Mexican War. The disease recurred during the Seminole War in Florida in 1857. Then his eyes became inflamed when he fought against the Modoc Indians at Lava Beds, California, in 1873.

When Daniel R. Hudson, whom Dey succeeded as first sergeant, accepted a first lieutenancy with the 18th Missouri, he had already served 12 years with the regular army, having enlisted in 1849. This portly, old regular soldier was looked upon by some members of the 18th Missouri as "something of a martinet, although he was a kind hearted man. The fact is that the officers and boys always thought he lacked sand, and he was not considered a good leader in dangerous places." Originally from Dinwiddie, Virginia, Hudson settled in St. Louis, Missouri, after resigning his commission in December 1864. He died there in 1892.

There were two Robert Armstrongs in Company F. Sergeant Armstrong from Norfolk, England, enlisted in 1848 and served with the company until 1862. He then received a commission with the 1st Missouri Light Artillery. He was the only casualty at Boonville in June 1861, receiving a non-incapacitating wound. The other Armstrong was from Philadelphia. He enlisted with the 3rd U.S. Infantry in 1850. He was later part of the unassigned regulars who fought with the 1st Missouri Artillery from 1862 to 1864 before joining Company F. He was taken prisoner at Atlanta on July 22, 1864. He remained in the service until he was discharged in 1885 "by act of Congress." He later applied for and was denied a pension for the loss of a thumb while cutting wood during his sixth enlistment.

Patrick Hennessy (1850–1869), from Cork, Ireland, was recruited by Brevet Major Philip Kearny in New York City. Hennessy began his career with the 3rd U.S. Artillery before joining Company F in 1861. He also was taken prisoner at Atlanta. He spent the rest of his career with the Ordnance Corps before resigning in 1869 "to enable him to support his family." He died in Albany, New York, in 1880.

John Martin (1864–1875), Moses Carmint (1856–1880), and John Nulty (1856–1889) just soldiered. Nulty applied for a pension, which was denied on the grounds that "the claimant is now on the retired list of the army." Carmint, who joined Company F in 1862 after having been given a disability discharge for rheumatism from the Pennsylvania Volunteer

Cavalry, remained with the 2nd U.S. Artillery until 1880, when he was given a second disability discharge for "chronic rheumatism and old age."

Nathaniel Gibbins, from Pittsburgh, Pennsylvania, began his career in 1857 with the 2nd Regiment of Dragoons. In 1861, he transferred into the 4th U.S. Artillery, and into the 2nd U.S. Artillery in 1862. He too was taken prisoner at Atlanta. He was discharged at age 45 in 1871 upon recommendation of his commanding officer while he was serving at the Vancouver Arsenal, Washington Territory. He spent most of his life in veterans' homes, before dying in the National Soldiers' Home, Washington, D.C. in 1916 at 76.

August Steffen (von Grahl) of Hralsund, Prussia, spent the majority of his 25-years' service (1857–1882) in administrative jobs both with the military and in the federal service. He was with Company F for a relatively short time in 1862. At one point in his career, he was sergeant major of the 2nd U.S. Artillery. He finished his career as a clerk in the AGO in Washington, D.C., where he lived and subsequently died in 1883.

Thomas Enright ended his military career after 24 years (1860–1884), "being broken down from hard service, and old age." He was discharged at Fort Douglas, Utah Territory, in 1884 from the 6th U.S. Infantry. His service record is difficult to decipher because he mangled his birth dates. He was born in Kerry County, Ireland, in 1826, came to the United States in 1848, and enlisted in Company F in 1860, claiming to be 29. Mathematically, the numbers add up to 34. (The records show that he was 24 when he enlisted!) He would have been 56 when he was discharged. He died in 1912 in the Soldiers' Home Hospital in Washington, D.C.

Despite having suffered "moon blindness," scurvy, and a wound at Atlanta, Patrick Meehan, of Sligo, Ireland, managed to survive 23-years' service (1860–1883) with the 2nd U.S. Infantry, the 1st Missouri Light Artillery, with Company F, and with the Ordnance Corps. He had no relatives, and "I have never married." After his retirement, he finished his days at the Soldiers' Home in Washington, D.C.

One of the strangest tales was that of John Shields' military life. The 19-year-old native of Limerick, Ireland, joined Company F in 1860. He reenlisted in 1864, but while on furlough in July 1864, he enlisted in the United States Navy. He served aboard the *Unadella, Princeton, North Carolina,* and *Rhode Island* as a landsman. He was discharged from the navy in August 1865. He then enlisted in the 2nd U.S. Cavalry in September 1865. He surrendered himself as a deserter from Company F as of July 1, 1864. He never returned to the company, but finished his 19-year military career with the cavalry. He died in 1918 in Mondak, Montana.

The last place of refuge for some of these regulars was the Soldiers' Homes or National Military Homes established throughout the country for disabled and aged veterans. Joining Enright, Gibbins, and Meehan at the Soldiers' Home in Washington, D.C. was the Mexican War veteran Charles Childs, who died there in 1898. Louis Emery, Joseph Keyes, who later moved to the home in Hampton, Virginia, closer to his adopted home in Richmond, Virginia, William Murray, and William Simpson were also in the home in Washington, D.C. Simpson, who was born in Caroline County, Maryland, died in Anacostia, Washington, D.C. and is buried in Prince Georges County, Maryland.

Louis Emery, a native of Baden, Germany, after his discharge in November 1865, spent the next 13 years in civilian life before reenlisting in 1878 in Company D, 7th U.S. Cavalry, after the Custer massacre at Little Big Horn. Emery only spent two years in the cavalry, being discharged in 1880 at Fort Yates, Dakota Territory, for chronic dyspepsia, hemorrhoids, and general debility. His commanding officer wrote on his discharge: "I know nothing special in regard to this man's diseases. They being of such complex nature that, in my opinion, nobody but a practising physician is qualified to give an opinion respecting them." Emery spent most of 1879 in company hospitals suffering from these various illnesses. During the war, he had suffered from deafness from the artillery fire at Vicksburg. He was only 40 years old then. At 52, while in the home in Washington, he applied for an increase of his pension because of the above complaints.

John Miller, who lost a leg at Atlanta, was an inmate at the National Military Home in Dayton, Ohio. Also there was Abraham Booth, of Burslim, England, who entered the home in 1900 and died there in 1911. John McIntyre, who was "completely broken down and worthless" because of syphilitic rheumatism, was in the Disabled Veterans' National Home in Washington, Ohio; Joseph Englebert lived in the Soldiers' Home in Sandusky, Ohio, where he died in March 1908.

Owen Donnelly, John Fisher, Henry B. Jewett, and John O'Brien lived in the Soldiers' Home in Los Angeles, California. Donnelly, who had been permanently injured in an accident in Sedalia, Missouri, in 1862, lived in Texas and Arizona after his discharge and before settling in California. Fisher, who stayed with the company when it went to the West Coast after the war, was discharged at Benicia, California. He stayed in California, lived at the home, and died there in November 1912. Jewett and O'Brien apparently left no records.

John Erasmy, who came from Milwaukee, Wisconsin, lived at the National Military Home in that city. At 62, he suffered from heart disease; he also claimed to have contracted rheumatism and suffered from general debility resulting from the "hard marching in the Spring of 1862 on the march to New Madrid, Mo."

Joseph Hendricks, who enlisted in the 5th Kansas Cavalry after his discharge from the company, died in February in the National Military Home at Leavenworth, Kansas. With him there was James Wallace, the Irishman from Cork, who was supposedly killed at Wilson's Creek in August 1861. After his discharge in 1864, Wallace settled in Brookville, Kansas. He died of cardiac arrest on January 2, 1922, at Leavenworth.

The task of gathering evidence as proof that a member of the company did in fact serve in the military, in the Civil War, and had suffered wounds or sickness while in the line of duty, was a sticky one. For one thing, the company's records prior to 1868 were lost at Kenai, Alaska, when the boat carrying men, supplies and records struck a rock and sank almost immediately. In 1863, Lieutenant Murray had complained that he could not give Sergeant Gus Dey much of a recommendation in Dey's application for a commission because the records had been lost. Then at Atlanta, when the company was overrun, Lieutenant Lemuel Smith, 5th U.S. Artillery, who assumed command of the company after Murray and Lieutenant Breckinridge were both captured, had trouble submitting the muster roll for April–June because the company's records were lost.

Furthermore, most of the applications for pensions were submitted years after the fact. Some could remember the names of comrades; others, like Dey, drew complete blanks. If they did remember names, they could not be sure where their old comrades lived. John Zimmer expressed a common frustration when he wrote in 1880 "that I have done all in my power, that was to be honestly done to secure additional evidence; that I advertised in several papers to learn the address of comrades but to no avail. And I again state, that I cannot furnish any record statement from hospitals, but was attended by different physicians in camp, whilst being moved from place to place, & again, that I recollect no name of any of those physicians. This was in the fall of 1863 in the neighborhood of Vicksburg, Miss. I further declare this to be *all* I have to say in my case." Zimmer also stated that two of his witnesses had been as accurate as they could possibly be under oath. But "Each [stated that] dates and particular circumstances could not be given by them. It being so long ago since we parted from service."

Eventually, pension attorneys partially solved the problem of accuracy by repetition. The witnesses were provided with the language of the claim. Each affirming testimony then took on the flavor of the original language. While most of the men hired pension attorneys to handle their affairs, one, Lorenzo Immell, himself became a pension attorney in St. Louis. His letterhead read: "Late Inspector of Artillery, 4th (IV) Army Corps, U.S. Volunteers. PENSION AND CLAIM ATTORNEY, Notary Public and Collector, Loans Negotiated." Still others were fortunate to have retained good pension attorneys, and found very good testimonial writers. Company F had its share of illiterates. But some of them, like George Myrick and Joseph Hendricks, had good recall so that they could dictate their statements to notaries. Some others were good writers, like Immell, John Kelly, William J. Williams, John Zimmer, George Seckler (who managed although he was semi-literate), and Richard A. Marsh (alias Robert Belt), who became an educator and eventually a county judge in Hidalgo County, Texas.

When Josiah Pond's widow needed to prove that hers was the only marriage to Pond, she wrote to Marsh, among others. Marsh responded with a flourish: "I condole with you on the death of your husband, whom I remember well as a member of Company F, 2nd Arty…I have no recollection of ever hearing that Comrade Pond was a married man…I am always ready to help the widow or orphans of an old comrade, and if there is any other evidence that I can furnish I will do it most cheerfully. Yours to Command."

John Zimmer not only provided affidavits to his old comrades, but he also actively solicited a return in kind. When he wrote an affidavit for Frederick Wiebezahl, he asked if Wiebezehl remembered his [Zimmer's] injury when his feet were crushed. "Do you know about this? Do you know when I was sick at Vicksburg Miss with Typhoid fever? If you can furnish testimony to the above, do so before a Notary Public. You will confer a poor fellow comrade a great great favor, Be Prompt." Zimmer not only described the incidents of his claim, he also framed the language for Wiebezahl. "Make it read like this: That John Zimmer late of Co F, 2nd Regt U.S. Art. In the summer of 1863, at the siege of Vicksburg Miss, from severe exposure, was stiff & sore, and from typhoid fever, after the siege at Vicksburg Miss, I firmly believe the same to have been the immediate cause of his rheumatism. Put it in the best words you can, and attend to it at once,—You will greatly oblige me, your fellow comrade."

Other frustrations for the veterans, or for family members of dead veterans, were the seemingly long delays for answers, or the disappointment of having pensions reduced. John Harrison Lane was particularly distressed when he learned that his pension was to be reduced from $12.00 to $8.00 per month. He protested not because of himself, but "I do not ask Charity, and would not even ask Justice, were it not for my four motherless, little children…I submit that while Mrs. Gen—draws 100.00 dollars per month and Mrs. Gen—2000.00 per year and spends more than that amount annually for Flowers for her receptions, my pitiful allowance per month must be reduced 33-1/3 per cent. I did my duty as faithfully as either of those Generals according to my station. I do not envy those ladies what they receive from the Government, money cannot repay their loss neither can it restore my health." Failing eyesight, deafness, and ruptures on both sides, chronic "Catahr and bronchitis, also a

gun shot wound in the left thigh received at Kenisaw Mountain, GA."
were the physical disabilities Lane suffered. Unfortunately, the AGO
report of February 24, 1898 sheds no light on the result of Lane's plea.

When Albert Boker, William Fallbright, Thomas Farrell, James
Fuller, James Garry, Henry Halteman, William Masters, Thomas Sieg,
and John Smith deserted in August 1865, rather than board transports
that carried the company to the West Coast, they did not realize then
the long-range effects their actions would have on their future lives.

When Boker, Halteman, and Fuller first applied for pensions, they
received the typical response from the AGO in Washington D.C. "Deserted Aug—'65 from (the name of the post). (Last rank). No record of
apprehension. Name is also borne as He is a deserter at large." On March
2, 1911, [Private -No. 249.] [H. R. 20603.] An Act For the Relief of Henry
Halteman was approved by the President. The act stipulated that
Halteman was to be "considered to have been honorably discharged from
the military service of the United States as a private in Company F,
Second Regiment of Artillery, on the eighteenth day of August, eighteen
hundred and sixty-five: Provided, That no pension shall accrue prior to
the passage of this Act." Halteman died in 1917. Albert Boker was
granted a similar pardon on May 26, 1902. He died August 4, 1902,
three months later, knowing that he had been honorably discharged.

James Fuller, who ended up living in Alma, Wisconsin, was also
exonerated by Special Act of Congress on July 22, 1891. A month later,
when Fuller submitted his claim for pension, he explained the reasons
for his desertion:

> On the 18th day of August 1865 [at Fort McHenry, Maryland] he
> being sick with chronic diarrhea obtained a pass or permit from
> his Commanding Officer among others Lieut. [Rezin Gist] Howell
> then commanding his company to go home. [Springfield, PA, just
> west of Philadelphia]. And that he then did go home in pursuance
> of said permit or pass and remained prostrate by such sickness for
> nearly four years thereafter, and did not know where to find said
> Company or Regiment. And being ignorant of military law & I did
> not know where to enquire for the whereabouts of said Company
> and supposed that as when he would be notified (would be ready
> and willing) to return to his duties as a soldier whenever called
> upon. He never reported and never received a discharge from the
> said organization.

Thomas Farrell was apprehended on July 1, 1872, but the record
on him is not complete. Master, Sieg, and Smith disappeared as far as
can be determined. William Fallbright died on June 28, 1884, in Philadelphia, Pennsylvania. His widow's claim for pension was denied: "Soldier having deserted from his command on Aug. 7, 1865, and failed to

receive a final honorable discharge,—claimant has no pensionable status under Act of June 27, 1890."

James Garry's action on March 2, 1895, was another story. The notary's statement, written from Amsterdam, New York, certified that James <u>McGarry</u> [underline mine] stated that he had served faithfully from 1860 until his discharge on or about July 1864. He had reenlisted in the company and had served his time. He had been a sergeant in Company F for "about 2 years and 6 months." But, unfortunately, he had lost his discharge and could not substantiate his claim. The AGO's response on April 5, 1895 was that a James Garry had in fact served with the company, and reenlisted as a sergeant. But he had "Deserted Aug 18, 1865, at Fort McHenry, MD., a Sergt. <u>He is a deserter at large.</u>" The report continued: "The name James McGarry is not borne on the muster rolls of company 'F' U.S. Artillery, during the period in question; nor is there any record of enlistment of any man by that name during the year 1860."

It would be fitting to close this research with a philosophic utterance by one of the enlisted men of the company which would summarize their total experience. After years of hard riding, either on horseback or as a teamster, or sitting on a caisson, eating dust and maggot-infested grain, or recalling the smell of death and the piercing screams of dying and wounded men and animals, and living in all climates in places where only regular army artillerymen would venture, their memories probably would not be of tactics, wars, campaigns or status in the military hierarchy. No words of wisdom would pour forth from field weary veterans like Dey, Keyes, Wallace, Williams, Marsh, Cavanagh, or Zimmer; their words would certainly be about such mundane things as survival and living. No diary entries or personal accounts have been found of a reunion under the Chinkapin oaks on "Bloody Hill" at Wilson's Creek, or of an outing at the end of Main Street in New Madrid, where the pier overlooks the Mississippi River and Island No. 10 is not far away, or of a GAR encampment at Farmington or Corinth—no account where a gem could be found and polished to shine like the rising sun over the Big Blue on the Missouri-Kansas border, or the sighting of the harvest moon on Clear Creek in Mississippi. Corporal John Miller's painful memory of a comrade's visit, as Miller laid on his cot in Atlanta aching from the leg that was no longer there, might be a fitting summary: "I was lying in bed when he came to see me & of course [I] did not feel like noticing anything ....in four days I was removed to Rome, GA, and never saw him again."[1]

Appendix A

Regimental and Company Histories

Table of Contents

Introduction

This appendix presents a list of the officers Gustav Dey either encountered or undoubtedly knew during his career with the 2nd United States Artillery. Histories of the regiment and specifically of the companies in which Dey served follow the list of officers. They were written in response to two different requests. The first request in July 1866 from Major John Calef, Adjutant, was for information about each company's service during the Civil War. These histories, at this author's discretion, cover only Companies I, F, E, and C, in which Gus Dey served during his military career.

The second request in 1890 was from Lieutenant William A. Simpson, Regimental Adjutant from 1889 to 1893. His compilation appeared in "Historical Sketches U.S. Army: The Second Regiment of Artillery," *Journal of the Military Service Institutions of the U.S.*, XIV:905–220 (1893). Reproduced in this appendix are "true copies" of the inputs

161

from Lieutenant Colonel Augustus A. Gibson, retired, Dey's commander in Company I from 1855–1857 and from Colonel John C. Tidball. (Use of italics is in accordance with current custom for foreign expressions, published works and names of vessels. This frequently replaces underlining or quotation marks used in the original handwritten documents.)

Gibson chose to confine his history to a nostalgic look at the regiment's duty in Buffalo and Rochester, New York during the "Patriot's war" in 1839. This was one of the few times that the companies were regimented. The Buffalo City Directory for 1840 noted that "The 2d Regiment of U.S. Artillery, is now quartered at the Barracks, in this city, with a full complement of 600 men, at a monthly expense of about $15,000." Other details of that description are included.

The second history is that written by Colonel John C. Tidball, retired, who began his career, after graduation from the U.S. Military Academy, with the 3rd Artillery before transferring to the 2nd Regiment in 1849. He commanded Company A during the Civil War, then ended the war as a brevet major general of volunteers. He retired in 1889. Tidball's history is fairly comprehensive. Not only does he present some insight into the regiment's experiences, he also offers some of his views of what role the artillery should play in the overall army organization.

Following these histories are short synopses of engagements during the Civil War of Companies I, F, E, and C written by the commanders of those units at that time. These synopses are presented separately because each company operated as individual units connected only by paper. It was only after the war that the companies were regimented for duty in California and Alaska.

The original manuscripts were found at the National Archives, Washington, D.C., in Record Group 391, *Preliminary Inventory of the Records of the United States Regular Army Mobile Units, 1821–1942*, "Records Relating to Regimental History, 1832–1893." Entry 64. The listing of officers was found in the same record group under "Descriptive Books for Batteries A-M. 1841–64." Entry 68.

Officers of the Second Artillery Regiment (c. 1854–1865)

Colonels

Matthew M. Payne, November 11, 1856. Resigned July 23, 1861.
John L. Gardner, July 23, 1861. Retired November 1, 1861.
William W. Morris, November 1, 1861 by promotion from 4th Artillery. Died at Fort McHenry, December 11, 1865.

Lieutenant Colonels

Justin Dimick, October 5, 1857. Promoted to colonel, October 26, 1861.
Horace Brooks, October 26, 1861. Promoted to colonel, 4th Artillery, August 1, 1863.

Lewis G. Arnold, August 1, 1863. Retired February 2, 1864.
William H. French, February 8, 1864.

Majors

Harvey Brown, January 9, 1851. Promoted to lieutenant colonel, 4th
Artillery, April 28, 1861.
Martin Burke, November 11, 1856. Promoted to lieutenant colonel, 3rd
Artillery, August 28, 1861.
Horace Brooks, April 28, 1861. Promoted to lieutenant colonel, 2nd Ar-
tillery, October 26, 1861.
Bennett H. Hill, August 26, 1861 by promotion from 1st Artillery.
Harvey A. Allen, August 1, 1863 by promotion.
Edward G. Beckwith, February 8, 1864 by promotion from 3rd Artillery.

Adjutants

Thomas J. Haines, 1st Lieutenant, October 1, 1855.
Thomas Grey, 1st Lieutenant, promoted to captain, November 4, 1863.
Joseph Gales Ramsey, 1st Lieutenant, December 10, 1863.
John H. Calef, 1st Lieutenant and brevet captain, November 18, 1864.

Quartermasters

John McLean Taylor, 1st Lieutenant, October 1, 1855.
Michael P. Small, 1st Lieutenant, July 10, 1861.
James Eveleth Wilson, 1st Lieutenant, December 10, 1863.

Captains

Horace Brooks, June 18, 1846.
Lewis G. Arnold, October 27, 1847.
Henry C. Pratt, April 21, 1848.
Arnold Elzey, February 14, 1849.
William F. Barry, July 1, 1852.
Henry J. Hunt, September 28, 1852.
Augustus A. Gibson, July 9, 1853. Promoted to major, 3rd Artillery, July
25, 1863.
William Hays, October 8, 1853.
Harvey A. Allen, November 25, 1854.
Samuel L. Anderson, March 8, 1855.
James Totten, October 20, 1855.
Albert J. S. Molinard, November 12, 1861. Wholly retired, October 3,
1863.

First Lieutenants

Marcus D. L. Simpson, October 27, 1847.
Anderson Merchant, April 21, 1848.
Julius A. deLagnel, January 26, 1849.

Henry Benson, March 2, 1853. Promoted to captain, May 14, 1861.
Armistead L. Long, July 1, 1854.
Henry A. Smalley, April 14, 1861.

First Lieutenants

Oliver D. Greene, April 25, 1861.
John W. Barriger, May 2, 1861.
John A. Darling, May 31, 1862, by promotion.
William Borrowe, August 1, 1863, by promotion.
Joseph C. Breckinridge, August 1, 1863, by promotion.
Albert M. Murray, March 30, 1864, by promotion.
John Fitzgerald, August 12, 1864, by promotion.
Gustav Dey, June 15, 1864, by promotion.
Rezin Howell, February 1, 1865.

Second Lieutenants

Joseph Peck Jones, January 27, 1856. Resigned February 8, 1861.
St. Clair Dearing, June 7, 1855. Resigned February 7, 1861.
William Borrowe, November 11, 1861.
Gustav Dey, October 31, 1862.
Franklin M. Ring, May 26, 1865.
John A. Darling, August 5, 1861.
Joseph C. Breckinridge, April 14, 1862.
Albert M. Murray, October 6, 1862.
John Fitzgerald, October 31, 1863.
Thomas D. Maurice, February 23, 1866 from volunteer service.

History of the Regiment in Buffalo, New York, 1839. A. A. Gibson, Lieutenant Colonel, Retired

In 1839 the regiment under Col. Bankhead was concentrated at Buffalo, N. Y., with the exception of Co. I at Rochester, in consequence of disturbances on the Canada border. Shortly anterior to this movement, it had been brought out of Florida exhausted and, I might say--decimated. It was the first and only instance before or since, within my knowledge, of the assemblage of an Artillery regiment for continual duty at a single post. A quadrangular tract of 13 acres was secured by the Government for a garrison site at the head of Main Street, about one mile from where the City Hall now exists, and extending across Delaware Street,--upon whose limits were erected--on the West, Officers' quarters--on the North and South, barracks--on the East, on Main Street, the guard house and sutler's store,--all of brick and one story with the exception of the Commanding Officer's quarters and one or two other buildings. Until these were completed for occupation in the Spring of

'40 the men were cantoned in hired buildings,--the Officers resided down town at the American Hotel--and during the winter the recruiting was lively. The stables for mounted Battery A, under 1st Lieutenant James Duncan, were near to and S. W. of the garrison.

The advantages of the location were its comparative isolation from the town and its proximity to the frontier. It was in the neighborhood of some of England's best troops--between whose officers and ours courtesies were exchanged in friendly accord. The tactical precision and the neat personnel of those troops gave to those of our regiment who went to see them an insight into and a standard of the work that was before them. The Colonel put his heart into elevating the regiment--and the Officers "caught on" in quick response. It so happened that never collectively, I venture to assert, has the regiment had better officers. Col. Bankhead was rather lymphatic--not extensively endowed by nature--but a portly gentleman of the old Virginia school compounded of pride and honor--in whose example was his chief force,--sincere, courteous and generally indulgent to his officers,--far from being a martinet, yet moderately firm, uniformly consistent in rule, and commanding the influence of personal respect.--He could not have been an unconscious subject of friendly yet acute criticism,--because the officers--many of them of superior ability--expected much from him and were determined to get it out of him. The Tactics was their pocket companion, and imperceptibly a school was evolved in which both master and pupil "got their lessons" practically-and got them well. Lieut. Col. Crane was soon promoted--and Fanning became his successor--the best drill-officer of the times. M. M. Payne was the Major,--a model soldier and the pride of the regiment. Equal attention was given to that part of discipline which relates to the men off duty--to their life in quarters and conduct at large--generating Company rivalry to its extreme limit, a rivalry contagious [not legible]. On Sundays those who wished to attend divine service were marched by music to the churches of their respective selection,--which during their absence the remainder were edified in quarters by the reading of chapters in Army Regulations. At first the church squad included indiscriminately all the men on duty--*nolens volens*, but upon reference to the War Dept. of the protests against such disregard of "Conscientious scruples" it was pronounced "unconstitutional."

There was a fine field for drills, battery and battalion below the garrison, called "Siberia." Duncan's was almost a separate Command-- He was gifted by nature for better service, -he had a genius for it, -and his drills were scenic.-

The stimulus of the beginning never relaxed while the regiment was in Buffalo. But there was that other side, not to be overlooked because it cannot be overestimated, of social intercourse with citizens of free-hearted hospitality--generous in their prosperity--whose favor the officers enjoyed without restriction. The City contained about 25000 people. It had already assumed the pretentious title of "Queen City of the West"--which its subsequent development has fully justified. It had a stirring population given to extraordinary enterprise while navigation was "open,"--but on the closing of the Canal their ardor was turned into the channel of social activities--in balls, parties, dinners, suppers, visits and all manner of amusements verging to excess, to which free access was enjoyed by the officers, not less to their improvement than their entertainment.

Those combined advantages--appreciated and worked for all they were worth, until August '41 it moved by canal to N. Y. Harbor--raised the regiment to such preeminence that it could challenge any other in the Army for superiority in tone --discipline--or esprit. They solidified it by adhesion which neither time nor dispersion could weaken. Does it remain to know how far it has recovered its prestige from the disastrous sundering of the old Army during the reballion [sic]--when it existed in fragments only, and in name?

That craze for a Light Battery organization--in principle the best, but in policy under our Institutions, the worst--weakened the unity and fraternity to which the regimental organization most conduces--But the revolutions of Science applied to invention and experiment in war and in peace have so modified the art and agencies of War that superior attainments will hereafter be required of the Artillerist--and the line of service between him and his adjunct of Infantry will be more definite and distinct,--with the opposite effect of more intimate association of the Artillerist and Engineer--and the more exclusive recognition of the Artillery Corps.-

November 25, 1890   Lt. Col. A. A. Gibson, Retired
Freeburg[?], MO.

[The Buffalo City Directory for 1840 included the following information about the roster of officers who were in the city for this assignment.]
MILITARY OF THE CITY OF BUFFALO
The 2d Regiment U.S. Artillery, is now quartered at the Barracks, in this city, with a full complement of 600 men, at a monthly expense of about $15,000.
OFFICERS,
Colonel--James Bankhead,
Lt. Colonel--J. B. Crane,
Major--M. M. Payne
Ass't Quarter Master--Edmund A. Ogden
Captains--James Green, John B[reckinridge] Grayson, S. McKenzie, G. S. Drane, C. S. Merchant, M. M. Clarke, W. C. De Hart, R. A. Zantzinger, C. F. Smith.

1st Lieutenants--James Duncan, H. C. Pratt, Horace Brooks, C. B. Daniels, Robert Allen, A. E. Jones, S. J. Bransford, Wm. Armstrong, Thos. P. Ridgeley [Ridgely], H. S. Kendrick, S. G. Arnold, R. A. Suther, Francis Woodbridge, W. W. Chapman, J. C. Casey, John Sedgwick, E. Shrivers, E. D. Townsend, J. F. Roland, M. S. Shackreford [M. L. Shackleford].

2d Lieutenants--W. F. Barry, W. A. Nichols, S. H. Allen, Leslie Chase, H. J. Hunt, W. B. Blair, A. A. Gibson. L. Pitkin, A. B. Lansing. ----Sutler--E. A. Ogden.

History of the Regiment, 1835–1890. Colonel J. C. Tidball, Retired
Second U.S. Artillery

In the Seminole War in Florida, 1835–40, the entire regiment was employed, and have a conspicuous part; serving always as infantry, in detachments of companies, and never as a whole regiment.

For an account of the services of the various companies see Sprague's *History of the Florida War*.

At Dade's Massacre, there were two companies--perhaps of artillery--and as Capt. Gardiner and Lieut. Bassinger of the 2d were killed, it is possible that one of the companies wiped out belonged to that regiment?

From Florida, all--perhaps all--of the regiment went, in 1838, to the Cherokee Country of Georgia and Alabama, and assisting in quelling the disturbances there, and emigrating the Indians to the Indian Territory.

From the Cherokee country the regiment went, in 1839, overland to the Canadian Frontier, at that time the scene of the Patriot disturbances [border conflicts including Americans who promoted Canadian independence]. The journey was made by marching, by river and by canal through Ohio; there were no railroads in those days west of the Alleghenies.

The regiment was stationed at various places along that frontier, but principally in Buffaloe [sic]. From the Canadian frontier the regiments [the 1st Artillery regiment was also on the frontier] went, in 1841, to Forts Adams, Trumbull, Columbus, Hamilton, etc. at most of which places they remained until some went west to Corpus Christi in 1845, and all in the following year to Mexico.

In the meanwhile Company A, commanded by Lieut. James Duncan, subsequently Brevet Col. Duncan, was mounted, in accordance with the law of 1812, authorizing one company of each regiment to be organized and equipped as light artillery.

Battery A was mounted in 1839, and its first service as such was at the Camp of Instruction at Trenton, N. J. in the summer of that year. The Captain--I think it was Joseph P. Taylor, afterwards Commissary

General, was permanently absent, and Duncan continued in command after he was promoted Captain, and thereafter promoted to Col. Inspector General in 1849.

Sedgwick then became Captain of it and continued until he was made Major of Cavalry in 1855, when Horace Brooks was assigned to the command of it. Brooks was relieved from it in 1857, and Barry assigned to it, and continued to command it until he was made Major of the 5th Arty, in 1862, when I was assigned to it and continued its Captain until promoted Major in 1867, when Ramsey fell heir to it. Since which time it has changed captains several times.

In this connection, it is proper to mention that soon after the first battle of Bull Run, *viz*, Sept. 1861, this battery, until this time only a mounted battery, was equipped as a Horse battery, and so continued until the close of the Civil War in July 1865.

In Nov. 1861, Benson's battery, M, was mounted as Horse Artillery, in March 1862 Robertson's battery B & L, combined was also mounted, and in 1863, one--I think, battery D, under Lieut. Williston, and another, (I have forgotten which) under Lieut. Butler[?] were also mounted as Horse Batteries, and all continued so mounted until July 1865.

In the fall of 1865 the regiment went to the Pacific Coast, and batteries A and M –the designated mounted batteries of the regiment– were remounted, as mounted batteries.

Battery A, was the first battery on this continent to be mounted as Horse Artillery. Ringgold, who commanded Battery C of the 3d Artillery, used, upon occasion to equip one of the sections (Platoons) of his battery as horse artillery, but the battery was not a Horse Artillery battery, and never used as such.

When Ringgold mounted his battery in 1838 it was a new thing in our service, and was called horse artillery, because it had horses. This confusion of terms continued until after the commencement of the rebellion. Genl Scott reported to the President, in the spring of 1861, that another horse battery had arrived at Washington, meaning, of course, a mounted (or Light) battery. (see Nicholay and Hays, *Life of Lincoln*.) This confusion of the terms misled Birkhimer in his admirable *History of the U. S. Artillery*. But the honor of having the first Horse Battery belongs to the 2d Regiment. At the time of mounting Battery A, I made a special inquiry as to the fact and knew it to be so.

The entire regiment went to the Mexican war, and took an active and gallant part; the most conspicuous was that of Duncan, with his battery A, which he had in nearly every battle, from Palo Alto to the City of Mexico.

During this war, *viz*. in 1846, two additional batteries, L and M, were added to each regiment. M of the 2d was raised and commanded by Captain, afterwards, Bvt. Major John F. Boland, and designated the additional light or mounted battery of the regiment, and this designation so continued until about 1868 when it was mounted, and never was remounted. After the Mexican war the regiment was assigned chiefly to the southern ports of the Atlantic; namely, Merchant at Southwell[?], N. C.; Larned at Augusta, Ga.; Smith, (C. F.) at St. Augustine; Swartwout at Beaufort, N. C.; Brooks in New Mexico; Kendrick in New Mexico; Luther at Fort Moultrie, S. C.; Roland at Savannah; Arnold at Fort Monroe; Woodbridge at Charleston; Pratt at Fort Monroe; and Sedgwick with light battery A at Baltimore. Headquarters at Fort Monroe.

In the summer of 1849 Luther and Roland exchanged posts; the former going to Savannah and the latter to Augusta Arsenal, Ga. where he was to mount his battery (M). But before he could do so Indians made trouble on Indian River, Florida, and we (I was with him as 2d Lieut. at the time) were ordered, first to Palatka, and afterwards to Indian River. So too were the companies of Merchant (then Elzey's), Larned, Swartwout, Smith & Woodbridge. Between Indian River and the Kissimmee, these companies, in conjunction with others from other regiments of artillery, did some scouting. But the chief occupation, during that winter and the following spring, was to construct a road from Indian River to the Kissimmee River. Westward of the latter river to Tampa, the road was built by the Seventh Infantry, assisted by some companies of Artillery. This road was an avenue through the pine barrens, forty feet wide from every tree and and [sic] scrub palmetto was grubbed, and the road raked and cleared of every twig and leaf. No one who has not seen the operation of grubbing out scrub palmetto can appreciate the perplexing nature of the work. Every swamp, and there were many of them, and of great extent, were corduroyed, and all streams bridged. The amount of work was enormous. That unique old character, General Twiggs, was the Department Commander, and it was said that he had a rooster tied on the top of his ambulance and when he drove over the road, if any portion of the road was sufficiently rough to flop the wings of the rooster, the command that built it would catch thunder. And he was most ingenious in devising ways of administering thunder on such occasions. Every one was afraid of him. His Texas surrender was among the least of his idiosyncrasies. For sheer hard work, deprivation, insufficiency and bad quality of food, unhealthiness of climate, and general insalubrity all around, this service was ahead of any that I have ever experienced.

In the late fall of 1850, the companies of Swartwout, Roland, and Elzey were withdrawn from Florida for service at Charleston Harbor, where, with one or two companies of the 4th, together with that of Luther, already there, they occupied Fort Moultrie, and Sumter, and Castle Pinckney. The people of South Carolina were then very noisy upon the subject of secession, and were having their war dance all around, to work themselves up to the scalping pitch. Larned and Woodbridge remained in Florida, and, in the spring of 1852, Swartwout returned there, where he died the following July, promoting Barry to company F.

In the summer of the same year--1852--yellow fever, then severely ravaging[?] in Charleston, struck Roland's company, occupying Castle Pinckney. This is a very small place and was without a hospital or any place that could be converted into one, and we had to depend upon occasional visits from a physician from Charleston. Roland took the fever and died in a few days, and so did several of the company. Lieut. Allen took it, but subsequently recovered. Lieut. Anderson--afterwards of the Confederate service, ran away from it, leaving me all alone. Being refused repeated applications to remove the healthy part of the company to some more suitable place, I finally called a boat and removed them to Fort Moultrie. This was the origin of the terrible yellow fever scourge of that year on Sullivan's Island, that raised such a controversy among medical men.

Roland's death promoted Hunt to company M. In the following year, 1853, Hunt with his company was sent to Indian Territory, (Fort Washita) where he remained until 1857 when he was sent to Leavenworth, to assist in quelling disturbances in Kansas. About this time his battery (M), still remaining one of the designated mounted batteries of the regiment, was mounted for the first time since the Mexican war. At the same time and for the same purpose, the other mounted battery (A) was sent from Baltimore to Leavenworth and both batteries were prepared for the march to Salt Lake. Brooks was then in command of battery A, but not being equal to the occasion was relieved and Barry designated in his stead. This caused considerable feeling in the regiment, but chiefly among those who were always on the lookout for something to feel about. These two batteries started 1858 for Utah, but got only as far as Fort Kearney. The Mormon troubles having been settled by this time. They both returned to Leavenworth. From whence, in a few months thereafter Hunt was sent to Fort Brown, Texas, where he remained until the surrender of that Department by Twiggs in the early part of 1861. He escaped this surrender, and got out of the country, leaving his horses, but saving his guns. Soon after reaching N. Y., Hunt with his guns, but without horses, sailed, Apr. 1861, with the expedition for the relief of Fort Pickens, Florida, where he remained until the latter part of June, when he sailed for N. Y., and getting horses for his battery, was in time to take part in the battle of Bull Run, July 21, in which he commanded his battery, although at that time a major in the 5th Arty. then just authorized. Upon Hunt's promotion, Benson was assigned to the command of battery M, and continued its commander until mortally wounded in a skirmish at Malvern Hill--in August, subsequent to the great battle of Malvern, Lieut. Pennington was then assigned to the command of the battery, and as lieutenant and captain continued its commander until his transfer with Ramsey to battery A, in 1881. Battery M, was, as before stated, dismounted at the Presidio about 1868, and never remounted.

Several other batteries of the regiment were sent to Kansas. Upon General Bankhead's death, Col. Payne became Col. of the 2d, but as the Governor of the Soldier's Home at Washington, the regiment was commanded by Dimick, the Lt. Col., with headquarters at Fort Leavenworth, where it continued, until Dimick was assigned to the Artillery Sch. of Practice at Ft. Monroe, 1859, when headquarters were moved there, and where they remained until after the commencement of the rebellion.

In 1853, some other Indian troubles in Florida, took a number of the companies back to that inhospitable region, where they continued for a couple of years or so, and besides doing a good deal of scouting had a number of skirmishes with the Seminoles; in one of which Lieut. Hartsuff, afterwards General Hartsuff, was severely wounded, and lay hid from the savages, in the water of a swamp for several days. After recovering from the wound, Hartsuff was one of a few who survived the wreck of the steamer, *Lady Elgin*, in Lake Michigan in 1857. His escape here was remarkable also; and it came to be said that Hartsuff was, unless hung, going to die a natural death,...

In 1856 the companies in Florida were brought out, and after a short stay at Ft. Independence and some other northern posts were sent, some to Kansas, some to Fort Ridgely, Ripley, and Snelling in Minnesota, and some elsewhere.

The two companies, Brooks' and Kendricks', in New Mexico remained there until 1857, when they--officers and non-commissioned officers, only--were brought into Fort Columbus. Kendricks having been appointed Professor of Chemistry at the Mil. Academy. Carlisle was promoted to his company (B), and was afterwards stationed with it at Fort Monroe until the spring of 1861, when he was brought to Washington, mounted his battery, and was at the battle of Bull Run.

My promotion to first lieutenancy took me to Kendricks company "B" then stationed at Fort Defiance at Canon Cito Bonito, New Mexico, near the N. E. corner of Arizona. After remaining there a short period, I was sent with Lieut. Whipple of the Topogs [Topographers], (afterwards Gen'l Whipple, Killed at Chancellorville) on an expedition for a railroad route to the Pacific--the 35th parallel route, through Arizona and southern California.

At the outbreak of the Secession, the companies and batteries were stationed as follows,

Brooks --------------------------- Ft. Leavenworth, Kansas
Barry (light battery A) -------   Do   Do
Hunt (light battery M) ------- Fort Brown, Texas
Hays ---------------------------- Fort Monroe, Va.
Carlisle -------------------------   Do   Do
Elezy --------------------------- Augusta Arsenal, Ga.

Gibson --------------------------- Fort Ridgely, Minnesota
Allen ----------------------------- Plattsburg, N. Y.
Arnold --------------------------- Dry Tortugas, Florida
Pratt ----------------------------- Mackinac, Michigan
Anderson ------------------------ Fayetteville Arsenal, N. Carolina
Totten --------------------------- Little Rock Arsenal, Arkansas

Floyd was then Secretary of War, and it was the policy of treason, then lurking around the administration at Washington, to scatter what little we had of a regular army, as much as possible, to out of the way places. The guards at the Southern Arsenals were merely to keep the hot heads from prematurely sacking them, and this precipitating hostilities before the time, came to pounce upon then, with their small guards, and secure their contents for rebellion.

Things began to look very threatening at the Capital in December 1860. Schemes were on foot to seize possession of the Government. Floyd however was gotten rid of and Holt, a truly loyal man, appointed Secty. of War, and immediately troops were called to Washington. The first to arrive was Barry's light battery A, which, leaving Leavenworth with horses, etc., about the 12th of January 1861, arrived at Washington Arsenal, on the 16. (I was then with it as a sub.) About a fortnight afterwards, several other companies, chiefly of the Second Artillery, arrived, and were quartered about the city in various places; and within a month or so Magruder's battery of the 1st Arty., also from Leavenworth, and the Instruction battery from West Point, under Lieut. Griffin; the Engineers company from the same place, and several other companies arrived in Washington.

Light battery A was however the first to arrive for the defence of the Capital, and had the honor of becoming the nucleus around which the grand Army of the Potomac eventually formed. This honor is not vitiated by the fact that battery A went with the relief expedition to Pickens in April; for it returned in time to be present at the battle of Bull Run. The entire battery, horses, guns and all, were taken to Pickens, as a ruse to deceive the enemy as to the destination of the expedition.

Nearly all the regular artillery of the army was mounted and organized with the Army of the Potomac. All of the companies of the 2d were mounted except H, I and K. The first and last of these served throughout the war at Pickens, and the other at Fort McHenry. "B" and "L" were, on account of the difficulty of getting men, united into one battery. Company C stationed at the Tortugas at the commencement of the war, and afterwards at Pickens, drifted over to Louisiana and, having mounted there, saw service in the Department of the Gulf. Company F--Totten's, after being routed out from Little Rock Arsenal, went to Missouri, and there, being mounted, saw service, and continued to the end of the war with the Western armies. All the other companies and batteries served with the Army of the Potomac from beginning at Bull Run to the end at Appomattox, and all became Horse batteries before the end of the war.

I will here mention that while the Army of the Potomac was lying at Harrison's Landing on the James River, a corporal of my battery, "A", died. Being a most excellent man and soldier, I was desirous of burying him with full military honors. I was however refused permission to fire three guns over his grave, and the thought suggested itself to me to sound Taps instead, which I did. The idea was taken up by others and soon became the custom. I believe it is now prescribed by regulations.

Battery A has therefore the honor of having introduced this custom into the service, and it is worthy of historical note.

The following officers seceshed, and joined in the rebellion:--Capts. Elezy and Anderson; Lieutenants Merchant, deLagnel, Long, Jones, Dearing and Butler.

There was an unusual number of staff officers appointed from the 2d in 1861. More in fact than from all other regiments of artillery combined. And as these officers generally held on to their regimental commissions, even after becoming captains, there was a great deal of absenteeism, making officers for batteries in the field very scarce. Batteries were generally commanded by first lieutenants and often by second lieutenants.

At the conclusion of the war the batteries were all dismounted and in August (1865) assembled at Fort McHenry, preparatory to sailing for California. This was the first and only time that the batteries of the regiment have ever been all together.

Arrived at San Francisco, one company was sent to San Diego, and afterwards to Yuma. Two were sent to the mouth of the Columbia River, one to Monterey (for a short period) afterwards to Alcatraz; two to Fort Point, and to Angel Island for a short time, and then to Black Point, one to Vancouver, one to San Juan Island. The two batteries (mounted) A, and M to the Presidio, and the other to Alcatraz Island.

When Alaska was purchased in 1867, the following batteries were sent to it:--

Dennison's "H"	to Sitka
Peirce's "E"	Tongass
Grey's "I" under Borrowe	Wrangell
Thompson's "G" under Huggins	Kodiak
Benjamin's "F" under MacGilvray	Kenai; at the head of Cook's Inlet.

When MacGilvray found the place to which he was ordered, it proved to be but a dreary waste of sphagnum and thicket. A few inches below the surface he found [perennial] ice. While searching along down the coast of the Inlet for a better place, his vessel, the bark *Torrent,* ice ran upon a rock and sank almost instantly. Being near the shore, all lives were saved, and provisions enough floated ashore to serve them until relief happened to come--one of the Russian Fur company's Steamers. After wintering at Kodiak, he proceeded, in the following spring, to St. Nicholas, and [sic] old trading post at the head of Cook's Inlet. At this dreary and forlorn place the company remained until the fall of 1870 at which time all the posts in Alaska were abandoned except the one at Sitka.

The post of Tongass was on a small island of that name, composed of rocks, trees, and moss, always dripping with wet. (It rains constantly on the Coast of Alaska.) It was with infinite labor that space was cleared, here and there, for tents, and it was even harder to construct huts. Of course there could be nothing like gardens, or even places to stretch clothes lines.

The post of Wrangel was on another island, one of that name, and it was similar in every respect to Tongass.

Sitka, being the headquarters of the Russian Fur Company, had plenty of houses, such as they were, and was more comfortable, but still required a great deal of labor to make it what it should be. Kodiak was similar to Sitka but more remote and out of the way of regular communications. No mails from October to April, and at other times, only by chance. That post of Alaska was made into a District, with the two posts of Kodiak and Kenai, and I was placed in command.

For the first two years after Alaska came into our possession, all parties desiring to do so went to the Seal Islands, in Behrings [sic] Sea, and slaughtered seals *ad libertum*. To put a stop to this, until Congress could enact laws for their protection, I was directed to place a guard on St. Paul's Island. Accordingly, I sent there twenty men under Lieut. Mast, who remained until the following summer, when they were relieved by another party under Lieut. Huggins.

Sitka was maintained as a two company post, and two companies of the 2d occupied it until relieved by the 4th Arty in the fall of 1872. At which time the whole regiment came east and were [sic] stationed on the coast of the Southern Atlantic States, and at Raleigh, N. C. At this period, all overt Ku Klux manifestations were subdued, and we had quiet, broken only by an occasional party sent with Treasury officials to the mountains to look out for moonshiners. Neither did the regiment have much, if anything, to do with election troubles. The Benzine Board of 1870 struck the 2d hard and much for the better. The vacancies were filled by transfers from infantry.

Some of which were good, some bad, and others medium.

When the Artillery School was established in 1868, Williston's battery K was transferred to it from the Pacific Coast. Subsequently Williston and Benjamin exchanged batteries; the former taking "F" and the latter "K", which remained at the Artillery School.

What individual batteries did in the Florida war can be best ascertained from Sprague's history of that war. And Ripley's or any other history of the Mexican war will give what they did in that war.

In the war of rebellion the batteries were conspicuously serviceable and active, but unfortunately no separate record was kept of these services. Here and there, they stand out in reports of division and corps operations; but as a rule their brilliant services have been lost to history.

The Rebellion Records, when completed, will contain valuable data, which, when picked out, will present the artillery in good light.

Nearly all of the artillery of the regular army was with the Army of the Potomac; and for a time was under General Barry, Chief of Artillery of that Army. He commenced a systematic record of all of its operations; but his successor, Gen'l Hunt, was not so systematic, and all was lost.

The organization and management of artillery in the field during the war was one of development. Some of the regiments, responding to the first call for volunteers in 1861, brought with them to the field, sections (platoons): Such was the case at the first Bull Run. These were, of course, of no account. Batteries were then attached to brigades; this was but little better. Afterwards, the batteries were attached to divisions only; this proved better still, but lacked greatly in that efficiency of which artillery was then capable. All of this was simply following after the old time customs and the infantry tactics of the smooth bore period when it was quite proper to distribute batteries along the line of battle at short intervals. All of this has however been changed by improvement in range, accuracy and power of artillery, requiring that it should be left to act freely; to take positions wherever its fire can be most effective, and this certainly will not be the case if confined to the narrow limits of a division of infantry.

It was observed that batteries attached to divisions of infantry rapidly deteriorated for want of proper supervision and means of supply, and in battle frequently stood idle because of the nature of the topography of the field, while but a short distance away, their services would have been most valuable, and could have been made so if they had not been tied to a limited area.

Finally the artillery of each army corps was consolidated into a brigade, with its own proper commander and supply departments. But by this time the habit of having batteries attached to divisions had become so strong that each division commander insisted on having charge of batteries during the march and in the battle.--They could not get along without them, they alleged--and this to a great extent nullified the good effect sought to be brought about by brigading the batteries. Notwithstanding this, there was sufficient gained in the direction of greater efficiency to warrant a very considerable diminution of the number of guns per thousand of infantry; thus disencumbering armies of much of their impedimenta.

European services provide in their drill, regulations for the assignment of batteries to divisions of infantry; but their divisions are as large as most of our corps were during the war; and from the very essence of our military policy it is not probable that our corps will, when war comes again, be greater in numbers.

An infantry division in our service is too small a body of men to have batteries of rifle cannon attached to it. Batteries so attached cannot be used to the best advantage. Although Corps Commanders have it in their power to order their artillery whenever they think best, it is almost impossible to get batteries away, even temporarily, from division commanders. They hatch up all sorts of excuses against it, causing delays and perplexities without number. I know this from my own experience, and all who had comprehensive experience, with artillery, during the war know it likewise.

The proposed new Drill Regulations for Infantry (Army & Navy Register, Oct. 18, 1890) provide for the assignment of batteries to divisions and even to brigades, thus going back to the days of the smoothbore, and losing all that was gained by the experience of the war.

These new Drill Regulations are intended to meet the new conditions of battle brought about by improvement in the range, accuracy, and rapidity of fire of the infantry arm. The same degree of improvement has been made in field artillery, and its efficiency should not be handicapped by obsolete customs. Drill Regulations for Infantry should leave the artillery to its own regulations, just as it leaves the cavalry and the other branches of the service. Artillery officers should see to it that this fatal error is not consummated in the Infantry drill book, and they should see to it that it is properly provided for in the new artillery drill book.

Field artillery should be formed into proper commands, with its own proper officers, etc., and not be attached, as an excrescence, to small bodies of infantry, where its services, however brilliant, are to a greater degree lost to history. The point which this digression is intended to point out.

So. Bethlehem, Pa. Jno C. Tidball
Nov. 21, 1890 U. S. Army.

Company I in the Civil War. Captain Thomas Grey

HQ Co I, 2d Arty
San Juan Island, WT
September 1, 1866

Major John H. Calef
Adjt 2d Arty
Fort Point, San Francisco, Cal.
Major

In reply to Circular--June 26, 1866 asking for the history from the Companies during the Rebellion,--I have the honor to state that the records of Co I 2d Artillery show its history to be as follows:

Left Fort Ridgely, Minn on the 13th and arrived at Fort McHenry, Md on the 18th of April 1861--where it remained on duty as a heavy Artillery Co until May the 12th 1864.

Serving as heavy Artillery on the Defences of Washington on the 11th, 12th, and 13th July 1864.

Left the Defences of Washington April 1st and arrived at Stevenson, Ala. April 16th 1865 where it remained on duty as Infantry until the 27th--Left for Chattanooga, Tenn. arriving there on the 20th and serving as Light Artillery at that place until August 5th 1865.

Left Chattanooga August 5 1865 and arrived at Fort McHenry, Md., August 12th 1865. Left there August 19th 1865 and reached San Francisco, Cal. September 19, 1865, which place it left on October 5th 1865 and reached this station on the 10th of same month.

The records of the Co. can be found as far back as follows:

Descriptive Book	to	Jany 1839
Letter "	"	October 1853
Order "	"	September 1857
Clothing "	"	" "
Morning Report	"	March 1866
Monthly Return	"	January 1854
Muster & Pay Rolls	"	February 1860

I am Sir

very respectfully

Your Obdt Serv

Thos Grey

Capt. 2d Arty

Cmdg

Company F in the Civil War. Lieutenant John Fitzgerald

Record of Company "F", 2nd U. S. Artillery commencing January 1859.

Company was stationed at Fort Reilly [sic] K. T. until June 1st 1859, on which date it left Fort Reilly for Fort Leavenworth K. T. Arrived at Fort Leavenworth June 1st 1859.

Sept. 9th 1860: Company marched from Fort Leavenworth and arrived at Fort Smith, Arkansas, September 29th having marched 330 miles in 106¼ hours marching time.

Oct. 10th 1860: Company left Fort Smith, Ark. for Fort Leavenworth, K. T. and marched to Cow Creek, 165 miles, when it was ordered to countermarch and return to Fort Smith via Fort Gibson. Left Cow Creek Oct 25th and arrived at Fort Smith November 3d 1860.

Nov. 27th 1860: Left Fort Smith and arrived at Little Rock, on the 6th of December, having marched in all from first leaving Fort Leavenworth, K. T. Sept. 9th, until arriving in Little Rock, Ark. Dec. 6th, 850 miles.

Feby 8th 1861: Evacuated Little Rock Arsenal, and went into camp about seven miles below Little Rock from which place Company embarked on Steamer *Medora*, Feby 12/61 for St. Louis, Mo, where it arrived Feby 22nd and took post in Jefferson Barracks, in obedience to Orders Nos. 3 & 6, dated Head Quarters Little Rock Arsenal, Ark. Feby 8th & 12th 1861, and S. O. No. 24, dated Hd Qrs, Dept of the West, St. Louis Mo Feby 23/61.

April 10/61: Left Jefferson Barracks and arrived at St. Louis Arsenal April 12, 1861.

May 10, 1861: Company took part in the capture of Camp Jackson, Mo.

[May] 12, " : Left St. Louis Arsenal and took post in St. Louis.

" 31, " : Left St. Louis and took post at Camp Harney near St. Louis.

June 12, " : Marched to St. Louis Arsenal from Camp Harney, and embarked on Steamers *Swan* & *Iatan* for Jefferson City, Mo. Arrived at Jefferson City on the 14th. Part of the command under Captain Totten crossed the river, same day, and captured Rebel Steamboat, *A. McDonnell*.

June 16/61: Sailed from Jefferson City to Rockport. Landed next day about 3 miles above Rockport and marched to Boonville Mo. and took part in the engagement there. One Sergeant wounded, one horse killed and one wounded.

June 19/61: Marched to Syracuse in pursuit of the rebels. Left Syracuse June 23d and marched back to Boonville.

July 3/61: Left Boonville and continued daily marches until arriving at Camp Sigel 12 miles from Springfield Mo. July 30th marched 13 miles to Camp McClellan.

August 1/61: Left Camp McClellan for points South where the enemy were concentrating. Found their pickets next day and drove them in. Came upon the enemy in force in the afternoon at Dug Springs Mo. and drove them from the field.

August 10/61: Company engaged at the Battle of Wilson's Creek, Mo from about 5 A. M. till 1 P. M. 4 privates killed and seven wounded. Every noncommissioned officer and soldier of the Company throughout the entire battle acted bravely and deserves the highest commendation.

It was believed that Privates Joseph Keyes, Jacob Miller, John Pratt, James Wallace of Co. "F", 2d Artillery were killed in the foregoing engagement at Wilson's Creek. They were left for dead where wounded, and the wounded on the field not being all brought into Springfield until after the army retired on Rolla their fate was not known for some time afterwards.

August 11th/61: Left Springfield Mo. arrived at Rolla Mo. August 17th. Aug. 22d moved from Rolla to Camp Lyon.

Sept. 10th/61: Left Camp Lyon and took the cars for St. Louis, Mo. arrived on the 11th; 26th left St. Louis abroad the *William L. Ewing.* arrived at Jefferson City Mo. Sept. 29th.

October 3/61: Left Jefferson City, arrived at Syracuse, MO. on the 8th.

" 21 " : Left Syracuse and arrived at Springfield, Mo. Nov.2d.

November 13/61: Left Springfield & Nov. 19th arrived at Sedalia, Mo. A Section of the Battery, one 12 pdr Howitzer, & one 6 pdr, under Capt. Howard, 1st Mo. Light Battery on Detached Service. Company left Sedalia December 15th & returned Dec. 21st.

February 3/62: Company marched to St. Louis, Mo. 100 miles. Left St. Louis Feby 25/62 on board Steamer *Edward Walsh* and reached Commerce Mo. Feby 28/62.

From March 2d to April 13th Company was stationed at New Madrid and took part in the bombardment of Fort Thompson.

April 13/62: Left New Madrid, Mo. on Steamer *Metropolitan* en route to Fort Pillow. Returned to New Madrid April 18th. Left New Madrid April 22d and arrived at Pittsburgh Landing, Tenn April 24th.

May 2d/1862: Advanced 12 miles toward Corinth Miss: on the 8th the battery was on reconnaissance in force under General Stanley. Shelling the enemy's pickets from their position twice: on the 17th advanced to Farmington, Miss. On the 24th a detachment with one Howitzer on reconnaissance shelling the enemy from their position. On the 28th advanced toward Corinth, Miss and engaged a Battery and large Infantry force of the enemy, silencing the Battery and driving back the Infantry after four hours fighting. Camped on the field: In this engagement four men were wounded, six horses killed & three wounded and one 12 pdr Howitzer disabled. And in a Section of the 10th Wisconsin Battery attached, there was one man killed and three wounded & three horses killed and two wounded. On the 30th Corinth was evacuated & Battery advanced to the crossing of the Charleston and Memphis railroad. Next day advanced to the Mobile and Ohio R. R.

June 2/62: Advanced 20 miles to Booneville, Miss on the Mobile and Ohio R. R., on the 12th returned to Camp on the Tuscumbia River. 24th advanced to Danville, Miss and on the 30th returned to Camp on Clear Creek, Miss.

August 21/62: Left camp on Clear Creek. Marched 20 miles and camped at Iuka, Miss on the 22d.

Sept. 12/62: Left Iuka. marched 20 miles and camped on Clear Creek, Miss. On the 18th marched back to Iuka, camping that night on the battlefield. 21st marched 12 miles and camped at Jacinto, Miss. 29th marched 8 miles and camped at Rienzi, Miss.

October 2/62: Left camp at Rienzi. Marched 17 miles toward Corinth and camped on Tuscumbia River. 3d marched 5 miles and formed

line of battle South of Corinth, taking position to the left of Fort Williams. On the 4th Battery engaged, supporting Fort of Siege guns under
Captain Williams, from 5 A. M. till 1 P. M. One private mortally wounded,
one Sergeant and one private wounded, 3 horses killed & 4 wounded.
On the 5th, 6th, 7th, 8th, 9th, 10th & 11th battery in pursuit of the
enemy on the Ripley road. Returned to Corinth on the 12th.

November 2/62: Left Camp near Corinth. marched 14 miles and
camped near Tuscumbia River. 3d marched 15 miles on the Memphis
road. Camped on the Little Hatchie; 4th marched 15 miles and camped
4 miles South of Grand Junction on the Holly Springs road. 5th 4 pieces
out on reconnaissance driving the enemy's pickets 4 miles. Moved camp
about 4 miles south to Davis Mills. 28th left camp at Davis Mills; 29th
camped near Holly Springs.

December 10/62: Left Holly Springs; on the 11th camped 2 miles
south of Oxford, Miss.; on the 17th Battery reviewed and Inspected by
Generals Grant, Hamilton, and Ross. 21st marched from Oxford and on
the 30th camped at Grand Junction, Tenn.

January 9/1863: Left camp near Grand Junction, Tenn. en route
for Corinth, Miss. Arrived there on the 13th.

April 20, 1863: Left Corinth in search of the Rebels. Skirmish at
Town Creek, Ala. on the 28th. Returned to Corinth May 2d. May 10th
left Corinth by rail for Memphis, Tenn.; arrived next day.

Sept. 22/63: Turned in old 4 Gun Battery to Ord Officer, Memphis,
Tenn. and received a new 6 Gun Battery, 12 pdr Napoleons.

October 18/63: Left Memphis, Tenn. and marched to Iuka, Miss.
Arriving there on the 27th.

November 2/63: Marched from Iuka and on the 13th camped at
Prospect, Tenn. station on the Nashville & Decatur R. R.

January 14/64: Marched from Prospect to Pulaski, Tenn, 18 miles.

February 21/64: Left Pulaski and marched to Prospect, Tenn.
Thence next day to Athens, Ala. 34 miles.

March 12/64: Marched from Athens to Decatur, Ala. 14 miles.

May 1/64: Left Decatur and marched to Woodville, Ala. 56 miles.
Got on board the cars at Woodville on the 4th & arrived at Chatta-
nooga, Tenn on the 5th. Marched thence to Resaca, Geo. Engaged at
Resaca on the 13th, 14th, & 15th. Left Resaca on the 16th and on the
18th reached Kingstown, Geo. & camped. Left Kingstown on the 25th.
On the 27th arrived at Dallas, Geo. and took up position. Engaged at
Dallas on the 29th & 30th.

June 1/64: Left Dallas & arrived at Acworth, Geo. on the 6th. Took
position in the lines at Kennesaw Mountain on the 15th. Engaged on
the 14th, 15th, 17th, 27th, 28th, 29th, 30th of June and on the 1st of
July. One pvte (volunteer attached) killed, one private wounded.

July 2/64: Left Kennesaw Mountain and marched to Marietta, Geo.
On the 4th Battle at Ruff's Mills, Geo. Shelling the Rebels 150 yds distance from their works & driving them back.

July 9/64: Camped on the Chattahoochie River.

" 14/64: One Sergeant, one private & one bugler killed by lightning.

July 16/64: Left camp at Chattahoochie and marched to Decatur about 6 miles from Atlanta, Geo. 21st took up position in the lines at Atlanta.

July 22/64: At 1 P. M. ordered back to assist in repelling an attack on the left flank. While marching through a thick wood, without Infantry support the Battery was suddenly surrounded by the enemy & captured. Lieut. A. Murray, comdg compy, Lieut. Breckinridge, one Sergeant, one Corp'l, 1 bugler, & 11 privates (6 volunteers attached) taken prisoners, 2 privates wounded, one Corp'l & one private killed.

July 25/64: 29 men attached to 15th Ohio battery, the remainder doing duty with Co. "H" 1st Mo. Light Arty. Company engaged with those Batteries during the siege of Atlanta until August 12th with the following casualties, 2 Privates killed, one corporal & 2 privates wounded, one private taken prisoner.

August 12/64: Company received a siege gun (4½ inch Rodman) and were engaged shelling the city of Atlanta until the 25th firing in all 1158 rounds, using up one gun and breaking two trails.

August 25/64: Company [retired to camp near the] Chattahoochie River about 8 miles form Atlanta. Part of the Company, serving with Co "H" 1st Mo. Light Artillery engaged at the Battle of Jonesboro, August 30th.

Sept. 13/64: Left camp at the Chattahoochie and marched to Atlanta; thence to Eastport 6 miles beyond Atlanta.

October 4/64: Moved from Eastport to Atlanta.

November 1/64: Left Atlanta on the cars for Nashville; arrived at Chattanooga on the 3d, waiting transportation till the 15th. On the 16th arrived at Nashville, Tenn.

Battery in position during the battles at Nashville, December 15th & 16th 1864.

April 11/65: Left Nashville on the cars for Bridgeport, Ala. arrived at Bridgeport on the 12th.

June 27th/65: Left Bridgeport on the cars for Chattanooga arriving same day.

August 5/65: Turned in Battery, Horses and all arms and equipments, and left Chattanooga by rail via Nashville, Louisville, Cincinnati, Columbus & Baltimore & Ohio R. R. and arrived at Baltimore, Md. on the 12th. Left Baltimore with the regiment, on board S. S. *Ben de Ford* on the 19th for San Francisco, Cal. Arrived at Aspinwall New Grenada on the 30th.

Sept. 1/65: Left Aspinwall, N. G. by rail, arrived at Panama, N. G. same day and embarked on Steamer *Sonora,* leaving Panama on the 3d. Arrived at Acapulco, Mexico on the 9th, leaving same day. Arrived at San Francisco, Cal. on the 19th at 4 P. M. Disembarked on the 20th and took up Quarters in Presidio Barracks,

September 26/65: Left Presidio on the 26th per Steamer for Benicia, Cal. arriving same day. Received battery and horses at Benicia.

December 18/65: Turned in Battery and horses and left Benicia Barracks per Steamer, arrived at Presidio Barracks on the 19th. Left Presidio on the 21st and took post at Fort Point receiving muskets & accoutrements.

April 1/66: Moved from Fort Point to Alcatraces [Alcatraz] Island.

Record of Officers serving with Company "F" 2d U. S. Artillery during the War from 1861 to 1866:

James Totten, Capt. 2d Artillery: Commanding Company till Sept. 22/61 & in the following engagements: Capture of Camp Jackson, Mo., Battles of Boonville, Dug Springs and Wilson's Creek, Mo.

G. O. Sokalski, 2d Lt. 2d Dragoons: Attached to Comp'y July 15/61. Comd'g Company from Sept. 22/61 till Dec. 26/61. Engaged at the Battles of Dug Springs & Wilson's Creek.

John A. Darling, 2d Lt. 2d U. S. Arty: Comd'g Company from Dec. 26/61, till Mar. 23/62 & at the Siege of New Madrid, Mo.

D. P. Walling, Lt. 2d Iowa Battery: Commanding Company from March 23/62, till April 29/62.

T. D. Maurice, Capt. 1st Mo. Lt. Arty.: Commanding Company from April 29/62. till Nov. 8/62. Comd'g Comp'y at Battles of Farmington, Miss, Iuka, Miss., & Corinth, Miss.

A. J. S. Molinard, Capt. 2d U. S. Arty.: Commanding Company from November 8/62 till November 17/62, and from January 16/63 till March 29/63.

J. D. McLean, 1st Lt. 8th Wisc. Battery: Attached from October 1862. Commanding Company from Nov. 17/62. till January 16/63.

Charles Green, 1st Lt. 1st Mo. Lt. Arty.: Commanding Company from March 29/63, till July 27/63.

A. M. Murray, 2d Lieut. 2d Arty.: Comd'g Comp'y from July 27/63 till July 22/64. Comd'g Comp'y in engagements at Resaca, Geo., Dallas, Kennesaw Mountain, Ruff's Mills, Geo. taken prisoner in battle before Atlanta, Geo. July 22/64. [Died in prison Sept. 1864.]

L. Smith, 2d Lt. 5th U. S. Arty.: Attached June 21/64. Commanding Comp'y from July 22/64 till March 8/65. Comd'g Comp'y during Siege of Atlanta, Geo. and at the Battles of Nashville, Geo.[sic].

R. G. Howell, 2d Lt. 2d Arty.: Comd'g Comp'y from March 8/65 till August 14/65. Served with comp'y at Siege of Atlanta & Battles of Nashville.

S. N. Benjamin, Capt. & Bvt Lt. Col. 2d Arty.: Commd'g Company from August 14/65 till April 13/66.

J. C. Breckinridge, 1st Lt. 2d Arty.: Commanding Company from April 13/66 till May 31/66.

J. Fitzgerald: Commanding Company since May 31/66.

List of Engagements taken part in by Co. "F" 2d U. S. Artillery during the War:
    May 10/61: Capture of Camp Jackson, Mo.
    June 17/61: Battle of Boonville, Mo.
    Aug. 3/61: Battle of Dug Springs, Mo.
    Aug. 10/61: Battle of Wilson's Creek, Mo.
    Mar. 2 to April 13th 1862: Siege of New Madrid.
    May 8/62: Skirmish near Corinth, Miss.
    May 24/62: Skirmish near Farmington, Miss.
    May 28/62: Battle of Farmington, Miss.
    Sep. 19/62: Battle of Iuka, Miss.
    Oct. 3 & 4/62: Battle of Corinth, Miss.
    [April 28/63: Skirmish at Town Creek, Ala.]
    May 13, 14, 15/1864: Battles at Resaca, Geo.
    May 28/64: Battles at Dallas, Geo.
    June 14 to July 1, 1864: Engaged at Kennesaw Mountain, Geo.
    July 4/64: Battle at Ruff's Mills, Geo.
    July 22/64: Battle at Atlanta, Geo.
    July 28/64: Battle at Atlanta, Geo.
    Aug. 12 to 25/64: Siege of Atlanta, Geo.
    Dec. 15 & 16/64: Battles at Nashville, Tenn.
        John Fitzgerald
            1st Lieut, 2nd Arty
            Comd'g Comp'y

Company E in the Civil War. Captain C. H. Peirce

Company "E" 2d U. S. Artillery
Fort Humboldt, Cal.
June 30th 1866

Sir:
    In compliance with Circular, received from Head Quarters on the Regiment, dated June 20th 1866.
    I have the honor to transmit the following list of <u>Battles & Skirmishes</u>, in which the Company has been engaged, during the recent <u>War of the Rebellion</u>, *viz*:

"Bull Run", Virginia,	July 21st 1861
"Yorktown", Virginia,	April 19th 1862 (Skirmish)
"Near Gaines House," Virginia,	May 31st 1862 (Skirmish)
"Near Gaines House", Virginia,	June 4th 1862 (Skirmish)
"Near Gaines House", Virginia,	June 11th 1862 (Skirmish)
"Golding Farm", Virginia,	June 27th 1862
"Turkey Bend", Virginia,	June 30th 1862
"Malvern Hill", Virginia,	July 1st 1862
"Bull Run", Virginia,	August 29th & 30th 1862
"Chantilly", Virginia,	September 1st 1862

"South Mountain, Maryland,   September 14th 1862
"Antietam", Maryland,   September 16th & 17th 1862
"Warrenton Sulphur Springs, Virginia,   November 16th 1862 (Skirmish)
"Fredericksburg", Virginia,   December 11th, 12th, 13th, &
                                         14th 1862
"Siege of Vicksburg", Miss.,   From June 20th to July 3d 1863
"Siege of Jackson", Miss.,   From July 11th to 17th 1863
"Campbell Station", Tenn.,   November 16th 1863
"Siege of Knoxville", Tenn.,   from November 18th to 28th
                                         1863
"Wilderness Run", Virginia,   May 4th 1864

                                         I am Sir Very respectfully
Bvt Major J. H. Calef, U. S. A.   Your Obt Svt.
Adjt 2d U. S. Arty   C. H. Peirce
Fort Point, Cal.   Capt. 2d U. S. Arty, Cmdg Co.

History of Company C in the Civil War. (unsigned)

[Punctuation changed for clarity by author.]

History of Company "C", 2nd U. S. Artillery during the recent war of the Rebellion.

The beginning of the year 1861 found the Company stationed at Fort Independence Boston Harbor, Mass. The Company left this place on board the *Joseph Whitney* on the 10th January 1861, and arrived at Fort Jefferson, Tortugas, Fla. 18th January 1861. Left Fort Jefferson, Fla. Sept. 9th 1861, in U. S. S. *Richmond*, [and] arrived at Fort Pickens, Fla. 13th Sept. 1861. The Company participated in the action of "Santa Rosa Island," Fla. October 9th 1861, and in the bombardment of "Fort Pickens," Fla. on the 21st and 22nd Novr. 1861, and 1st January 1862. Next the Company was engaged in bombarding the enemies lines on the night of the 9th May 1862, crossed the bay on board the steamer *Harriet Lane* to Fort Barrancas. On the 10th marched from Fort Barrancas to Pensacola, Fla., arriving at 6 P. M. May 12th 1862.

On the 1st of September 1862 the Company left Pensacola, Fla. on board the Steamer *Ocean Queen*. Arrived at New Orleans, La. on the 2nd. Left on the 22nd for Metairie Bridge, La. Arriving the same day, and went back to New Orleans, La. again on 7th Novr. 1862. Proceeded to Baton Rouge, La. from there on the 18th Decr. 1862, arriving on the 22nd Decr. 1862. The battery left Baton Rouge, La. March 14th 1863 on the *Port Hudson*. Returned to Baton Rouge, La. 21st March 1863. Embarked on board the steamer *St. Mary's* on the 29th March 1863. Disembarked and marched along the Bayou LaFourche on the 31st March 1863. Arrived at Thibodans, La. April 2nd 1863. At Bayou Boeuf, 5th April 1863. At Brashear City, 9th April 1863. Embarked on steamer, *Laurel Hill* 11th April 1863. Arrived at Porter's Landing 13th April 1863. Advanced on the enemies lines at "Irish Bend" 14th April 1863, engaged with the whole battery. 1 Private Killed, 5 Privates wounded. The engagement lasted about 5 hours.

The battery marched on the 15th April 1863; arrived at Newtown, La. on the 16th; at Vermillion Village on the 17th; at Opolousa on the 20th; and at Barry's Landing on the 26th. The whole distance marched from Baton Rouge to this post is 300 miles.

Left Barry's Landing 5th May 1863; arrived at Wells Landing on the 8th; left on the 13th; arrived at Symmesport, La. on the 16th; embarked here on board the steamers *Laurel Hill* and *St. Charles* on the 21st; arrived and landed at Bayou Sara, La. the same night; marched next morning and before Port Hudson, La. 23rd May 1863.

The Company was engaged in the siege of Port Hudson from its commencement to its surrender 8th July 1863, and in particular in the assaults made on the 27th May and 14th June.

After the surrender of Port Hudson, the Battery was detached and formed part of the garrison of Port Hudson until the 2nd August, when it left, and arrived at Carroltown, La. the 5th August; and at New Orleans, La. the 11th August. Left New Orleans, La. on board the transport, *Yatan* the 31st October 1863. Arrived at Baton Rouge, La. the 3rd November 1863.

The Company from here went on board the transport *Laurel Hill* 23rd March 1864 to Alexandria, La. arriving March 25th 1864. Left Alexandria, La. May 11th 1864, arriving at Symmesport, La. May 17th; left here 19th arriving Morganza, La. 23rd.

Embarked on the Steamer *Ida Handy* June 19th 1864. Arrived at Tunicia Bend, La. June 20th; left same day, arrived at Fort Adams, Miss. June 21st. Embarked again on board steamer *Universe;* arrived at Morganza, La. June 21st 1864. Left Morganza July 2nd 1864. Arrived at New Orleans July 3rd 1864. Embarked on board steamer *Gayoo* July 27th 1864. Arrived at New York August 4th, and at Washington, D. C. August 5th 1864.

From Camp Barry, Washington, D. C., went to Camp Bailey, Bladensburg, Md. July 13th 1865. From here July 25th 1865 to Fort McHenry, Baltimore, Md. Embarked August 18th 1865 for California. Arrived at San Francisco September 19, 1865. Left here October 6th on board steamer *Sierra Nevada* for Fort Stevens, Oregon, arriving October 8th 1865.

The Company participated in the following battles during the Rebellion:

"Santa Rosa Island," Florida, October 9th 1861.

Bombardment of "Fort Pickens," Fla. November 21st & 22nd 1861, and Jan'y 1st 1862.

"Irish Bend," April 14th 1863.

Siege of "Port Hudson" from May 23rd 1863 till its surrender, July 1st 1863.

Appendix B

🌑

Rosters, Company I and Company F

This appendix contains data on the enlisted men of Companies I and F, 2nd U.S. Artillery, who served with Gustav Dey during his military service from 1854 to 1865. Except as specifically noted, these data were gathered from the following record groups (RG) at the National Archives, Washington, D.C.

RG 15—*Records of the Veterans Administration*
Microfilm T288, "General Index to Pension Files, 1861–1934."
Microfilm T289, "Organization Index of Veterans Who Served Between 1861 and 1900." Roll 714, Company F.

RG 94—*Records of the Adjutant General's Office, 1780's–1917.*
Muster Rolls, Companies I and F, 1854–1865.
Microfilm M727, "Returns from Regular Army Artillery Regiments, June 1821–Jan. 1901." Rolls 12 and 13.
Microfilm M233, "Register of Enlistments in the US Army, 1798–1914." Rolls 24 through 30.

RG 391—*Preliminary inventory of the records of the United States Regular Army Mobile Units, 1821–1942.*
Entry 48, "Letters Sent. Dec. 1844–Feb. 1901."
Entry 53, "Letters Received. 1846–1901."
Entry 55, "Regimental Orders Issued. Jan. 1838–Feb. 1901."
Entry 58, "Special Orders Received. 1853–65."
Entry 61, "Letters, Orders, and Reports Received From or Relating to Members of the 2d Artillery ('Name File'). 1861–66."
Entry 64, "Records Relating to Regimental History. 1832–93."
Entry 67, "Regimental Descriptive Books. 1860–78."
Entry 68, "Descriptive Books for Batteries A–M. 1841–64."

186

Entry 72, "Descriptive Book of Recruits. Jan. 1847–Mar. 1856."
Entry 73, "Recruiting Returns. 1853–98."
Entry 74, "Recruiting Accounts, Descriptive Lists and Accounts of Pay and Clothing. 1857, 1861–68, and 1895–1903."
Entry 76, "Miscellaneous Records. 1860–1900."

Although all the sources were researched, the bulk of the information pertinent to an individual's service record is found in:

(1) The Muster Rolls (RG 94), which were bimonthly status reports submitted by the company commander to regimental headquarters. Each contains a list and present duty of every company officer and enlisted man. The Muster Rolls include regimental orders, special orders, promotions, demotions, transfers (in and out), numbers present or on sick call, disciplinary actions, discharges, deaths and desertions. Included are listings of members of other units who are on temporary detached service with the company. Also included are the status of instruction, arms and accoutrements, and a Record of Events generally describing company movements on scout or reconnaissance, or after action conditions.

(2) The Returns (RG 94, Microfilm M727), which were monthly reports containing much of the same information found in the Muster Rolls, generally in a more condensed form.

(3) Entry 48, "Letters Sent;" Entry 53, "Letters Received;" Entry 55, "Regimental Orders Issued;" Entry 58, "Special Orders Received;" and Entry 68, "Descriptive Books for Batteries A–M;" all of which support material found in the Muster Rolls.

In the Company F roster, the information found in the above-cited sources is supplemented with data from the individual's pension file (RG 15) for the Civil War and post-war periods.

The original records were compiled by several hands and inevitably reflect a number of apparent discrepancies. These were sorted out as fully as possible, and are reflected in the individual entries. Additional sources which were used to obtain information of specific men are cited in the relevant individual's service summary.

Brackets are used for author's comments, highlighting significant items, or when conflicting data is found in different sources. The narrative for the individual entries contain several, frequently repeated abbreviations. Consequently, standard punctuation for the abbreviations were usually omitted in the narrative while included in the tabled data. Modern Postal Codes were used for the states and territories instead of traditional abbreviations in both the tabled data and narrative.

Following is a table of abbreviations (with and without punctuation) used in these rosters. The table excludes modern state Postal Codes but includes similar codes for territories.

Abbreviation	Definition	Abbreviation	Definition
—	no data found	Lt.	Lieutenant
AGO	Adjutant General's Office	lt.	light
Ars(.)	Arsenal	Ltr(s)	Letter(s)
Art	Artillery	M	Microfilm
AWOL	Absent without leave	Maj(.)	Major
Bks(.)	Barracks	MR	Muster Rolls
brn.	brown	MRF	Muster Rolls, Company F
c.	about *(circa)*	MRI	Muster Rolls, Company I
Capt(.)	Captain	Mt	Mountain
Cav.	Cavalry	nd	no date
Cmdg	Commanding	No.	Number
Cmplx.	Complexion	NT	Nebraska Territory
Co	Company	Or#	Order Number
Co.	County	*OR: Armies*	*The War of the Rebellion: A*
Col(.)	Colonel		*Compilation of the Official*
Cpl(.)	Corporal		*Record of the Union and*
Dept	Department		*Confederate Armies*
Dist.	District	Pvt(.)	Private
DT	Dakota Territory	Regt	Regiment
Ft.	Fort	RG	Record Group
Gen(.)	General	Sgt(.)	Sergeant
GO#	General Order Number	SO#	Special Order Number
HQs	Headquarters	Terr(.)	Territory
Inf	Infantry	Vol(s)	Volunteer(s)
KT	Kansas Territory	WDC	Washington, D.C.
Lt Art	Light Artillery	WT	Washington Territory

ROSTER: Company I

SURNAME / ALTERNATE SPELLINGS, Given Name(s), Initial(s) & Birthplace

Prior Occupation	Height	Cmplx.	Hair	Eyes
ENLISTMENT: Date	Age	Place		By Whom

BACHEMAN / BRACKEMAN / BACKMAN, John   Bavaria, Germany
shoemaker   5' 7³/₄"   fair   brown   blue
5 Dec 1855   34   Camp Daniels, FL   Lt. Grey
7 Nov 1860   —   —   —
     Listed as Cpl in MRI, April–June 1857 (Or#23, HQs, 2nd Art, Ft. Monroe, VA, 12 June 1857). Promoted to Sgt (Or#8, HQs, 2nd Art, Ft. McHenry, MD, 15 Feb 1859).

BADY, Charles [see BRADY / BADY, Charles]

BARRY, Henry   Long Island, NY
laborer   5' 4³/₄"   fair   brown   hazel
17 Jan 1856   22   Philadelphia, PA   Lt. Burns
     Joined Co at Ft. Deynaud, FL from Gen Dept, 26 March 1856. Drummed out of the Service, 9 Feb 1861 at Ft. Monroe, VA. A Pvt.

BECKMAN, John   Bavaria, Germany
   varnisher   5' 6"   fair   brown   hazel
   25 Aug 1854   22   New York, NY   Col. Brown
   Joined Co at Ft. Deynaud, FL from Gen Dept 18 Jan 1855. Deserted 22 March
1855 from Ft. Deynaud, FL.

BENTLEY, Charles H.   Clinton Co., NY
   shoemaker   5' 9"   fair   sandy   blue
   12 Feb 1856   22   New York, NY   Lt. Frazer
   Joined Co at Ft. Deynaud, FL from Gen Dept 26 March 1856. Discharged 10
Nov 1859, by order, WDC. A Pvt.

BERKLANTH, John   Uri, Switzerland
   upholsterer   5' 8"   ruddy   brown   blue
   15 April 1854   21   New York, NY   Col. Brown
   Joined Co at Ft. Deynaud, FL from Gen Dept 18 Jan 1855. Discharged 16 Nov
1856 at Ft. Columbus (Governor's Island, NY). Surgeon's certificate of disability
(Ltr HQs, 2nd Art, Ft. Columbus, NY, 24 Nov 1856). A Pvt.

BIANCHI, Matteo   Bergane, Lombardy [Italy]
   sailor   5' 5"   florid   black   hazel
   20 Dec 1853   21   Pittsburgh, PA   Capt. Ketcham
   20 Dec 1858   26   Ft. Monroe, VA   —
   Appointed Cpl 7 July 1857 in place of Patrick Flynn [see subsequent listing]
who resigned (Or#26, HQs, 2nd Art, Ft. Monroe, VA, 8 July 1857).

BOLL, Max   Culaz, Poland
   painter   5' 8¹/₂"   fair   brown   blue
   8 Feb 1854   22   New York, NY   Col. Brown
   8 Dec 1859   27   Ft. Monroe, VA   Lt. Grey
   Discharged 1 Nov 1862 for disability. Was with Co K, 3rd US Art. A Cpl.

BRACKEMAN, John [see BACHEMAN / BRACKEMAN / BACKMAN, John]

BRADY / BADY, Charles   Posen, Prussia
   soldier   5' 8¹/₄"   fair   auburn   black
   27 Dec 1853   29   St. Louis, MO   Maj. Gatlin
   Joined Co 4 April 1854 from Gen Dept. Discharged 2 Aug 1855 at Camp Daniels,
FL. Surgeon's certificate of disability. Approved HQs, Dept of Army, NY, 14 July
1855.

BRADY, William   Dublin, Ireland
   tailor   5' 4¹/₂"   fair   brown   blue
   7 Dec 1854   21   Boston, MA   Lt. Davis
   Joined Co at Ft. Deynaud, FL from Gen Dept 18 Jan 1855. Discharged 8 Oct
1857 at Ft. Monroe, VA. Surgeon's certificate of disability. A Pvt.

BRYANT, Franklin
   [See Co F roster for BRYAN / BRYANT, Franklin. Joined Co I at Ft. Monroe, VA
by assignment.]

CARROLL, John P.   Kilkenny, Ireland
  clerk   5' 8"   sallow   brown   blue
  10 Dec 1853   24   Newport, KY   Col. Hoffman
  11 Oct 1858   29   Ft. Monroe, VA   —
  [No service record shown.]

CHAMBERS, Charles   Dublin, Ireland
  carpenter   5' 7"   ruddy   brown   grey
  18 Oct 1853   —   Newport, KY   Col. Hoffman
  28 Sept 1858   —   Ft. Monroe, VA   —
  Promoted to Cpl 21 July 1856 (Or#20, HQs, 2nd Art, Ft. Myers, FL, 24 July
  1856). Appointed Artificer [nd] (MRF, June–Aug 1857). Discharged 28 July 1868
  at San Francisco, CA. Expiration of service.

CHAMBERS, John   Lancaster, PA
  soldier   5' 8³/₄"   fair   brown   grey
  23 May 1853   35   Hampton, VA   Capt. Clark
  23 March 1858   40   Ft. Monroe, VA   —
  Sgt John Chambers, Co C, 2nd US Art, applied for transfer to Co F, 31 March
  1854 (Ltr Maj Woodbridge, 31 March 1854). Appointed 1st Sgt, Co F, 1 June 1854
  (Ltr 24 June 1854, Barrancas Bks, FL, Maj Woodbridge, Cmdg Co). Transferred to
  Co I, 1 Sept 1857 (SO#24, HQs, 2nd Art, Ft. Monroe, VA, 3 Sept 1857), to replace
  Sgt Gustavus Dey [see subsequent listing in Co F roster], who was transferred to
  Co F. Discharged 23 March 1858 for reenlistment. His 6th.

COLLINS, Amos I.   Montgomery, NY
  boatman   5' 6¹/₂"   ruddy   brown   blue
  4 Dec 1854   34   Albany, NY   Lt. Miller
  Joined Co at Ft. Deynaud, FL from Gen Dept 18 Jan 1855. Deserted 3 March
  1858 from Ft. Monroe, VA. Rejoined Co 1 June 1858 from desertion.

CRILLAN / CRELLAN, John   Isle of Man, England
  laborer   5' 7¹/₂"   sallow   brown   blue
  11 Feb 1854   34   St. Louis, MO   Maj. Gatlin
  10 Dec 1858   —   Ft. Monroe, VA   —
  Died 27 Nov 1859 of drowning at Ft. Monroe, VA. Body never found.

CUMMINS, Elinda   Tioga, PA
  laborer   6' 1¹/₂"   fair   brown   grey
  9 Jan 1854   21   Newport, KY   Col. Hoffman
  Discharged 13 Sept 1855 at Camp Daniels, FL. Surgeon's certificate of disability. A Pvt [listed as Sgt in RG 391, Entry 68].

DAY, Julius   Iredell, NC
  carpenter   5' 11"   fair   brown   blue
  27 Aug 1857   23   Charlotte, NC   Lt. J. P. Jones
  Joined Co by assignment at Ft. Monroe, VA. Deserted 20 Nov 1857. A Pvt.

DEY, Gustavus Adolphus
  [See Co F roster. Joined Co I from Gen Dept 18 Jan 1855.]

DIEZ, Joseph [see DUZ / DIEZ, Joseph]

DILLON, Michael   Limerick, Ireland
  laborer   5' 8"   ruddy   brown   grey
  1 Dec 1854   27   Philadelphia, PA   Lt. Burns
  2 Oct 1859   32   Ft. Monroe, VA   —
  Joined Co from Gen Dept 18 Jan 1855.

DOHERTY, John   Cork, Ireland
  soldier   5' 6"   ruddy   brown   blue
  19 Sept 1854   21   Ft. Meade, FL   Lt. Vincent
  Appointed Cpl, 1 Nov 1857. Died 12 March 1858 at Ft. Monroe, VA of consumption. [His wife applied to be his legal representative with the power to sign receipted vouchers (Ltr 18 March 1858; RG 391, Entry 48).]

DOHN, Charles   Easton, PA
  baker   5' 5"   fair   brown   hazel
  16 Dec 1854   21   New York, NY   Lt. Garnett
  Joined Co at Ft. Deynaud, FL from Gen Dept 18 Jan 1855. Deserted 17 July 1857. Rejoined Co 30 Sept 1857 at Ft. Monroe, VA from desertion. Discharged 11 Nov 1857 at Ft. Monroe, VA from action of a General Court-Martial.

DONNON, David   —, Ireland
  soldier   5' 9"   dark   dark   blue
  17 Sept 1844   30   Ft. Hamilton, NY   Lt. Loeser
  17 July 1849   35   Ft. Moultrie, SC   Lt. Wela
  17 May 1854   40   Ft. Meade, FL   Lt. Rhett
  Discharged 20 July 1857 at Ft. Monroe, VA. Surgeon's certificate of disability. A Sgt.

DOUGLAS, Robert   Donegal, Ireland
  laborer   5' 6"   light   black   hazel
  22 May 1851   23   Boston, MA   Capt. Merchant
  Discharged 21 May 1856 at camp near Depot No. 2, Big Cypress, FL. Expiration of service.

DUNES, Henry   Wurttemberg, Germany
  brickmaker   5' 7½"   fair   brown   grey
  26 Jan 1854   31   New York, NY   —
  26 Jan 1858   —   Ft. Monroe, VA   —
  Discharged 26 Sept 1868 at San Juan Island, WT. Expiration of service.

DURHAM, Stewart   Edgefield, SC
  potter   5' 8"   sallow   brown   hazel
  27 Aug 1857   27   Charlotte, NC   Lt. J. P. Jones
  20 Aug 1862   32   Ft. McHenry, MD   Lt. Grey
  Joined Co by assignment at Ft. Monroe, VA [nd]. Appointed Cpl (Or#27, HQs, 2nd Art, Ft. McHenry, MD, 10 Aug 1862).

DUZ / DIEZ, Joseph   Bavaria, Germany
  clerk   5' 11½"   fair   brown   grey
  23 May 1854   22   New York, NY   Col. Brown
  Joined Co at Ft. Deynaud, FL from Gen Dept 18 Jan 1855. Died 9 April 1857 at Ft. Monroe, VA. Disease. [No other particulars noted.]

ELLETT, James M.   King William Co., VA
   carpenter   5' 8½"   fair   dark   blue
   25 Feb 1853   21   Richmond, VA   Maj. Anderson
   Joined Co 11 June 1857 by transfer from Co G, 2nd US Art (SO#18, HQs, 2nd
Art, Ft. Monroe, VA, 10 June 1857). Discharged 25 Feb 1858 at Ft. Monroe, VA.
Expiration of service.

ERNEST, Charles   Baden, Germany
   tailor   5' 11½"   fair   brown   grey
   8 March 1854   21   St. Louis, MO   Maj. Gatlin
   Appointed Cpl, 1 Oct 1857 at Ft. Monroe, VA. Discharged 8 March 1859 at Ft.
Monroe. Expiration of service. A Pvt.

EVERETT, Ignatius   Mayo, Ireland
   laborer   5' 11½"   fair   sandy   grey
   2 Dec 1854   28   Buffalo, NY   Lt. Stevenson
   Joined Co at Ft. Deynaud, FL from Gen Dept 18 Jan 1855. Appointed Cpl, 1
July 1856 (Or#20, HQs, 2nd Art, Ft. Myers, FL, 24 July 1856). Appointed Cpl, 1
Oct 1857 (Or#39, HQs, 2nd Art, Ft. Monroe, VA, 18 Oct 1857). Promoted to Sgt 1
Nov 1857 (Or#41, HQs, 2nd Art, Ft. Monroe, VA, 2 Nov 1857). Discharged 2 Dec
1859 at Ft. Monroe, VA. Expiration of service. A Pvt.

FALK, Charles   Berne, Switzerland
   farmer   5' 6"   florid   brown   blue
   14 May 1851   23   Buffalo, NY   Col. Smith
   Died 7 March 1856 at Ft. Deynaud, FL of acute dysentery.

FALTZ, William   Rowan, NC
   painter   6' 2"   fair   brown   dark
   1 Sept 1857   27   Salisbury, NC   Lt. J. P. Jones
   [No service record found.]

FARRELL, Lawrence   Longford, Ireland
   laborer   5' 8"   fair   fair   grey
   2 Dec 1854   21   Boston, MA   Lt. Flint
   Joined Co at Ft. Deynaud, FL from Gen Dept 18 Jan 1855. Discharged 2 Dec
1859 at Ft. Monroe, VA. Expiration of service.

FEENEY, Charles   Sligo, Ireland
   soldier   5' 5¾"   dark   brown   blue
   26 Nov 1853   30   Pittsburgh, PA   Capt. Ketchum
   27 Sept 1858   35   Hampton, VA   Lt. Grey
   [Reenlisted 27 Sept 1858 "At Fort Moultrie, S.C., Private" (M233, Roll 24).]

FIRTH, William   Lancaster, England
   laborer   5' 6"   dark   dark   brown
   27 Sept 1858   27   Hampton, VA   Lt. Grey
   Discharged 19 May 1860 by sentence of General Court-Martial, Ft. Monroe, VA.
A Pvt.

FLYNN, Patrick   Roscommon, Ireland
   soldier   5' 5½"   ruddy   dark brn.   grey
   4 Sept 1854   35[33]   Ft. Meade, FL   Lt. Vincent

Into 2nd enlistment, resigned as Cpl (Or#26, HQs, 2nd Art, Ft. Monroe, VA, 8 July 1857). Sick in hospital. Discharged 15 Oct 1857 at Ft. Monroe, VA. Surgeon's certificate of disability. A Pvt.

FORNEY / FORNOY, John A.   Lincoln, NC
tailor   5' 5¹/₂"   light   light   grey
3 Aug 1854   35   Ft. Meade, FL   Lt. Vincent
Discharged 3 Aug 1859 at Ft. Monroe, VA. Expiration of service. A Pvt.

FULTZ, William
[no descriptive data]
[no enlistment data]
Joined Co by assignment at Ft. Monroe, VA. [No other data.]

GAUSSENDORF, Oscar A.   Saxony, Germany
waiter   5' 6¹/₂"   fair   brown   blue
4 Nov 1858   22   New York, NY   Lt. Sweeny
   Transferred to Co I, 1 May 1859 (SO#28, HQs, 2nd Art, Ft. McHenry, MD, 13 April 1859). Deserted 16 May 1859 from Ft. Monroe, VA.

GILL, George W.   Cork, Ireland
soldier   5' 7¹/₄"   fair   black   black
21 Dec 1853   25   St. Louis, MO   Maj. Gatlin
   Joined Co 4 April 1854 from Gen Dept. An Artificer. Deserted 21 March 1855 from Ft. Deynaud, FL.

GILLON, James M.   Edinburgh, Scotland
bricklayer   5' 5"   —   —   —
19 Jan 1854   21   New York, NY   Col. Brown
   Discharged 31 July 1857 at Ft. Monroe, VA. Surgeon's certificate of disability. A Pvt.

GINGER, John   London, England
laborer   5' 8¹/₂"   fair   auburn   blue
5 Dec 1854   28   Buffalo, NY   Capt. Stevenson
   Joined Co at Ft. Deynaud, FL from Gen Dept 18 Jan 1855. Deserted June 1857 from Ft. Monroe, VA.

GRAHAM, William   Philadelphia, PA
soldier   5' 9"   fair   lt. brn.   brown
7 Dec 1854   28   Philadelphia, PA   Lt. Burns
   Joined Co at Ft. Deynaud, FL from Gen Dept 18 Jan 1855. Rejoined Co by assignment at Ft. Monroe, VA. Discharged 7 Dec 1859 at Ft. Monroe. Expiration of service. A Pvt. [Must have reenlisted.] Appointed Cpl, 18 March 1861 (Or#13, HQs, 2nd Art, Ft. McHenry, MD, 8 June 1861).

GRAVES, Nathaniel   Thomaston, ME
farmer   5' 7"   dark   brown   blue
30 May 1851   24   Boston, MA   Capt. Merchant
Discharged 10 Oct 1854 at Ft. Meade, FL. Surgeon's certificate of disability.

HALL, Alexander   Tyrone, Ireland
  moulder   5' 5³/₄"   fair   fair   blue
  31 Jan 1856   22   New York, NY   Lt. Sargent
  Joined Co at Ft. Deynaud, FL from Gen Dept 26 March 1856. Deserted 17 Sept
1858.

HALL, Hugh W.   Liverpool, England
  porter   5' 7"   fair   brown   blue
  13 June 1851   21   Buffalo, NY   Col. Smith
  Discharged 12 June 1856 at Ft. Deynaud, FL. Expiration of service. A Pvt.

HANCOCK, John J.   Caswell, NC
  carpenter   5' 10"   fair   brown   hazel
  29 Aug 1857   19   Charlotte, NC   Lt. J. P. Jones
  Joined Co by assignment. Discharged 28 July 1858 by order of the AGO at Ft.
Monroe, VA. A Pvt.

HANKINSON, John [see HENKINSON / HANKINSON, John]

HARNEY, Thomas   Tipperary, Ireland
  farmer   5' 5³/₄"   fair   brown   grey
  24 Jan 1856   22   Boston, MA   Lt. Archer
  Joined Co at Ft. Deynaud, FL from Gen Dept 26 March 1856. Discharged 24
Jan 1861 at Ft. Monroe, VA. A Pvt.

HAYES / HAYS, Michael   Tipperary, Ireland
  laborer   5' 11¹/₄"   ruddy   brown   grey
  13 June 1851   22   New York, NY   Capt. Westcott
  Discharged 12 June 1856 at Ft. Deynaud, FL. Expiration of service.

HENKINSON / HANKINSON, John   Meath, Ireland
  harness maker   5' 7"   sandy   auburn   grey
  28 Nov 1854   22   Philadelphia, PA   Lt. Burns
  29 Sept 1859   27   Ft. Monroe, VA   —
  29 Jan 1864   32   Ft. Meade, MD   Lt. Grey
  [See GO#46, HQs, VIII Army Corps, Baltimore, MD, 24 Oct 1862 in which he
was accused of stealing a saddle horse. Found not guilty.]

HENNESSEY / HENNESSY, Michael   Limerick, Ireland
  wool comber   5' 7"   fair   brown   blue
  28 Nov 1853   27   New York, NY   Col. Brown
  Recommended to be Cpl 5 Sept 1854. Reduced from Cpl to Pvt, Garrison Court-
Martial (Or#43, HQs, 2nd Art, Ft. Myers, FL, 2 April 1857). Deserted 23 July 1857
from Ft. Monroe, VA.

HOWELL, Henry A.   Jefferson, VA
  farmer   5' 4¹/₄"   fair   brown   hazel
  29 Dec 1853   23   St. Louis, MO   —
  Discharged 28 Dec 1858 at Ft. Monroe, VA. Expiration of service. A Pvt.

HUGHES, Michael   Cork, Ireland
  laborer   5' 6"   fair   lt. brn.   blue
  12 July 1854   24   New York, NY   Col. Brown

Joined Co at Ft. Deynaud, FL from Gen Dept 18 Jan 1855. Died 6 March 1857 at Ft. Monroe, VA. Reported deserted 6 March 1857, on the Return of Co F, 2nd Art. His body was found in Mill Creek near Ft. Monroe. Died from drowning. A Pvt.

HUNTER, John   New York, NY
clerk   5' 7¹/₂"   fair   brown   blue
29 Sept 1858   25   Hampton, VA   Lt. Grey
Appointed Cpl, 1 May 1860. Promoted to Sgt Maj 3rd US Art [nd]. Transferred to 4th US Art (SO#70, HQs, 2nd Art, Ft. McHenry, MD, 1 May 1861) at Ft. McHenry.

JACOBS, Barney   Baun, Prussia
boy   4' 8¹/₄"   dark   light   blue
12 May 1857   15   New York, NY   Lt. Updegraff
Discharged 12 May 1862 at Ft. McHenry, MD. Expiration of service. A Musician.

JOHNSON, Alexander   Cambridge, NY
weaver   5' 9¹/₂"   light   brown   grey
8 Dec 1854   24   Philadelphia, PA   Lt. Burns
Joined Co at Ft. Deynaud, FL from Gen Dept 18 Jan 1855. Discharged 10 Oct 1855 at Camp Daniels, FL. Surgeon's certificate of disability.

JOHNSON, Almon   Otsego, NY
machinist   5' 5"   fair   brown   blue
1 Nov 1855   37   Camp Daniels, FL   Lt. Grey
Joined Co by enlistment. Discharged 1 Nov 1860. Expiration of service.

JORDAN, Charles   Bavaria, Germany
cloth weaver   5' 7"   fair   lt. brn.   grey
11 Aug 1854   21   New York, NY   Col. Brown
Joined Co at Ft. Deynaud, FL from Gen Dept 18 Jan 1855. Deserted 31 May 1857 from Ft. Monroe, VA.

KAMPF, Frederick [see KEMP / KAMPF, Frederick]

KEIFF / KRIFF, James   Kilkenny, Ireland
laborer   5' 7¹/₂"   ruddy   auburn   blue
28 Oct 1854   24   Buffalo, NY   Lt. Stevenson
Joined Co at Ft. Deynaud, FL from Gen Dept 18 Jan 1855, as Artificer. Discharged 28 Oct 1859 at Ft. Monroe, VA. Expiration of service. A Pvt.

KELL, Charles   Burlington, PA
laborer   5' 8"   dark   brown   brown
1 Feb 1856   25   Philadelphia, PA   Lt. Flint
Deserted 27 April 1857 from Ft. Monroe, VA.

KEMP / KAMPF, Frederick   Luhl [Sule?], Prussia
shoemaker   5' 4¹/₂"   fair   brown   grey
24 July 1854   22   New York, NY   Col. Brown
Joined Co at Ft. Deynaud, FL from Gen Dept 18 Jan 1855. Deserted 18 July 1857 from Ft. Monroe, VA.

KEOUGH, James   Galveston, TX
  scholar   5' 7"   ruddy/fair   brown   hazel/dark
  15 Dec 1852   14   New York, NY   Col. [illegible]
  28 Nov 1857   19   Hampton, VA   Lt. Grey
  Deserted 1 Jan 1858 from Ft. Monroe, VA. A Musician.

KILROY, Martin V.   Buffalo, NY
  tailor   5' 5"   light   brown   blue
  4 Jan 1854   23   New York, NY   Col. Brown
  19 Nov 1858   28   Ft. Monroe, VA   Lt. Grey
  Discharged 12 Feb 1860 by sentence of General Court-Martial at Ft. Monroe,
VA. A Pvt.

KLEIN, William   Luxembourg, France
  carpenter   6' 3"   sallow   black   hazel
  4 Sept 1854   27   New York, NY   Col. Brown
  Joined Co at Ft. Deynaud, FL from Gen Dept 18 Jan 1855. Deserted 22 March
1855 from Ft. Deynaud.

KNOPPEL, John   Coblenz, Germany
  farmer   5' 6½"   fair   brown   blue
  3 Dec 1853   —   Chicago, IL   Lt. Furnley
  Discharged 2 Dec 1858 at Ft. Monroe, VA. Expiration of service. A Pvt.

KOCH, Joseph   Rerne, Germany
  turner   5' 10½"   fair   brown   hazel
  20 May 1854   24   New York, NY   Col. Brown
  2 April 1859   29   Ft. Monroe, VA   Lt. Grey
  18 Jan 1864   34   Ft. McHenry, MD   Capt. Grey
  Joined Co at Ft. Deynaud, FL from Gen Dept 18 Jan 1855. Transferred to Regimental Band (Or#45, HQs, 2nd Art, Ft. Brooke, FL, 12 Nov 1856). Transferred
from Band back to Co I, 1 Sept 1862 (SO#12, HQs, 2nd Art, Ft. McHenry, MD, 22
Aug 1862).

KRIFF, James [see KEIFF / KRIFF, James]

KROPPE / KROPEFF / KROFPPE, Fernick / Frederick   Bavaria, Germany
  clerk   5' 5½"   fair   sandy   blue
  2 Aug 1854   22   New York, NY   Col. Brown
  2 June 1859   27   Ft. Monroe, VA   Lt. Grey
  21 Feb 1864   34   Ft. McHenry, MD   Capt. Grey
  Joined Co at Ft. Deynaud, FL 18 Jan 1855. Transferred to Regimental Band
(Or#45, HQs 2nd Art, Ft. Brooke, FL 12 Nov 1856). Transferred back to Co I, 1
Sept 1862 (SO#12, HQs, 2nd Art, Ft. McHenry, MD, 22 Aug 1862).

LOHMEYER, Henry   Hanover, Germany
  soldier   5' 6"   fair   brown   blue
  7 Dec 1853   28   New York, NY   Col. Brown
  7 Nov 1858   33   Hampton, VA   Lt. Grey
  7 Aug 1863   38   Washington, DC   —
  Joined Co at Ft. Deynaud, FL from Gen Dept 18 Jan 1855. Appointed Cpl (Or#4,
HQs, 2nd Art, Ft. Hamilton, NY, 18 Jan 1858). Promoted to Sgt 24 May 1861

(Or#13, HQs, 2nd Art, Ft. McHenry, MD, 8 June 1861). Promoted to 1st Sgt. [See RG 391, Entry 76, dated 19 Jan 1862, in which the non-commissioned officers, musicians and privates of Co I signed an Oath of Allegiance. 1st Sgt Lohmeyer headed the list of signers.]

McANALLY, William	Mayo, Ireland			
laborer	5' 5¹/₂"	fair	fair	grey
9 Feb 1856	21	New York, NY		Lt. Sargent
7 Dec 1860	26	Ft. Ridgely, MN		—

Joined Co at Ft. Deynaud, FL from Gen Dept 26 March 1856. Appointed Cpl (SO#30, HQs, 2nd Art, Ft. Monroe, VA, 6 Sept 1859). Promoted to Sgt (SO#21, HQs, 2nd Art, Ft. McHenry, MD, 10 July 1861).

McANNALLY, Henry	Kildare, Ireland			
—	5' 6³/₄"	fair	brown	grey
12 Dec 1853	24	St. Louis, MO		Maj. Gatlin

Discharged 27 Dec 1858 at Ft. Monroe, VA. Expiration of service. A Pvt.

McCABE, James	Lukem, Ireland			
laborer	5' 7¹/₂"	fair	brown	blue
23 April 1851	22	Providence, RI		Maj. Potter
23 April 1856	27	Ft. Deynaud, FL		—
3 Sept 1858	29	Hampton, VA		Lt. Grey
12 Aug 1863	34	—		—

Recommended to be Cpl, 1 Sept 1854 (Ltr 21 Oct 1854, Lt. G. Hartsuff, Cmdg Co, Ft. Meade, FL). Reenlisted 12 Aug 1863 with Co K, 3rd US Art.

McGUIRE, John	Fermanagh, Ireland			
tailor	5' 7³/₄"	fair	dark	brown
30 Jan 1856	29	New York, NY		Lt. Frazer
30 Jan 1861	34	—		—

Joined Co at Ft. Deynaud, FL from Gen Dept 26 March 1856.

McINERNEY, Daniel J.	Cork, Ireland			
clerk	5' 6³/₄"	fair	fair	blue
5 Dec 1854	21	New York, NY		Lt. Garnett

Joined Co at Ft. Deynaud, FL from Gen Dept 18 Jan 1855. Discharged at Ft. Monroe, VA by order of the AGO, 1 May 1859. A Pvt.

McKENNA, Bernard	Antrim, Ireland			
laborer	5' 9"	ruddy	brown	blue
27 Dec 1853	28	Newport, KY		—

Absent. In confinement at Ft. Columbus, NY. [Date of desertion and apprehension not found.] Rejoined Co from desertion (MRI Feb–April 1857). Discharged 27 Dec 1858 at Ft. Monroe, VA. Expiration of service. A Pvt.

McKEON, Andrew	Antrim, Ireland			
laborer	5' 5³/₄"	fair	brown	hazel
21 July 1851	21	New York, NY;		
		(Whitehall Street)		Capt. Hayden

To be made Cpl, 1 April 1854 (per 1st Lt Rhett, Ft. Meade, FL, 5 April 1854). Ltr 22 April 1854 canceling recommendation above for "highly improper &

misobedientlike conduct." Tried by Garrison Court-Martial (Ltr from Lt Rhett to Regt HQs, Ft. Meade, FL). Discharged 21 July 1856. Expiration of service. A Cpl.

MAHONEY, William   Tipperary, Ireland
laborer   5' 11½"   dark   dark   hazel
4 Dec 1854   24   New York, NY   Lt. Garnett
17 Oct 1859   29   Ft. Monroe, VA   —
Joined Co at Ft. Deynaud, FL from Gen Dept 18 Jan 1855. Appointed Artificer [nd]. Reduced to Pvt from Artificer 20 April 1857 by order of Capt Gibson. Reenlisted 17 Oct 1859 as Artificer. Died of apoplexy 30 July 1860 at Ft. Ridgely, MN.

MAXWELL, James   Londonderry, Ireland
soldier   5' 8"   light   fair   blue
26 April 1853   25   Ft. Meade, FL   Lt. Butler
25 Feb 1858   30   Hampton, VA   Lt. Grey
Was Co 1st Sgt when he reenlisted in 1858. Went from Cpl to Sgt on 1 May 1861; to Pvt on 10 July 1861; to Cpl on 1 March 1862. Discharged 26 Feb 1863 [into his 4th enlistment]. Expiration of service. A Sgt.

MEIR / MEIER, Herman   Minden, Prussia
laborer   5' 6"   fair   light   blue
22 Feb 1856   23   Philadelphia, PA   Lt. Flint
Joined Co at Ft. Deynaud, FL from Gen Dept 26 March 1856. Deserted 31 May 1857 from Ft. Monroe, VA.

MILLER / MULLER, Henry   Bavaria, Germany
painter   5' 5"   ruddy   brown   grey
3 Nov 1854   22   New York, NY   Col. Brown
Joined Co at Ft. Deynaud, FL from Gen Dept 18 Jan 1855. Deserted 6 Dec 1855 from Ft. Deynaud.

MORRIS, James   Tipperary, Ireland
laborer   5' 10"   fair   brown   grey
22 Dec 1853   23   St. Louis, MO   Maj. Gatlin
Discharge 22 Dec 1855 at Ft. Deynaud, FL. Surgeon's certificate of disability: 2/3 pension. A Pvt.

MORSE, Robert B.   Utica, NY
laborer   5' 10"   dark   brown   blue
20[30] Aug 1853   22   Toledo, OH   Capt. Stevenson
Subject of General Court-Martial (SO#12, HQs, Dept of East, Baltimore, MD, 14 Feb 1857). Transferred from Co F to Co I (SO#5, HQs, 2nd Art, Ft. Hamilton, NY, 6 April 1858). Discharged 19 Aug 1858 at Ft. Monroe, VA. Expiration of service. A Pvt.

MULLER, Henry [see MILLER / MULLER, Henry]

NELSON, Alexander   Fermanagh, Ireland
currier   5' 5"   fair   black   blue
16 Dec 1854   31   Boston, MA   Lt. Davis
Joined Co at Ft. Deynaud, FL from Gen Dept 18 Jan 1855. Deserted 14 Oct 1855 from Camp Daniels, FL.

NEUMAN / NEUMANN, William   Saxony, Germany
butcher   5' 6"   fair   brown   blue
21 Aug 1854   22   New York, NY   Col. Brown
Joined Co at Ft. Deynaud, FL from Gen Dept 18 Jan 1855. Discharged 21 Aug 1859. Expiration of service. A Pvt.

NEWSOM, Cornelius   Cabarras, NC
laborer   5' 10"   sallow   brown   blue
27 Aug 1857   27   Salisbury, NC   Lt. J. P. Jones
Joined Co by assignment at Ft. Monroe, VA (SO#24, HQs, 2nd Art, Ft. Monroe, VA, 3 Sept 1857).

PENDER / PINDAR, James   Dublin, Ireland
laborer   5' 10½"   fair   brown   blue
6 Feb 1856   22   Philadelphia, PA   Lt. Flint
Deserted 23 July 1857 from Ft. Monroe, VA.

PHEALY, John   Sligo, Ireland
laborer   5' 8"   florid   brown   blue
30 May 1851   23   Buffalo, NY   Col. Smith
Discharge 29 May 1856 at camp near Depot No. 2, Big Cypress, FL. Expiration of service.

PINDAR, James [see PENDER / PINDAR, James]

POLKOW, Frederick   Mechlenburg, Germany
soldier   5' 7"   dark   brown   blue
17 Dec 1853   34   Chicago, IL   Lt. Turnley
20 Oct 1858   39   Hampton, VA   Lt. Grey
Discharged 13 April 1863 at camp near Acquia, VA. Disability. A Pvt.

POULSON, Peter F.   Gluckstadt, Germany
soldier   5' 9¼"   sallow   brown   blue
11 Dec 1853   37   St. Louis, MO   Maj. Gatlin
4 Dec 1858   42   Ft. Monroe, VA   Lt. Grey
Discharged 8 Aug 1862 at Ft. Monroe, VA. Disability. A Pvt.

PRINZING, Daniel [David]   Ulm, Germany
farmer   5' 8½"   fair   light   grey
11 Feb 1856   21   Philadelphia, PA   Lt. Flint
Deserted 17 July 1857 from Ft. Monroe, VA.

REDAN / RODIN, William R.   Pickens Dist., NC
—   5' 10"   light   light   blue
19 Aug 1857   20yrs 9mo Charlotte, NC   Lt. J. P. Jones
Joined Co by assignment at Ft. Monroe, VA. Deserted 27 Dec 1858 from Ft. Monroe.

RITCH, William G.   Union, NC
carpenter   5' 9"   fair   light   blue
22 Aug 1857   21   Salisbury, NC   Lt. J. P. Jones
Joined Co by assignment at Ft. Monroe, VA. Discharged 22 Aug 1862 at Ft. McHenry, MD. Expiration of service. A Pvt.

ROBINSON, Gilbert   Tyrone, Ireland
  painter   5' 9"   light   brown   grey
  6 Jan 1854   21   New York, NY   Col. Brown
  5 Nov 1858   26   Hampton, VA   Lt. Grey
  Appointed Cpl, 1 June 1854 at Ft. Meade, FL. Discharged 25 Feb 1860 at Ft.
Monroe, VA by order of AGO. A Sgt.

RODIN, William R. [see REDAN / RODIN, William R.]

ROSSLER, John   Wurttemberg, Germany
  farmer   5' 8½"   fair   light   grey
  4[31] Jan 1856   22   Philadelphia, PA   Lt. Flint
  Deserted 17 July 1857 from Ft. Monroe, VA.

SCHMIDT, Frederick   Weissenburg, France
  waiter   5' 5"   light   lt. brn.   hazel
  2 June 1854   20   New York, NY   Col. Brown
  Joined Co at Ft. Deynaud, FL from Gen Dept 18 Jan 1855. Discharged 24 May
1857 at Ft. Monroe, VA. Surgeon's certificate of disability. [See M233, Roll 24:
died 19 July 1856 of acute dysentery at Ft. Myers, FL. A Pvt. This record is
confused with Frederick C. Schudt and seems irresolvable. See next listing.]

SCHUDT, Frederick C. Frankfurt, Germany
  clerk   5' 7"   fair   lt. brn.   blue
  20 Aug 1854   34   New York, NY   Col. Brown
  Joined Co at Ft. Deynaud, FL from Gen Dept 18 Jan 1855. Died 19 July 1856 at
Ft. Myers, FL of acute dysentery. [See M233, Roll 24: discharged 24 May 1857
from Ft. Monroe, VA, Surgeon's certificate of disability. A Pvt. See Frederick
Schmidt listing above.]

SMITH, James   Limerick, Ireland
  farmer   5' 9½"   fair   brown   blue
  1 May 1851   32   New York, NY   Maj. Johnson
  1 March 1856   37   Ft. Deynaud, FL   Lt. Grey
  Appointed to Cpl, 1 July 1854. Recommended for promotion to Sgt 29 Oct 1856.
Denied promotion due to previous Court-Martial; but appealed by Cmdg Officer,
Capt A. A. Gibson, for "long term of faithful service, again worthy of appointment."
Was a Sgt when he reenlisted on 1 March 1856. Then reduced to Cpl in April 1857.
Promoted to Sgt 20 July 1857. Reduced to Pvt 10 Aug 1857. Discharged 1 March
1861 by order of the Secretary of War at WDC. A Pvt. [Final note: "Pvt. Smith in
Insane Asylum in Washington, D.C. since Aug. 22, 1858 (M727, Roll 12)."]

STELZER, John J.   Wurttemberg, Germany
  shoemaker   5' 5"   fair   honey   hazel
  31 Jan 1854   21   New York, NY   Col. Brown
  Discharged 31 Jan 1859 at Ft. Monroe, VA. Expiration of service. A Pvt.

STEPHEN, George   Bavaria, Germany
  farmer   5' 2½"   dark   brown   black
  5 Jan 1855   17   New York, NY   Lt. Garnett
  9 Jan 1859   21   Ft. Monroe, VA   —
  Joined Co at Ft. Monroe, VA from Gen Dept at Ft. Columbus, NY, 1 Sept 1857. A
Musician.

STOLL, Urban   Strassburg, France
  soldier   5' 7¹/₂"   fair   grey   hazel
  2 Dec 1854   34   New York, NY   Col. Brown
  Joined Co at Ft. Deynaud, FL from Gen Dept 18 Jan 1855. Died 2 March 1855
at Ft. Myers, FL of acute dysentery. A Pvt.

STROUS / STROWSE, Peter   Cimahausen, Germany
  baker   5' 7"   fair   brown   grey
  14 Feb 1854   24   New York, NY   —
  Deserted 13 March 1854. Apprehended 15 May 1854. Joined Co at Ft. Meade,
FL from desertion 15 May 1854. Discharged 13 Feb 1859 at Ft. Monroe, VA. Expiration of Service. A Pvt.

SULLIVAN, Cornelius   County Kerry, Ireland
  laborer   5' 7¹/₄"   fair   dark   blue
  14 Dec 1853   26   Newport, KY   Col. Hoffman
  19 Nov 1858   31   Hampton, VA   Lt. Grey
  Deserted 19 Jan 1859. A Pvt.

TALLY, Sandford   Halifax, VA
  laborer   5' 9¹/₂"   dark   black   black
  20 July 1857   26   Salisbury, NC   Lt. J. P. Jones
  Joined Co by assignment at Ft. Monroe, VA. Discharged 20 Aug 1862 at Ft.
McHenry, MD. Expiration of service. A Pvt.

WALKER, Joseph [see WALTERS / WALKER, Joseph]

WALSH / WELSH, Lawrence   Kilkenny, Ireland
  laborer   5' 5³/₄"   fair   light   blue
  22 Dec 1853   26   St. Louis, MO   Maj. Gatlin
  26 Nov 1858   31   Hampton, VA   Lt. Grey
  Joined Co from Gen Dept 4 April 1854.

WALTERS / WALKER, Joseph   Elegentry, Germany
  shoemaker   5' 4¹/₂"   honey   black   blue
  15 May 1854   29   New York, NY   Col. Brown
  Joined Co at Ft. Deynaud, FL from Gen Dept 18 Jan 1855. Discharged 15 May
1859 at Ft. Monroe, VA. Expiration of service. A Pvt.

WELSH, Lawrence [see WALSH / WELSH, Lawrence]

WILLIAMS, David G.
  [no descriptive data]
  [no enlistment data, except that he enlisted at Newport, KY]
  Appointed Artificer 20 April 1857. Appointed Cpl from Artificer 20 July 1857
(Or#27, HQs, 2nd Art, Ft. Monroe, VA, 21 July 1857). Promoted to Sgt (Or#29,
HQs, 2nd Art, Ft. Monroe, VA, 10 Aug 1857).

WILSON, John P.   Alexander, NC
  laborer   5' 9³/₄"   fair   dark   hazel
  29 Aug 1857   21   Charlotte, NC   Lt. J. P. Jones
  Assigned to Co (SO#24, HQs, 2nd Art, Ft. Monroe, VA, 3 Sept 1857).

ROSTER: Company F

SURNAME / ALTERNATE SPELLINGS, Given Name(s), Initial(s) & Birthplace

Prior Occupation	Height	Cmplx.	Hair	Eyes
ENLISTMENT: Date	Age	Place		By Whom

ABERNATHY, James W.   Lincoln, NC

brickmaker	5' 9"	fair	light	blue
8 Aug 1857	—	Charlotte, NC		Lt. J. P. Jones

Joined Co 15 Aug 1857 at Ft. Monroe, VA. Died 26 May 1861 from disease at St. Louis, MO.

ADAMS, John   Randolph Co., NC

farmer (carpenter)	6' 0"	dark	dark	brown
30 Nov 1859	28	Ft. Leavenworth, KT		Lt. Pratt

Deserted 10 Feb 1860 from Ft. Leavenworth, KT.

AKEHURST, Charles W.   New Hartford, NY

laborer	5' 7³/₄"	fair	brown	blue
13 Nov 1860	c. 22	St. Louis, MO		Lt. O'Connell

General services recruit. Attached to Co M, 1st MO Lt Art from 1861 to 1864. Transferred to Co F, 2nd US Art (SO#21, HQs, Dept of Army, WDC, 14 Jan 1864). Discharged at Benicia Bks, CA, 13 Nov 1865. Expiration of service. A Pvt. Died of cancer at age 53 on 6 Jan 1891. Buried at Forest Hill Cemetery, Utica, NY. Contracted malarial disease at Black River, MS, between Jackson and Vicksburg, in 1863 during the Vicksburg campaign.

ALBER, Louis   —, Germany

baker	5' 9"	light	brown	brown
30 Dec 1857	29	Ft. Leavenworth, KT		Lt. J. P. Jones

Deserted 14 March 1858 from cantonment at Ft. Leavenworth, KT.

ANDERSON, James   Lockport, NY

teamster	5' 6"	fair	brown	grey
11 March 1860	21	Ft. Leavenworth, KT		Lt. Barriger

Deserted 14 June 1860 from Ft. Leavenworth, KT.

ARMSTRONG, Robert   Norfolk, England

soldier	5' 6"	fair	brown	grey
— March 1848	—	—		—
31 March 1853	26	Ft. Capron, FL		Lt. Taylor
16 Feb 1858	31	Ft. Monroe, VA		Lt. Grey

Appointed Sgt 1 May 1854. In confinement at Ft. Leavenworth, KT, having been reported as a deserter since 12 March 1858. Reduced to Pvt from Cpl as of that date (Or#31, HQs, 2nd Art, Ft. Hamilton, NY, 13 Aug 1858). Promoted to Sgt 5 May 1860 at Ft. Leavenworth, KT (Ltr from Capt Totten to HQs, 1 June 1860). Wounded 16 June 1861 at Battle of Boonville, MO.

ARMSTRONG, Robert
[no descriptive data]

2 May 1850	21	Philadelphia, PA		—
23 Oct 1855	26	Philadelphia, PA		—

17 Nov 1860	31	Newport Bks., KY	Lt. Wilkins
14 Dec 1865	36	Frankford Ars.;	
		at Philadelphia, PA	—
26 Dec 1868	39	New Orleans, LA	—
1 July 1871	42	Ft. McHenry, MD	—
24 July 1876	47	Ft. Point, San Jose, CA	—
25 July 1881	52	—	—

Assigned to Co G, 3rd US Inf, 1850. Reenlisted 1855. Assigned to Co I, 1st US Art. Transferred from Newport Bks, KY to Jefferson Bks, MO, Feb 1861. Transferred to Co L, 1st MO Lt Art at Jefferson City, MO, Oct 1861. Transferred to Co M, 1st MO Lt Art, Feb 1862. Transferred 25 May 1864 to Co F, 2nd US Art. Taken prisoner at Atlanta, GA 22 July 1864. Released Sept 1864. Transferred to Co K, 1st US Art, Aug 1865. Assigned to Ordnance Dept, Frankford Ars, Philadelphia, PA, Dec 1865. Discharged 14 Dec 1868. Reenlisted 26 Dec 1868. Discharged 5 June 1871 at New Orleans, LA (GO#217, HQs, Dept of Army, WDC). Assigned to Co E, 4th US Art, 1871. Discharged 1 July 1876 from Co E, 4th US Art at Ft. Stevens, OR. Assigned to Co F, 4th US Art, 1876. Discharged 23 July 1881 at Ft. Point, CA. Reenlisted with Co M, 4th US Art. Approved for discharge 14 Feb 1885 at Ft. Preble, ME. Discharged 13 May 1885 by Act of Congress. Applied for pension for loss of thumb in wood cutting accident during his sixth enlistment. Application denied.

ATKINSON, Joseph		Isle of Wight, VA	
farmer	5' 7"	ruddy	red	grey
1 Nov 1857	23	Charlotte, NC	Lt. J. P. Jones

Transferred into Co from temporary attachment (Or#148, HQs, Ft. Riley, KT, 9 Dec 1858). Discharged 4 April 1859 from Ft. Riley, KT. Surgeon's certificate of disability. [Shown as deserted 9 Sept 1859 (M233, Roll 26).]

AULD, Elijah M.		Steubenville, OH	
printer	5' 8"	fair	black	hazel
12 Nov 1860	28	Newport, KY	Lt. Wilkins

Assigned to Co F. Transferred to Jefferson Bks, MO, 5 Feb 1861. On detached service with Co M, 1st MO Lt Art. Returned to Co F in Jan 1865. Transferred from Co F, 2nd US Art, to Co K, 1st US Art. Discharged 15 Nov 1865. Expiration of service. A Pvt. Born 7 Oct 1832. Died 14 Feb 1910. Buried in Cadiz Cemetery, Cadiz, OH. Suffered severe injury to his hearing, and contracted chills and fever during the Vicksburg campaign in 1863.

AUSTIN / AUSTEN, William		Cleveland, OH	
—	5' 6"	fair	black	grey
15 Nov 1860	23	Newport, KY	Lt. Wilkins
21 July 1864	27	near Atlanta, GA	—

Joined Co by transfer from general service recruits (SO#22, HQs, Dept of West, Springfield, MO, 7 July 1861). Deserted 7 Nov 1864.

BAKER, Gilbert		McKean, PA	
farmer	5' 6³/₄"	fair	brown	blue
26 Jan 1852	21	Syracuse, NY	Capt. Robinson
29 Dec 1856	26	Hampton, VA	Lt. J. P. Jones

Deserted 29 Jan 1858 from cantonment near Ft. Leavenworth, KT. Discharged 12 Aug 1862 at St. Louis, MO. Expiration of service.

BAKER, John A.   Shelby, IL
   laborer   5' 10¹/₂"   fair   brown   grey
   10 May 1860   22   Ft. Leavenworth, KT   Lt. Barriger
   Deserted 5[29] July 1860 from Ft. Leavenworth, KT.

BAKER, Julius A.   Big Lick, Stanley Co., NC
   laborer   5' 7¹/₄"   fair   light   grey
   12 Aug 1857   21   Charlotte, NC   Lt. J. P. Jones
   23 Dec 1863   27   St. Louis, MO   —
   Joined Co 15 Aug 1857. Discharged 14 Aug 1862 from St. Louis, MO. Expiration of service. A Pvt. From Sept 1862 to Dec 1863, drove a team for the US Government in Leavenworth, KS. Then enlisted in Co G, 2nd MO Lt Art. Discharged 23 Aug 1865 at Benton Bks, St. Louis, MO. Expiration of service. A Cpl. Born 24 Aug 1837. Died 6 Aug 1909 in Charlotte, NC.

BARRY, Garrett   Monongahela, PA
   laborer   5' 5"   florid   brown   brown
   15 Dec 1860   22   Newport, KY   Lt. Wilkins
   Unassigned recruit. Joined Co from Co M, 1st MO Lt Art (SO#21, HQs, Dept of Army, WDC, 14 Jan 1864). Killed 22 July 1864 in battle near Atlanta, GA.

BECK, Henry [alias for ELLER, Henry]   Utica, NY
   [no other descriptive data]
   27 Nov 1860   18   Milwaukee, WI*   Lt. J. P. Jones
                                       *[error (?), probably St. Louis, MO]
   Regular army recruit on duty with Co M, 1st MO Lt Art. Transferred to Co F (SO#21, HQs, Dept of Army, WDC, 14 Jan 1864). Died in Gayoso General Hospital, Memphis, TN, 28 July 1864 from a gunshot wound to the right shoulder, received at Atlanta, GA 22 July 1864. A Pvt.

BELCHER, William   Spartansburg, NC
   brickmaker   —   fair   light   blue
   10 Aug 1857   21   Charlotte, NC   Lt. J. P. Jones
   Joined Co 15 Aug 1857 as recruit. Deserted 28 May1858 from encampment at Indian Creek, KT.

BELL, William B.   Nicholas, KY
   physician   6' 0"   fair   brown   grey
   22 Feb 1860   21[23]   Ft. Leavenworth, KT Lt. Pratt
   Died of disease 21 Sept 1862 at Jefferson Bks, MO. A Pvt.

BELT, Robert [alias for MARSH, Richard Alvis]   Morganfield, KY
   student   5' 9¹/₂"   light   light   blue/grey
   3 Oct 1860   18   Newport, KY   Lt. Wilkins
   1 July 1864   22   Atlanta, GA   Lt. Murray
   19 Sept 1865   23   Cincinnati, OH   —
   24 June 1869   27   Cincinnati, OH   —
   28 May 1870   28   —   —
   Joined Co by transfer from general service recruits (SO#22, HQs, Dept of West, Springfield, MO, 7 July 1861). Appointed Cpl, 1 Jan 1864. Discharged 1 July 1864 to reenlist in Co F. Discharged 25 Jan 1865 to accept commission with TN Vols. War ended before his unit could be mustered in. Discharged 28 March 1869 at Ft.

Buford, DT. Enlisted 24 June 1869. Deserted 26 March 1870 from Newport Bks, KY. Enlisted 28 May 1870 in Co A, 15th US Inf; transferred to general services, Dept of NM. Discharged 2 June 1873. A 1st Sgt. Claims to have suffered frostbite of the left foot during detached service with a section of Co F on march from West Point, MO to Independence, MO in Jan 1862. Born 29 Oct 1843 [or 6 June 1842, or 4 Nov 1844]. Died in Mercedes, TX, 17 Aug 1917. Buried in Edinburgh, TX. Death certificate lists occupation as "Retired Teacher." [The details in this file are somewhat confusing, probably because of the alias and the individual strove to maintain his privacy, or because of the elapsed years when some of the information was provided.] Married Virginia Johnston y Cantu (age 14) in 1887 and had nine children. Mrs. Marsh received a widow's pension until her death (at age 93) in Feb 1966.

BENNICK / RENNICK, Franz A. —, Sweden
druggist 5' 8¹/₃" fair brown blue
14 July 1858 26 Ft. Leavenworth, KT Lt. J. P. Jones
Joined Co by enlistment. Died 2 Nov 1858 in hospital at Ft. Riley, KT, "by discharge of a pistol in the hands of Sergt. Peter Soukin [Socin] at Ft. Riley." A Pvt. An inventory of his personal effects showed he had "a Uniform Coat; 1 Pr. Trowsers [sic]; 1 Great Coat; and 1 blanket, — all worn."

BERLING, Frederick, E. O. Saxony, Germany
farmer 5' 5³/₄" fair fair blue
20 Oct 1860 23 Chicago, IL Lt. J. P. Jones
20 July 1864 27 near Atlanta, GA Lt. L. Smith
20 July 1867 30 Ft. Vancouver, WT Lt. Gilvray
Joined Co by transfer from general service recruits (SO#22, HQs, Dept of West, Springfield, MO, 7 July 1861). Appointed Cpl [nd]. Appointed Sgt 1 May 1864 (GO#7, HQs, 2nd Art, Ft. McHenry, MD, 9 March 1865). Reenlisted as Sgt. Discharged 21 July 1870 at Ft. Kodiak, AK. Expiration of service.

BINGHAM, William A. Prince George Co., VA
tailor 5' 5" fair sandy blue
1 Jan 1857 26 Hampton, VA Lt. Merchant
Discharged 1 Jan 1862 at Sedalia, MO. Expiration of service. A Pvt.

BLACK, Robert J. Aurelius, NY
farmer 5' 7" fair auburn hazel
19 Nov 1860 22 St. Louis, MO Lt. O'Connell
Joined Co by transfer from general service recruits (SO#22, HQs, Dept of West, Springfield, MO, 7 July 1861). Wounded 10 Aug 1861 at Battle of Wilson's Creek, MO. On 28 May 1862, at Farmington, MS, shot in the right shoulder, and kicked in the left shoulder by a dying horse. Remained in the field hospital for one month before being sent to the General Hospital at Evansville, IN. There for three months before rejoining the Co on 1 Oct 1862. Appointed Cpl 28 April 1863. Promoted to Sgt 3 Sept 1863. Discharged 5 Nov 1865 at New Orleans, LA. Expiration of service. Cpl with Co K, 1st US Art. Died in Thayer, KS on 10 May 1908.

BOKER, Albert —, Germany
— 5' 6" light light blue
20 July 1861 20 — —
1 Dec 1863 22 Prospect, TN Lt. Murray
Discharged 30 Nov 1863 from the 11th MO Vol Inf. Received a $25 bounty for enlisting in the regular army with Co F, 2nd US Art. Deserted 7 Aug 1865 enroute

from Chattanooga, TN to Baltimore, MD. A Pvt. Was granted an honorable discharge by a special act of Congress, approved by the President, 26 May 1902. This special act granted an honorable discharge "from said service and battery August 7th, 1865; provided, that no pay, bounty or other emoluments shall become due or payable by the passage of this bill." Died 4 Aug 1902; suffered from Bright's disease, prostration and "mental derangement at times."

BOLT, William
[no descriptive data]
[no enlistment data]
Died 21 Sept 1861 at Jefferson Bks, MO.

BOOTH, Abraham   Burslim, England
potter   5' 5³/₄"   ruddy   light   grey
13 Dec 1860   26   Newport, KY   Lt. Wilkins
General service recruit. Transferred to Jefferson Bks, MO 8 Jan 1861. Appears on MR of a detachment of the 4th US Art Jan–Feb 1861, a Pvt, present for duty at St. Louis Arsenal. Then present for duty with same detachment at Boonville, MO during May–June 1861. In summer of 1861, was assigned to Co M, 1st MO Lt Art by order of Gen Lyon. Joined Co F, 2nd US Art, from Co M, 1st MO Lt Art (SO#21, HQs, Dept of Army, WDC, 14 Jan 1864). Discharged 13 Dec 1865 at Benicia, CA. Expiration of service. A Pvt. After his discharge, lived in Beaver Falls, PA. Entered the National Military Home [Soldiers' Home] in Dayton, OH on 26 April 1900. Died there 15 March 1911.

BORDEN, Frederick   New York, NY
porter   5' 1"   black   dark   black
1 Jan 1855   16   New York, NY   Lt. Garnett
Discharged 1 Jan 1860 at Ft. Leavenworth, KT. Expiration of service. A Musician.

BOURKE, Michael   Galway, Ireland
soldier   5' 4¹/₂"   sallow   brown   grey
30 Nov 1860   26   St. Louis, MO   Lt. O'Connell
Transferred from general service recruits (SO#22, HQs, Dept of West, Springfield, MO, 7 July 1861). Died 28 Nov 1863 at Overton Hospital, Memphis, TN of chronic diarrhea. A Pvt.

BRENNAN, James   County Kings, Ireland
mason   5' 5"   fair   dark   blue
26 Nov 1860   32   Newport, KY   Lt. Wilkins
Transferred from general service recruits (SO#22, HQs, Dept of West, Springfield, MO, 7 July 1861). Sent to General Hospital, Army of the MS, 3 May 1862. Discharged 7 Oct 1862 at Newport, KY. Surgeon's certificate of disability (Ltr attached to MRF Aug–Oct 1862). A Pvt. "Said soldier was engaged in cleaning his revolver, after a skirmish with the enemy about 4 miles from Corinth, Mississippi, in the latter part of April 1862. While so engaged, the weapon was accidentally discharged, and his left hand injured thereby." The injury rendered him unfit for service.

BREWER, Raleigh   Kershaw Dist., NC
painter   5' 7"   dark   black   dark
12 Aug 1857   19yrs10mo   Charlotte, NC   Lt. J. P. Jones
26 Aug 1863   —   Ft. Leavenworth, KS   —

Joined Co 15 Aug 1857 at Ft. Monroe, VA. Appointed Cpl [May 1862 ?]. Discharged Aug 1862 at St. Louis, MO. Expiration of service. A Cpl. Worked as a teamster at Ft. Leavenworth, KS. Enlisted in 1863 with Co M, 5th KS Vol Cav, which became Co B, 15th KS Vol Cav. Mustered out 19 Oct 1865. A Sgt. Died 19 Jan 1907.

BROWN, Charles H.	Belleville, Canada			
teamster	6' 0"	fair	black	hazel
1 Dec 1860	22	Little Rock Ars., AR		Lt. Merchant

Deserted 13 March 1861 from Jefferson Bks, MO.

BROWN, Henry W.	Portsmouth, VA			
soldier	5' 8½"	dark	brown	grey
5 Dec 1855	38	Barrancas Bks., FL		Lt. Bingham
6 Oct 1860	—	Ft. Smith, AR		Lt. Riddick

[Above was his 7th enlistment (RG 391, Entry 68).]
Discharged 19 Jan 1862 at Sedalia, MO "by Order" [no other details given].

BRYAN / BRYANT, Franklin	Davidson, NC			
soldier	5' 9"	fair	brown	grey
22 June 1857	23	Salisbury, NC		Lt. J. P. Jones
22 June 1862	28	Ft. McHenry, MD		Lt. Grey

Transferred to Co I (SO#4, HQs, 2nd Art, Ft. McHenry, MD, 31 May 1862). Reenlisted 22 June 1862 for three years. Transferred to Co F, 1 Oct 1862. Discharged 23 April 1868. Expiration of service. Third enlistment.

BURKE, Richard	Connaught, Ireland			
peddler	5' 7½"[5]	fair	light	blue
28 Jan 1859	22	Ft. Riley, KT		Lt. Taylor

Discharged 28 Jan 1864 at Pulaski, TN. Expiration of service.

BURNS / BYRNE, Andrew	Dublin, Ireland			
laborer	5' 8¾"	fair	light	grey
6 Sept 1859	21	Ft. Leavenworth, KT		Lt. Haines

Deserted 21 April 1861 from St. Louis Ars, MO.

BUSCHELBERG, Victor	Darmstadt, Germany			
soldier	5' 8½"	—	sandy	brown
8 May 1860	29	Ft. Leavenworth, KT		—

Deserted 1 March 1862 from St. Louis, MO.

BUSSARD, Charles A. [alias for BUSSARD, Osee A.]				Akron, OH
carriagemaker	5' 7¾"	ruddy	sandy	grey
13 May 1861	21	Cincinnati, OH		Lt. Sweitzer
2 Sept 1864	24	Cincinnati, OH		—

Unassigned recruit. Joined Co F, 2nd US Art. Detached to Co M, 1st MO Lt Art. Served with that unit until reassigned to Co F, 2nd US Art (SO#21, HQs, Dept of Army, WDC, 14 Jan 1864). Discharged 28 May 1864. Expiration of service. A Pvt. Reenlisted in 1864 with Co K, 2nd MO Vol Cav, "Merrill's Horse." Discharged 15 June 1865. His name was distorted on his first enlistment; was advised to keep name "Charles A." to eliminate any confusion. Died in Marion, OH, 18 Dec 1908. Was working in Columbia, SC when the War began. To escape, enlisted in the

Columbia Flying Artillery. Managed to work his way "through the lines and reached Cincinnati." Enlisted in Co F, 2nd US Art. At Big Shanty, GA on or about 1 May 1865, developed rheumatism from exposure in a violent rain storm, and chilling winds. Affliction rendered him incapable of performing his duty, "except [he could] accompany his command back to Chattanooga, Tenn., where in a short time, to wit, three or four weeks, [he was] discharged."

BYRNE, Andrew [see BURNS / BYRNE, Andrew]

CAMP, Vardry   Cleveland Co., NC
    laborer   5' 9"   light   light   blue
    6 Aug 1857   23   Charlotte, NC   Lt. J. P. Jones
    Joined Co 15 Aug 1857 as recruit. Severely wounded 28 May 1862 near Farmington, MS. Sent to General Hospital, Army of the MS. Discharged 12 Aug 1862 at Corinth, MS [St. Louis, MO]. Expiration of service.

CAMPBELL, Peter   Amherst Co., VA
    farmer   5' 11½"[7]   fair   brown   blue
    1 April 1861   27   Jefferson Bks., MO   Capt. Totten
    Severely wounded 28 May 1862 near Farmington, MS. Sent to General Hospital, Army of the MS, 29 May 1862. Discharged 4 Nov 1862 at St. Louis, MO. Surgeon's certificate of disability. A Pvt.

CAMPBELL, Thomas   Lubrim [?], Ireland
    soldier   5' 7"   dark   dark   black
    30 Sept 1863   26   New York, NY   Capt. Hildt
    Paid $50 bounty for enlisting. Deserted 27 Nov 1864.

CARMINT / CARMAN, Moses V.   Tyrone, Ireland
    driver   5' 7½"   fair   brown   grey
    29 May 1856   (Co I, 10th Regt US Inf)
    11 Sept 1861   (Co D, PA Vol Cav)
    26 March 1862   —   Philadelphia, PA   Lt. Peirce
    16 Sept 1865   (Co D & B, 14th US Inf)
    31 Oct 1868   (Co M, 2nd US Art)
    28 Nov 1871   (Co G, 2nd US Art)
    30 Nov 1876   (Co G, 2nd US Art), in Camp,
                     nine miles from Ft. Sill, Indian Territory
    Was discharged 25 Jan 1862 from Co D, PA Vol Cav on a Surgeon's certificate of disability "Rheumatism." Paid $50 bounty on reenlistment with Co F, 2nd US Art on 26 March 1862. All other discharges were for "expiration of service" until his discharge from Co G, 2nd US Art on 3 May 1880 with another Surgeon's certificate of disability: "because of chronic rheumatism and old age." Went to San Antonio, TX, on his retirement. Was discharged from Ft. Brown, TX.

CARNEY, James   Cambridge, MA
    laborer   5' 7½"   ruddy   red   blue
    6 Dec 1849   24   Boston, MA   Lt. Jordan
    5 Oct 1854   29   Barrancas Bks., FL   Maj. Woodbridge
    5 Aug 1859   34   —   —
    Discharged 1 Aug 1868 from Co A. Expiration of service.

CARTER, George W.   Stanley Co., NC
  carpenter   5' 8"   fair   light   grey
  7 Oct 1857   21   Salisbury, NC   Lt. J. P. Jones
  Transferred from temporary attachment (Or#148, HQs, Ft. Riley, KT, 9 Dec 1858).
Discharged 4 April 1859 at Ft. Riley, KT. Surgeon's certificate of disability. Also
served with Co B, 2nd US Art. A Pvt.

CASPER, William F.   —, Virginia
  shoemaker   5' 9"   sallow   brown   blue
  22 Aug 1857   21[17]   Salisbury, NC   Lt. J. P. Jones
  22 June 1862   —   Ft. McHenry, MD   Lt. Grey
  Joined Co I, 2nd US Art 3 Sept 1857 at Ft. Monroe, VA by assignment. Reen-
listed 22 June 1862 at Ft. McHenry, MD for three years. Transferred to Co F, 23
June 1862. Discharged 22 June 1865 at Ft. Stevenson, AL. Expiration of service.
A Pvt. While still with Co I at Ft. McHenry in early 1862, but on detail with the
Ordnance Dept, Casper, a Virginian, was accused by one of his comrades of disloy-
alty. Casper wrote an appeal to the Cmdg Officer of the Regt, 2nd US Art, Col W.
W. Morris, "that I have never made remarks, that could injure the service and the
Government." In addition to affirmations from some of his comrades, the Ord-
nance Sgt Maj, G. H. Dailey, wrote: "I have no hesitation in saying that I firmly
believe that Casper would turn his face to the enemy as willingly as nine tenths of
the soldiers stationed at Fort McHenry [RG 391, Entry 61]." Died 20 Dec 1875 in
Baltimore, MD of Bright's disease at age 35. Buried in the Baltimore Cemetery,
Baltimore, MD.

CAVANAGH / KAVANAGH, Peter   Cork, Ireland
  carpenter   5' 10"   ruddy   brown   grey
  29 Aug 1860   33[36]   Newport, KY   Lt. Wilkins
  1 July 1864   35[40]   near Atlanta, GA   Lt. L. Smith
  Joined Co F as Pvt (SO#21, HQs, Dept of Army, WDC, 14 Jan 1864) from detached service with Co M, 1st MO Lt Art [made Cpl, 1 Feb 1862; Sgt, 16 Aug 1863].
Discharged 1 July 1867 at Ft. Vancouver, WT. Expiration of service. A Sgt. Died
and buried in Cappancur, County Offaly, Ireland, 10 March 1871. Married Margaret Tiernan in Nov 1867 upon return from US. Two daughters: Margaret and
Mary Ann. Wife died in 1930. Fought in the MO campaign. In MS at Farmington,
Blackland, Iuka, Corinth, and sieges of Vicksburg and Jackson; in the Red River
and Meridian Expeditions; at Ruff's Mill, and Atlanta, GA; and at Nashville, TN.
[Personal data and some military data per author's correspondence with Cavanagh's
great-grandson, Michael A. MacNamara, Newgarden, Castleconnell, County Limerick, Ireland.]

CHILDS, Charles Thorp [alias THORP, Charles / Isaacher]   Philadelphia, PA
  carpenter   5' 8"   ruddy   brown   blue
  10 Jan 1846   22   New Orleans, LA   —
  2 Dec 1851   27   Pittsburgh, PA   —
  20 Dec 1860   36   St. Louis, MO   Lt. O'Connell
  1 July 1864   40   near Atlanta, GA   Lt. Smith
  13 July 1868   44   Vancouver Ars., WT   —
  Charles Childs enlisted in 1846 and was wounded in the thigh during the Mexican War. The bullet was never removed. Discharged for disability 1 Feb 1848
from Co B, 8th US Inf at Mexico City. Enlisted in 1851 as Issacher Thorp in Co B,
2nd US Art. Discharged at Ft. Defiance, MN, 2 Dec 1856. A Pvt. Enlisted as

Charles Thorp in 1860 in St. Louis, MO with Co F, 2nd US Art. Retained that
name through the remainder of his enlistments. Was discharged 13 July 1871 at
Vancouver Ars, WT. A Cpl. The bullet in his left thigh eventually moved into his
leg. Admitted to the hospital at the Soldiers' Home in WDC on 8 Feb 1898. His leg
was amputated, but gangrene had set in. Died 11 Feb 1898. His effects were
returned to his wife on 21 Feb 1898 with a note which inventoried his belongings:
"One Hat, One red cotton handkerchief, one Tobacco pipe, one tobacco Bag, and
One Overcoat all of which are much worn and of little value. He left no money,
private papers, or Certificate of Discharge from the Army. His pension Certificate
has been returned to the Pension Bureau."

CLARK / CLARKE, Charles   Seneca, NY
  soldier   5' 9"   fair   brown   blue
  4 June 1839   25   Detroit, MI   —
  11 May 1844   30   Ft. Columbus, NY   —
  26 May 1849   35   Ft. Moultrie, SC   —
  25 May 1854   40   Barrancas Bks., FL   Lt. Molinard
  17 April 1858   45   Ft. Monroe, VA   Lt. Grey
    Enlisted in Co C, 2nd US Art, 1839. Transferred to Co K, 2nd US Art, July
1846; and to Co F, 2nd US Art, Dec 1847. Last enlistment was his 5th. Left in Ft.
Monroe, VA by Co F as too old for field service. Rejoined Co F and was discharged
31 May 1862 at Ft. Leavenworth, KS for disability. "He has served the Government long & faithfully (for more than twenty two years), & is virtually worn out in
the service."

COLLINS, John [alias FLYNN, Michael]   Salem Co., NJ
  laborer   5' 3½"   dark   black   hazel
  24 Aug 1863   16   Harrisburg, PA   Lt. Snyder
    Paid $175 for enlisting. Enlisted as John Collins. Joined Co F, 2nd US Art
from Ft. Columbus, New York Harbor. Deserted 18 Aug 1865. Apprehended 30
Aug 1865 and held at Ft. McHenry, MD as AWOL, "[He and his brother, Michael
Collins,] awaiting transportation to join their Company." Discharged 24 Aug
1868 at Ft. Stevens, OR. Expiration of service. A Pvt with Co C, 2nd US Art, to
which he had been transferred on 26 May 1865. [See next listing for Michael
Collins, brother. No pension file found on Michael.] Needed affidavits from former
comrades to prove that Michael Flynn was the same as John Collins. Two of
them identified him in 1897 or 1898 from the Soldiers' Home in Los Angeles, CA.
They had been in correspondence with him for years. Flynn lived in Philadelphia, PA. They received from him "a tin type of himself which they recognize as
their comrade..." Flynn also indicated that he had a tattoo, "Anchor and Shield
India Ink on left arm." Died 13 Aug 1913 at Philadelphia Hospital, following
throat operation.

COLLINS, Michael [alias? – no pension file found] Wilmington, DE
  farmer   5' 6"   dark   black   brown
  24 Aug 1863   19   Harrisburg, PA   Lt. Snyder
    Paid $175 bounty for enlisting. Deserter 18 Aug 1865. Apprehended from
AWOL 30 Aug 1865 and held at Ft. McHenry, MD. "Awaiting transportation to
join [his] Company." Discharged 24 Aug 1868 from Ft. Stevens, OR. Expiration
of service. A Pvt with Co C. [See above listing for brother John Collins, alias
Michael Flynn.]

CONNELL, Dennis   Armagh [Limerick], Ireland
   laborer   6' ¹/₄"   ruddy   brown   blue
   29 Dec 1849   23   Harrisburg, PA   Lt. Schneider
   28 Oct 1854   28   Barrancas Bks., FL   Maj. Woodbridge
   1 Sept 1859   33   Ft. Leavenworth, KT   —
Deserted in 1851. Apprehended [date not legible]. Discharged 28 Oct 1854 at
Barrancas Bks, FL for reenlistment. A Pvt. Appointed Sgt from Pvt (Or#45, HQs,
2nd Art, Ft. Hamilton, NY, 30 Dec 1858). [Subsequently reduced in rank?] Pvt
Connell was to be promoted to Sgt effective 4 May 1860. "Dennis Connell was
reduced to the ranks by a Garrison Courts Martial at Ft. Leavenworth, K.T., Order
No. 108 May 3, 1860 and on my account only" per 1st Lt Anderson Merchant, 4
May 1860, Ft. Leavenworth, KT (RG 391, Entry 48, loose Ltr). Deserted 21 Sept
1861 from Jefferson Bks, MO.

COONS, George   Elizabeth, PA
   soldier   5' 7"   ruddy   brown   blue
   28 Aug 1860   33   Chicago, IL   Lt. J. P. Jones
   Transferred from general service recruits (SO#22, HQs, Dept of West, Springfield, MO, 7 July 1861). Deserted 21 Sept 1861 from St. Louis, MO.

COTTON, William Lewis Shelby Co., IN
   farmer   5' 8"   fair   brown   brown
   16 April 1860   21   Ft. Leavenworth, KT   Lt. Barriger
Deserted 6 May 1860, less than a month after enlisting.

CROSBY, James Henderson   York Dist., SC
   carpenter   5' 9"   dark   dark   hazel
   5 Aug 1857   21   Charlotte, NC   Lt. J. P. Jones
   Joined Co as recruit 15 Aug 1857. Wounded 10 Aug 1861 at Battle of Wilson's
Creek, MO. The wound was made by a minie ball which entered in the inner side
of the right leg, passed obliquely through the lower third of the tibia, and embedded itself in the inner side of the fibula. It was extracted by cutting down on the
other side of the leg. Discharged 7 Jan 1862 at St. Louis, MO on a Surgeon's
certificate of disability. After his discharge, served as a mess cook for the US
Government at Rolla and St. Louis, MO. Drove a street car in St. Louis. Then
again became head cook for the Government at Little Rock, AR. He and his assistant cook were captured by the Confederates and taken to Magnolia, AR. Then
sent "to the prison pen at Sweezeport Louissia [Shreveport, LA]." In prison four
months before being exchanged and returned to Little Rock. Born 12 Sept 1825 in
Yorkville, SC; died 4 Sept 1915 in Statesville, NC.

DARBY, Thomas   London, England
   clerk   5' 9¹/₄"   light   brown   blue
   19 Nov 1855   31   Barrancas Bks., FL   Lt. J. D. Bingham
Discharged at Ft. Smith, AR 19 Nov 1860. Expiration of service. A Pvt.

DAVIS, Samuel L.   Davy Co., NC
   teamster   6' 0"   ruddy   brown   brown
   2 Nov 1857   28   Charlotte, NC   Lt. J. P. Jones
   Transferred from temporary attachment (Or#148, HQs, Ft. Riley, KT, 9 Dec 1858).
Discharged at Corinth, MS on 3 Nov 1862. Expiration of service. A Pvt [at Grand
Junction, TN as of 2 Nov 1862 (M233, Roll 26)].

DENNIS, Fred [also FREED, Dennis]   Londonderry, Ireland
   laborer   5' 7½"   fair   brown   blue
   19 Aug 1863   23   New York, NY   Capt. Hildt
   Deserted from Buffalo, NY before joining Co, 25 Oct 1863.

DEWEY, Lewis Edward   Conneaut, OH
   farmer   5' 9½"   light   brown   blue
   23 Oct 1860   17   Chicago, IL   Lt. J. P. Jones
   General service recruit assigned to Co F, 2nd US Art from Newport Bks, KY, 7 July 1861. Appointed Cpl, 1 Nov 1863. Transferred to Co L, 1st US Art, and discharged 23 Oct 1865 from Ft. McHenry, MD [or Ft. Schuyler, NY]. "When I enlisted, I gave my age as 21. My true age at that time was 17 years, 5 months & 13 days. This was so I would not be rejected because of age." Born 13 Nov 1845. Died of Bright's disease on 11 Feb 1918 at Fairmount, NE. Buried in Edgar, NE.

DEY, Gustavus Adolphus   Konigsburg, Prussia
   farmer   5' 8¼"   fair   brown   grey
   18 Dec 1854   27   New York, NY   Lt. R. Garnett
   18 Oct 1859   32   Ft. Leavenworth, KT   Lt. Haines
   Joined Co I at Ft. Deynaud, FL from Gen Dept 18 Jan 1855. Appointed Cpl, 1 Dec 1856 (Or#54, HQs, 2nd Art, Ft. Hamilton, NY, 23 Dec 1856). Appoint Sgt 1 June 1857 (Or#23, HQs, 2nd Art, Ft. Monroe, VA 12 June 1857). Transferred to Co F, 1 Sept 1857 (SO#24, HQs, 2nd Art, Ft. Monroe, VA, 3 Sept 1857). Reduced to Pvt by General Garrison Court-Martial (SO#208, HQs, Ft. Leavenworth, KT, 30 Nov 1857). Appointed Cpl, 18 Nov 1858 at Ft. Riley, KT (Or#45, HQs, 2nd Art, Ft. Hamilton, NY, 30 Dec 1858). Reenlisted 18 Oct 1859. Promoted to Sgt 1 April 1861 (Or#48, HQs, 2nd Art, Ft. Monroe, VA, 6 April 1861). Promoted to 1st Sgt 1 May 1862. Wounded at Battle of Corinth, MS, 4 Oct 1862. Relieved as 1st Sgt 1 Nov 1862. Reinstated as 1st Sgt June 1863. Discharged 26 Nov 1863 by reason of promotion to 2nd Lt, Co F, 2nd US Art, as of 31 Oct 1863. Assigned to duty in Co (SO#175, HQs, Fuller's Brigade, 7 Dec 1863). Ordered by Gen Grenville Dodge to join his new Co E at Knoxville, TN (SO#18, HQs, Left Wing, XVI Army Corps, Pulaski, TN, 18 Jan 1864). Joined Co E at Ft. Sanders, TN, 28 Jan 1864, 1st Division, IX Army Corps, Dept of OH. Promoted to 1st Lt 15 June 1864. Commanded Co C, Camp Barry, WDC, April–June 1865. AWOL as of 30 June 1865. Dropped from rolls 6 Oct 1865. Died 14 Feb 1882 in Dunkirk, NY. Buried in Forest Hill Cemetery, Fredonia, NY.

DILLON, Owen   —, Ireland
   soldier   5' 6"   fair   light   blue
   29 Dec 1860   21   Newport Bks., KY   Lt.Wilkins
   1 July 1864   24   near Atlanta, GA   Lt. Smith
   1 July 1867   27   Ft. Vancouver, WT   Lt. McGilvray
   General service recruit assigned to Co F, 2nd US Art on 7 July 1861. Appointed Cpl, 1 June 1868. Discharged 1 July 1870 at Ft. Kodiak, AK. Expiration of service. Third enlistment. A Cpl. Died 10 July 1895. Buried in National Cemetery, San Francisco, CA. Named guardian of Sgt Thomas Grant's daughter, Johanna, after Grant's death. [See subsequent listing for Grant.]

DONIGAN, Bernard [see DUNNIGAN / DONIGAN, Bernard]

DONNELLY, Owen   Tyrone, Ireland
farmer   5' 5¹/₂"   light   light   grey
21 June 1859   22   Ft. Leavenworth, KT   Lt. Bailey
Discharged at St. Louis, MO 8 May 1862. [His pension file indicates that he was discharged at Jefferson Bks, MO on 12 Nov 1862.] Surgeon's certificate of disability. A Pvt. While on duty at camp three miles from Sedalia, MO, on or about Feb 1862, "or immediately after the 2d Battle of Springfield [probably part of the Fremont campaign in southwest MO?], while leading his horse to water, he was kicked in the right knee by the animal and had the right knee pan or cap seriously fractured and said fracture rendered him unfit for further service." His medical record shows that he was sent to City General Hospital in St. Louis, MO for "Rheumatismus, diagnosis also appears as Synovitis. Vul Sclopet [?] & Debility." On 11 April 1862, sent to New House of Refuge, General Military Hospital, St. Louis, MO, diagnosed with "Vul Sclop R. Knee." "Discharged from service May 8/62, cause, Partially [illegible] fracture of right patella." After his discharge, lived in TX and Florence, AZ from whence his pension claim was filed.

DOOLING, Richard   Kilkenny, Ireland
laborer   5' 10¹/₂"   fair   brown   blue
26 May 1860   26   Ft. Leavenworth, KT   Lt. Barriger
Discharged at St. Louis, MO, 19 Sept 1861 for wounds received at the Battle of Wilson's Creek, 10 Aug 1861. A Pvt. Received a gun shot wound in the left arm; "ball cut out." On his disability certificate, Capt Totten, Cmdg Co F, 2nd US Art, noted that Dooling's character was "Very Good." His pension application, #75, was filed 4 Oct 1861 in St. Louis, MO.

DOYLE, William   Dublin, Ireland
laborer   5' 6¹/₂"   fair   light   blue
25 Oct 1859   21   Ft. Leavenworth, KT   Lt. Haines
Deserted from Jefferson Bks, MO, 7 April 1861.

DULKEWITZ, Charles   Augustow, Poland
soda water maker   5' 6"   fair   brown   hazel
12 Oct 1853   21   New York, NY   Col. Casey
1 Sept 1858   26   Ft. Leavenworth, KT   —
29 July 1863   31   Memphis, TN   Lt. Murray
Joined Co F by transfer from Co A, 3rd US Art (SO#301, HQs, Ft. Leavenworth, KT, 21 Aug 1858), as Sgt. Appointed Farrier 9 Nov 1862. Deserted 1 Sept 1863 from camp near Iuka, MS.

DUNNIGAN / DONIGAN, Bernard   Manchester, England
soldier   5' 7"   fair   brown   grey
22 April 1854   21   New Orleans, LA   Lt. Taylor
24 June 1859   26   [3rd enlistment, a Pvt]   —
Deserted 3 July 1854 from Co M, 2nd US Art, from Baton Rouge, LA. Enlisted in Navy. Apprehended 3 Nov 1854 and claimed by Maj Woodbridge, Cmdg Co F (Ltr 3 Nov 1854, Barrancas Bks, FL, RG 391, Entry 53). Appointed Cpl, 1 Sept 1857. Promoted to Sgt 1 Sept 1862. Promoted to 1st Sgt. Recommended for commission after Battle of Corinth, 4 Oct 1862. Never appointed. Discharged 29 May 1863 (GO#96, HQs, XVI Army Corps).

EBEYCHIEN, Christian
[no descriptive data]
[no enlistment data]
Transferred from general service recruits (SO#22, HQs, Dept of West, Springfield, MO, 7 July 1861). Deserted from St. Louis, MO, 21 Sept 1861.

ECHO, Boston K.   Cumberland Co., OH
    farmer   5' 8"   fair   brown   blue
    5 Oct 1863   19   Harrisburg, PA   Lt. Snyder
    Paid bounty of $200 for enlisting. Appointed Cpl, 1 June 1868. Discharged at
Ft. Kodiak, AK, 5 Oct 1868. Expiration of service. A Pvt.

ELLER, Henry [see BECK, Henry]

EMERY, Louis   Baden, Germany
    gardener   5' 5½"   fair   auburn   blue
    21 Nov 1860   [19]   Newport Bks., KY   Lt. Wilkins
    20 Aug 1878   37   New York, NY   Capt. Chaffee
    First assigned to Co F, 2nd US Art. Transferred to Co K, 1st US Art in Nov
1865. Discharged at New Orleans, LA, 21 Nov 1865. Expiration of service. A Pvt.
Reenlisted in Co D, 7th US Cav in 1878. Discharged 8 Aug 1880 at Ft. Yates, DT,
Surgeon's certificate of disability, general debility. Also had suffered deafness at
the Siege of Vicksburg, MS, in June 1863. Application for increased pension at age
52, submitted from the Soldiers' Home, WDC, 6 Dec 1890.

ENGLEBERT / ENGLEBECK, Joseph Wayne, Co., IN
    painter   5' 6½"   fair   sandy   blue
    27 May 1861   18   Cincinnati, OH   Lt. Sweitzer
    7 Sept 1864   21   Cincinnati, OH   —
    Unassigned recruit. Joined Co from Co M, 1st MO Lt Art (SO#21, HQs, Dept of
Army, WDC, 14 Jan 1864). Discharged 27 May 1864 at Vicksburg, MS. Expiration
of service. A Pvt. Reenlisted in Sept 1864 in Co K, 13th OH Vol Cav. Discharged
at camp near Petersburg, VA 8 June 1865. AGO record in his pension file shows
him as an unassigned recruit at Carlisle Bks, PA, in June 1861. At the same time,
the record shows him as transferred to a Regiment of Mounted Rifles, unspecified.
Also shown later (1864) to have been assigned to Co F, 2nd US Art, and then placed
on detached service with Co M, 1st MO Lt Art. In a general affidavit, a comrade
claims him to have contracted rheumatism at Pittsburg Landing, TN in April 1862,
and also to have suffered deafness of the right ear caused by cannon firing. At the
Siege of Vicksburg, MS, contracted typhoid fever in the summer of 1863. Spent
about 7 weeks in the military hospital at Vicksburg recovering from his illness.
Died in the Soldiers' Home in Sandusky, Erie Co., OH, 24 March 1908.

ENRIGHT, Thomas   County Kerry, Ireland
    laborer   5' 4½"   ruddy   brown   hazel
    3 Dec 1860   24[32]   Detroit, MI   Lt. Fink
    3 Jan 1866   29[38]   —   —
    23 Jan 1869   32[41]   —   —
    24 Jan 1872   35[44]   —   —
    24 Jan 1877   40[49]   —   —
    24 Jan 1882   45[54]   Ft. Thornburgh;
                                      in UT Territory   Lt. Dinkins

Unassigned recruit. Joined Co from Co M, 1st MO Lt Art (SO#21, Hqs, Dept of Army, WDC, 14 Jan 1864). Discharged 3 Dec 1865 at Benicia, CA. Expiration of service. A Pvt. The remainder of his service was with Companies I, F and D, 6th US Inf. In 1869, was discharged at Charleston, SC. In 1872, discharged at Ft. Hays, KS. Was discharged on 3 May 1884 at Ft. Douglas, UT Terr after 23 years service, "being broken down from hard service, and old age." Born in Ballylongford, County Kerry, Ireland, on 25 Feb 1828; came to the US in 1848. Claims to have been "about 29 years old when I enlisted." [If birth date is correct, Enright would have been 32 years old, not 29, when he enlisted. However, the record shows him as 24 years old at his first enlistment!] Died 12 Dec 1912 in the Soldiers' Home Hospital, WDC.

ERASMY, John   Milwaukee, WI
laborer   5' 6"   ruddy   black   brown
5 Nov 1860   [30]   Chicago, IL   Lt. J. P. Jones
     Assigned to Co F, 2nd US Art. Was attached to Co M, 1st MO Lt Art from Jan 1861 to Feb 1864. Transferred to Co K, 1st US Art in Aug 1865. Discharged at Baltimore, MD on 5 Nov 1865. Expiration of service. A Pvt. Contracted rheumatism, and suffered from general debility, as a result of "hard marching in the Spring of 1862 on the march to New Madrid, Mo." Suffered from heart disease, and at the age of 62, resided in the National Military Home in Milwaukee, WI.

EVERT, Charles   Gottenburg, Sweden
painter   5' 9¼"   fair   light   grey
27 Dec 1860   22   Newport, KY   Lt. Wilkins
     Transferred from general service recruits (SO#22, Hqs, Dept of West, Springfield, MO, 7 July 1861). Deserted from St. Louis, MO, 21 Sept 1861.

FAGG, James A.   Richmond, VA
carpenter   5' 9"   fair   brown   grey
7 Dec 1860   22   Little Rock Ars., AR   Lt. Merchant
Discharged at Jefferson Bks, MO, 1 April 1861. Disability. A Pvt.

FAHRENBAKER, Joseph   —, Germany
soldier   5' 6"   dark   black   grey
20 July 1861   20   Olney, IL   —
1 Dec 1863   23   Prospect, TN   Lt. Murray
     Enlisted in Co E, 11th MO Inf. Discharged 30 Nov 1863. Reenlisted in Co F, 2nd US Art. Received $25 bounty. Transferred to Co L, 26 May 1868. Discharged 1 Dec 1868 at Ft. Vancouver, WT. Expiration of service. A Pvt. Was disabled in the summer of 1867 at Vancouver, WT. While driving a team of mules, the mule which he was riding fell, throwing him on the hames [part of horse collar], causing a rupture. Died 7 July 1900 in Bogota, Jasper Co., IL.

FALLBRIGHT, William   Philadelphia, PA
shoemaker   —   —   —   —
3 Oct 1855   21   Philadelphia, PA   —
27 Dec 1860   26   Newport Bks., KY   Lt. Wilkins
     Deserted 24 April 1856; apprehended 29 Apr 1856, Ft. Stanton, NM. Deserted 2 June 1856, while awaiting sentence of General Court-Martial. Apprehended 22 Aug 1856 near San Antonio, NM. Deserted from confinement 26 May 1857; apprehended same day; tried by General Court-Martial and found guilty of all three

desertions (per SO#65 of 1856, and SO#15 of 1858, Dept of NM). Sentenced to be confined for the remainder of his enlistment. Discharged 3 Oct 1860 at Pecos River, TX. Expiration of service. A Pvt. Reenlisted in Co F, 2nd US Art in Dec 1860. On detached service with Companies M and H, 1st MO Lt Art from 1862 to 1864. Was with a section of Co M at Vicksburg, MS in 1863–64. Transferred back to Co F (SO#21, HQs, Dept of Army, WDC, 14 Jan 1864). Deserted from Louisville, KY, 7 Aug 1865. An Artificer. Died 28 June 1884 of heart disease and strangulated hernia in Frankford, Philadelphia, PA. Widow's pension claim rejected, 3 Oct 1902: "Soldier having deserted from his command on Aug. 7, 1865, and failed to receive a final honorable discharge, claimant has no pensionable status under Act of June 27, 1890."

FARRELEY, Garrett   Donegal, Ireland
—   5' 6³/₄"   fair   brown   blue
19 June 1862   22   New York, NY   Lt. Sprole
Discharged 19 June 1865 at Bridgeport, AL. Expiration of service.

FARRELL, Thomas   Londonderry, Ireland
bricklayer   5' 6³/₄"   fair   —   —
25 Aug 1863   26¹/₂   New York, NY   Lt. Hildt
Deserted 19 Aug 1865. Apprehended 1 July 1872 and erroneously...[not legible].

FELKER, John   Quincy, IL
musician   5' ¹/₂"   fair   light   blue
1 Jan 1863   16   Corinth, MS   Capt. Molinard
Bugler, enlisted for 5 years at Corinth. Killed by lightning near the Chattahoochee River, GA, 14 July 1864. [See subsequent listings for John Pratt and Thomas Smith.]

FISHER, John Jackson   Pottsville, PA
carpenter   5' 8¹/₂"   ruddy   brown   grey
5 Dec 1860   22   Chicago, IL   Lt. J. P. Jones
Regular recruit on detached service with Co M, 1st MO Lt Art from the 4th US Art. Transferred to Co F (SO#21, HQs, Dept of Army, WDC, 14 Jan 1864). Taken prisoner near Atlanta, GA, 22 July 1864. Exchanged on 18 or 22 Sept 1864 at a point between Lovejoy and Rough and Ready, GA. Discharged at Benicia Bks, CA, 5 Dec 1865. Expiration of service. A Pvt. Born 15 July 1838 [or 1839]. Died 15 Nov 1912 in Los Angeles, CA. In addition to the illnesses contracted at Andersonville during his captivity, previously had suffered from "sun pain" or "sun stroke" at the time of the capture of Island No. 10, MO, April 1862. Then, along with most of the detachment from Co M, 1st MO Lt Art, during the Vicksburg Campaign, became sick from using water from Baker's Creek, which had become contaminated from the unburied bodies of the dead from the Battle of Champion's Hill, 16 May 1863.

FLYNN, Michael [see COLLINS, John]

FORAN, Michael   Tipperary, Ireland
laborer   5' 7"   fair   brown   grey
6 July 1860   24   Ft. Leavenworth, KT   Lt. Barriger
Discharged at Jefferson Bks, MO, 1 April 1861 by sentence of General Court-Martial (SO#35, HQs, Dept of West, St. Louis, MO, 1 April 1861).

FRANK, John H. / Jacob —, Germany
  butcher 5' 8" ruddy sandy hazel
  24 Jan 1852 27[?] Syracuse, NY Capt. Robinson
  24 Dec 1856 — Hampton, VA Lt. Merchant
  At reenlistment in Co F on 24 Dec 1856, was a Sgt. Appointed Cpl 22 Aug 1859
  at Ft. Leavenworth, KT (SO#28, HQs, Ft. Leavenworth, KT, 24 Aug 1859). Died at
  Ft. Leavenworth, KT, 1 July 1860 of apoplexy. At the time of his death, he owed
  the laundress, Mrs. Brown, $4.00 and the sutler, Hiram Rich, $23.30.

FRANKLIN, Vardy Lehigh[?], Co., PA
  farmer 5' 5" sallow brown grey
  13[16] Sept 1863 18 Harrisburg, PA Lt. Snyder
  Joined Co from depot; received $50 bounty for enlisting. Killed at the battle
  near Atlanta, GA, 22 July 1864. A Pvt.

FREED, Dennis [see DENNIS, Fred]

FULLER, James H. Springfield, PA
  — 5' 1/6" dark dark light
  10 Sept 1863 44 Towanda, PA Lt. Pike
  Deserted 18 Aug 1865. Released from service, 22 July 1891 by Act of Congress
  which approved his application. Contended in pension testimony 22 Aug 1891
  that "on the 18th day of August 1865 [at Ft. McHenry, MD] he being then sick with
  chronic Diarrhea obtained a pass or permit from his Commanding Officer among
  others Lieut. [Rezin Gist] Howell then commanding his company to go home. And
  that he then did go home in pursuance of said permit or pass and remained pros-
  trate by such sickness for nearly four years thereafter, and did not know where to
  find his said Company or Regiment. And being ignorant of military laws & rules
  [he] did not know where to enquire for the whereabouts of said company and supposed that as when needed he would be notified (would be ready & willing) to
  return to his duties as a soldier whenever called upon. He never reported and
  never received a discharge from the said organization." He then lived in Alma city,
  Waseca Co., WI.

FULTON, Joseph Derry, Ireland
  laborer 5' 9½" fair auburn blue
  13 July 1853 21 Philadelphia, PA Capt. Burbank
  Joined Co by transfer from Co A, 2nd US Art (Or#23, HQs, 2nd Art Battalion,
  Ft. Leavenworth, KT, 1 May 1858). Discharged at Ft. Leavenworth, KT, 13 July
  1858. Expiration of service. [Disability (RG 391, Entry 68).] A Sgt.

GARRY, James H. [alias McGARRY, James H.] —
  — 5' 7¾" ruddy black hazel
  31 July 1860 21[30] Chicago, IL Lt. O'Connell
  1 July 1864 25½[34] camp near Atlanta, GA Lt. Murray
  Transferred to Co F, 2nd US Art from general service recruits (SO#22, HQs,
  Dept of West, Springfield, MO, 7 July 1861). Promoted to Cpl, 1 Oct 1862. Reduced
  to Pvt 30 May 1863. Appointed Cpl 3 Sept 1863. Promoted to Sgt 3 Jan 1864
  (GO#7, HQs, 2nd Art, Ft. McHenry, MD, 9 March 1865 [delayed paperwork]). Discharged 1 July 1864 for reenlistment, same Co. A Sgt. Deserted 18 Aug 1865 from
  Ft. McHenry, MD. Applied for disability pension in July 1894, under the name of
  James H. McGarry. Claims to have lost his discharge papers. Rejected. No indica-
  tion in file as to disposition for desertion. Born about 1830; lived in Amsterdam, NY.

GIBBINS, Nathaniel   Pittsburgh, PA
  soldier   5' 6"   ruddy   brown   hazel
  13 March1857   18   Pittsburgh, PA   —
  13 March 1862   23   New Madrid, MO   Lt. Darling
  10 April 1865   26   Pittsburgh, PA   Lt. Williams
  10 April 1868   29   Vancouver Ars., WT   —
  Assigned to Troop E, 2nd Regt Dragoons, 1857. Transferred to Battery B, 4th
US Art, 14 March 1860. Deserted 11 Oct 1861 from St. Joseph, MO. [Records fail
to show the date he rejoined the service from reported desertion. No record of trial
for desertion or evidence of restoration to duty without trial or order.] Temporarily
assigned to Co F, 2nd US Art, 20 Feb 1862. Discharged 13 March 1862, expiration
of service. Reenlisted in Co F same day. Taken prisoner near Atlanta, GA 22 July
1864. Was imprisoned at Andersonville, and at Florence, SC. Exchanged at Savannah, GA 17 Dec 1864. Reported at Annapolis, MD 24 Dec 1864. Discharged at
Camp Parole, MD, 13 March 1865 [or at Little Rock, AR on 19 March 1865; a Sgt
(M233, Roll 27)?]. Reenlisted in Co F, 10 April 1865. Temporarily attached to Co K
(SO#38, HQs, 2nd Art, Ft. McHenry, MD, 20 April 1865). Transportation requested
for Gibbins and his wife [Mary Carnes Muhlrelin, laundress in same Co] to Bridgeport, AL to join Co F, 31 May 1865. Appointed Cpl, 1 June 1865. [See Ltrs 14 Jan,
13 April, 22 April, and 31 May 1865; RG 391, Entry 48.] Appointed Sgt 1 Sept
1865. "Discharged at Vancouver Arsenal, W.T., Feby 19/71 per S.O. No. 43, A.G.O.
1871, a Corporal. Was discharged upon the recommendation of his immediate
commanding officer." Died 19 Aug 1916 at age 79 in the National Soldiers' Home,
WDC. Had also been an inmate in the National Military Homes in Montgomery
Co., OH, and Marion, IN.

GLENDENING / GLENDENNING, Reuben L.   —, PA
  farmer   5' 6¼"   light   sandy   grey
  25 Oct 1860   21   Cleveland, OH   Lt. Clendon
  8 July 1864   —   Atlanta, GA   —
  Transferred from general service recruits (SO#22, HQs, Dept of West, Springfield, MO, 7 July 1861). Discharged 1 July 1867. Expiration of service.

GOLDRICK, Patrick   Sligo, Ireland
  tinsmith   5' 7"   ruddy   red   grey
  30 Oct 1854   22   Buffalo, NY   Capt. Stevenson
  1 Oct 1859   27   Ft. Leavenworth, KT   —
  Joined Co I, 2nd US Art from Gen Dept, Ft. Columbus, NY 18 Jan 1855. Transferred to Co F, 1 Sept 1857 at Ft. Monroe, VA (SO#24, HQs, 2nd Art, Ft. Monroe,
VA, 3 Sept 1857). Discharged 30 Oct 1859 at Ft. Leavenworth, KT (M233, Roll 24).
[Conflicts with RG 391, Entry 68, which shows he reenlisted in Co on 1 Oct 1859.]

GOSLING, Joseph   Cincinnati, OH
  cook   5' 8½"   fair   light   blue
  13 June 1859   21½   Ft. Leavenworth, KT   Lt. Bailey
  Deserted from Ft. Leavenworth, KT 10 July 1859 [with less than one month's
service].

GRANT, Thomas   Tipperary, Ireland
  soldier   5' 6"   fair   auburn   hazel
  31 Aug 1860   22   Newport, KY   Lt. Wilkins
  20 July 1864   26   Atlanta, GA   Lt. Murray

Transferred to Co F, 2nd US Art from general service recruits (SO#22, HQs, Dept of West, Springfield, MO, 7 July 1861). Appointed Cpl [nd]. Promoted to Sgt 1 Sept 1862 (GO#7, HQs, 2nd Art, Ft. Mchenry, MD, 9 March 1865 [significantly delayed paperwork!]). Appointed 1st Sgt upon accidental death of 1st Sgt John Pratt (14 July 1864). 1st Sgt at Benicia, CA, Oct 1865. Appointed Sgt 20 July 1867 into 3rd enlistment. Died of "Oedamaglottis" [excessive fluid swelling between vocal cords] 4 Dec 1868 at Ft. Kodiak, AK. Married a minor, Mary Ann Whelan in San Francisco, CA, 24 Sept 1865. Subsequently named a comrade, Owen Dillon [see previous listing] as guardian of his daughter, Johannah.

HALTEMAN, Henry   Dayton, OH
laborer   5' 5½"   florid   lt. brn.   hazel
18 Dec 1860   19   Newport, KY   Lt. Wilkins
Transferred to Co F, 2nd US Art from general service recruits (SO#22, HQs, Dept of West, Springfield, MO, 7 July 1861). Deserted 18 Aug 1865 from Ft. McHenry, MD. A Pvt. Pension application submitted 1 Feb 1883 on grounds of having contracted rheumatism and deafness in Feb or March 1861, through exposure. Was treated in the St. Louis Ars Hospital. Claim rejected because of charge of desertion not removed from his record. On 2 March 1911, through an act of Congress: "[Private—No. 249] [H.R. 20603.] An Act For the relief of Henry Halteman. ...now resident of Ohio, shall hereafter be held and considered to be honorably discharged from the military service of the United States as a private in Battery F, Second United States Artillery, on the eighteenth day of August, eighteen hundred and sixty-five: Provided, That no pension shall accrue prior to the passage of this act." Died 14 April 1917, Dayton, OH.

HAND, Randolph [see RANDOLPH, John]   Hathaway, NY
carpenter   5' 7"   ruddy   brown   hazel
24 Nov 1860   27   St. Louis, MO   Lt. O'Connell
Transferred to Co F, 2nd US Art from general service recruits (SO#22, HQs, Dept of West, Springfield, MO, 7 July 1861). Died 4 Oct 1862 of wounds in the Battle of Corinth, MS. A Pvt.

HART, Martin   Dublin, Ireland
soldier   5' 4"   fair   black   blue
1 April 1853   23   Ft. Capron, FL   —
Resigned as Cpl on 31 Aug 1856 (Or#37, HQs, 2nd Art, Ft. Hamilton, NY, 21 Sept 1856). Discharged 1 April 1858 at Ft. Monroe, VA. A Pvt.

HAUSER, John   —, Germany
carpenter   5' 6¼"   fair   black   blue
27 Dec 1860   21   Newport, KY   Lt. Wilkins
Transferred to Co F, 2nd US Art from general service recruits (SO#22, HQs, Dept of West, Springfield, MO, 7 July 1861). Deserted 21 Sept 1861 from St. Louis, MO.

HAVENS, Luther   Exeter, WI
farmer   —   —   —   —
11 Sept 1861   24   Camp Randall;
                                     at Madison, WI   Capt. S. Estes
Enrolled as Pvt in Co H, 8th WI Vol Inf. Detached to Co F, 2nd US Art, 10 Aug 1862. "Luther Havens, Private, 2d US Arty., Co. F, Captd. Atlanta, Ga. July 22,

1864. [Was imprisoned in Andersonville.] Delivered N.E. Bridge, N.C., Feby. 27, '65. Arrived College Green Bks., Mch. 10, '65. Sent to Camp Parole. The name appears in the Camp Parole books but opposite in pencil 'Did not Report' — Clothing A/C $49.15. Pay A/C $– (RG 391, Entry 61)." Was mustered out of service by reason of expiration of three years service, effective 27 Oct 1864. Died 11 March 1866, Dayton, WI, after having filed application for pension on 16 Feb 1866.

HENDRICKS, Joseph A. Mecklenburg, NC
wagon maker	5' 10"	fair	brown	grey
12 Aug 1857	22	Charlotte, NC		Lt. J. P. Jones
24 July 1863	28	Leavenworth, KS		—

Discharged 12 Aug 1862 at Camp Clear Creek, near Corinth, MS. Expiration of service. A Pvt. Enlisted in 1863 in Co M, 5th KS Cav. Transferred to Co B, 15th KS Cav. Deserted 25 Aug 1865. Returned voluntarily 29 Sept 1865. Mustered out with the Co at Ft. Leavenworth, KS, in Oct 1865. Claimed chronic rheumatism contracted in 1864 at the Trading Post "on the line of the States of Kansas and Missouri." According to a comrade, was on scout and carrying dispatches, "For several weeks, about that time [1864], the labor was very severe. We frequently received orders like this, 'put this through, don't spare horse flesh.' For several weeks we had little rest, day or night." Born 3 March 1835. Died 3 Feb 1913, at the National Military Home, Leavenworth, KS. Buried in Mount Muncie Cemetery, Leavenworth, KS.

HENNESSY, Patrick Cork, Ireland
laborer	5' 10¼"	fair	brown	hazel
26 June 1850	21	New York, NY		Maj. P. Kearney
17 Sept 1855	26	—		—
14 Nov 1860	31	St. Louis, MO		Lt. O'Connell
24 Nov 1865	36	Watervleit Ars.; at Troy, NY		—
25 Nov 1868	39	Watervleit Ars.; at Troy, NY		—

Assigned to Co C, 3rd US Art from general depot, Carlisle Bks, PA, 1850. Discharged 26 June 1855 at Ft. Washita, Indian Terr. Assigned to Co D, Mounted Rifles, 1855. Discharged 17 Sept 1860 at Ft. Union, NM. A Pvt. Transferred to Co F from general service recruits (SO#22, HQs, Dept of West, Springfield, MO, 7 July 1861). Promoted to Cpl, 1 Oct 1862. Promoted to Sgt 1 July 1863. Taken prisoner near Atlanta, GA, 22 July 1864. Transferred to Co L, 1st US Art. Discharged 14 Nov 1865 at Ft. Schuyler, NY. Expiration of service. A Pvt. Assigned to Ordnance Corps, 1865. Discharged 24 Nov 1868. Expiration of service. A Cpl. Reenlisted in same organization, 1868. "Discharged by virtue of Special Orders, No. 153, Hdqrs. of the Army dated June 25, 1869, at Watervliet Arsenal, NY, A Private, (upon his request, to enable him to support his family)." While imprisoned at Andersonville, GA, in 1864, Sgt Hennessy contracted malaria and developed liver problems. After his parole at Rough and Ready, GA, he spent time in the General Hospital in Nashville, TN. Then in Nov 1864, he was sent to the General Hospital at Jefferson Bks, MO. Born 1829. Died 17 June 1880 of malaria and cirrhosis of the liver. Buried in St. Mary's Cemetery, Albany, NY.

HILL, Milton Mecklenburg, NC
| cabinet maker | 5' 8" | fair | brown | grey |
| 13 Aug 1857 | 25 | Charlotte, NC | | Lt. J. P. Jones |

Deserted 16 Dec 1857 from Ft. Leavenworth, KT.

HOCKSTADTER, Andrew Bavaria, Germany
farmer   5' 7½"   fair   brown   blue
4 Nov 1854   22   New York, NY   Col. Brown
5 Nov 1859   27   Ft. Leavenworth, KT   —
Joined Co I from Gen Dept, Ft. Columbus, NY, 18 Jan 1855. Transferred to Co
F, 1 Sept 1857 (SO#24, HQs, 2nd Art, Ft. Monroe, VA, 3 Sept 1857). Discharged 23
May 1861 by order of Cmdg Gen, Dept of West, at St. Louis, MO. Became 1st Sgt,
Co K, 1st MO Lt Art. [See *OR: Armies*, Volume XVII, Series I, page 270, for cita-
tion at Battle of Corinth, MS.]

HOGAN, Patrick   —, Ireland
laborer   5' 8"   ruddy   brown   hazel
31 Oct 1860   23   St. Louis, MO   Lt. O'Connell
1 July 1864   —   near Atlanta, GA   —
Unassigned recruit. Joined from Co M, 1st MO Lt Art (SO#21, HQs, Dept of
Army, WDC, 14 Jan 1864). Discharged 1 July 1867. Expiration of Service.

HOWARD, William   Londonderry, Ireland
sail maker   5' 8"   fair   brown   blue
10 April 1860   28   Ft. Leavenworth, KT   Lt. Barriger
Deserted from Ft. Leavenworth, KT, 20 June 1860 [or 14 June 1860 per RG 391,
Entry 68].

HUBER, Jacob
[no descriptive data]
15 Dec 1860   —   St. Louis, MO   Lt. O'Connell
Unassigned recruit from Co M, 1st MO Lt Art (SO#21, HQs, Dept of Army, WDC,
14 Jan 1864). Wounded near Atlanta, GA, 22 July 1864. In General Hospital at
Marietta, GA 12 Aug 1864.

HUDSON, Daniel R.   Dinwiddie, VA
soldier   5' 11½"   sallow   brown   grey
15 Oct 1849   22   —   —
23 Oct 1854   27   Barrancas Bks., FL   Maj. Woodbridge
23 Aug 1859   32   Ft. Leavenworth, KT   Lt. Haines
28 March 1862   35   St. Louis, MO   —
Enlisted in Co C, 2nd US Art, 1849. Discharged in 1854. Reenlisted in Co F,
2nd US Art. Appointed 1st Sgt 15 Jan 1861 at Little Rock Ars, AR. Supposedly
deserted from St. Louis, MO, 16 March 1862. Also applied for Regimental Ordnance Sgt, 1 March 1862. AGO charge of AWOL and desertion dropped. Was
discharged 16 March 1862 by reason of promotion, 1st Lt, Co B, 18th MO Vol Inf.
Taken prisoner at Shiloh, TN, 6 April 1862. Confined in prison in Macon, GA.
Paroled at Aikens Landing, SC on 12 Oct 1862. Placed in command of Co A, 18th
MO Vol Inf. Promoted to Capt, Co A, 16 Sept 1863. Supposedly wounded at
Kennesaw Mt, GA, 16 June 1864. Was discharged 27 Dec 1864 on tender of resignation. Applied for commission in the Veterans' Reserve Corps, 17 Jan 1865. Died
of chronic diarrhea on 21 June 1892 in St. Louis, MO. Buried in Calvary Cemetery. Contemporary commentaries about Hudson reveal some of his characteris-
tics: "...he was [a] large portly gentleman, and able [to] eat heartily and take his
drinks like the ballance [sic] of the boys." "I loaned him my horse to go out to his
command [at Pittsburg Landing / Shiloh], and he and [the] horse were both gobbled
up by the rebels, on the way. I never saw the Capt. any more till after the close of

the war, and I have never met the said horse to this day—I often wish I could for he was a $200 horse." "I liked the Captain he was a kind hearted old fellow. ... I think almost any private in the company, however, would have been a better leader in battle than he. The Capt. was not generally liked in the regiment on that account."

HUGGINS, William C.   Chesterfield Dist., SC
carpenter   5' 11½"   fair   light   hazel
1 Aug 1857   21   Charlotte, NC   Lt. J. P. Jones
Died at Ft. Leavenworth, KT, 26 Nov 1857. A Pvt.

IMMELL, Lorenzo Dow   Ross Co., OH
plasterer   5' 9"   —   —   —
12 Aug 1860   23   Ft. Leavenworth, KT   Lt. Barriger
19 Feb 1862   25   St. Louis, MO   —
Appointed Cpl at Jefferson Bks, MO, 1 April 1861. Discharged at St. Louis, MO, 19 Feb 1862 to accept commission as 2nd Lt with 1st MO Lt Art (SO#155, HQs, Dept of MO, St. Louis, MO, 21 Feb 1862). Reportedly wounded in right shoulder at Battle of Wilson's Creek, 10 Aug 1861. Injury to right eye and ear in action at Farmington, MO, 28 May 1862. Gunshot wound in the nose at Battle of Corinth, 4 Oct 1862. Shell wound in right instep during the Battle of Resaca, GA, 15 May 1864. Also served with 12th WI Lt Art. Was awarded the Medal of Honor in 1890 for bravery at the Battle of Wilson's Creek, MO. In 1890, Immell transmitted letters from two comrades with his request for the Medal of Honor. William J. Williams [see subsequent listing] wrote: "I was a private in Capt. Jas. Totton's [Totten] Co. F, 2nd U. S. Artillery, and was acting gunner of the third piece in the battle. I remember seeing him [Immell] advance between the enemy and our lines and cut loose the lead team, which had been killed, then mount the saddle horse of the swing team and save the caisson of Corporal Writtenberry's [Wrightenburg – see subsequent listing] piece, which had been abandoned by all drivers and men, and I remember our whole line cheering him. I also saw him take a mule, put it in place of one of the wheel horses which had been shot, take an ax and cut a small tree, on which the piece was fast, and save the gun; also saw him advance, under a hot fire, and get a horse belonging to the enemy, the rider of which I had killed, Immell having had his horse shot under him in the fore part of the engagement." Recommending award, Maj Gen J.M. Schofield wrote: "My own personal observation of the conduct of Battery F, Second U. S. Artillery, at the battle of Wilson's Creek, enables me to fully corroborate the record made upon the muster roll, viz; that 'every non-commissioned officer and soldier of the company throughout the entire battle acted bravely and deserves the highest commendation.' I saw a part of the conduct described, viz; the cutting out of dead horses, and the replacing of them, so as to make up teams sufficient to haul off the guns after the battle." (Immell, Medal of Honor file, National Archives, Washington, DC.) Was also cited by Gen Rosecrans for meritorious service at the Battles of Iuka and Corinth, MS. Was discharged at Benton Bks, St. Louis, MO, 28 July 1865. Born 18 June 1837. Died in St. Louis on 31 Oct 1912. Buried in Jefferson Barracks National Cemetery, MO.

JAMISON, Joseph   Edinburgh, Scotland
painter   5' 5¼"   fair   brown   hazel
1 Feb 1857   27   San Diego, CA   Capt. Burton
Transferred from Co F, 3rd US Art to Co F, 2nd US Art (SO#301, HQs, Ft. Leavenworth, KT, 21 Aug 1858). Discharged 1 Feb 1862 at Sedalia, MO. Expiration of service.

KAVANAGH, Peter [see CAVANAGH / KAVANAGH, Peter]

KELLETT / KILLETT, Francis		Cavan, Ireland		
laborer	5' 7"	fair	brown	blue
16 Dec 1854	31	New York, NY		Lt. Garnett

Joined Co I from Gen Dept, Ft. Columbus, NY, 18 Jan 1855. Transferred to Co F 1 Sept 1857 (SO#24, HQs, 2nd Art, Ft. Monroe, VA, 3 Sept 1857). Discharged at Ft. Leavenworth, KT, 16 Dec 1859. Expiration of service.

KELLY, Henry H. / John H.		Kalamazoo, MI		
clock maker	5' 7"	ruddy	brown	blue
26 Oct 1860	21	Detroit, MI		Lt. Fink
1 July 1864	24	near Atlanta, GA		Lt. Smith

Regular army recruit on detached service with 1st MO Lt Art. Transferred to Co F (SO#21, HQs, Dept of Army, WDC, 14 Jan 1864). Taken prisoner near Atlanta, GA, 22 July 1864. Appointed Cpl 20 Dec 1865. Promoted to Sgt 1 April 1867. Discharged 1 July 1867 at Ft. Vancouver, WT. Expiration of service. A Sgt.

KELLY, John		—, Ireland		
—	5' 9"	—	—	—
24 Dec 1860	17	Newport Bks., KY		—
8 June 1866	23	Ft. Ontario, NY		—
15 March 1870	27	Indianapolis, IN		—

Enlisted as unassigned recruit; assigned to Co M, 1st MO Lt Art. Received a gunshot wound in right leg at Wilson's Creek, 10 Aug 1861. Sent to New House of Refuge, St. Louis, MO for treatment. Claimed disability for chronic diarrhea and deafness from the Vicksburg campaign in 1863. Joined Co F, 2nd US Art, from Co M, 1st MO Lt Art (SO#21, HQs, Dept of Army, WDC, 14 Jan 1864). Taken prisoner at Atlanta, GA on 22 July 1864. Discharged 25 Dec 1865 at Ft. Point, CA. Expiration of service. Enlisted in 4th US Inf in 1866. Discharged 8 June 1870 at Ft. Laramie, WY. Enlisted in 11th US Inf in 1870. Deserted 3 Aug 1870. A Pvt. Suffered from rheumatism and a weak back from Civil War service. Admitted in 1893 to have deserted because of "Ill usage and unmerited abuse From Lieutenant Derby and Sergt. Barnes." In 1890 applied for a discharge but was told to "surrender myself to the nearest military authority and as I did not think it was right for me to do so, and if I did [I] would leave my family in needy circumstances I left the [charge] stand as I feared to do anything more." Later used an old comrade, L. D. Immell [see previous listing] as his pension attorney. Died 3 March 1901 at Anderson, IN.

KELLY, William		—, England		
farmer	5' 6"	ruddy	sandy	grey
30 Nov 1860	22	St. Louis, MO		Lt. O'Connell

Transferred from general service recruits (SO#22, HQs, Dept of West, Springfield, MO, 7 July 1861). [Deserted 8 June 1861 (M233, Roll 27).] Appointed Cpl, 1 July 1862. Reduced to Pvt 7 May 1863. Discharged 30 Nov 1865 at Benicia, CA. Expiration of service. A Pvt.

KEYES, Joseph		Limerick, Ireland		
stone cutter	5' 9"	fair	black	brown
2 Jan 1861	28	St. Louis, MO		—
24 March 1864	31	Hart Island, New York Harbor		Capt. Downey

Joined Co F, 2nd US Art, July 1861 from general services, St. Louis Ars, MO. Missing and supposedly killed at Battle of Wilson's Creek, MO, 10 Aug 1861. Actually wounded at Wilson's Creek; sick at Hospital in Springfield, MO, since 11[14?] Aug 1861. In and out of hospitals at St. Louis, MO from Aug 1861 to Dec 1863. Discharged 28 Jan 1864 at Pulaski, TN. Expiration of service. A Pvt. Enlisted 24 March 1864 in the Veterans Reserve Corps, Co H, 82nd NY Vols. Transferred a month later to 4th US Art. Shortly after the Battle of the Wilderness, his wounds again festered. Sent to Emory Hospital in WDC; thence to David's Island [Ft. Slocum], NY; then returned to Ft. Washington, MD. Discharged 1 April 1865 at Ft. Washington on Surgeon's certificate of disability. A Pvt. Born 10 May 1833. Died 8 June 1910. Buried in Maury Cemetery, Richmond, VA. At the Battle of Wilson's Creek, received a gunshot wound through the right breast, passing through the shoulder, breaking the bone. Also under the same arm received another buckshot wound. Laid on the battlefield for three days, before the Confederates took him to the Springfield, MO, Court House, which was being used as a hospital. Remained there until Gen Fremont retook Springfield in Oct 1861.

KILLETT, Francis [see KELLETT / KILLETT, Francis]

KIRKLAND, David   Butler Co., PA
  farmer   5' 8½"   —   —   —
  6 Aug 1860   21   Ft. Leavenworth, KT   Lt. Barriger
  Appointed Cpl, 1 June 1862. Promoted to Sgt 12 Oct 1862 (GO#7, HQs, 2nd Art, Ft. McHenry, MD, 9 March 1865 [significantly delayed paperwork!]). Appointed 1st Sgt 1 Oct 1864. Born c. 1840. Died 26 July 1894. Buried in Homewood Cemetery, Washington, PA.

KOPPE / KOEPPE, Edward   Dresden, Germany
  sugar maker   5' 6"   fair   sandy   grey
  24 July 1854   24   New York, NY   Col. Brown
  Joined Co I from Gen Dept, Ft. Columbus, NY, 18 Jan 1855. Transferred to Co F, 1 Sept 1857 (SO#24, HQs, 2nd Art, Ft. Monroe, VA, 3 Sept 1857). Deserted 13 Dec 1857 from Ft. Leavenworth, KT.

LANE, John Harrison   Columbus, OH
  —   5' 8"   light   dark   grey
  16 Jan 1860   21   Ft. Leavenworth, KT   Lt. Pratt
  Discharged 16 Jan 1865 at Nashville, TN. Expiration of service. A Pvt. Born 5 Nov 1839. Died 31 Aug 1911, Monte Vista, CO. Claims to have served in army commands with Capt [John H.] Dickerson at Omaha and Ft. Kearney, NT in 1856; with Lt G. K. [Gouverneur Kemble] Warren in the Black Hills in 1857; and with Capt [Frederick] Steele at Ft. Ripley, MN. No army records to substantiate the claim. Also claimed to have suffered a rupture, deafness, and eye problems from "premature discharge of cannon" in 1864. Worked five years as a night watchman in the Commissary Dept in St. Louis, MO [nd], and for seven years with the "Rocky Mountain News" [Denver, CO, nd].

LEAHY, Thomas   Kilkenny, Ireland
  laborer   5' 6½"   fair   brown   grey
  1 Feb 1857   27   San Diego, CA   Capt. Burton
  Transferred into Co from Co B, 3rd US Art (SO#301, HQs, Ft. Leavenworth, KT, 21 Aug 1858). Discharged 1 Feb 1862 at Sedalia, MO. Expiration of service.

LEAVITTE / LEAVITTEE, James Henry   Quebec, Canada
  clerk   5' 7"   fair   brown   grey
  18 Jan 1861   22[25]   Little Rock Ars., AR   Capt. Totten
  Deserted from St. Louis Ars, MO, 21 April 1861, after three months' service.

LEE, Samuel Geles   Middletown, OH
  farmer   5' 8"   sandy   brown   blue
  24 April 1860   26   Ft. Leavenworth, KT   Lt. Barriger
  Deserted 5 July 1860 from Ft. Leavenworth, KT, after less than three months'
  service.

LEWIS, Charles K.   Champagne Co., OH
  farmer   5' 11"   fair   red   grey
  12 July 1860   22   Ft. Leavenworth, KT   Lt. Barriger
  Appointed Cpl, 1 July 1864. Discharged 13 July 1865 at Chattanooga, TN.
  Expiration of service. A Pvt.

LONG, Matthew   Tipperary, Ireland
  moulder   5' 6"   ruddy   brown   brown
  29 Nov 1854   21   Albany, NY   Lt. Miller
  29 Nov 1859   26   Ft. Leavenworth, KT   —
  Joined Co I from Gen Dept, Ft. Columbus, NY, 18 Jan 1855. Transferred to Co
  F, 1 Sept 1857 (SO#24, HQs, 2nd Art, Ft. Monroe, VA, 3 Sept 1857).

LOWRY, John   Washington, PA
  soldier   5' 7³/₄"   fair   dark   hazel
  16 Feb 1855   28   —   —
  30 Nov 1860   33   St. Louis, MO   Lt. O'Connell
  Assigned to Co B, 1st US Dragoons, 1855. Deserted 5 Jan 1857; apprehended
  27 Sept 1857. Transferred to Co F, 1st US Art. Discharged 6 Nov 1860. Expiration of service. A Pvt. Transferred from general service recruits to Co F, 2nd US
  Art (SO#22, HQs, Dept of West, Springfield, MO, 7 July 1861). Appointed Farrier
  6 Feb 1863. Transferred to Co K, 1st US Art. Discharged 30 Nov 1865 at Baltimore, MD. A Blacksmith. Suffered impaired hearing from the concussion and
  firing of artillery at the Battle of Corinth, MS. At Kennesaw Mt, GA in June 1864,
  while serving as No. 1 on a piece, left foot broken when the piece recoiled and ran
  over his foot. In Sept 1865, at Ft. McHenry, MD, kicked in the left arm and groin
  while shoeing a horse. One comrade recalled: "When Lowry was sober he was a
  good man. But when he got whare [sic] there was whiskey he was worthless." Of
  the accident at Ft. McHenry, the same comrade noted: "If Lowry had been sober, I
  don't think he would have been hurt. He was drinking. Col. [William Montrose]
  Graham ordered him to work." Died in 1891 or 1893.

LUZ, John   Wurttemberg, Germany
  rope maker   5' 10"   florid   brown   hazel
  16 June 1854   31   New York, NY   Col. Brown
  Joined Co I from Gen Dept, 18 Jan 1855. Transferred to Co F, 1 Sept 1857
  (SO#24, HQs, 2nd Art, Ft. Monroe, VA, 3 Sept 1857). Discharged 16 June 1859 at
  Ft. Leavenworth, KT. Expiration of service.

McCARTY / McCARTHY, Timothy   County Cork, Ireland
  boot shoemaker   5' 6"   fair   brown   blue
  20 May 1861   23   Philadelphia, PA   Lt. Peirce
  Discharged 20 May 1864 at Kingston, GA. Expiration of service. A Pvt.

McGARRY, James H. [see GARRY, James H.]

McGEE, Patrick   Donegal, Ireland
  laborer   5' 5"   dark   brown   grey
  7 Dec 1854   21   Boston, MA   Lt. Flint
  Discharged 7 Dec 1859 at Ft. Leavenworth, KT. Expiration of service. A Pvt.

McGINNIS, Franklin S. [enlisted as Frank]   Charlotte, NC
  farmer   5' 9"   fair   brown   grey
  12 Oct 1857   21   Charlotte, NC   Lt. J. P. Jones
    Transferred to Co F, 2nd US Art from Co B, 2nd US Art, 9 Dec 1858 (Or#148,
  HQs, Ft. Riley, KT, 9 Dec 1858). Served as Orderly to the Gen Cmdg Dept of West
  at HQs, St. Louis, MO. Sent by Capt Totten as requested by the Cmdg Gen (SO#8,
  HQs, Dept of West, St. Louis, MO, 28 Feb 1861). Appointed Cpl 20 May 1861.
  Promoted to Sgt 23 Feb 1862. Discharged 12 Oct 1862 at camp near Corinth, MS.
  Expiration of service. A Sgt. Was employed as an independent scout under Gen
  Grenville Dodge. Was captured at Tishimingo Co., MS, 4 July 1863. Confined in
  Castle Thunder, Richmond, VA. His statement under oath in Richmond, 18 Sept
  1863 was "That he is 21 years old, is a native of North Carolina, served for 5 years
  in Co. F 2d Arty. Regt. U.S. Regulars, was discharged on Expiration of his term of
  service in 1862,—since that time has been hired to the Sutler of 66th Illinois Regiment, owns a farm in Kansas, and considers that his home. He has no connection
  with the Army—is a citizen of Kansas." The Confederate Secretary of War ordered
  that he be retained as an Alien Enemy. Born 12 Oct 1835. Died 31 Aug 1908 in
  Lincolnton, NC. Claimed that in Aug 1862, near camp at Clear Creek, MS, while
  going out to drill, his horse threw him, injuring his right arm. [Also claimed to
  have fallen off his horse. And again that his horse fell on him.] He also claimed
  that he was cut across the abdomen with a butcher knife in a wagon train fight at
  or near Corinth, MS [nd].

McGINNISS / McGINNESS, William   Chester Co., PA
  surveyor   5' 5½"   fair   brown   grey
  18 June 1860   31   Ft. Leavenworth, KT   Lt. Barriger
    Appointed Cpl, 1 Jan 1861 at Little Rock Ars, AR. Discharged 3 May 1861 at St.
  Louis, MO (SO#74, HQs, Dept of West, St. Louis, MO, 30 May 1861). A Cpl. [See
  Ltr from Col Frank Blair, 1st MO Vols, dated 29 May 1861, asking that McGinniss
  be discharged so that he could join Blair's regiment (RG 391, Entry 61; also RG
  393, Entry 5489).]

McINERNEY, James   Clare, Ireland
  farmer   5' 9"   fair   sandy   blue
  8 July 1858   23   Ft. Leavenworth, KT   Lt. J. P. Jones
  Deserted 25 May 1859 from Ft. Riley, KT.

McINTYRE, Francis   Tyrone, Ireland
  laborer   5' 10"   fair   brown   blue
  3 Sept 1858   23   Ft. Leavenworth, KT   Lt. J. P. Jones
    Appointed Cpl 7 Sept 1861 at Camp McKinstry, Fairfield, MO. Promoted to Sgt
  25 Feb 1862. Appointed 1st Sgt 1 Nov 1862 vice Gustavus Dey [see previous list-
  ing], who was wounded at Corinth, MS. Relieved as 1st Sgt 20 Feb 1863 by Bernard Dunnigan [see previous listing]. Discharged 3 Sept 1863 at Prospect, TN.
  Expiration of service. A Sgt.

McINTYRE, John   Fermanagh, Ireland
laborer   5' 9"   fair   brown   blue
31 May 1861   22   New York, NY   Capt. H. C. Bankhead
7 July 1864   25   —   —
21 Aug 1867   28   Ft. Lafayette, NY   Lt. Osbury
Discharged 21 May 1864 at Owens Mills, GA. Expiration of service. A Pvt. Enlisted in Co I, 6th US Inf, 1864. Enlisted in Battery C, 1st US Art, 1867. Discharged 18 Feb 1869 at Ft. Hamilton, NY for disability. Suffered from syphilitic rheumatism, "principally affecting right knee joint, with positive change of structure. The glands of the neck are enlarged & he is completely broken down and worthless." Lived for a while in Baltimore, MD, and at the National Home for Disabled Veteran Soldiers, Washington, OH.

McKEE, James   —, Illinois
farmer   5' 10"   ruddy   light   grey
5 Oct 1863   20   Chicago, IL   Capt. Benedict
Three year enlistment. Deserted 27 Oct 1863 from Odeon, IL before joining Co.

McSHANE, David M. / Daniel   Cork, Ireland
laborer   5' 6"   ruddy   brown   blue
24 April 1860   29   Ft. Leavenworth, KT   Lt. Barriger
Appointed Cpl 28 April 1863. Died of apoplexy 29 Nov 1863 at Prospect, TN. A Sgt.

MADDEN, William [see MURRAY, William]

MAGOWEN, Patrick   Troy, NY
carpenter   5' 7¼"   fair   brown   blue
16 Nov 1855   29   Barrancas Bks., FL   Lt. Bingham
Appointed Artificer [nd]. Discharged at Little Rock Ars, AR 16 Nov 1860. Expiration of service. A Pvt [at Ft. Leavenworth, KT 17 Nov 1860 (M233, Roll 25)].

MAHONEY, John   Cork, Ireland
soldier   5' 9"   florid   brown   grey
7 July 1854   26   Barancas Bks., FL   Lt. Molinard
6 May 1859   31   Ft. Riley, KT   —
Was a Pvt at reenlistment at Ft. Riley, 6 May 1859. Relieved from duty as 1st Sgt to Sgt at Little Rock Ars, AR, 15 Jan 1861.

MAISCH, Joseph   Bjorn, Germany
gardener   5' 7½"   florid   sandy   hazel
31 July 1863   43   Buffalo, NY   Capt. Tidball
Taken prisoner in battle near Atlanta, GA, 22 July 1864.

MALONEY, James   Kerry, Ireland
plasterer   5' 9¼"   fair   brown   grey
8 June 1860   23   Ft. Leavenworth, KT   —
Deserted from Ft. Leavenworth 8 Sept 1860.

MARSH, Richard Alvis [see BELT, Robert]

MARTIN, John   Armagh [Limerick], Ireland
  soldier   5' 8½"   fair   auburn   hazel
  21 March 1854   27   New Orleans, LA   Lt. Taylor
  26 March 1859   32   Ft. Riley, KT   Lt. Taylor
  1 Feb 1864   37   Pulaski, TN   Lt. Murray
  29March 1867   42   —   —
  29 March 1870   45   Ft. Kenai, AK   Lt. Crawford
  Transferred to Co F, 2nd US Art, from Co A, 3rd US Art (SO#301, HQs, Ft.
Leavenworth, KT, 21 Aug 1858). Last served in Light Battery, Co M, 2nd US Art.
Reenlistment in 1870 was his sixth.

MASTER / MASTERS, William   Cologne, Prussia
  painter   5' 8"   fair   black   blue
  2 Sept 1863   32   Memphis, TN   Lt. Murray
  Wounded at Rome Cross Roads, GA, 16 May 1864. Not allowed furlough while
in hospital. Deserted 16 Aug 1865. [See Ltrs in file (RG 391, Entry 61; and M233,
Roll 28). Masters on detached service at HQs, Dept of MO, as clerk, draftsman
and engineer.]

MEEHAN / MEHAN, Patrick   Sligo, Ireland
  lumberjack   5' 8"   fair   sandy   blue
  19 Oct 1860   22   Chicago, IL   Lt. J. P. Jones
  1 July 1864   26   Atlanta, GA   Lt. Smith
  17 July 1867   29   Benicia, CA   —
  21 July 1870   32   Benicia, CA   —
  24 July 1875   37   Benicia, CA   —
  25 Nov 1878   40   —   —
  Assigned to Co B, 2nd US Inf, 1860. Transferred to 4th US Art; then to Co M,
1st MO Lt Art. Unassigned recruit; joined Co F from Co M, 1st MO Lt Art (SO#21,
HQs, Dept of Army, WDC, 14 Jan 1864). Wounded 11 Aug 1864 at battle near
Atlanta, GA; in hospital at Marietta, GA, 12 Aug. Discharged 1 July 1867 at Ft.
Vancouver, WT. Enlisted in Ordnance Dept, 1867. Reenlisted in same organization in 1875. Discharged 4 July 1876. Reenlisted in same organization, 25 Nov
1878. Discharged at Benicia, CA, 23 July 1883. Born c. 1835. Came to the US
from Ireland in 1846, lived in Oconto, WI, and "was lumbering." About six months
prior to enlistment, "I was on the steamer Lady Elgin on Lake Michigan (both
Steamer & Capt. Lost). Have no relatives in this Country & I have never married." Died 16 Nov 1898 in the Soldiers' Home, WDC. Claimed to have contracted
scurvy from exposure and poor food during the Springfield, MO campaign in 1861.
Was stricken with moon blindness in June 1862. Also received a wound in the
right hip at Atlanta in Aug 1864. [See also, Ltr from Lt L. Smith, Cmdg Co F to
aide de camp, East Point, GA, 27 Sept 1864, requesting a sick furlough for Meehan
who had been absent, "wounded at Hospital at Marietta (RG 391, Entry 61)."]

MEIERS / MEYERS / MYERS, George Rhumpfaly, Germany
  painter   5' [?"]   fair   brown   hazel
  3 Jan 1861   22   Newport, KY   Lt. Wilkins
  Transferred from general service recruits (SO#22, HQs, Dept of West, Springfield, MO, 7 July 1861). Appointed Cpl 28 Aug 1863. Promoted to Sgt 26 Nov 1863
vice John Pratt [see subsequent listing], who was promoted to 1st Sgt. Discharged
at Prospect, TN, 3 Jan 1864. Expiration of service. A Sgt.

MEIGHAN, John   Donegal, Ireland
  laborer   5' 10"   fair   brown   hazel
  16 Aug 1858   24   Ft. Leavenworth, KT   Lt. J. P. Jones
  Deserted from Ft. Leavenworth 12 July 1859.

MENDENEZ, Christian   Werdenberg, Switzerland
  —   5' 4½"   ruddy   brown   blue
  16 Oct 1860   21   Milwaukee, WI   Lt. J. P. Jones
  Transferred from general service recruits (SO#22, HQs, Dept of West, Springfield, MO, 7 July 1861). Deserted from New Madrid, MO 13 April 1862.

MEYER, Joseph Henry   Bavaria, Germany
  —   6' 2½"   light   brown   grey
  26 May 1860   28   Ft. Leavenworth, KT   Lt. Barriger
  Discharged 27 May 1861 at St. Louis, MO. Surgeon's certificate of disability. A
  Pvt.

MEYERS, George [see MEIERS / MEYERS / MYERS, George]

MILLER, John   Dunnigan, Germany
  laborer   5' 6"   fair   brown   hazel
  31 Jan 1856   24   Philadelphia, PA   Lt. Flint
  6 Dec 1860   29   Chicago, IL   Lt. J. P. Jones
  1[14] July 1864   33   near Atlanta, GA   Lt. L. Smith
  Assigned to Co G, 2nd US Art, 1856. Discharged 23 Nov 1860 at Ft. Mackinac,
  MI. A Pvt. Transferred to Co F from general service recruits (SO# 22, Dept of
  West, Springfield, MO, 7 July 1861) [mistakenly identified as Jacob Miller in MRF
  June–Aug 1861]. Missing; supposed killed at Battle of Wilson's Creek, MO, 10
  Aug 1861. Rejoined Co at Rolla, MO, 7 Sept 1861. Deserted from Commerce, MO,
  1 March 1862 [deserted from St. Louis, MO, 1 March 1862 per MRF Feb–April
  1862]. Appointed Cpl, 1 Nov 1863. Discharged 14 July 1864 for reenlistment in
  Co F. Severely wounded in right knee, causing amputation of leg, near Atlanta,
  GA, 11 Aug 1864. In General Hospital, Marietta, GA, 12 Aug 1864. Sent to Gen-
  eral Hospital, Camp Dennison, OH. There fitted with an artificial leg by Douglas
  Bly Company, manufacturer of artificial limbs. Discharged 14 June 1865 at Ft.
  McHenry, MD on a Surgeon's certificate of entire disability. A Cpl. Eventually
  entered National Military Home, Montgomery Co., OH. Born c. 1832. Died 1903
  or 1904.

MITCHELL, John R.   —, England
  gardener   6' 1"   ruddy   light   blue
  2 Aug 1860   21   Ft. Leavenworth, KT   Lt. Barriger
  Slightly wounded at the Battle of Corinth, MS, 4 Oct 1862. Served as Officers'
  cook from 19 Sept 1864 to [?] for Lt Lemuel Smith. Discharged 2 Aug 1865 at
  Chattanooga, TN. Expiration of service. A Pvt. Became a resident of Detroit, MI.
  Claimed wound at Corinth from a shell which hit his left hand on the knuckle of
  the 2nd forefinger, injuring the bone and ligament. Also claimed to have been
  treated at the General Hospital at Corinth on 7 Oct 1862. [Official records only
  state that he was slightly wounded, and not hospitalized.] Born c. 1839. Died in
  Jan 1879 of spinal meningitis in West Carroll Parish, LA.

MOOSE, George Willis   Sparta, NY
farmer   5' 8"   light   brown   grey
10 April 1860   21   Ft. Leavenworth, KT   Lt. Barriger
Discharged 10 April 1865 at Nashville, TN. Expiration of service.

MOOSER, William   Zurich, Switzerland
soldier   5' 7³/₄"   fair   light   blue
17 Jan 1861   24   St. Louis, MO   Lt. O'Connell
Transferred from general service recruits (SO#22, HQs, Dept of West, Springfield, MO, 7 July 1861). Deserted 21[19] Sept 1861 from St. Louis, MO.

MURPHY, Jeremiah   Cork, Ireland
soldier   5' 5"   fair   brown   blue
12 Dec 1860   23   St. Louis, MO   Lt. O'Connell
1 July 1864   27   Atlanta, GA   Lt. Smith
Discharged 1 July 1867. Expiration of service.

MURPHY, Patrick   Kerry, Ireland
laborer   5' 7"   fair   brown   blue
28 April 1860   24   Ft. Leavenworth, KT   Lt. Barriger
1 July 1864   28   near Atlanta, GA   —
13 July 1867   32   Ft. Vancouver, WT   —
12 Aug 1870   35   Sitka, AK   —
Discharged 1 July 1867. Expiration of service. Reenlisted 13 July 1867. Discharged 13 July 1870 at Ft. Kenai, AK. Expiration of service. Reenlisted 12 Aug
1870 at Sitka, AK.

MURRAY, William [alias MADDEN, William]   Halifax, Nova Scotia
painter   5' 6¹/₂"   fair   brown   grey
13 May 1846   —   —   —   —
28 July 1851   —   —   —   —
19 March 1860   —   Ft. Leavenworth, KT   —
1 July 1864   —   near Atlanta, GA   —
2 Dec 1865 [as MADDEN, William]   —   —
18 Jan 1869   —   —   —   —
19 Jan 1872   —   —   —   —
3 Aug 1874 [as MURRAY, William]   —   —
Assigned to Co I, 2nd US Art, 1846. Transferred to Co L, 2nd US Art, 4 Oct
1848. Discharged 12 May 1851. Assigned to Co K, 2nd US Art, 1851. Discharged
28 July 1856. Assigned to Co F, 2nd US Art, 1860. Discharged 1 July 1864 by
reenlistment in same Co. Taken prisoner near Atlanta, GA 22 July 1864. Assigned to temporary duty with Co K, 2nd US Art (SO#34, HQs, 2nd Art, Ft. McHenry,
MD, 23 Oct 1864). "Corp. Wm Murray of your Co., now confined at Provost Guard
at these HQs [Ft. McHenry, MD, 2nd US Art Regt] has reported without papers
whatever (RG 391, Entry 48, Ltr 16 March 1865)." Deserted 2 Dec 1865 from
Benicia, CA. Enlisted 2 Dec 1865 as William Madden; assigned to Co G, 9th US
Inf. Being a deserter from Co F, this enlistment and the next two were in violation
of the 50th Article of War. Discharged 2 Dec 1868. Reenlisted in same organization on 18 Jan 1869. Transferred to Co G, 12th US Inf, 17 April 1869. Discharged
18 Jan 1872. Reenlisted in same organization. Surrendered as deserter [as Murray]
from Co F, 2nd US Art on 16 Nov 1872, and dropped from rolls of Co G, 12 US Inf,
[as Madden]. "He was restored to duty without trial per SO#331, dated HdQts of

the Army A.G.O., Washington, Dec. 17 '72, and transferred to Co G, 12th US Inf under the name of William Murray (to serve balance of original enlistment in [Co] F, 2nd Art)." MR for Jan–Feb 1873, Co G, 12th US Inf, reported him [as Murray] "Present for duty." Discharged 29 July 1874. Reenlisted in same organization. Discharged 2 Aug 1879. Expiration of service. A Pvt. Murray filed for disability pension in Aug 1884, claiming injured sight. Claimed that he contracted inflammation of left eye while serving with Co G, 12th US Inf, against the Modoc Indians at Lava Beds, CA, March 1873. In 1885, while a resident at the Soldiers' Home, WDC, gave testimony for Patrick Meehan, a comrade [see previous listing], relative to his (Murray's) knowledge of scurvy and his own suffering from the disease on campaigns in the Mexican War, and in Florida with the 2nd US Art.

MYERS, George [see MEIERS / MEYERS / MYERS, George]

MYRICK, Franklin Daniel Alexander   Davidson, NC
farmer   5' 7"   fair   brown   brown
12 Oct 1857   23   Salisbury, NC   Lt. J. P. Jones
23 Dec 1863   29   St. Louis, MO   —
Transferred to Co F, 2nd US Art from temporary attachment (Or#148, HQs, Ft. Riley, KT, 9 Dec 1858). Discharged 12 Oct 1862 at Camp Clear Creek, MS. Expiration of service. A Pvt. Reenlisted in Co G, 2nd MO Lt Art. Discharged 22 Aug 1865 at Benton Bks, MO. A Sgt. Born c. 1834. Died 3 April 1892. Buried in Odd Fellows Cemetery, St. Louis, MO. Claimed to have developed rheumatism, kidney and liver disease from exposure during 1864. There being no room in the hospitals at Memphis, TN, was treated in his tent at camp.

MYRICK, George   Davidson, NC
farmer   5' 11"   fair   brown   brown
23 Sept 1857   22   Salisbury, NC   Lt. J. P. Jones
Transferred into Co from temporary attachment with Co B (Or#148, HQs, Ft. Riley, KT, 9 Dec 1858). Discharged at Jacinto, MS [camp near Corinth, MS (M233, Roll 25)], 23 Sept 1862. Expiration of service. A Pvt. [Later enlisted in Co M, 5th KS Cav at Leavenworth, KS. Served with Joseph Hendricks and Raleigh Brewer. See previous listings.]

NASH, George Samuel   Hamilton, Canada
farmer   5' 10"   fair   auburn   hazel
12 July 1860   26   Ft. Leavenworth, KT   Lt. Barriger
Discharged 12 July 1865 at Chattanooga, TN. Expiration of service. A Pvt. Died 30 March 1898 in Palmyra, Lenawee Co., MI; buried in Palmyra. Claimed chronic diarrhea, resulting from over-exposure, exposure without tents, and drinking of "unhealthy slimy water" at Sedalia, MO in Aug 1862. [Co F was in Sedalia 19 Nov 1861 to 3 Feb 1862.] Was admitted to City General Hospital, St. Louis, MO, 10 Feb 1862 with rheumatism and pneumonia. Returned to duty 20 Feb 1862. Readmitted to General Hospital, Benton Bks, MO on 20 Feb 1862, "diagnosis not stated." Returned to duty 12 July 1862 at camp near Iuka, MS.

NEWBOLDT, Francis   Hanover, Germany
soldier   5' 6½"   fair   light   blue
13 Sept 1858   27   Ft. Leavenworth, KT   Lt. Robertson
Deserted 9 Sept 1859. Apprehended 10 Sept 1860. Transferred from Co A, 2nd US Art to Co F (SO#161, HQs, Dept of Army, WDC, 8 April 1863). Discharged 3 Sept 1863. Expiration of service. A Pvt.

NOLAN, Stephen   Carlow, Ireland
  bricklayer   5' 11³/₄"   fair   brown   grey
  15 July 1858   25   Ft. Leavenworth, KT   Lt. J. P. Jones
  Appointed Cpl, 1 Jan 1861, Little Rock Ars, AR. Discharged 15 June 1863 at
Memphis, TN. Expiration of service. A Pvt. Claimed that, while the battery was
changing position at the Battle of Wilson's Creek, MO, he was struck across the
eyes by a tree limb, causing failing sight in right eye. Also claimed that during the
siege of Corinth, MS, spring of 1862, "in response to Call No. 2... [a] fracture of my
right arm [was] caused by me being thrown from the limber of the caison [sic] on
which I was mounted." Treated at the field hospital near Pittsburg Landing, TN,
at St. Louis Arsenal and at Benton Bks, MO. Returned to Co in June–July 1862
and participated in the Battles at Iuka and Corinth, MS.

NOLDAY, Augustus   Munster, Germany
  carpenter   5' 11¹/₂"   light   fair   grey
  9 June 1859   21   Ft. Leavenworth, KT   Lt. Bailey
  Deserted 15 April 1860 from Ft. Leavenworth, KT.

NOLL, George   Baden, Germany
  farmer   5' 5"   fair   brown   grey
  1 April 1863   35   Corinth, MS   Lt. C. Green
  Taken prisoner near Atlanta, GA, 22 July 1864. Confined in Andersonville Prison,
GA. Paroled at Rough and Ready, GA, 18 or 22 Sept 1864. Discharged 1 April
1868 at Vancouver, WT. Expiration of service. A Pvt. Suffered from rheumatism
brought about by hardships during his imprisonment. Verifying testimony was
given by Michael Tierney [see subsequent listing], a comrade in Co F, and Noll's
brother-in-law. Subsequently, a neighbor claimed that "[Tierney] took an advantage of his (Noll's) ignorance and getting Noll's ranch for much less than its real
value [dated 4 April 1894, La Center, WA]." Noll died 8 May 1892.

NULTY, Michael [alias for NULTY, John]   Cavan, Ireland
  laborer   5' 7"   fair   black   blue
  26 Jan 1856   21   New York, NY   Lt. Frazer
  10 Jan 1861   26   Little Rock Ars., AR   Capt. Totten
  Appointed Cpl, 1 Oct 1862. Promoted to Sgt 1 Nov 1863. Discharged 10 Jan
1864 at Prospect, TN. Expiration of service. Remained in military service. Retired 8 June 1889. A Sgt. Resided in South Deerfield, MA. Died 19 May 1895.
Claim for disability pension, filed 11 Aug 1890, rejected "on the ground that the
claimant is now on the retired list of the Army."

O'BRIEN, Edward   Brooklyn, NY
  soldier   5' 7"   light   red   blue
  1 Jan 1860   23   Ft. Leavenworth, KT   Lt. Pratt
  Deserted 6 Sept 1860 from Ft. Leavenworth, KT.

O'BRIEN, Patrick   Cork, Ireland
  soldier   5' 9"   florid   sandy   grey
  9 Jan 1860   23   Ft. Leavenworth, KT   Lt. Pratt
  Appointed Cpl 5 May 1860 at Ft. Leavenworth, KT (Or#25, HQs, 2nd Art, Ft.
McHenry, MD, 15 June 1860). Appointed Cpl 28 April 1863. Discharged 9 Jan
1865 at Nashville, TN. Expiration of service.

O'DONNELL, Bernard   Monaghan (Kerry), Ireland
  laborer   5' 9"   fair   dark   blue

[Data above may not be totally correct. Found in M233, Roll 24, page 170 at end of the page, and appears incomplete.]

| 15 Dec 1854 | 30 | New York, NY | Lt. Garnett |

General Court-Martial #127, 30 July 1857, HQs, 2nd US Art, Ft. Monroe, VA. General Garrison Court-Martial (SO#208, HQs, Ft. Leavenworth, KT, 30 Nov 1857; and SO#226, HQs, Ft. Leavenworth, KT, 18 Dec 1857). <u>Drummed out of the Service</u>, General Court-Martial #18, 23 Sept 1859, at Ft. Leavenworth, KT, Dept of West.

O'REILLY, John   Tipperary, Ireland

| cook | 5' 7" | fair | brown | blue |
| 5 Aug 1858 | 24 | Ft. Leavenworth, KT | Lt. J. P. Jones |

Deserted 5 Jan 1859; 8 June 1859; 1 May 1861. In confinement since 1 May 1861 at St. Louis, MO for desertion. Discharged 1 Aug 1861 (RG 391, Entry 68) by order of Gen Nathaniel Lyon: "Worthlessness!"

OSBORNE / OSBORN, Alfred L.   Hartford, CT

carpenter	5' 10½"	dark	light	hazel
25 March 1853	31	St. Louis, MO	—
5 July 1859	37	Ft. Leavenworth, KT	Lt. Haines

Assigned to Co B, 3rd US Art. Transferred to Ordnance Dept, Ft. Monroe, VA 1 June 1857. Discharged 25 March 1858 at Ft. Monroe Ars. Expiration of service. A Carriage Maker. Second enlistment 1859, assigned to Co F, 2nd US Art. Appointed Artificer 1 July 1861. Discharged 5 July 1864 at Kennesaw Mt, GA. Expiration of service. An Artificer. Married Bridget McIntyre, who was a laundress for Co C, and later for Co F, 2nd US Art, on 22 April 1855 at Ft. Washita, Indian Terr. They were married "in Major [Henry Jackson] Hunt's parlor, Lieut. Goodloe and McCaskey as witnesses." Osborn died 24 Nov 1906 in Carlisle, AR. Was born c. 1822. Wife was born 1839 in Ireland. They would have been 33 and 16 years old, respectively, at marriage. Pension claim based on "partial deafness of both ears caused by concussion of artillery" that incurred at the Battle of Wilson's Creek, MO, 10 Aug 1861.

PAUL, George W.   Rhea Co., TN

| farmer | 6' 0" | fair | brown | grey |
| 9 Aug 1860 | 22 | Ft. Leavenworth, KT | Lt. Barriger |

Deserted 6 or 16 Oct 1860 from Ft. Smith, AR.

PAYNE, William   New York, NY

farmer	5' 9"	light	light	blue
2 Sept 1861	23	Plymouth, WI	—
1 Dec 1863	25	Prospect, TN	Lt. Murray

Enlisted in 8th WI Vol Inf. Discharged 30 Nov 1863 for reenlistment in Co F, 2nd US Art. Paid $25 bounty for enlisting. Had been on detached service with Co F from July 1862 to 31 Oct 1863. Discharged 1 Dec 1868 at Vancouver, WT. Expiration of service. A Pvt. After discharge, returned to WI. Lived in Marchfield, WI. Occupation: Laborer and teamster.

PERRY, William   Schuykill Co., PA

| soldier | 5' 11" | fair | brown | blue |
| 22 Nov 1854 | 23 | Barrancas Bks., FL | Maj. Woodbridge |

Discharged 22 Nov 1859 at Ft. Leavenworth, KT. Expiration of service. A Pvt. Also was with Co G, 1st US Art.

POND, Josiah   Charles City, VA
  machinist   5' 8"   brown   black   dark
  20 Nov 1854   22   Baltimore, MD   Capt. McConnell
  1 Oct 1859   27   Ft. Leavenworth, KT   Lt. Haines
Deserted 20 May 1856. Apprehended 31 May 1856. General Court-Martial
(SO#12, HQs, Dept of East, Baltimore, MD, 14 Feb 1857). Discharged 2 Oct 1862.
Surgeon's certificate of disability at Keokuk, IA. During the march to Springfield,
MO, in late July / early Aug 1861, was run over by a piece of artillery, causing
rupture to his left side and enlargement of the testicle. After discharge, lived for a
while in Evansville, IN. Died 28 Dec 1908 in Richmond, VA. Buried in Oakwood
Cemetery. Discharge exam noted: "Varicocele chronic cystitis probably following
gonorrhea."

PORTER, William   Essex, NY
  brickmaker   5' 9"   fair   brown   blue
  15 Nov 1860   25   St. Louis, MO   Lt. McConnell
  Transferred from general service recruits (SO#22, HQs, Dept of West, Springfield, MO, 7 July 1861). Wounded at Battle of Wilson's Creek, MO, 10 Aug 1861.
Sent to hospital at St. Louis, MO. Discharged 21 Sept 1861 at St. Louis. Surgeon's
certificate of disability, from wound suffered at Wilson's Creek. A Pvt.

PRATT, John   Cavan, Ireland
  laborer   5' 6"   light   brown   blue
  28 Nov 1854   23   Philadelphia, PA   Lt. Burns
  1 Oct 1859   28   Ft. Leavenworth, KT   —
  Appointed Cpl, 1 April 1857 (Or#13, HQs, 2nd Art, Ft. Hamilton, NY, 7 April
1857). Wounded at Battle of Wilson's Creek, MO, 10 Aug 1861. Appointed Cpl, 1
May 1862. Promoted to Sgt, 1 July 1862. Promoted to 1st Sgt vice Gustavus Dey
[see previous listing] 26 Nov 1863. Killed by lightning 14 July 1864 near the
Chattahoochee River, GA.

PULTZ, Michael
  [no descriptive data]
  [no enlistment data]
  Transferred from Co I, 2nd US Art to Co F, 1 Sept 1857 (SO#24, HQs, 2nd Art,
Ft. Monroe, VA, 3 Sept 1857).

RACE, William H.   Detroit, MI
  tinsmith   5' 10"   light   lt. brn.   blue
  10 Aug 1860   c. 23   Detroit, MI   Lt. Fink
  Unassigned recruit; joined Co F from Co M, 1st MO Lt Art (SO#21, HQs, Dept of
Army, WDC, 14 Jan 1864). Severely wounded in the right arm 22 July 1864 at
battle near Atlanta, GA. Was treated at the General Field Hospital at Atlanta;
and in hospitals in Marietta, GA, and at Nashville, TN. Discharged 10 Aug 1865.
Expiration of service. A Pvt.

RAMSBOTTOM, Thomas Queens, Ireland
  clerk   5' 8"   dark   black   hazel
  15 Dec 1854   21   New York, NY   Lt. Garnett
  Deserted 16 July 1856 (M233, Roll 24). General Court-Martial (SO#12, Dept of
East, Baltimore, MD, 14 Feb 1857). Discharged 22 Nov [5 Dec] 1859 at Ft.
Leavenworth, KT. Expiration of service.

RANDALL, John   Kent, England
laborer   5' 10"   fair   dark   grey
24 July 1858   25   Ft. Leavenworth, KT   Lt. J. P. Jones
Discharged 24 July 1863 at Memphis, TN. Expiration of service. A Pvt. Served
in the Ordnance Dept in the South selling off captured materiel. Born in 1833;
died on 24 April 1901 of cancer of the intestines at East St. Louis, IL.

RANDOLPH, John
[no descriptive data]
[no enlistment data]
Mortally wounded and died 4 Oct 1862 at Corinth, MS. [See previous listing for
Randolph Hand. This may be a case of confusing two names. Have not been able
to resolve.]

RATCHFORD, William Campbell   Walton, GA
carpenter   5' 8½"   dark   brown   brown
2 Nov 1857   22   Charlotte, NC   Lt. J. P. Jones
Transferred to Co F from temporary attachment (Or#148, HQs, Ft. Riley, KT, 9
Dec 1858). Died 4 April 1862 [or 15 June 1862 (RG 391, Entry 68)] at New House
of Refuge, St. Louis, MO of chronic diarrhea. On 24 April 1882, mother filed a
pension application, claiming that her son died of wounds received at the Battle of
Wilson's Creek, 10 Aug 1861. The official records [AGO] do no confirm claim. Born
c. 1835.

REAGEN, Joseph [see REGAN / REAGEN, Joseph]

REED / REID, William   —, Indiana
blacksmith   5' 10"   fair   brown   grey
1 May 1860   23   Ft. Leavenworth, KT   —
Deserted 8 Sept 1860 from Ft. Leavenworth, KT.

REGAN / REAGEN, Joseph   Buffalo, NY
sailor   6' 0"   dark   dark   brown
21 March 1863   21   Buffalo, NY   Lt. Long
Deserted 28 March 1863. Apprehended 16 April 1863. Deserted 27 Oct 1863
from Odeon, IL, before joining Co F.

REID, William [see REED / REID, William]

REILLY / RIELY, George   Albany, NY
sailor   5' 5¾"   —   brown   blue
1 May 1857   21   Hampton, VA   Capt. Totten
Enlistment was for 2 years and 15 days. Deserted 12 Dec 1857 from Ft.
Leavenworth, KT. Apprehended and tried for desertion (SO#4, HQs, Dept of West,
St. Louis, MO, 30 March 1858). Drummed out of the Service 30 March 1858.

RENNICK, Franz A. [see BENNICK / RENNICK, Franz A.]

REYNOLDS, James   Carlow, Ireland
laborer   5' 8"   fair   honey   grey
27 Nov 1854   20   New York, NY   Lt. Garnett
1 Oct 1859   25   Ft. Leavenworth, KT   —
Deserted 10 March 1860 from Ft. Leavenworth, KT.

RIELY, George [see REILLY / RIELY, George]

RITCHIE, Charles   —, Ireland
laborer   5' 8½"   ruddy   black   blue
15 Nov 1860   —   St. Louis, MO   Lt. O'Connell
Regular army recruit on detached service, 1st MO Lt Art. Transferred to Co F
(SO#21, HQs, Dept of Army, WDC, 14 Jan 1864). Killed 22 July 1864 in battle
near Atlanta, GA.

ROBERTS, William   Gosport, England
—   5' 5"   fair   brown   dark
26 April 1860   23   Ft. Leavenworth, KT   Lt. Barriger
Died 12 June 1861. Drowned at St. Louis Ars, MO. A Musician.

ROBIE, Edward W.   Georgetown, KY
—   5' 8"   fair   —   blue
8 Dec 1860   26   St. Louis, MO   Lt. O'Connell
Transferred from general service recruits. Deserted 26 July 1861 near Ozark,
MO.

ROBINSON, John   Meath, Ireland
soldier   5' 7"   dark   black   grey
22 July 1854   21   Barrancas Bks., FL   Lt. Molinard
22 July 1859   26   Ft. Leavenworth, KT   —
Appointed Cpl, 1 Jan 1858 (Or#2, HQs, 2nd Art, Ft. Hamilton, NY, 12 Jan 1858).

ROGERS, James   Jefferson Co., NY
soldier   5' 9"   dark   brown   grey
1 Dec 1863   28   Prospect, TN   Lt. Murray
Enlisted from 8th WI Vol Inf. Paid $25 bounty for enlisting. [Discharged 24
March 1864 (M233, Roll 28), or deserted 24 March 1864 from Decatur, AL (RG 94,
M727, Return for March 1864).]

ROLLER, Henry   Wurttemberg, Germany
shoemaker   5' 5¼"   dark   black   hazel
22 Jan 1855   30   Newport, KY   Maj. Backus
1 July 1860   —   Ft. Leavenworth, KT   Lt. Barriger
Enlisted in Co I, 7th US Inf, 1855. Discharged 22 Jan 1860, at Camp Floyd, UT.
Reenlisted in Co F, 2nd US Art. Discharged 12 Dec 1861 at St. Louis, MO. Surgeon's
certificate of disability. On 13 July 1861, on march from Boonville, MO, about 20
miles from Springfield, Roller was run over by a caisson. His left arm and leg were
broken. His left arm then had to be amputated. Below his signature on the Certificate of Disability, Capt Totten changed the form to read: "Commanding Company at the [time] of Roller's misfortune." Roller's pension claim #456 was filed 21
Feb 1862. Lived in Cincinnati, OH after discharge.

ROOKE, George   Cornwall, England
tailor   5' 8"   fair   fair   blue
5 Aug 1854   21   Boston, MA   Lt. Flint
8 June 1859   26   Ft. Leavenworth, KT   —
General Garrison Court-Martial (SO#208, HQs, Ft. Leavenworth, KT, 30 Nov
1857). Discharged 15 Dec 1859 at Ft. Leavenworth, KT. Ordinary disability.

ROSS, William B.   Lycoming Co., PA
farmer   5' 9"   fair   brown   blue
24 April 1860   27   Ft. Leavenworth, KT   Lt. Barriger
Deserted 3 July 1860 (M233, Roll 28).

ROTH, Jacob   —
laborer   5' 6½"   fair   brown   hazel
28 Nov 1860   22   Newport, KY   Lt. Wilkins
Transferred from general service recruits (SO#22, HQs, Dept of West, Springfield, MO, 7 July 1861). Deserted 21 Sept 1861 from St. Louis, MO.

RUPPRECHT, Henry F.   Luxembourg, Germany
painter   5' 4½"   light   light   grey
21 March 1859   32   Ft. Riley, KT   Lt. Taylor
Deserted 10 July 1859 from Ft. Leavenworth, KT.

RUSH, Joseph   Mayo, Ireland
tailor   5' 7½"   dark   brown   hazel
6 Dec 1854   21   Philadelphia, PA   Lt. Burns
20 Dec 1859   26   Ft. Leavenworth, KT   —
Deserted 21 Sept 1855 from Barrancas Bks, FL. Apprehended and joined Co from desertion 20 Dec 1857 at Ft. Leavenworth, KT. Discharged 2 March 1862 at New Madrid, MO. Expiration of service. A Pvt.

RUSS, John   Mecklenburg, NC
laborer   5' 9¾"   fair   light   blue
12 Aug 1857   25   Charlotte, NC   Lt. J. P. Jones
Deserted 4 Dec 1857 from Ft. Leavenworth, KT.

RUSSELL, John J.   Dublin, Ireland
soldier   6' 1"   dark   brown   blue
16 Sept 1859   28   Ft. Leavenworth, KT   Lt. Haines
Deserted 7 April 1861 from Jefferson Bks, MO.

RUSSELL, Michael   [County] Kings, Ireland
"boy"   4' 10"   fair   brown   blue
1 Nov 1855   13   New York, NY   Lt. Frazer
Discharged 1 Nov 1860 enroute to Ft. Smith, AR. Expiration of service. A Musician.

RYAN, John   Kilkenny, Ireland
bricklayer   5' 9½"   light   sandy   blue
4 Dec 1854   31   New York, NY   Lt. Garnett
4 Dec 1859   36   Ft. Leavenworth, KT   —
Appointed Cpl 2 Dec 1857. Reduced to Pvt 21 Dec 1857 (SO#237, HQs, Battalion, Ft. Leavenworth, KT, 21 Dec 1857 and Or#50, HQs, 2nd Art, Ft. Hamilton, NY, 23 Dec 1857). [The following is from the AGO file.] John Ryan enlisted 19 March 1860 at Albany, NY. Unassigned recruit at Carlisle Bks, PA, was transferred to Regt of Mounted Rifles [subsequently became 3rd US Cav] 17 May 1861. Deserted, then apprehended by Civil Authority on 24 Sept 1861. Returned to duty with 3rd US Cav. Transferred to Co M, 1st MO Lt Art, 25 April 1862. Assigned to Co F, 2nd US Art, Jan 1864 (SO#21, HQs, Dept of Army, WDC, 14 Jan 1864). Discharged for expiration of service 19 March 1864 from Co M, 1st MO Lt Art.

SCHLUSSER, Max   Uldersdorf, Prussia
soldier   5' 11½"   fair   light   blue
10[19] Oct 1863   34   New York, NY   Capt. Hildt
Died 23 Aug 1864 of chronic diarrhea at field hospital, Rome, GA. A Pvt.

SCHREIBER, Carl   Baden, Germany
soldier   5' 9"   fair   brown   grey
16 Feb 1863   27   Philadelphia, PA   Lt. Peirce
Deserted 26 Oct 1863 from Cleveland, OH before joining Co.

SECKLER, George W.   Herkimer Co., NY
shoemaker   5' 1"   fair   brown   grey
8 June 1859   23   Ft. Leavenworth, KT   Lt. Bailey
Discharged 8 June 1864 at Acworth, GA. Expiration of service. A Pvt. Born in
Little Falls, Herkimer Co., NY, 10 April 1836. Died 10 March 1915 at Galway,
Saratoga Co., NY. Claimed deafness in left ear from exposure and from firing of
artillery during the battle at Dallas, GA, 28 May 1864.

SEDGWICK, John W.   Oneida Co., NY
farmer   5' 0"   fair   black   grey
7 July 1854   33   Barrancas Bks., FL   Lt. Molinard
Deserted 14 Dec 1857 from Ft. Leavenworth, KT.

SELLERS, Andrew J.   Pope Co., IL
farmer   6' 1"   fair   brown   grey
16 March 1860   22   Ft. Leavenworth, KT   Lt. Barriger
Deserted 13 March 1861 from Jefferson Bks, MO.

SHERRILL, Hiram C.[A.] Iredell, NC
blacksmith   5' 9"   fair   dark   blue
7 Aug 1857   22   Charlotte, NC   Lt. J. P. Jones
Deserted 30 Jan 1858 from cantonment near Ft. Leavenworth, KT.

SHIELDS, Christopher   County Longford, Ireland
clerk   5' 4½"   fair   light   blue
3 Sept 1863   22   Philadelphia, PA   Lt. Peirce
Received a $225 bounty for enlisting for 5 years. Transferred to Co C 26 May
1868. Discharged 3 Sept 1868 at Portland, OR. Expiration of service. A Pvt.

SHIELDS, John   Limerick, Ireland
laborer   5' 5"   dark   brown   brown
9 Nov 1860   19   St. Louis, MO   Lt. O'Connell
1 July 1864   23   —   —
24 Oct 1864   23   US Navy, Phil., PA   —
5 Sept 1865   24   —   —
24 May 1869   28   —   —
3 Sept 1874   33   —   —
Assigned to Co F, 2nd US Art, 1860. Discharged for reenlistment in same Co, 1
July 1864. Deserted while on furlough in July 1864. Enlisted in US Navy, 1864;
served aboard *Unadella*, *Princeton*, *North Carolina*, and *Rhode Island* as a
landsman. Discharged from Navy 25 Aug 1865. Enlisted in Troop D, 2nd US Cav,
1865. Surrendered as a deserter and was transferred to Troop D, 2nd US Cav to

serve term of enlistment as of 1 July 1864. Discharged 5 Sept 1868. Expiration of service. A Pvt. Reenlisted in Cav. Discharged 2 Sept 1879. Expiration of service. A Pvt with Co G, 2nd US Cav to which he was transferred. Born 25 March 1841. Died 22 Nov 1918 in Mondak, MT. Buried in Culbertson, MT.

SIEG, Thomas	Harrisburg, PA			
drayman	5' 11"	fair	light	brown
20 Aug 1863	20	Harrisburg, PA		Lt. Snyder
Deserted 18 Aug 1865.				

SIMON, Henry	Berlin, Germany			
tailor	5' 6½"	fair	brown	blue
2 Dec 1846	38	Philadelphia, PA		—
28 Feb 1849	41	St. Louis, MO		—
1 April 1861	53	Jefferson Bks., MO		Capt. Totten

Assigned to Co E, 1st Regt, PA Vols, 1846. Discharged 5 Aug 1848. Assigned to Co F, 3rd US Inf, 1849. Discharged 28 Feb 1854 at San Diego, CA. Expiration of service. A Pvt. Enlisted in Co F, 2nd US Art, 1861. In Oct 1861, near St. Louis, MO, while watering his horse, the animal "became unmanagable [sic] and he was thrown from his horse and the horse fell on him, and he was struck in the abdomen by the huff [sic] of the horse." Was treated at the hospital at St. Louis Ars. While trying to reach Co F, traveled with a battery of the 1st MN Art. At the General Hospital in Shiloh, TN, surgeons operated on him to save his life [supposedly was castrated during the operation]. Was then sent by hospital boat to Evansville, IN; then by rail to the General Hospital at Terre Haute, IN, where he was discharged 18 Sept 1862 on a Surgeon's certificate of disability. A Pvt. Mistakenly reported as deserting 1 March 1862 from Commerce, MO.

SIMPSON, William Alexander	Caroline Co., MD			
painter	5' 11½"	dark	dark	hazel
25 June 1859	30	Ft. Leavenworth, KT		Lt. Bailey

Discharged 19 Jan 1862 at Sedalia, MO for disability. A Pvt. At Battle of Boonville, 17 June 1861, taken ill from rheumatism, due to exposure during the campaign in MO. Sent to the post hospital at Jefferson Bks, MO. Then went into the post hospital at Ft. Leavenworth, KS "as a citizen refugee." Eventually was sent to the Soldiers' Home in WDC. Died 30 March 1897 in Anacostia, WDC. Buried in Prince Georges Co., MD.

SINSINHEIMER / SINSHEIMER, Elias	Baden, Germany			
clerk	5' 4½"	fair	brown	grey
— 1858	22	—		—
10 Nov 1863	27	Pulaski [Prospect], TN		Lt. Murray

Received bounty of $225 for second enlistment. Transferred to Co C, 26 May 1868. Discharged in 1868 at Ft. Stevens, OR. Expiration of service. A Cpl with Co C, 2nd US Art.

SISSON, Oscar O.	Black River Falls, WI		
[no other descriptive data]			
13 Sept 1861	—	Madison, WI	—
2 Dec 1863	—	Prospect, TN	Lt. Dey

Enrolled in 8th Regt WI Inf, La Crosse, WI, 29 Aug 1861. Enlisted in same unit as a Cpl. Was on detached service with Co F, 2nd US Art. Discharged from WI unit to reenlist with Co F in Dec 1863. A Farrier. Discharged 2 Dec 1868 at the Presidio, San Francisco, CA. Expiration of service. A Sgt. Spent most of his military service in and out of hospitals suffering from rheumatism.

SKIPP, John H.   Sunbury, PA
—   5' 9"   fair   auburn   hazel
19 Nov 1860 21   St. Louis, MO   Lt. O'Connell
1 July 1864 26   Atlanta, GA   Lt. Smith
6 July 1867 29   Ft. Vancouver, WT   Lt. McGilvray
Appointed Cpl, 1 July 1864. Reduced in rank and discharged 1 July 1867. Expiration of service. Reenlisted 6 July 1867. Deserted from Ft. Vancouver, WT, 8 Aug 1868. Surrendered himself 2 Dec 1868 at Ft. Vancouver, WT. Deserted 15 March 1869.

SMITH, John   Danflos, Germany
soldier   5' 10"   dark   brown   grey
1 Dec 1863   35   Prospect, TN   Lt. Dey
Appointed Cpl, 1 Jan 1864. Deserted 7 Aug 1865.

SMITH, Louis   Paris, France
laborer   5' 7½"   dark   dark   blue
23 Aug 1858 34   Ft. Leavenworth, KT Lt. J. P. Jones
[Enlisted in St. Louis, MO; joined Co at Ft. Leavenworth, KT.] Deserted 27 May 1859 from Ft. Riley, KT.

SMITH, Luke   Cavan, Ireland
soldier   5' 7"   fair   brown   blue
29 Aug 1854 33   Barrancas Bks., FL   Maj. Woodbridge
Deserted 7 May 1859 from Ft. Riley, KT. He was into his 2nd enlistment.

SMITH, Mahlon B.   Ancaster, Canada
surveyor   5' 7¾"   florid   auburn   blue
25 Aug 1858 31   Rochester, NY   Lt. Holabird
Enlisted in Co G, 3rd US Art. Transferred to Co F, 2nd US Art (SO#38, HQs, Dept of Army, NY, 12 March 1861). Deserted Co, 1 April 1861. Joined Co at Commerce, MO, 28 Feb 1862. Discharged 27 Sept 1862 at St. Louis, MO for disability which read "Very great General Debility and Emaciation. Off duty since about first of March. In this Hospital [Benton Bks, St. Louis, MO] three months." Suffered from consumption ("Superadded to Hereditary predisposition") and secondary syphilis. Died 17 Oct 1862 after discharge in post hospital, Benton Bks, MO. A Pvt.

SMITH, Samuel
[no descriptive data]
24 Jan 1861 28   St. Louis, MO   Lt. O'Connell
6 Dec 1865   33   Benicia, CA   Lt. Buckmayer[?]
Regular army recruit on detached service with 1st MO Lt Art. Transferred to Co F, (SO#21, HQs, Dept of Army, WDC, 14 Jan 1864). Deserted 15 June 1864 from Odeon, IL, on way to join Co. Reported as deserted on 1 July 1864. Transferred to Co L, 2nd US Art, 26 May 1868. Discharged 23 Jan 1868. Expiration of service.

SMITH, Thomas			Liverpool, England
   groom			5' 6¹/₂"		ruddy		sandy		grey
   2 Sept 1863		30		Buffalo, NY			Capt. Tidball
   Killed by lightning 14 July 1864 near the Chattahoochee River, GA. A Pvt.

SMITH, William
   [no descriptive data]
   [no enlistment data]
   Transferred to Co F, 2nd US Art from general service recruits (SO#22, HQs, Dept of West, Springfield, MO, 7 July 1861). Transferred from Co F [no data given (MRF April–May 1862)].

SOCIN, Peter			Basel, Switzerland
   cooper			5' 9"		dark		brown		blue
   23 Feb 1855		29		Barrancas Bks., FL		Maj. Woodbridge
   Appointed Cpl, 1 April 1857 (Or#13, HQs, 2nd Art, Ft. Hamilton, NY, 7 April 1857). Appointed Sgt, 2 Nov 1857 (Or#13, HQs, 2nd Art Battalion, cantonment near Ft. Leavenworth, KT, 2 Dec 1857) vice Gustavus Dey [see previous listing], who was demoted to Pvt. Discharged 8 Nov 1858 at Ft. Riley, KT with Surgeon's certificate of disability. A Sgt. [See previous listing for Franz Bennick, who was killed on 2 Nov 1858 "by discharge of a pistol in the hands of Sergt. Peter Soukin [Socin] at Ft. Riley."]

STEELE, Josiah			—, New Jersey
   soldier			6' 3"		light		auburn		dark
   2 Sept 1861		21		Plymouth, WI			—
   1 Dec 1863		23		Prospect, TN			Lt. Murray
   Enlisted in 8th WI Inf. Discharged 30 Nov 1863 for reenlistment with Co F, 2nd US Art. Received $25 bounty for enlisting. Appointed Cpl, 1 Jan 1864. Killed 22 July 1864 in battle near Atlanta, GA. A Cpl. Born 7 April 1839. Pension claim filed by father, William Steele of Plymouth, Sheboygan Co., WI, in 1886.

STEFAN, Joseph [see STEPHAN / STEFAN, Joseph]

STEFFEN, August [or VonGRAHL, August Steffen] Hralsund, Prussia
   soldier			5' 8³/₄"		—		—		—
   16 May 1857		29
   28 May 1862		34		Ft. McHenry, MD		Lt. Grey
   9 March 1865		37		—			—
   23 May 1868		40		—			—
   1 July 1876		46		Washington, DC		AGO
   1 July 1881		51		Washington, DC		AGO
   Assigned to Co B, 2nd US Art, 1857. Discharged 16 May 1862 at Mt Prospect, VA. Expiration of service. A Sgt. Reenlisted in Co F, 2nd US Art, 1862. Transferred to Co I, same Regt, 31 Dec 1862. Appointed Sgt Maj, 2nd US Art Regt, 31 Oct 1863. Discharged and reenlisted 9 March 1865. Reduced in rank and transferred to Co B, 2nd US Art, 31 Oct 1865. Discharged Alcatraz Island, CA, 28 March 1868. A Sgt. Reenlisted in Co C, 1st US Art, 1868. Discharged 12 Nov 1868 at WDC, by reason of appointment to civil clerk in AGO. A Cpl. From 1 July 1876 to Aug 1882, was a General Service Clerk in the AGO's office; "and his duties as such were analogous to those of a civil clerk." Discharged 11 Aug 1882 "by order of Secretary of War (having been appointed to a clerkship class #1, A.G.O.) at

Washington, D.C., a Private." Died 18 May 1883 in WDC, at 70 years, 7 months. Buried in Prospect Hill Cemetery. Death certificate states he was born in Vorwitz, Germany; lived at 223–4½ Street, South West, WDC, and had been a resident for 16 years.

STEPHAN / STEFAN, Joseph   —, Hungary
  soldier   5' 6"   dark   dark   dark
  9 Feb 1861   31   Little Rock Ars., AR   Capt. Totten
  9 Dec 1863   32   Prospect, TN   Lt. Murray
"Paroled prisoner at Holly Springs, Miss." [no date; near Corinth (MRF Oct–Dec 1862)]. Deserted 5 Nov 1864. Apprehended 7 Nov 1864. Discharged 9 Dec 1868 at Cape Disappointment, WT. Expiration of service. A Pvt.

STEWART, David   Derry, Ireland
  laborer   5' 7"   ruddy   dark   grey
  25 Nov 1854   29   New York, NY   Lt. Garnett
  Died at 2:00 a.m. of delirium tremens 22 July 1859 in hospital at Ft. Leavenworth, KT.

STILLER, Henry C.   Hesse Cassel, Germany
  laborer   5' 5"   fair   lt. brn.   hazel
  20 Aug 1854   22   New York, NY   Col. Brown
  24 June 1859   27   Ft. Leavenworth, KT   —
  Transferred from Co I, 1 Sept 1857 (SO#24, HQs, 2nd Art, Ft. Monroe, VA, 3 Sept 1857). Wounded at the Battle of Wilson's Creek, MO, 10 Aug 1861.

STRANGE, James M.   York Dist., NC
  farmer   5' 11"   fair   brown   hazel
  19 Nov 1857   21   Charlotte, NC   Lt. J. P. Jones
  Transferred to Co F, 2nd US Art from temporary attachment (Or#148, HQs, Ft. Riley, KT, 9 Dec 1858). Discharged 19 Nov 1862 at Grand Junction, TN [or at Davis' Mill, MS]. Expiration of service. A Pvt. [See *OR: Armies*, Volume XVII, Series I, page 248, for Strange's action at Battle of Corinth, MS.] Claimed pension for piles developed on the retreat from Wilson's Creek to Rolla, MO in Aug 1861. "I cannt [sic] say what caus [sic] them unless it was pushing at a caeshon [caisson] that was left on the Battle field." Was also shot in the hip accidentally by a Provost Guard in Memphis, TN in 1864. Lived in Pulaski and Perry Counties, AR, after discharge. Died 23 March 1900.

STREET, Darius   Toronto, Canada
  wagon maker   5' 6½"   ruddy   brown   grey
  1 June 1856   30   San Diego, CA   Capt. [illegible]
  Transferred from Co C, 3rd US Art (SO#301, HQs, Ft. Leavenworth, KT, 21 Aug 1858). Discharged 1 June 1861 at St. Louis, MO. Expiration of service. A Pvt.

STROH, John G.   Wurttemberg, Germany
  farmer   5' 5"   fair   black   hazel
  22 Feb 1854   33   Newport, KY   Col. Hoffman
  Transferred from Co I to Co F, 1 Sept 1857 (SO#24, HQs, 2nd Art, Ft. Monroe, VA, 3 Sept 1857). Discharged 22 Feb 1859 at Ft. Riley, KT. Expiration of service. A Pvt.

STROMENGER, Peter   —, Germany
—   5' 6¹/₂"   fair   —   dark
10 Dec 1860   —   Chicago, IL   —
Unassigned recruit; sent to Newport Bks, KY. Assigned to Co M, 1st MO Lt Art, Oct 1861. Transferred to Co F, 2nd US Art (SO#21, HQs, Dept of Army, WDC, 14 Jan 1864). Discharged 10 Dec 1865. Expiration of service. A Pvt. Claimed he suffered from rheumatism as a result of exposure in inclement weather during the campaigns in MO and MS. Died 25 June 1900 at Montevideo, Chippewa Co., MN.

STUMPF, Eugene   —, Germany
laborer   5' 4¹/₂"   fair   light   hazel
1 Dec 1860   22   Newport, KY   Lt. Wilkins
Transferred from general service recruits (SO#22, HQs, Dept of West, Springfield, MO, 7 July 1861). Deserted 21 Sept 1861 from St. Louis, MO.

SUTLIFF, William H.   Warren, OH
carpenter   5' 10"   fair   brown   blue
4 June 1860   24   Ft. Leavenworth, KT —
Deserted 29 March 1861 from Jefferson Bks, MO.

SWEENEY, Daniel   Cork, Ireland
laborer   5' 7"   fair   brown   grey
6 July 1855   22   San Francisco, CA   Capt. Keyes
1 July 1860   27   Ft. Leavenworth, KT Lt. Barriger
1 July 1864   31   Atlanta, GA   Lt. Smith
Transferred from Co A, 3rd US Art, (SO#301, HQs, Ft. Leavenworth, KT, 21 Aug 1858). Discharged 1 July 1867. Expiration of service.

TAPPLER / TAPPLE, Charles W.   Baden, Germany
baker   5' 5¹/₂"   fair   brown   grey
23 Feb 1855   24   Barrancas Bks., FL   Maj. Woodbridge
Deserted 20 May 1856 from Barrancas Bks, FL. Apprehended 31 May 1856. General Court-Martial (SO#12, HQs, Dept of East, Baltimore, MD, 14 Feb 1857) for desertion. Rejoined Co. Discharged 5 March 1860. Expiration of service.

THOMPSON, Arthur   Wattesville, OH
soldier   5' 9"   fair   dark   black
1 March 1864   24   Athens, AL   Lt. Murray
Reenlisted from the 43rd OH Vol Inf, and appointed Cpl in Co F, 2nd US Art, 1 March 1864. Discharged 1 March 1867. Expiration of service.

THORP, Charles / Isaacher [see CHILDS, Charles Thorp]

TIERNEY, Michael   Clare, Ireland
laborer   5' 5³/₄"   fair   brown   grey
2 Sept 1863   25   Buffalo, NY   Capt. Tidball
Received $225 bounty for five year enlistment. Transferred to Co C, 2nd US Art, 26 May 1868. Discharged 2 Sept 1868 at Ft. Vancouver, WT. Expiration of service. A Pvt.

TILLS, Newton   London, England
soldier   5' 8¹/₂"   dark   black   grey
1 July 1864   26   Atlanta, GA   Lt. Smith
Discharged 1 July 1867. Expiration of service.

TIPPET, John   Cornwall, England
  painter   5' 8½"   fair   brown   blue
  22 Sept 1858   21   Ft. Leavenworth, KT   Lt. J. P. Jones
Severely wounded 28 May 1862 near Farmington, MS. Discharged 28 June
1862 for disability at Danville, MS. A Pvt. Died 28 Feb 1894 of enlarged prostate
in Chicago, IL. Claimed wound at Farmington disabled him from performing in
his post war trade as a printer. Wound in left forearm caused by a shell "so shaped
as to make four very bad wounds." Admitted to field hospital at Farmington, MS 1
June 1862. Remained a month; then sent back to his Co with orders to be given a
disability discharge.

TONRY / YOUNG, Bartholomew   Roscommon, Ireland
  farmer   5' 6½"   fair   brown   blue
  11 May 1860   24   Ft. Leavenworth, KT   Lt. Barriger
Deserted 22 March 1861 from Jefferson Bks, MO.

TONRY / YOUNG, Martin Roscommon, Ireland
  farmer   5' 6½"   fair   brown   blue
  11 May 1860   27   Ft. Leavenworth, KT   Lt. Barriger
Joined by enlistment. Deserted 22 July 1860 from Ft. Leavenworth, KT.

TRACY / TRACEY, William   Jefferson Co., NY
  farmer   5' 9"   fair   light   hazel
  22 March 1860   22   Ft. Leavenworth, KT   Lt. Barriger
Deserted 9 April 1860 from Ft. Leavenworth, KT, after less than one month's
service.

TWINAME, James E.   New York, NY
  bricklayer   5' 11"   dark   dark   blue
  28 Aug 1860   28   Milwaukee, WI   Lt. J. P. Jones
Unassigned. Transferred from Newport Bks, KY to Co M, 1st MO Lt Art, Oct
1861. Transferred to Co F, 2nd US Art, (SO#21, HQs, Dept of Army, WDC, 14 Jan
1864). Discharged 28 Aug 1865 at Ft. McHenry, MD. Expiration of service. A Pvt.
According to the Co records, three men were struck by lightning and killed on 14
July 1864 near the Chattahoochee River, GA. Not noted was that Pvt Twiname,
while on guard duty, was struck in the back and knocked unconscious by the same
bolt of lightning. Was never hospitalized but was, according to a comrade, "excused from duty a great deal." Born 11 Nov 1832. Died 23 July 1917 in Indianapolis, IN.

VALLENDER / VOLLANDER, John   New Prussia, Germany
  harness maker/saddler 5' 6"   dark   brown   blue
  3 Dec 1860   27   Newport, KY   Lt. Wilkins
  9 Dec 1866   33   —   —
  4 Jan [Feb] 1870   37   Cincinnati, OH   —
Unassigned recruit. As a consequence of battle conditions at New Madrid, MO
and Vicksburg, MS, experienced rheumatism, deafness, and became "completely
broken down in health." Was assigned to Co B, 2nd Regt, Vol Invalid Corps doing
guard duty at Detroit and Pontiac, MI, 1863; reassigned to the Invalid Corps of
the regular army, Ft. McHenry, MD, 1864. Transferred from 1st MO Lt Art to Co
F (SO#21, HQs, Dept of Army, WDC, 14 Jan 1864). Left in hospital at Ft. McHenry,
MD when Co F embarked for CA, 3 Oct 1865 (RG 391, Entry 48). Disability

discharge for chronic rheumatism and deafness. Enlisted in Co B, 2nd US Inf, 1866. Discharged 8 Dec 1869. Expiration of service. Enlisted in Co K, 1st US Art, 1870. Disability discharge 15 Feb 1871 at Ft. Riley, KS. Died of Bright's disease on 8 April 1908 in Enterprise, KS. In his discharge in 1871, his Cmdg Officer wrote: "This soldier entered my Barracks in an intoxicated condition and made an assault on one of the other men who was quietly sleeping in his bunk. The assault was made with a Sabre and the attacked party defended himself with the Lance weapon. In the conflict, Pvt. Vallender received a sabre cut in the hand & has been in the hospital ever since. I do not think this soldier is entitled to any consideration on the part of the government." He was discharged because of the disability to his hand, which was quite non-functional.

VAUGHT, James Charles   Logan Co., KY
    farmer   5' 8"   florid   light   blue
    1 May 1860   23   Ft. Leavenworth, KY   Lt. Barriger
    Joined Co by enlistment. Appointed Cpl, 1 Jan 1864 (GO#7, HQs, 2nd Art, Ft. McHenry, MD, 9 March 1865 [delayed paperwork]). Discharged 1 May 1865. Expiration of service. A Cpl. Was Co Saddler. After discharge, served on the St. Louis Police Force. Born 22 Feb 1835. Died 21 Dec 1873. Buried in the Bellefonte Cemetery, St. Louis, MO. Vaught's widow remarried in 1874. Her second husband was "habitually intoxicated" and deserted her after one year. Her third marriage lasted from 1889 to 1928, when she was again widowed. The next year, at age 81, she applied for a widow's pension based on Vaught's service. It was denied on 24 Nov 1930 on grounds "that claimant having lived in open and notorious adulterous cohabitation [presumably her third marriage!] since soldier's death and since the passage of the Act of Aug. 7, 1882, has under the provisions of said Act forfeited any right to pension which she might have as soldier's former widow."

VOLLANDER, John [see VALLENDER / VOLLANDER, John]

VonGRAHL, August Steffen [see STEFFEN, August]

WACHSMAN, Albert   Sonderhausen, Germany
    carpenter   5' 8"   sallow   brown   hazel
    8 Aug 1854   21   New York, NY   Col. Brown
    10 June 1859   25   Ft. Leavenworth, KT   —
    Joined Co I at Ft. Deynaud, FL 18 Jan 1855 from Gen Dept, Ft. Columbus, NY. Transferred to Co F, 1 Sept 1857 (SO#24, HQs, 2nd Art, Ft. Monroe, VA, 3 Sept 1857). Appointed Cpl 22 Aug 1859 at Ft. Leavenworth, KT. Appointed Sgt 1 Sept 1861. Discharged 2 June 1862 at Camp Clear Creek, MS, to accept commission with MO Vol. Became a Capt with Battery A, 2nd MO and 1st MO Lt Art (Heitman, *Register*, volume 2). Discharged at Benton Bks, St. Louis, MO, 28 Aug 1865. Married Virginia K. Bridger, daughter of Jim Bridger, famed Indian scout. Born 21 Dec 1833. Died in Kansas City, MO, 10 Jan 1883. Buried in old section 8, Union Cemetery, Kansas City, MO. At time of his death, was the Westport [Kansas City, MO] Justice of the Peace (*Soldiers Buried at Union Cemetery, Kansas City, MO*, 1988, volume 2, Union Cemetery Historical Society, Kansas City, MO). Credited with writing a biography of his father-in-law, Jim Bridger. Shortly after being commissioned in the Vol service, in July 1862 at Sedalia, MO, while on drill with his battery, his horse fell with him, severely bruising his left leg and dislocating his arm. Then on the march from Westport, MO to Sedalia from 28 Dec 1863 to 5 Jan 1864, exposed to severe weather, took cold which developed into chronic dysentery. Also suffered from rheumatism as a result of the earlier accident.

WAGNER, Lewis / Louis   Wurttemberg, Germany
  tanner   5' 7¹/₂"   fair   brown   grey
  13 Jan 1854   30   Newport, KY   Col. Hoffman
  Discharged 13 Jan 1859 at Ft. Riley, KT. Expiration of service. A Pvt. [Served
  also with Co I.]

WALLACE, James   Cork, Ireland
  —   5' 10"   fair   sandy   blue
  19 July 1859   22   Ft. Leavenworth, KT   —
  Believed killed at the Battle of Wilson's Creek, MO, 10 Aug 1861. Admitted to
General Hospital, Springfield, MO, 10 Aug 1861 with severe gun shot wound in
left side near 7th rib "the ball entering & piercing the cavity of the chest & lodging
in the back where it still remains." Rejoined Co 1 Sept 1861 at Rolla, MO. Admitted 9 Sept 1861 in New House of Refuge, St. Louis, MO. Returned to duty 28 Nov
1861, "with remark: 'Recommend for discharge to his Co. Com.,' noted opposite his
name." Appointed Cpl 7 May 1863 at camp near Memphis, TN. Discharged 19
July 1864 at Decatur, GA. Expiration of service. Born 19 July 1837 [1836]. Died
2 Jan 1922 of cardiac arrest in National Military Home, Leavenworth, KS.

WALSH, John   —, Ireland
  forge hand   5' 7"   fair   black   grey
  24 April 1860   24   Ft. Leavenworth, KT   Lt. Barriger
  Artificer. Discharged 24 April 1865 at Bridgeport, AL. Expiration of service. A
Pvt. Claimed total deafness of right ear and severe deafness in left ear from artillery firing during the siege and Battle of Corinth, MS, 1862. Lived in Hutchinson,
KS after discharge.

WARES, John   Tyrone, Ireland
  laborer   5' 4¹/₂"   fair   brown   blue
  13 Nov 1855   21   Boston, MA   Lt. Archer
  1 Nov 1860   26   enroute to Ft. Smith, AR   Lt. Stanley
  Transferred from Co G, 3rd US Art (SO#301, HQs, Ft. Leavenworth, KT, 21 Aug
1858). Erroneously reported as having deserted from St. Louis, MO, 19 Sept 1861
(MRF Aug–Oct 1861; RG 391, Entry 68).

WARRINER, Robert   Lancastershire, England
  sailor   5' 6"   fair   brown   brown
  7 Dec 1853   22   New York, NY   Col. Brown
  9 Oct 1858   27   Ft. Leavenworth, KT   Lt. J. P. Jones
  9 Aug 1863   32   Memphis, TN   Lt. Murray
  Transferred from Co I to Co F, 1 Sept 1857 (SO#24, HQs, 2nd Art, Ft. Monroe,
VA, 3 Sept 1857). Paid $200 bounty for third enlistment. Died 21 July 1867 at Ft.
Vancouver, WT, of "Phethesis Palmonolis" [?].

WATKINS, Isaac   Delaware, NY
  blacksmith   5' 5"   sallow   red   grey
  4 Jan 1856   22   Philadelphia, PA   Lt. Flint
  Joined Co I at Ft. Deynaud, FL 26 March 1856 from Gen Dept, Ft. Columbus,
NY. Transferred to Co F, 1 Sept 1857 (SO#24, HQs, 2nd Art, Ft. Monroe, VA, 3
Sept 1857). Deserted 25 March 1858 from Ft. Leavenworth, KT.

WEIBEZAHL, Frederick   —, Germany
blacksmith   5' 8"   dark   brown   grey
7 July 1855   18   —   —
1 Nov 1860   23   Newport, KY   Lt. Wilkins
Enlisted in Co D, 3rd US Inf. Discharged 6 July 1860 at Pecos River, TX. Expiration of service. Enlisted as a general service recruit. Assigned to Co F. Detached to Co M, 1st MO Lt Art. An Artificer. Returned to Co F (SO#21, HQs, Dept of Army, WDC, 14 Jan 1864). Disability discharge, 10 Feb 1864 for chronic hepatitis. Born 1837. Died 29 July 1892 in Providence Hospital, WDC. Buried in the National Cemetery at Soldiers' Home, WDC. Had a blacksmith business at Ninth Street between Rhode Island Avenue and R Street in WDC. The hepatitis occurred during the Vicksburg campaign, when the entire Co M was infected. Later claimed pension for having been wounded in foot. The claim was disputed because of evidence that he shot himself in the foot rather than engage in battle. This was not plausible to his comrades, who said that as the harness mender for the battery, he was never committed to battle. Received pension only for hepatitis.

WILLIAMS, William J.   Charlotte, NC
carpenter   5' 8"   fair   light   hazel
12 Aug 1857   21   Charlotte, NC   Lt. J. P. Jones
General Garrison Court-Martial (SO#226, HQs, Ft. Leavenworth, KT, 18 Dec 1857). Discharged 12 Aug 1862 at Corinth, MS. Expiration of service. A Pvt. "i have not seen a Relation since August 12th 1857. My Father, Mother Sisters and Brothers are all Dead since shortly after the War. ...i remember that the officer that enlisted me hesitated to take me for i was short a few months of being twenty one but our Amorer [?] a Judge vouched for me..." Sedalia, MO, 2 Jan 1862: "While on detail as teamster hauling wood and water for the Company, the team scared without any fault of his own and ran off throwing him off the saddle mule which fell upon him and injured him, causing Kidney and Bladder disease to such extent as to render him unable to do any kind of duty for several months." Left in the hospital at Sedalia when the Co moved south in Feb 1862 for the attack on New Madrid, MO and Island No. 10. Also injured at Farmington, MS, 28 May 1862, when "the swing saddle horse was shot, reared up, then fell throw[ing] him between the tongue, and fell on him, mashing the right hand." The accident knocked out two front teeth, broke his nose and badly disfigured him. Then on 30 May 1903, during the flood in Armourdale [Kansas City, MO] contracted rheumatism from exposure to the elements. Born in Charlotte, SC, 22 April 1837. Died 25 March 1909, Kansas City, MO.

WILSON, George W.   Mason City, IL
farmer   5' 8"   fair   brown   grey
24 April 1860   22   Ft. Leavenworth, KT   Lt. Barriger
Deserted 13 March 1861.

WOODS, James   Buffalo, NY
teamster   5' 5"   fair   brown   brown
24 Dec 1860   21   Chicago, IL   Lt. J. P. Jones
Transferred from general service recruits (SO#22, HQs, Dept of West, Springfield, MO, 7 July 1861). Appointed Bugler 1 Sept 1862. Taken prisoner 22 July 1864 near Atlanta, GA. Discharged 24 Dec 1865 at Ft. Point, CA. Expiration of service. A Bugler.

WRIGHT, Marion   DeKalb Co., GA
  soldier   5' 11"   ruddy   auburn   blue
  15 May 1860   26   Ft. Leavenworth, KT   Lt. Barriger
  Deserted 28 July 1860 from Ft. Leavenworth, KT. Was into his second enlistment.

WRIGHTENBURG, William   Allamans, Orange Co., NC
  cooper   5' 8[9]"   dark   brown   grey
  21 Oct 1857   24   Charlotte, NC   Lt. J. P. Jones
  22 July 1863   30   —   —
  Transferred into Co F, 2nd US Art, from temporary attachment (Or#148, HQs,
  Ft. Riley, KT, 9 Dec 1858). Appointed Cpl, 1 April 1861 at Jefferson Bks, MO.
  Promoted to Sgt, 23 Feb 1862. Discharged 21 Oct 1862 at camp near Corinth, MS.
  Expiration of service. A Sgt. Enrolled in Co E, 14 KS Cav. Held ranks of Pvt and
  Sgt from July to 19 Oct 1863. Commissioned 2nd Lt on 19 Oct 1863. Transferred
  to Co L, 14th KS Cav. Tendered resignation and discharged (SO#30, AR) on 11 Feb
  1865 "because of 'limited education.' " Claimed to have been wounded by a buckshot to the ankle during the Battle of Wilson's Creek and by a gunshot to the hip at
  the Battle of Corinth. Supposedly treated in field hospital, Corinth, 4 Oct 1862.
  Regimental Casualty Returns for 1861 and 1862 do not list him as wounded. In
  1870, moved to CA, and lived in Kern and Los Angeles Counties. Testified (April
  1894) to being quite destitute: "I am without means to travel or make search for
  these men [former comrades] ...I have come on foot 40 miles to find a Notary and
  make this affidavit." [Signed with his mark at Fairmount, CA.]

WUSSHASSKIESE, Charles   Baden, Germany
  tailor   5' 8½"   fair   lt. brn.   blue
  14[10] July 1856   21   Barrancas Bks., FL   Lt. Merchant
  Deserted 26 May 1858 from camp 9 miles from Ft. Leavenworth, KT.

YOUNG, Bartholomew [see TONRY / YOUNG, Bartholomew]

YOUNG, Cyrus H.   Lancaster Co., PA
  cooper   5' 10"   ruddy   auburn   dark
  28 Nov 1860   24   Newport, KY   Lt. Wilkins
  16 Aug 1864   29   Lancaster, PA   —
  Transferred into Co F, 2nd US Art, from general service recruits (SO#22, HQs,
  Dept of West, Springfield, MO, 7 July 1861). Wounded 10 Aug 1861 at Battle of
  Wilson's Creek, MO. Rejoined Co at Camp Sigel [nd] (RG 391, Entry 68). Discharged 17 Sept 1861 at St. Louis, MO for disability from wounds suffered at
  Wilson's Creek. A Pvt. While holding horses of the battery, it being in action, and
  he being a driver, received a gunshot wound in the left leg, just above the knee.
  The bullet was embedded in the bone, and was not extracted. Carried the bullet
  for two years; then had it extracted. Was then enrolled, 16 Aug 1864, in Independent Battery C, PA Lt Art. Transferred to Co M, 5th PA Heavy Art in Jan 1865.
  Discharged with Co on 30 June 1865 at WDC. Born 20 Dec 1836, Warwick Town-
  ship, Lancaster Co., PA. Died 27 Dec 1911 in Northumberland, PA.

YOUNG, Daniel   Byrone, Germany
  musician   5' 9"   dark   brown   hazel
  7 Aug 1863   29   Buffalo, NY   Capt. Tidball
  Deserted 25 Oct 1863 from Buffalo, NY, before joining Co.

YOUNG, Martin [see TONRY / YOUNG, Martin]

ZIMMER, John   Germany [or Ohio]
laborer   5' 7½"   florid   brown   blue
14 Jan 1861   —   Cleveland, OH   Lt. Clinton
Regular army recruit temporarily on detached service with 1st MO Lt Art. Returned to Co F, 2nd US Art (SO#21, HQs, Dept of Army, WDC, 14 Jan 1864). Discharged same day at Vicksburg, MS. Expiration of service. Born c. 1835. Notation in pension file: "Sailed on barge *Neptune* [on way to US from Germany?]." Died 3 May 1886, in New Riegel, OH. Claimed to have crushed his ankle while driving left wheel team of three teams pulling a 10-lb Parrott. John Vallender [see previous listing] testified that "while going into action at Point Pleasant, Mo. [the New Madrid / Island No. 10 campaign], Said John Zimmer was driving wheel team on 1st piece, and on going up a lane and passing through a bars [opening in a fence] into a field, the Lieut. in command ordered the move toward the left to be made suddenly, which brought the Said John Zimmer between left horse and fence post, and unable to extricate himself at once; team was halted and turned to the right, and at same time jamming Said John Zimmer's feet against the fence post, injuring both ankles, left one the most, and unable to walk at that time and for several weeks thereafter." Zimmer also contracted typhoid fever during the Vicksburg, MS campaign.

****

DISPOSITION OF ENLISTMENTS, Company F, 1857–1865 and beyond:

	Enlisted in Company			General Service Recruits SO#22	SO#21	Company
	1857–60	1861–63	1863–64	7 July 1861	14 Jan 1864	Totals
Deserted	32	16	12	11	1	72
Discharged:						
Expiration of service	13	49	11	15	15	103
Disability	5	14		4	2	25
Dishonorable	1	1				2
Useless		1				1
Died / Killed	4	9	5	4	3	25
Commissioned in:						
Regular army		1				1
Volunteer army		4				4
Career Soldier		10	1			11
Data inconclusive		5	1	1	1	8
Totals:	55	110	30	35	22	252

Appendix C

List of Honorable Mentions for Meritorious and Distinguished Service during the "Battle of Corinth" on the 3d and 4th days of October A.D. 1862

In his official report of the Battle of Corinth, Major General William Starke Rosecrans took pains to recognize all the especially valorous soldiers who fought: "To signalize in this report all those officers and men whose actions in the battle deserve mention would unnecessarily lengthen this report. I must therefore refer to sub-reports and special mentions, and to a special paper herewith, wherein those most conspicuous, to the number of 109 officers and men, are mentioned." [There are more than 109 names mentioned because the paper also includes names of individuals who distinguished themselves in the Battle of Iuka, September 19, 1862.]

The General's reference to the special paper is contained in *OR: Armies*, Series I, Volume XVII, Part I, page 170. The special paper itself is filed in the National Archives, Washington, DC, under Record Group 94, "Office of the Adjutant General, War Records Office, Union Battle Reports," Box 27. At the suggestion of the author, Mike Musick of the National Archives was able to locate the document.

As far as can be determined, this is the first time the special paper has been presented in its entirety in any published work. It is reproduced here, with additions in brackets to indicate information found by the author to clarify some of the entries, particularly to complete the names of individuals cited. The author has also taken the liberty to make obvious spelling and punctuation changes from the handwritten document.

NAME / REMARKS	RANK	Co.	REGIMENT
SEARS, [Cyrus]	Lieut.		[11th Ohio Battery]
NEIL, [Henry M.]	Lieut.		[" " "]

Reported by Lt. Col. Lothrop for gallant conduct, battle of Iuka.

WHITE	Corpl.
HILL	"

Recommended for service rendered at battle Iuka, for favorable notice, Comdg. Genl., by Genl. Hamilton.

CRAIG, [D. A.]	Captain	H	17th Iowa
GARRETT, [Jesse B.]	Lieut.	A	" "
JOHNSON, [Charles P.]	"	A	" "
RICE, [Alphonso A.]	"	I	" "
NULL [HULL, Amaziah]	"	E	" "
SNODGRASS, [John C.]	"	I	" "
MORRIS, [Robert S.]	"	F	" "
STAPLETON, [Martin]	"	C	" "

Reported by Capt. John L. Young, commanding 17th Iowa Regt., as having behaved in a very brave and unflinching manner and as deserving credit at the Battle of Iuka, Miss.

JONES, S. E.	1st Sergt.		12th Wis. Battery
COTY, Philander	Sergt.		[" " "]

Reported by Lieut. Immel for gallantry at the Battle of Iuka.

WILKER, John	Captain	26 Mo.
RICE, T. M.	Captain	26 Mo.
ROBINSON, Wm. M.	[Captain]	26 Mo.
SCHERMAN, F. G.	Lt. & Adjt.	26 Mo.
BROWN, C. F.	Lt. & RMQ [QM]	26 Mo.

Reported for having conducted themselves with rare coolness, bravery, gallantry & nobleness at the battle of Iuka and for efficiency in camp; by Lt. Col. John H. Holman, Comdg., 26 Mo. Vol.

MAUPINS, J. W.	2d Lieut.	F	26 Mo.
CROWELL, Robt. C.	Capt.		26 Mo.
DENNY, D. R.	1st Lieut.		26 Mo.
CROWE, L. T.	2d Lieut.	E	26 Mo.
SCHIRMER, [Laurenzo]	1st Lieut.	H	26 Mo.
DARIUS, J. M.	1st "	C	26 Mo.

Reported by Col. [Geo. B.] Boomer of the 26th Mo. Vol. for having shown distinguished gallantry and energy at the battle of Iuka Miss. [Boomer wounded in battle.]

RUGG, D. W. [DeWitt] C.	Lt. Col.	48 Ind.
STANFIELD, [Edward P.]	AAg.	48 Ind.
ELLIS, [William R.]	Sergt. Major	48 Ind.

Mentioned by Col. Norman Eddy, 48th Ind. Vol., for having shown meritorious conduct at the battle of Iuka. The Lt. Col's. gallantry is reported as conspicuous at every point of danger.

WHITE, [Henry A.]	Lieut.	G	48 Ind.
BINGHAM, Newton	1st Sergt.	F	48 "
SMITH, [John H.]	Captain	A	48 "

Reported by Lt. Col. Rugg as having displayed remarkable bravery.

IMMEL, [Lorenzo D.]   Lt.   1 Mo. Arty., Comdg. 12 Arty. [Wis.]
     Reported by Lt. Col. Boomer as having shown in the battle of Iuka bravery and gallant
conduct for which he cannot receive too much praise.

WILLIAMS,
     G. [George] A.   Captain   1st Infty.
     Gallant conduct at Corinth while commdg. heavy batteries, recommended for Brig. Genl. Vol.
by Brig. Genl. [David S.] Stanley.

ROBINETTE,
     H. C. [Henry Clay]   1st Lieut.   1st Infty.
     Very distinguished conduct at Corinth where he was wounded, recommend for brevet by Brig.
Genl. Stanley.

MOWER, Jos. A.   Colonel   11th Missouri
     Comdg. 2d Brigade 2d Division. Conspicuous in the battles of Iuka and Corinth. On the 3d led
his brigade gallantly, and drove the enemy. Wounded on the 4th Oct. and taken prisoner, escaped
without being pardoned. Recommended to the Govt. as an experienced Brigade commander and
gallant leader by Brig. Genl. Stanley.

WEBER, A. [Andrew] J.   Major   11th Missouri
     Distinguished in action of 4th Oct. at Corinth, - per report Genl. Stanley, recommended for
promotion to Lt. Col.

KENDALL, C. [Cyrus] D.   2d Lieut.   11th Missouri
     Remaining in the field during whole engagement of 4th Oct. after receiving two flesh wounds.
Mentioned by Major Weber, Comdg.

SIMMONS, Wm. S.   Corporal   C   11th Missouri
FYFFE, James A.   "   G   "   "
FRAKES, Jefferson   Private   C   "   "
     Exhibited great bravery on field 4th Oct. Reported by Major Weber, Commdg.

SPAULDING,
     Z. [Zephaniah] S.   Major   27th Ohio
     Distinguished in action of the 4th at Corinth. Mentioned by Genl. Stanley.

EATON, [John]   Chaplain   27th Ohio
     Thanks are due him for arduous labor the days of the battle and caring for the wounded.
Stanley's report.

GOULD, [Orrin B.]   Private   G   27th Ohio
     Captured the colors of the 9th Texas, displayed courage. Mentioned by Z. S. Spaulding, Major
Comdg., and Genl. Stanley.

SPRAGUE, J. [John] W.   Colonel   63d Ohio
     Behaved with great bravery, on the 4th Oct. under murderous fire. Mentioned by Genl.
Stanley.

FRY, [Benjamin St. James] Chaplain   63d Ohio
     Thanks are due him for arduous duties.

BROWN, [Charles E.]   Captain   63d Ohio
    Behaved with distinguished gallantry. Mentioned by Genl. Stanley.

ROBBINS, [George W.]   Lt. Col.   [8th Wis. Inf.]
    Wounded on 3d Oct., is highly recommended by Brig. Genl. Stanley.

JEFFERSON, [John W.]   Major   8th Wisconsin
    Wounded severely on the 3d. Commanded on the 4th.

GILLMORE, [Robert A.]   Major   26 Ills. Infty.
    Commanded Regt. with credit on 3d per report Genl. Stanley.

REED, Geo. H.   1st Lieut.   B   26 Ills. Vol.
    Wounded on 4th Oct., distinguished himself, mentioned by Major Commdg.

KERLIN, G. W.   1st Lieut.   D   26 Ills.
    Distinguished himself on the 4th Oct. battle Corinth, mentioned by Maj. Gillmore, Comdg.

KING, S. Noble   1st Lieut.   A   26 Ills.
    Distinguished himself on the 4th Oct. 1862 at Corinth. Mentioned by Major Gillmore.

BAKER, S. [Samuel] R.   Capt.   47th Ills.
    Commanded Regt. with credit on 3d Oct.

SWAYNE, Wager   Colonel   43d Ohio
HERRICK, [Walter F.]   Major   "   "
PARKS [PARK, Horace]   Capt.   "   "
KINNEY, [John P.]   Lieut.   "   "
    These officers were under the personal observation of Genl. Stanley and deserve mention for conduct. Battle Corinth.

NOYES, [Edward F.]   Colonel   [39th Ohio]
McDOWELL, [Henry T.]   Major   [39th Ohio]
WEBER, [Andrew J.]   Adjt. [Major]   [11th Mo.]
LOTHROP, [W. H.]   Capt.
DUSTAN, [C. W.]   Capt. Adjt.   Staff Col. Fuller - 10 Missouri
BROOKINGS, [Charles H.] Lieut.   aide-de-camp [Stanley]
SINCLAIR, [W. H.]   Lieut.   aide-de-camp [Stanley]
BROWN, [Charles E.]   Capt.   63d Ohio
MAURICE, T. [Thomas] D.   Capt.   F   2d Arty.
    These officers deserve mention from personal observations of Brig. Genl. Stanley. [Capt. Maurice was further cited:] Behaved with distinguished gallantry, particular mention made by Gen. Stanley.

DEY, Gustave   1st Sergt.   F   2d Arty.
    Recommended for honorable mention in Genl's. report for gallantry and coolness on the 4th Oct. though wounded by a shell. Mentioned by Captain Maurice.

McGINNISS
[McGINNIS, Frank S.]   Sergt.   F   2d Arty.
    Recommend for promotion by Capt. Maurice; he has been discharged his term having expired.

GEARY
   [GARRY, James H.]   Private   F   2d Arty.
HENNESSEY, [Patrick]   "   "   " "
   Capt. Maurice mentions these [men] as having behaved bravely.

HUBBARD, L. [Lucius] F.   Colonel   5th Minn.
   Behaved with distinguished gallantry. Mentioned by Genl. Stanley.

GERE, Wm. B.   Lt. Col.   5th Minn.
   By his efforts and example inspired the men and was of essential service upon the field. Mentioned by Col. Hubbard.

TULE [?], A. A.   1st Lieut.   A   A. Adjt. 5th Minn.
   Rendered most efficient service and bore himself gallantly throughout the action, mentioned by Col. Hubbard.

LAMBERG, [Carl A.]   [1st] Lieut.   [3d Mich. Battery]
   Deserves great credit for his service in the 3d Mich. Battery. Mentioned by Genl. Stanley.

Name	Rank	Unit
ROBINSON, Geo.	2d Lt.	3d Mich. Batty.
SHIER, Henry	1st Sergt.	" " "
HYZER, W. W.	Sergt.	" " "
WALLING, D. [Daniel] P.	1st Lt.	2d Iowa Batty.
REED, Chas. F.	2d Lt.	" " "
RAYNOLDS [?], Lewis	1st Sergt.	" " "
KELLOGG, J. [Jay] W.	Sergt.	" " "
COONS, John W.	"	" " "
TALLIE, Thos.	"	" " "
SHELBY, Harry D.	Corporal	" " "
ATKINSON, Albert [G.]	"	" " "
BURKE, John	"	" " "
DAVIS, Oliver [P.]	"	" " "
SOBER, Morris	"	" " "
NORTON, Chas.	"	" " "
FISH, James	Private	" " "
HOLT, J. L. [James Lyman]	"	" " "
DAVIDSON, D. B.	"	" " "

   [Note: above should be LAWSON, Daniel or David B.]

Name	Rank	Unit
McKINLY, F. [Francis]	"	" " "
JONES, Orlin E.	"	" " "
BURNS, Silas [D.]	"	" " "
RICE, W. Scott	"	" " "

   These Officers, Non-Commissioned officers and privates are recommended by their respective commanders. Report [by] Genl. Stanley.

BUFORD,
   N. [Napoleon] B.   Brig. Genl.   [Cmdg. 1st Brig.]
   Mentioned as having handled his brigade on the 4th at Corinth with a skill and bravery worthy of his high reputation, by Brig. Gen. Hamilton.

HOLMES, S. [Samuel] A.   Colonel   [Cmdg. 2d Brig.]
   Mentioned by Gen. Hamilton as having handled the Brigade of Gen. Sullivan, after the Genl. received his injury, with a discretion and gallantry unsurpassed during the action of 4th Oct.

SULLIVAN,
J. [Jeremiah] C.   Brig. Genl.   [Cmdg. 2d Brig.]
    Gen. Hamilton reports that on the 4th Oct. "Springing from his sick bed" and bravely led the 56th Ills. and 17th Iowa Regts., and took the lead in the charge against the rebels; recaptured the Earthwork battery and guns of the 1st Mo. Battery (Davis Division).

HORNEY, [Leonidas]   [Major]   10 Missouri [Inf.]
    Gen. Hamilton reports his having stood his ground against the panic stricken regiment that gave way, in its front, and even as its front was uncovered by retiring soldiers opening on the enemy and joining in the advance of the Division, aided to recapture Battery.

SANBORN, J. [John] B.	Colonel	4 Minn.
MATTHIES, C. [Charles] L.	"	5th Iowa
ALEXANDER, J. [Jesse] I.	"	59 Ind.
HOLMES, J. [John] H.	Lt. Col.	26 Mo.
RUGG, DW. [DeWitt] C.	" "	48 Ind.
RAUM, G. [Green] B.	" "	56 Ills.
HORNEY, L. [Leonidas]	Major	10 Mo.
LANNING, R. [Richard] P.	"	80 Ohio [Killed 4th Oct.]
BANBURY, J. [Jabez]	"	17th Iowa [from the 5th Iowa, Cmdg. 17th]

    Gen. Hamilton reports that these officers were all that officers should be, leading and inspiring their men by their dauntless bravery at the battle of Corinth.

McCALLA, [Nathaniel]   Major   10 Iowa
    Mentioned by Genl. Hamilton as all that an officer should be at the battle of Corinth; inspired his men by his dauntless bravery, etc.

POWELL, A. [Albert] M.   Major   Chief of Arty. - 3d Div.
    Mentioned by Gen. Hamilton as one "to whom the country is greatly indebted" for conspicuous bravery and the masterful manner in which his batteries were brought to the front and handled.

DILLON, [Henry]	Capt.		6 Wisconsin
NEIL, [Henry M.]	Lieut.		11 Ohio Arty.
IMMEL, [Lorenzo]	Lieut.		12 Wis. Arty.
McMURRAY, [Junius W.]	Lieut.	M	1st Mo.

    Mentioned for having contributed to the victory 4th Oct., and of whom Gen. Hamilton says he cannot say too much.

SAWYER, R. M.	Capt.	[AAG]
SCOTT [MOTT], J. W.	Capt. & C. S.	[Staff]
PEARCE, E. T.	[Lieut.]	aide-de-camp
WHEELER, W. F.	[Lieut.]	aide-de-camp

    Mentioned by Gen. Hamilton for bravery and promptness on 4th Oct. for rallying great numbers of Davis' Div. and taking them back to [the] field.

MURPHY, L. [J.] H.   Surgeon   [Acting. Medical Dir.]
    For taking care of wounded.

BATES, [Kinzie]	Lieut.	1st Arty.
HOSMER, [Charles Hawes]	"	" "
MACE [?]	"	" "

    Mentioned by Capt. William for good conduct at Battle of Corinth.

ROBINETTE, [Henry Clay]   Lieut.   1st Arty.
CULLEN, [Edgar M.]   "   "   "
    Capt. Williams calls special attention for part taken 4th Oct.

BRANAGAN, [Patrick]   1st Sergt.   I   1st Arty.
HEIN, [Leonard]   [']   C   "   "
JACOBI, [Otto]   [']   D   "   "
McGUIRE, [Edward]   Sergt.   "   "
McDONALD, [Patrick]   "   "   "
GALLAGHER, [Patrick]   "   "   "
WATERS, [John]   Lance Corporal   "   "
    Capt. Williams calls attention for good behavior in the Battle of Corinth.

HICKENLOOPER,
   [Andrew]   Capt.   5th Ohio Battery, Chief Arty., 6th Div.
    Mentioned by Genl. McArthur for good management, battle of Corinth.

WHITE, H. B.   Capt.   10 Ohio Arty.
CLAYTON, [William Z.]   Sergt. [Lieut.]   1st Minn.
    These officers distinguished themselves and ought to be promoted, McArthur reports.

WILLARD, [Lot S.]   Lieut.   aide-de-camp
McARTHUR, [James G.]   Lieut.   aide-de-camp
    Commended as efficient officers and deserving promotion, by Genl. McArthur.

ZEIGLER, [John R.]   Capt.   11 Ills. Cav.
LEWMAN, [Moses T.]   Lieut.   11 Ills. Cav.
HIGLEY, [M. A.]   Lieut.   A. Div. Qr. Master
    These officers are entitled to thanks for part taken, battle of Corinth and commended as efficient officers by Genl. McArthur.

Appendix D

The Dey/Day Family Genealogy Compiled by Nancy Day Ingrisano

Gustav(us) Adolphus Dey -m.(2)- Victoria Gunther -m.(1)- Charles B. Taylor
1828-1882   1867   1824/5-1890   1851   1817-1864

                                                              ┌Zachary Taylor: 1854-?
                                                              └William B. Taylor: 1863-?

Gustav Adolph Dey / Day─┘ -m.(1)- Christina Kolpack -m.(2)- Rudolph Gollnik
1869-1921   c.1903   1879/80-1936/7   1867-1937

         Ernest Christian Day┐ -m.-   Helen Nieman
         1904-1941   │ 1924   1900-1957

    Edna Louisa Day: 1905-1978┐ [see below]
  Edward Howard Day: 1911-1952┤ [see below]
   Elmer Walter Day: 1914-1971┤ [see below]
Ethel Victoria Day: 1916-1950/55(?)┤ [see below]

    Charles Dersam -m.(1)- Edna Louisa Day -m.(2)- William Roman
    c.1897-1977   c.1926   1905-1978   1959   Patynowski / Patty
                    div.:1958   1913-1977

      Joan Ellen Dersam┐ -m.-   Richard Warren Schoelles
      1930-   │ 1953   1931-1992

    Douglas John Schoelles┐ -m.-   Isabel Beasley
    1963-   │ 1992   1965-

   Lynne Elisabeth Schoelles┐ -m.-   Andrew John D'Hondt
   1966-   │ 1990   1964-

Timothy Steven Syakovich┐
1983-   │ ┌Erin Nicole D'Hondt: 1987-
                         │ └─Lauren Michelle D'Hondt: 1989-

William David Schoelles: 1970- ┘

257

Edward Howard Day -m.- Helen Josephine Lesswing
1911-1952   1941   1910-1982

    Carol Christine Day┤   -m.-   Paul Edward Bieron
         1942-   1964   1942-

                          ├Lisa Helene Bieron   -m.-   Paul Charles Hoffman
                          1965-   1990   1965-

                                    ├Olivia Grace Hoffman: 1994-
                                    └Carolyn Faith Hoffman: 1997-

                          ├Brian Francis Bieron   -m.-   Kimberly Ann Summers
                          1966-   1990   1966-

                                    ├James Christopher Bieron: 1992-
                                    └Julianne Day Bieron: 1997-

                          ├Kristin Marie Bieron   -m.-   William Joseph Maher, Jr.
                          1968-   1992   1966-

                                    ├Daniel William Maher: 1995-
                                    └David James Maher: 1997-

    Kathleen Mary Day┤   -m.-   Thomas Edward Latham
         1944-   1966-   1942-

                          └Richard Thomas Latham   -m.-   Annette Louise Munson
                           1967-   1996   1966-

                                    ├Steven Victor Latham: 1996-

    Nancy Helen Day┤ -m.(2)-   Michael Nicholas Ingrisano -m.(1)- Bettyjeanne
         1945-   1986   1921-   1945   Louise Hill
                                                                        1922-1985

Elmer Walter Day   -m.-   Mary Jane Brown
1914-1971   1942   1921-1989

Jane Davis Butzner   -m.(1)-   --Christian Charles Day   -m.(2)-   Janet Anita Weaver Mason
1947-   1968   1946-   1978   1938-1993
              div: 1970

Ann Marie Kochan   -m.(3)-
1955-   1995
                                    Lawrence Baron--   -m.-   --Kimberly Anita Mason
                                                    1988   1962-
                                                 div: 1996

                                    Michael Lewis Cohen   -m.-   --Hilary Elizabeth Mason
                                    1968-   1993   1970-

                                                             --David Eric Cohen: 1995-

Brian Matthew Israel   -m.-   --Christine Jane Day
1951-1986   1978   1953-

Henry I. Michael   -m.(1)-   **Ethel Victoria Day**   -m.(2)?-   William Peet / Peat
1914-   c.1933/4   1916-1950-5?
              div.   --(?)Christine

William Day Michael--   -m.-   Diane H. McKno
1937-   1958
                   div: 1976

                   --Pamela Ann Michael: 1959-

                   --Kathleen Irene Michael   -m.-   Edward Krukowski
                     1961-   1995   1960-

                   --Tracey Anne Michael   -m.-   James Roetzer
                     1963-   1983
                                  div: 1993

                                      --James Michael Roetzer: 1984-
                                      --Jena Lea Roetzer: 1986-

                   --William Henry Michael: 1965-

David Edward Michael--   -m.-   Sally Mitchell
1938-   1964
                    div.

                    --David James Michael: 1965-
                    --Karen Elizabeth Michael: 1967-
                    --Susan Elaine Michael: 1970-
                    --Daniel Edward Michael: 1972-

ﶺotes

───────────────────────────── 💣

CHAPTER 1

1. The background material for this chapter was digested from James W. Covington, *The Seminoles of Florida* (Gainesville: University of Florida Press, 1993), and Alfred Jackson Hanna and Kathryn Abbey Hanna, *Lake Okeechobee* (New York: The Bobbs-Merrill Company, 1948).

   Richard Brooke Garnett, Va., USMA 1841. Resigned 1861 to join Confederacy. Killed at Gettysburg in 1863, leading his brigade. Brig. Gen. Francis B. Heitman, *Historical Register and Dictionary of the United States Army* (Washington, D.C., 1903), vol. 1.; Mark M. Boatner, III, *The Civil War Dictionary* (New York: David McKay Company, Inc., 1959), p. 324.

2. "Register of Enlistments in the United States Army. 1789–1914." Vol. 49–50, No. 315. And "Register of Enlistments..." Microfilm 233 (hereafter M + number), Roll 25, line 5 (hereafter R.+ number). Record Group 94 (hereafter RG + number).

   The specifications for an artilleryman were found in the returns of Company F, 2nd U.S. Art. From a return from Company M, same regiment. *Records of the Adjutant General's Office* (hereafter AGO), *1780–1917*. M 727, "Returns from Regular Army Artillery Regiments, June 1821–Jan. 1901," R. 12. Company F returns for December 1858. RG 94.

3. Muster rolls, Company I (hereafter: MRI), Dec. 1854–Jan. 1855. RG 94. Also *Preliminary Inventory of the Records of the United States Regular Army Mobile Units, 1842–1942.* "Descriptive Books for Batteries A-M, 1841–1864," l. 228, Company I. RG 391, Entry 68 (hereafter E.+ number).

   John Munroe, Scotland, USMA 1814. Veteran of 2nd Seminole and Mexican Wars. Died April 28, 1861. Heitman, *Register*, vol. 1.

   Fort Thompson was on the Caloosahatchee River, near the mouth of Lake Flirt. Only description provided by Heitman, *Register*, vol. 2.

   The muster rolls do not describe how the recruits reached Florida from Fort Columbus, N.Y. Edward M. Coffman, *The Old Army: A Portrait of the American Army in Peacetime, 1784–1898* (New York: Oxford University Press, 1986), describes the movement of troops "in the crowded holds of seagoing vessels, on the decks of canal boats or river steamboats," p. 160. Having experienced such a voyage on the return from Europe in WWII, the writer well knows the discomfort of being crammed into the hold of a liberty ship.

For these recruits, the voyage to Fla. may well have been the reverse of the trip which brought them to Fort Monroe, Va., in 1857. For the return, the company boarded a coastal schooner at Punta Rassa, sailed to Key West, and then up the coast to Va. (See MRI, Feb.–Apr. 1857. RG 94.)

To get to Fort Thompson, the troops may have marched from Fort Myers along established trails along the Caloosahatchee to Lake Flirt, or they may have used alligator or gondola boats which were coming into use. These flat-bottomed boats were thirty feet long, pointed at both ends, and could navigate in water twenty-four to thirty-six inches deep. Covington, *Seminoles*, p. 136. Occasionally, small steamers like the *Texas Ranger* were available. This vessel eventually was made available to troops among the forts on the Caloosahatchee. See later in this chapter.

4. *Records of the U.S. Army Continental Commands, 1821–1920*, M 1090, "Memoirs of Reconnaissance with Maps During the Florida Campaign, April 1854–February 1858." RG 393. These reports were complete with hand-drawn maps showing the locations of forts along the Caloosahatchee to Lake Okeechobee. The two forts pertinent to Company I's tour in Fla. were Deynaud and Simmons, which were within "12,041 feet" of each other.

   James W. Covington, "An Episode in the Third Seminole War," *Florida Historical Quarterly*, vol. 45, no. 1 (July 1966), p. 50 and note 14, same page.

5. August Abel Gibson, Maine, USMA 1839. Served with the 2nd Regt. from 1839 to 1862, when he was appointed Col. with the 2nd Pa. Vol. Art. Returned to rank in the regular army in 1863. Retired in 1870. Died in 1893. Heitman, *Register*, vol. 1.

6. MRI, Oct.–Dec. 1854. RG 94. Gibson succeeded Capt. Roland Augustus Luther, who died on July 3, 1853. Gibson was promoted to Capt. on July 9, 1853. For officer's conduct, see Coffman, *The Old Army*, p. 52.

7. George Lucas Hartsuff, N.Y., USMA 1852. Suffered two severe wounds during the 3rd Seminole War, one of which eventually caused his death in 1874. He was again severely wounded at Antietam during the Civil War. Promoted to Maj. Gen. and commanded the XXIII Corps. Remained in the army until retired as Maj. Gen. "for disability from wounds received in battle." Ezra J. Warner, *Generals in Blue* (Baton Rouge: Louisiana State University Press, 1981 printing). Also Heitman, *Register*, vol. 1.

   Stephen H. Weed, N.Y., USMA 1854. Promoted to Brig. Gen. Vols. in June 1863. Killed less than a month later at Gettysburg while holding Little Round Top. The place is now marked "Weed's Hill." Heitman, *Register*, vol. 1; Boatner, *Dictionary*.

   Jefferson H. Nones, Md., Midshipman, USN 1840–1856. Joined the 2nd Art. in 1847. Resigned commission in March 1856. Died 1903. Heitman, *Register*, vol. 1. Nones, 1st Lt., was sick at Wilmington, Del. He left the company, Oct. 1853. MRI, Oct.–Dec. 1854. RG 94.

   Thomas Smith Rhett, S.C., USMA 1848. Resigned 2nd Art., 1855 and worked as a bank clerk in Baltimore, Md., 1855–1861. Joined CSA in 1861. Died 1893. Heitman, *Register*, vol. 1. In the CSA, he was appointed Capt. in the Provisional Army of the Confederate States on Nov. 19, 1861. As a Col. of Art., was placed in charge of all batteries defending Richmond in May 1862. In 1863, sent abroad to purchase arms for the CSA. Died in 1893. Robert K. Krick, *Lee's Colonels* (Dayton: Morningside Bookshop, 1979).

8. MRI, Oct.–Dec. 1854, and Dec. 1854–Feb. 1855. RG 94.

9. Thomas A. Gonzalez, *The Caloosahatchee* (Fort Myers Beach: The Island Press Publishers, 1982), a facsimile reprint of the 1932 edition.

The spelling of Deynaud as opposed to Denaud in present-day usage follows the army's usage at that time. Actually the fort was located on land belonging to a Frenchman named Denaud, who for many years had been trading with the Seminoles in that vicinity. Gonzalez, *Caloosahatchee*, p. 48.

See also Florida State Historical marker F282. This marker, near the site of the old fort, noted that the fort was reopened in 1855 soon after the outbreak of the war. Company quarters, hospital, guardhouse, sutler's store, and a stable were built. "A few months after a fire ravaged the post in 1856, another site on the bank of the river one mile west was chosen." There is nothing in the muster remarks and returns noting that a fire caused the abandonment of the fort.

10. RG 392, M 1090.

11. William Hays, Va., USMA 1840. Fought in the Mexican and Seminole Wars. Brevetted Brig. Gen. for meritorious service during the Civil War. Died 1875. Heitman, *Register*, vol. 1; Gonzalez, *Caloosahatchee*, p. 49.

12. Jan. 22, 1855, M 1090, RG 393.

    Henry Clay Pratt, Mass., USMA 1837. Brevetted Capt. for bravery during the Mexican War. Was a Maj. in the Paymaster Dept. during the Civil War. Retired in 1879. Died 1884. Heitman *Register*, vol. 1.

13. Forts Keais and Doane were located near the Big Cypress Swamp and Depot No. 1. Heitman, *Register*, vol. 2, pp. 513 and 495 respectively. M 1090, RG 393.

14. MRI, Dec. 1854–Feb. 1855. RG 94.

15. MRI, Feb.–Apr. 1855. RG 94.

16. Harvey Brown, N.J., USMA 1818. Fought in the 2nd Seminole War and the Mexican War. Commanded Fort Pickens, Fla., in 1861–1862; and finally took command of the defenses of N.Y. in 1862–1863. Retired in 1863. Died in 1874. Heitman, *Register*, vol. 1; Boatner, *Dictionary*, p. 90.

17. *Letters Sent, Register of Letters Received and Letters Received by Headquarters Troops in Florida and Headquarters, Department of Florida, 1850–1858*, Mar. 5 and 10, 1855. M 1084, RG 393.

18. MRI, Feb.–Apr. 1855, and MRI, Apr.– June 1855. RG 94. The seven sick soldiers were Charles Bady, Elida Cummings, Charles Falk, Alexander Johnson (at Fort Myers), James Morris, Frederick Schudt (at Fort Myers), and Cornelius Sullivan.

    Albert Julian Stiffan Molinard, N.Y., USMA 1851. Served his entire career with the 2nd Art. Wholly retired in Oct. 1863. Died Sept. 1872. Heitman, *Register*, vol. 1.

    Molinard was born in New York City, N.Y., July 2, 1828. His father, J. Molinard, formerly a soldier in the French army, taught French at the USMA from 1830–1839. The father began applying for an appointment for his son in 1843. The endorsements read like a "Who's Who" in N.Y. State at that time: Rufus King, Van Buren, Van Rensselear, Corning, etc. But the appointment did not come until 1847. The young Molinard failed his physical because of shortsightedness, "attributing his failure to the excitement of the moment." He finally was accepted in July 1847. "Records Relating to USMA Cadets." M 688, R. 148, No. 200. RG 94.

19. William Selby Harney, La., entered the army in 1818. Fought brilliantly in the 2nd Seminole and Mexican Wars. Commanded troops in the Dept. of Fla. during the 3rd Seminole War, and in the Kansas Territory. Was made Comdr. of the Dept. of the West before being relieved by Brig. Gen. Nathaniel Lyon. Retired in 1863. Was brevetted Maj. Gen. in 1865. Died in 1885. Heitman, *Register*, vol. 1; Warner, *Generals in Blue*. May 15, 16, 26, 1855, M 1084, RG 393.

20. MRI, Apr.–June 1855. RG 94.

21. Heitman, *Register*, vol. 2, p. 493.

22. Gonzalez, *Caloosahatchee*, p. 22.

23. David Emanuel Twiggs, Ga., served in the War of 1812, Black Hawk, Seminole, Mexican and Civil Wars. Was commissioned a Maj. Gen. in the CSA, in command of the District of Louisiana. Died in 1862. Heitman, *Register*, vol. 1.

    Abraham C. Myers, S.C., USMA 1833. Served in the early Seminole Wars and the Mexican War. Appointed QMG of the CSA before resigning in August 1863. Died June 1889. Heitman, *Register*, vol. 1; Boatner, *Dictionary*, p. 577.

24. Henry Benson, N.J., a ranker, was commissioned in the 2nd Art. In June 1848. A Capt., he died of wounds sustained at Malvern Hill, Va., in Aug. 1862. Heitman, *Register*, vol. 1.

    Gonzalez, *Caloosahatchee*, pp. 20–21. Hendry wrote his reminiscences in 1886 for the *Fort Myers Press*. Karl H. Gismar, *The Story of Fort Myers* (Fort Myers Beach: Island Press Publishers, 1982), p. 65.

25. Gonzalez, *Caloosahatchee*, p. 23.

26. MRI, June–Aug. 1855. RG 94.

    Thomas Grey, Ireland, ranker from 1838 until he was commissioned a 2nd Lt., 2nd Art., in June 1855. Served as Regt. Adj. during the Civil War. Retired in 1870. Died in 1872. Heitman, *Register*, vol. 1.

27. MRI, June–Aug. 1855. General courts-martial, Special Orders (hereafter SO) No. 63, HQ, Dept. of the East, Baltimore, Md., June 9, 1855. RG 94.

28. MRI, Aug.–Oct. 1855. RG 94.

29. MRI, Oct.– Dec. 1855. RG 94.

30. Covington, "An Episode," pp. 48–49.

31. M 1090, RG 393.

32. "Introduction" to M 1090, RG 393.

33. Covington, "An Episode," p. 45.

34. Covington, "An Episode," pp. 46–47.

35. MRI, Oct.–Dec. 1855. RG 94.

    Frank Hunt Larned began his career as a 2nd Lt. of Inf. Transferred to the 2nd Art. in 1848. Retired in 1867. Died in 1891. Heitman, *Register*, vol. 1.

36. Gonzalez, *Caloosahatchee,* p. 24; Gismer, *Fort Myers*, p. 7.

37. Covington, "An Episode," pp. 51–52.

    Lewis Golding Arnold, N.J., USMA 1837. Served in the Mexican War, 3rd Seminole, and Civil Wars. Retired in 1864. Died in 1871. Heitman, *Register*, vol. 1.

38. MRI, Dec. 1855–Feb. 1856. RG 94.

39. M 1084, RG 94.

40. Lt. Arnold to Harney, commanding troops Caloosahatchee, Fort Myers, Fla., Jan. 24, 1856. *Orders and Special Orders Issued 1855–April 1858*, Dept. of Fla. RG 393, E. 1642.

41. MRI, Dec. 1855–Feb. 1856. RG 94.

42. MRI, Dec. 1855–Feb. 1856, and MRI, Feb.–Apr. 1856. RG 94.

43. Covington, "An Episode," p. 49 and note 12, same page.

44. Grismer, *Fort Myers*, p. 72; Gonzalez, *Caloosahatchee*, p. 52.

45. M 1090, RG 393. There is nothing to indicate that the regulars were eligible to collect these bounties.

46. MRI, Feb.–Apr. 1856. RG 94. And "Register of Enlistments in the U.S. Army, 1798–1914." M 233, R. 24. RG 94.

In 1862, Nones applied for a commission from Maj. Gen. Benjamin F. Butler, who was recruiting troops in Mass. There is no evidence that his letter was answered or any evidence that he served during the Civil War. The letter was found in RG 391, E. 61.

The record of the action which took place on Apr. 6–7 was found in "Records Relating to Regimental History, 1832–1893," under General Orders (hereafter GO) No. 14, HQ, Army, N.Y., N.Y., Nov. 17, 1857. The order signed by Irvin McDowell, Asst. Adj. Gen., extols the bravery of the men who participated and expresses that the General-in-Chief found this action as "too interesting to be omitted from general orders." Pvt. John Simons, Company L, 2nd Art., was killed. Cpl. Joseph Parson and Pvt. George Muller, John Strobell, Company C, 2nd Art., and Pvt. Thomas Newton, Company L, 1st Art., were severely wounded; and Pvts. Silas M. Watkins and William Abbott, Company C, 2nd Art., were slightly wounded. RG 391, E. 64.

47. MRI, Apr.–June 1856, RG 94. M 1090, RG 393.

48. MRI, Apr.–June 1856. RG 94.

49. William E. Birkhimer, *Historical Sketch of the Artillery, United States Army* (New York: Greenwood Press, 1986), pp. 116–118. And MRI, Apr.–June 1856. RG 94.

50. MRI, June–Aug. 1856. RG 94. Kroppe is listed variously as Fernick Kroppe, Fropeff, and Krofppe.

Because of the similarity, Frederick Schudt and Frederick Schmidt were often confused in the records. The muster rolls show that Schudt died at Fort Myers on July 19, 1856. In the MRI for Apr.–June 1857, Frederick Schmidt is shown as having been discharged at Fort Monroe, Va., on May 24, 1857.

The muster rolls, though they occasionally provide confusing information, are generally more accurate since the records were prepared by personnel in the field. The Register of Enlistments was maintained at the AGO on Washington, D.C. and, although generally accurate, was more prone to error.

51. MRI, Aug.–Oct. 1856. RG 94.

Judson David Bingham, N.Y., USMA 1854. Joined the Q.M. Dept. shortly after the outbreak of the Civil War. Remained with the Q.M. and was made a Brig. Gen. in 1865. Retired in May 1895. Heitman, *Register*, vol. 1.

52. MRI, Oct.–Dec. 1856. RG 94. The record of events indicated that the company marched from Fort Myers to Deynaud during the night in what must have been hostile country.

Also MRI, Dec. 1856–Feb. 1857. RG 94. Dey's promotion also appeared in "Regimental Orders Issued, 1838–1901, Order No. 54, HQ, 2nd Art., Fort Hamilton, N.Y., Dec. 23, 1856. RG 391. E.55.

53. MRI, Dec. 1856–Feb. 1857. RG 94.

54. Report March 10, 1857. RG 393, E. 1642.

55. MRI, Feb.–Apr. 1857. RG 94.

56. "List of Locations of Headquarters and Batteries, 1821–1900." RG 391, E. 70. Heitman, *Register*, vol. 2.

Matthew Mountjoy Payne, Va., fought in War of 1812, in the 2nd and 3rd Seminole and Mexican Wars. He resigned in July 1862 and died in Aug. 1862. Heitman, *Register*, vol. 1.

57. "Introduction." M 1090, RG 393. Also Grismer, *Fort Myers*, pp. 74–77.

Gustavus Loomis, Vt., USMA 1811. Fought in the War of 1812; served on the frontier, and fought in the 2nd Seminole and Mexican Wars. Retired in June 1863. Heitman, *Register*, vol. 1; Boatner, *Dictionary*.

58. The total, 102, represents the number where fairly complete information was found. It does not, however, represent the total number of biographical sketches shown in Appendix B. More names were added as information was found. This information was included for genealogical references.

CHAPTER 2

1. The background material for this chapter was extracted from: Richard P. Weinert and Col. Robert Arthur, *Defender of the Chesapeake* (Shippensburg, Pa.: White Mane Press, third edition, 1989); Phyllis I. McClellan, *The Artillerymen of Historic Fort Monroe, Virginia* (Bowie: Heritage Books, Inc., 1991); Birkhimer, *The Artillery*.

2. Order No. 46, HQ, 2nd Art., Fort Brooke, Fla., Nov. 22, 1856. RG 391, E. 55.

3. Order No. 49, HQ, 2nd Art., Tampa, Fla., Nov. 26, 1856. RG 391, E. 55.

4. Order No. 22, IAW GO No. 6, HQ, Dept. of the Army, N.Y., May 7, 1857. RG 391, E. 55.

5. MRI, Feb.–Apr. 1857. RG 94. For McKenna see also SO No. 16, HQ, 2nd Art., Fort Hamilton, N.Y., May 25, 1857. RG 391, E. 55.

6. "Carded Medical Records, 1821–1884." RG 94. McClellan, *Artillerymen*, p. 53, noted that "The first hospital was located inside the fort and was described as a three-story brick building of 12 rooms with a slate roof, cistern, and pillared structure in the first and second floors."

7. MRI, Apr.–June 1857. RG 94. Also Order No. 33, HQ, 2nd Art., Fort Monroe, Va., June 12, 1857. In the same order, Bacheman and Smith were promoted to Cpl., and Dey to Sgt. RG 391, E. 55, p. 152.

   General Wool retired in 1863 and died in 1869 in Troy, N.Y., age eighty-five. Heitman, *Register,* vol. 1; Boatner, *Dictionary*; and Warner, *Generals.*

8. MRI, June–Aug. 1857. Also "Carded Medical Records" for Dey's sick call. RG 94.

9. *Letters Received, 1846–1901.* This exchange covers the short period from July 11 to July 18. RG 391, E. 53.

10. MRI, Aug.–Oct. 1857. RG 94.

11. "Carded Medical Records." RG 94. The record is not clear since it shows Dey being admitted as Corporal Dey on July 30, 1857, and returning to duty on Sept. 1. The next entry, however, shows him as Sgt. and as having been admitted on Aug. 8, and returned to duty on Aug. 30.

12. MRI, Aug.–Oct. 1857. RG 94. Also SO No. 23, HQ, 2nd Art., Fort Monroe, Va., Sept. 3, 1857, and SO No. 24, same date. RG 391, E. 55.

13. MRI, Aug.–Oct. 1857. RG 94. General courts-martial, SO No. 12, Dept. of the East, Baltimore, Md., Feb. 14, 1857. According to McClellan, *Artillerymen*, p. 50, "The guard room and jail was located within the inner walls of this gateway [West Sallyport, Fort Monroe]."

14. Weinert, *Defender*, pp. 84–85.

CHAPTER 3

1. Francis Woodbridge, Vt., USMA 1837. Brevetted for gallantry during the Mexican War. Died in 1855.

   James Totten, Pa., USMA 1841. Joined the 2nd Art. as a Bvt. Lt. Was brevetted for gallantry and meritorious service for the battles of Boonville and Wilson's Creek, Mo., and Mobile, Ala. Achieved rank of Brig. Gen. Dismissed from the service in July 1870. Died in 1871. See also Jay Monaghan, *Civil War on the Western Border* (Lincoln, Nebr.: Bison Books, 1984).

Anderson Merchant, Va., 2nd Lt., 2nd Art., since 1847. Resigned from the Union army in 1861. Joined the CSA where he served from 1861–1865 as a Capt. of artillery. Died in 1896.

M. D. L. Simpson, N.Y., USMA 1846. Served in the Mexican War where he was cited for gallantry and meritorious service. Attained rank of Maj. Gen. for meritorious service during the Civil War.

Joseph Peck Jones, N.C., Cadet, USMA, July 1, 1849 to Jan. 10, 1850. 2nd Lt., 2nd Art., June 1856. Resigned Jan. 28, 1861. Lt. Col., 5 N.C. Vols., CSA, 1861–1865.

Note: all biographical summaries from Heitman, *Register*, vol. 1.

"Regimental Orders Issued, Jan. 1838–Feb. 1901." SO No. 23, Sept. 3, 1857; SO No. 24, same date, HQ, 2nd Art., Fort Monroe, Va. RG 391, E. 55.

2. SO No. 25, Sept. 4, 1857. RG 391, E. 55.

3. Muster Roll, Company F (hereafter shown as MRF), Aug.–Oct. 1857. RG 94. Birkheimer, *Artillery*, p. 362.

4. Information on the B&O supplied telephonically by with Ms. Ann Calhoun, Librarian, B&O Museum, Baltimore, Md., Jan. 31, 1992. Other information taken from *Battlefields of the Civil War*, produced by the *National Geographic Magazine*, n.d. This map shows an excellent picture of the railroad networks during the Civil War.

5. "Returns from U.S. Military Posts, 1800–1916." RG 94, M 617, R. 611. Fort Leavenworth.

Elvid Hunt, *History of Fort Leavenworth, 1827–1937* (Fort Leavenworth: The Command and General Staff School, 1937), pp. 81–82, 98.

6. On the issue of supplying the frontier army, see Raymond L. Welty, "Supplying the Frontier Military Posts," *Kansas Historical Quarterly*, vol. 7 (1938), pp. 154–169.

7. Most of the political background for this discussion was digested from the following sources: Jay Monaghan, *Civil War*; John G. Nicolay and John Hay, *Abraham Lincoln: A History*, as published in *The Century Illustrated Monthly Magazine*, vol. 34, New Series (May 1887–Oct. 1887), pp. 82–100, 203–219, and 369–396; *Report of the Special Committee on the Troubles in Kansas*, House of Representatives, 34th Congress, 1st Session, Report No. 200, Washington, D.C., 1856; Kenneth Stampp, *America in 1857, A Nation on the Brink* (New York: Oxford University Press, 1990), chap. 6.

8. Thomas West Sherman, R.I., USMA 1836. Served in the Mexican and Civil Wars. Retired as a Maj. Gen. in 1879. Died in 1879. Heitman, *Register*, vol. 1.

9. "General and Special Orders Received from Troops Serving in Kansas, May 1857–May 1858," SO No. 77, Sept. 26, 1857. HQ Troops Serving in Kansas, Fort Leavenworth. RG 393, E. 5490.

10. Alfred Pleasonton, D.C., USMA 1844. Served in the Mexican and Civil Wars. Cited for gallantry and meritorious service at Antietam, Gettysburg, and against General Price in Missouri. Achieved rank of Maj. Gen. during the war. Died in 1897. Heitman, *Register*, vol. 1.

11. Camp Walker may have been named after the then governor, Robert Walker. According to the MRF, it was located near Lawrence. Heitman, *Register*, vol. 2, has no location for this camp. Information from Mrs. Iona Spencer, historian, Lecompton Historical Society was inconclusive and vague. Letter, March 8, 1991.

12. Lecompton was the first capital of the territory, and sat squarely in the middle of the political upheaval of the period. When Kans. attained statehood in 1861, the capital moved to Topeka. Today, Lecompton, a small town, is overshadowed by the university town of Lawrence and Topeka. Also MRF, Aug.–Oct. 1857. RG 94.

13. Nicolay and Hay, *Lincoln*, pp. 376–377.

14. SO No. 89, Oct. 9, 1857. SO No. 111, Nov. 7, 1857. RG 393, E. 5490. MRF, Oct.–
    Dec. 1857. RG 94. Cincinnati was an area slightly west of the city of Leavenworth
    and due south of where the federal prison now stands (about 1.5 miles west of
    the southern entrance to present-day Fort Leavenworth). In 1898, the govern-
    ment began building the federal prison there. German workers on the project
    built and settled a community just south of the prison site which they called
    Cincinnati. Leavenworth citizens called it "Goosetown" because of the many geese
    which the settlers raised and allowed to roam freely in the streets. Mary Jo Winder,
    "The Leavenworth Historic Resource Survey," (1985), p. 15. Furnished by Pamela
    J. Kontowitz, asst. admin., Leavenworth County Historical Society, Leavenworth,
    Kans. Evidence that the hamlet existed before then was found in the 1860 U.S.
    Census.

15. MRF, Oct.–Dec. 1857. RG 94. "Register of Proceedings of Regimental and Garri-
    son Court Martials Received by the Acting Judge Advocate," Dept. of the West.
    RG 393, E. 5581. The author has not been able to locate SO No. 208, showing the
    charges against Sergeant Dey. The reference includes an abstract of the SO show-
    ing that it resulted from the findings of the court-martial board appointed by SO
    No. 200; that twelve enlisted men were tried in that CM; and that remarks had
    been "Forwarded to Headquarters, Army, December 12, 1857." In RG 391, Entry
    48, "Letters Sent, Dec. 1844–Feb. 1901," a volume including letters from Jan. 1
    1855 to Apr. 20, 1866, p. 138, there is a letter from the commanding officer of the
    2nd U.S. Art., dated Dec. 12, 1857, requesting that the warrants against Gustav
    Dey, late Sgt. in Company F, be sent to headquarters. The CO also wanted to
    know how Dey was reduced in rank, and "if by a Garrison Court Martial, that a
    transcript of the order be transmitted as required." The answer to that request
    may well have been the abstract noted. Research through the records of the Dept.
    of the Army also failed to reveal the contents of Dey's court-martial proceedings.
    Search through RG 391, E. 53, "Letters Received, 1846–1901," still failed to un-
    lock the secret of this action. There are very few letters in this file for the 1857–
    1858 period. See "General and Special Orders Issued by Troops Serving in Kan-
    sas, May 1857–May 1858," SO No. 13, Jan. 10, 1858, for the court-martial cita-
    tions for the other enlisted men involved. Perhaps these, too, were the charges
    against Dey.

16. MRF, Oct.–Dec. 1857.

17. SO No. 124, Nov. 18, 1857; SO No. 136, Dec. 3, 1857. RG 393, E. 5508.

18. *Transactions of the Kansas State Historical Society* (hereafter *Transactions*), ed-
    ited by F. G. Adams, Secretary, vol. 5 (1896). "Governor Denver's Administra-
    tion," pp. 464–561. SO No. 4, Jan. 2, 1858, HQ, Fort Leavenworth, Kans. RG 393,
    E. 5490.

19. The material about the Planters Hotel was found in *Other Days...Other Ways*,
    (1961), a booklet written by the Leavenworth Branch of the American Association
    of University Women as part of the city's centennial celebration of the state's
    admission into the Union in 1861. Leavenworth County Historical Society.

20. SO No. 11, Jan. 10, 1858; SO No. 19, Jan. 20, 1858. RG 393, E. 5508.

21. SO No. 22, Jan. 29, 1858. RG 393, E. 5508 and E. 5490.

22. SO No. 6, Jan. 12, 1858. RG 393, E. 5508. Coffman, *The Old Army*, pp. 112–113,
    and note 16, chapter 3, where he discusses the importance of laundresses on a
    military post. On p. 113, Lt. George Hazzard, 4th Art., "complained in December
    1857 that the camp women at Fort Leavenworth did not have housing suitable
    for the winter. We estimated that the number of women laundresses present was
    double the official allowance of four per company."

23. *Transactions,* pp. 472–473.

24. MRF, Dec.–Feb. 1858. RG 94.

25. *Transactions,* pp. 478, 481; Christopher Phillips, *Damned Yankee: The Life of General Nathaniel Lyon* (Columbia, Mo.: University of Missouri Press, 1990), p. 114; Monaghan, *Civil War,* p. 102.

26. Louise Barry, "The Fort Leavenworth-Fort Gibson Military Road and the Founding of Fort Scott," *Kansas Historical Review,* vol. 11, no. 2 (May 1942), pp. 115–129; Eloise Frisbee Robbins, "The Original Military Post Road Between Fort Leavenworth and Fort Scott," *Kansas History,* vol. 1, no. 2 (Summer 1978), pp. 90–100; National Park Service pamphlet on the National Historic Site Fort Scott.

27. MRF, Feb.–Apr. 1858. RG 94. The ritual, as ordered by General Harney, is described in detail by Coffman, *Old Army,* p. 197, and by John D. Billings, *Hard Tack and Coffee* (Bowie, Md.: Heritage Books, Inc., 1990 reprint), pp. 155–156.

28. SO No. 59, Apr. 27, 1858. RG 393, E. 5490. And MRF, Feb.–Apr. 1858. RG 94.

Thomas John Wood, Ky., USMA 1845. Served in the Mexican and Civil Wars. Became a Maj. Gen. of Vols. In 1865. Cited for gallantry at Chickamauga, Ga., and at the battle of Nashville, Tenn. Retired with rank of Maj. Gen. He was the last survivor of his academy class, dying in 1906. Heitman, *Register,* vol. 1; Warner, *Generals in Blue.*

29. MRF, Feb.–Apr. 1858. RG 94. And MRF, Apr.–June 1858. RG 94.

30. "General and Special Orders, May–Aug. 1858, Dept. of Utah," GO No. 2, May 5, 1858. RG 393, E. 5026. Troops Serving in Kansas, SO No. 63, May 12, 1858. RG 393, E. 5490. "Special Orders, Jan. 1858–May 1861." Dept. of the West, St. Louis, Mo., May 24, 1858. RG 393, E. 5489.

31. Phillips, *Damned Yankee,* p. 135.

Nathaniel Lyon, Conn., USMA 1841. 2nd Lt., 2nd Inf. Cited for gallantry and meritorious conduct during the Mexican War. Made Brig. Gen. U.S. Vols. May 1861. Killed at the battle of Wilson's Creek, Mo., Aug. 10, 1861. Heitman, *Register,* vol. 1.

32. Dean S. Thomas, *Cannons: An Introduction to Civil War Artillery* (Gettysburg, Pa.: Thomas Publications, 1985), p. 68.

33. MRF, Apr.–June 1858. RG 94.

34. "Records Relating to Regimental History, 1832–93." Company H stayed at Fort Riley until Feb. 1860. RG 391, E. 64. MRF, Aug.–Oct. 1858. RG 94. Also "Special Orders, Jan. 1858–Nov. 1861." Dept. of Mo. Return of an attachment of Company F, Oct. 1858. RG 393, E. 5489.

Oliver Duff Greene, N.Y., USMA 1853. Served in Civil War. Cited for gallantry and meritorious service at Bull Run, Crampton's Gap, and Antietam, for which he was awarded a Medal of Honor in 1893. Retired in 1897. Heitman, *Register,* vol. 1.

35. MRF, Oct.–Dec. 1858. RG 94. "Returns from Regular Army Artillery Regiments, 1821–1901." RG 94, M 727, R. 12, Return for November 1858. "Register of Enlistments in the U.S. Army, 1798–1914." RG 94, M 233, R. 26, shows Rennick's death by pistol. Order No. 45, HQ, 2nd Art., Fort Hamilton, N.Y., Dec. 30, 1858, Dey's promotion. RG 391, E. 55.

36. "Carded Medical Records," Dey, June 18–24, 1859. RG 94. See also RG 393, E. 5489, p. 98.

37. MRF, Aug.–Oct. 1859, Dec. 1858–Feb. 1859. RG 94.

38. MRF, Oct.–Dec. 1859. RG 94.

39. Return for Dec. 1859. RG 94, M 727, R. 12.

40. MRF, Feb.–Apr. 1860, Apr.–June 1860. RG 94.

St. Clair Dearing, Ga. Appointed 2nd Lt., 4th Inf., in 1855. Transferred to the 2nd Art. in Feb. 1858. Resigned to join CSA in 1861. Served with the 25th N.C. Vols. as Lt. Col. in 1861. Declined reelection in Apr. 1862 with what he later called "petulance." Was Lt. of cavalry in Nov. 1864. In Apr. 1865, tried to recruit Negroes for the CSA in Ga. Heitman, *Register*, vol. 1; Robert K. Krick, *Lee's Colonels* (Dayton, Ohio: Morningside Bookshop, 1979), pp. 102–103.

41. MRF, June–Aug. 1860. RG 94.

42. MRF, Aug.–Oct. 1860. RG 94.

CHAPTER 4

1. Edward C. Bearss and Arrell M. Gibson, *Fort Smith* (Norman, Okla.: University of Oklahoma Press, second edition, 1979), various pages. Also note 31, p. 232, citing GO No. 4, Aug. 19, 1859, War Dept., AGO, Letters Sent File. RG 94.

2. MRF, Aug.–Oct. 1860. RG 94. Also "Returns from U.S. Military Posts, 1801–1916." Oct. 1860, RG 94, M 617, R. 1188, Fort Smith.

3. SO No. 110, HQs, 2nd Art., Sept. 20, 1860. Received at Fort Smith on Sept. 30, 1860, RG 94, M 617.

4. Bruce Catton, *The Coming Fury* (Garden City, N.Y.: Doubleday, 1961), p. 122; Francis Paul Pruscha, *A Guide to the Military Posts of the United States, 1789–1895* (Madison, Wisc.: The State Historical Society of Wisconsin, 1964), pp. 20–21.

5. MRF, Oct.–Dec. 1860; Returns Co. F, Nov. 1860; M 727; and Return for Oct. 1860, M 617, R. 1188. RG 94.

6. E. B. Long, *The Civil War Day by Day* (Garden City, N.Y.: Doubleday, 1971), pp. 2–3.

7. Return for Nov. 1860, RG 94, M 617, R. 1188.

8. MRF, Oct.–Dec. 1860; Return for Co. F, Dec. 1860, M 727; and Return for Dec. 1860, M 617, R. 1188. RG 94.

9. SO No. 183, HQs. Dept. of the West, St. Louis, Mo., Dec. 29, 1860. RG 393, M 233, R. 26, E. 5489.

10. "Letters, Orders, and Reports Received From or Relating to Members of the 2nd U.S. Artillery ("Name File") 1861–66." RG 391, E. 61.

11. W. E. Woodruff, *With the Light Guns in '61–'65* (Little Rock, Ark.: Central Printing Company, 1903. Facsimile Edition reprinted by Eagle Press of Little Rock, no date), p. 9. William Totten served with the U.S. Army from Mar. 3, 1812. He was four years a Cpl.; five years, an ordnance Sgt.; and up to Aug. 21, 1836, served as hospital steward. James, his son, it was said "was born in the Army." On April 3, 1837, James, writing from Fort Monroe, Va., accepted his appointment to the USMA, adding: "My Father is now absent in Arkansas, and will most freely give his sanction to my acceptance when he returns." "Records Relating to USMA Cadets." M 688, No. 249. RG 94.

12. Woodruff, *Light Guns*, pp. 9–10.

13. Ibid., p. 10.

14. Long, *The Civil War Day by Day*, pp. 17, 21, 22.

15. Woodruff, *Light Guns*, p. 10; Catton, *The Coming Fury*, p. 195; Page Smith, *Trial By Fire* (New York, N.Y.: McGraw-Hill Book Company, 1982), p. 111; James M. McPherson, *Battle Cry of Freedom* (New York, N.Y.: Oxford University Press, 1988), p. 282.

16. Robert N. Scott et al., ed. *War of the Rebellion: A Compilation of the Official Records of the Union and Confederate Armies* (Washington, D.C.: U.S. Congress, 1881–1901), ser. 1, vol. 1, pp. 638–645. Hereafter *OR: Armies*. And "Letters Received," Department of the West. RG 393, E. 5486, Box 12.

17. Woodruff, *Light Guns*, p. 12. Patrick Cleburne achieved fame as a leading Confederate Gen. He was killed at the battle of Franklin in Nov. 1864. Ezra J. Warner, *Generals In Gray* (Baton Rouge, La.: Louisiana State University Press, 1959), pp. 53–54.

18. Woodruff, *Light Guns*, p. 12.

19. *OR: Armies*, ser. 1, vol. 1, p. 643.

20. Ibid., "Confederate Correspondence," pp. 681–682.

21. *OR: Armies*, ser. 1, vol. 1, pp. 644–645.

22. Ibid., p. 645. Orders No. 3, HQ, Little Rock Arsenal, Little Rock, Ark., February 8, 1861.

23. *OR: Armies*, ser. 1, vol. 1, p. 646. Orders No. 6, Camp at Fletcher's Landing, Vicinity of Little Rock, Ark., Feb. 12, 1861.

24. Woodruff, *Light Guns*, p. 13; Catton, *The Coming Fury*, p. 195.

CHAPTER 5

1. Some of the background material was excerpted from the following sources: Phillips, *Damned Yankee*, p. 141; Ray W. Irwin, editor, "Missouri in Crisis: The Journal of Captain Albert Tracy, 1861," *Missouri Historical Review*, pt. 1: vol. 51 (Oct. 1956; hereafter *MHR*, 51: no.: page); James W. Covington, "The Camp Jackson Affair," *MHR*, 55:3 (April 1961); Arthur Roy Kirkpatrick, "Missouri in the Early Months of the Civil War," *MHR*, 55:3 (April 1961).

2. Phillips, *Damned Yankee*, pp. 139–141.

3. Irwin, *MHR*, 51:10–11.

4. SO No. 24, Feb. 23, 1861, HQ, Dept. of the West, St. Louis, Mo. RG 393, E. 5489.

5. Phillips, *Damned Yankee*, p. 153 and note 50. The editorial appeared in the *Missouri Democrat*, March 31, 1861. The citation about General Harney is from Phillips.

6. Philip Thomas Tucker, *Westerners in Gray* (Jefferson, N.C.: McFarland & Company, Inc., 1995), pp. 19–20.

7. MRF, Dec. 1860–Feb. 1861, and Feb.–Apr. 1861. RG 94. Also Order No. 8, HQ, 2nd Art., Fort Monroe, Va., Apr. 6, 1861. RG 391, E. 55.

8. Irwin, *MHR*, 51:18; MRF, Feb.–Apr. 1861. RG 94; *OR: Armies*, ser. 1, vol. 1, Correspondence, Union, Apr. 9 and Apr. 10, 1861, HQ, Dept. of the West, Jefferson Barracks, St. Louis, Mo., pp. 663–664; and SO No. 53, HQ, Dept. of the West, St. Louis, April 12, 1861. RG 393, E. 5489.

   Albert Tracy, N.Y., Maine, 1st Lt. Inf. Served in Mexican War. Lt. Col. for service in Civil War. Died June 1893. Heitman, *Register*, vol. 1.

9. Letter Townsend to Harney, April 15, 1861, HQ, Dept. of the Army, Washington, D.C. RG 391, E. 61.

10. MRF, Feb.–Apr. 1861. RG 94. Letter Merchant to Lt. W. L. Lothrop, 4th U.S. Art., St. Louis Arsenal, April 22, 1861. RG 391, E. 61.

11. Covington, *MHR*, 55:3:199.

12. Ibid., 55:3:200–201.

13. *OR: Armies*, ser. 1, vol. 1, p. 676, St. Louis Arsenal, Apr. 30, 1861.

14. Covington, *MHR*, 55:3:205.

   Thomas William Sweeny, Ireland, 2nd Lt. Inf. Lost an arm during the Mexican War. Rose to rank of Brig. Gen., Mo. Vols., in 1861. Retired from the army in May 1870 as Brig. Gen. Died in 1892.

   Francis Preston Blair, Ky., Mo., Col., 1st Mo. Inf., April 1861. Col., 1st Mo. Art., June 1861. Maj. Gen., Vols., 1862. Resigned 1865. Died July 1875.

   Franz Sigel, Germany, Mo., Col., Mo. Inf., May 1861. Brig. Gen., Vols., May 1861. Maj. Gen., Vols., Mar. 1862. Resigned May 1865. Died Aug. 1902.

   All biographies from Heitman, *Register*, vol. 1.

15. Covington, *MRH*, 55:3:208–210.

16. "Consolidated Morning Report," "Orders Issued by Gen. James Totten, Camp Harney, St. Louis, May–June 1861." RG 393, E. 2868. [The rating given Totten apparently was temporary.]

17. May 13, 1861, HQ, U.S. Troops, St. Louis, Mo. RG 393, E. 2828; MRF, Apr.–June 1861. RG94. Also "Return for June 1861." Company F. RG 94, M 727, R. 12.

   Up to this point in the search through the records of Company F, this is the first documented mention of its organization as a four-gun battery, of two sections of two guns each.

18. MRF, Apr.–June 1861. RG 94. GO No. 24, May 22, 1861, AGO, WDC, 1861.

   Henry Adams Smalley, Vt., USMA 1854. Col., 5th Vt. Vols., Sept. 1861. Resigned 1862. Capt., 2nd U.S. Art. Resigned May 1865. Died 1888.

   John Walker Barriger, Ky., USMA 1856. Brevetted Capt. for meritorious service at Bull Run, July 1861. Achieved rank of Brig. Gen. by 1865 for faithful and meritorious service.

   Biographies from Heitman, *Register*, vol. 1.

19. Letter, Blair to Harney, St. Louis Arsenal, May 29, 1861. RG 391, E. 61. MRF, Apr.–June 1861. RG 94.

20. Order No. 6, HQ, U.S. Troops, St. Louis, Mo., May 30, 1861.

21. Heitman, *Register*, vol. 1.

22. Phillips, *Damned Yankee*, pp. 208–209.

   Peter Valentine Hagner, D.C., USMA 1836. Brevetted for bravery in the Mexican War. Ranked to Brig. Gen. in Civil War for meritorious and faithful service in the Ordnance Dept. Died March 1893. Heitman, *Register*, vol. 1.

23. *OR: Armies*, ser. 1, vol. 3, p. 381.

24. Phillips, *Damned Yankee*, p. 210.

25. Colonel Thomas L. Snead, "The First year of the War in Missouri," *Battles and Leaders of the Civil War*, vol. 1 (Secaucus, N.J.: Castle, 1887), p. 267.

26. MRF, Apr.–June 1861. RG 94. The training by Company F is discussed in Daniel R. Hudson's pension file. He was 1st. Sgt. of Company F at that time. RG 15.

27. "Federals Capture Jefferson City," *MHR*, 56:4 (June 1952).

28. MRF, Apr.–June 1861. RG 94. Also "Return for June 1861." RG 94, M 727, R. 12. The return shows that four horses were wounded, rather than the two mentioned in the MRF.

29. Snead, *Battles and Leaders*, pp. 267–268; William F. Switzler, "Battle of Boonville," *Encyclopedia of the History of Missouri—A Compendium of History and Biography for Ready Reference*, edited by Howard L. Conrad, vol. 1 (N.Y., N.Y., 1901). See also "The Battle of Boonville," from the Kansas City *Times*, June 12, 1929, *MHR*, 24 (July 1930), pp. 621–622, "Missouri History Not Found in Textbook."

30. William A. Simpson's pension file. RG 15.

31. Snead, Battles and Leaders, p. 269; Wiley Britton, The Civil War on the Border (N.Y., N.Y.: G. P. Putnam's Sons, 1899), vol. 1, third edition, revised, pp. 69–71; Edward C. Bearss, The Battle of Wilson's Creek (Springfield, Mo.: Wilson's Creek Battlefield Foundation, 1988), third edition, p. 4.

32. Patrick Meehan's pension file, and testimony by Owen Dillon, same file. Both men were eventually permanently assigned to Company F in July 1864. RG 15.

Warren L. Lothrop, Maine. Ranker. Rose from Pvt. to 1st Sgt., Engineers. 2nd Lt., 4th Art., 1857. Brevetted Maj. for conspicuous service at New Madrid, Mo., in 1862. Promoted to Lt. Col. in March 1862 for gallantry and meritorious service. Died in Oct. 1866.

33. Henry Roller's pension file. Claim No. 456. Disability discharge signed by Capt. James Totten. RG 15.

34. Camp Sigel was named in honor of Gen. Franz Sigel, who commanded troops made up mainly of Germans from St. Louis. RG 393, E. 5486.

John McAllister Schofield, N.Y., USMA 1853. Reached rank of Maj. Gen., Vols., in 1863. Mustered out of service in Nov. 1864 as Brig. Gen. Was Sec. of War, 1868–1869. Commander-in-Chief of the army, 1888–1895. Retired 1895 as Lt. Gen. Awarded Medal of Honor for conspicuous gallantry at the battle of Wilson's Creek. David Stanley was rather derisive of Schofield's honor: "He was on Lyon's staff but this morning asked to join his regiment, the 1st Missouri Infantry, of which he is a major. For this he wears a medal on rather flimsy grounds." David S. Stanley, Personal Memoirs of Major General David S. Stanley (Gaithersburg, Md.: Olde Soldier Books, Inc., reprinted 1987), p. 74. Stanley also received the Medal of Honor.

Chester Harding, Mass., Lt. Col., Asst. Adj. Gen., Mo. Vols., 1861. Brevetted Brig. Gen. for Civil War service. Mustered out in 1865. Died 1875. Heitman, Register, vol. 1.

35. MRF, June–Aug. 1861. RG 94. Also SO No. 22, July 7, 1861, Army of the West, Springfield, Mo. RG 393, E. 5489.

Throughout the Missouri campaign, Lyon complained about shortages of men and supplies. No one was in charge of the Dept. of the West until Maj. Gen. John C. Fremont was appointed to command on July 3, 1861. But he did not report until July 25. Hence, the staff at headquarters was reluctant to honor Lyon's requests. When Fremont did report, he still did not send the troops which Lyon felt he needed to face the Confederate force, which he believed to be about 30,000. The actual number proved to be just over 10,000, outmanning Lyon's army by almost two to one, as it moved toward Springfield.

George Oscar Sokalski, N.Y., USMA 1860. 2nd Lt., 2nd Dragoons and 2nd Cavalry. Capt., 2nd Cavalry, 1864. Dismissed 1866; reinstated 1866. Died 1867. Heitman, Register, vol. 1.

36. Bearss, Wilson's Creek, pp. 9–11; Return I. Holcombe and W. S. Adams, An Account of the Battle of Wilson's Creek, or Oak Hills (Springfield, Mo.: Independent Printing Co., 1985, reprint of 1885 edition); Elmo Ingethron, Borderland Rebellion (Branson, Mo.: The Ozarks Mountaineer, 1980, fourth printing), pp. 62–69; Eugene Fitch Ware, The Lyon Campaign: Being a History of the First Iowa Infantry (Topeka, Kans.: 1907, reprinted by The Camp Pope Book Shop, Iowa City, Ia., 1991), pp. 224–227. A note about Ware, when his three-month enlistment was over, he reenlisted in the 4th Ia. Cavalry. Late in 1863, he transferred as a commissioned officer to the 7th Ia. Cavalry. A Capt., he mustered out in May 1866 and returned to his home town of Burlington, Ia. In 1867, he moved to Fort Scott, Kans., where he lived until 1893. He moved to Topeka that year. He was named commissioner of pensions by President Theodore Roosevelt in 1902.

Dr. James C. Malin, now deceased, was professor of history at the University of Kansas, Lawrence, and a noted historian of both national and Kansas history. Malin studied the works of Eugene Ware, who wrote under the pen name of "Ironquill." Dr. Malin's study was published as "The Burlington, Iowa, Apprenticeship of the Kansas Poet Eugene Fitch Ware, 'Ironquill.' " *Iowa Journal of History*, n.d.

The skirmish at Forsyth is not mentioned in Company F's "Remarks" in either the muster roll or the return for June–Aug., 1861. Nor is it mentioned in a "Record of Company 'F,' 2nd U.S. Artillery Commencing January 1857," written by John Fitzgerald, 1st Lt., commanding company in 1866. Fitzgerald does mention the skirmish in the list of engagements which are included in the report. The entire report is found in an appendix to this study. The report was found in "Records Relating to Regimental History, 1832–93." RG 391, E. 64. The skirmish at Forsyth is recorded also in Heitman, *Register*, vol. 2.

David Sloan Stanley, Ohio, USMA 1852. Capt., Cavalry, 1861. Brig. Gen., Vols., Sept. 1861. Maj. Gen., Vols., Nov. 1862. Honorably mustered out of Vols., Feb. 1866. Awarded Medal of Honor in Mar. 1893 for bravery in battle of Franklin, Tenn., Nov. 1864. Died Mar. 1902. Heitman, *Register*, vol. 1.

37. Josiah Pond's pension file, RG 15. MRF, June–Aug. 1861. RG 94.

38. Holcombe and Adams, *Oak Hills*, p. 12.

39. Joseph A. Mudd, "What I Saw at Wilson's Creek," *MHR*, 7:2:93 (January 1913).

40. MRF, June–Aug. 1861; Holcombe and Adams, *Oak Hills*, p. 12.

Frederick Steele, N.Y., USMA 1843. Fought in Mexican War. Maj. Gen. of Vols., 1862. Died in 1868.

41. Joe M. Scott, *Four Years Service in the Southern Army* (Fayetteville, Ark.: Washington County Historical Society, 1992), pp. 1–2.

42. Bearss, *Wilson's Creek*, p. 16; *OR: Armies*, ser. 1, vol. 3, p. 49.

CHAPTER 6

1. MRF, June–Aug. 1861. RG 94; Bearss, *Wilson's Creek*, pp. 27–28. The others present at the Aug. 4 council of war were Generals Sweeny and Sigel, Majors Sturgis, Schofield, Isaac F. Shepherd (AAG, Mo.) and H. A. Conant (1st Mo. Regt.), and Lt. G. A. Shaeffer.

2. Phillips, *Damned Yankee*, pp. 242–243.

3. Phillips, *Damned Yankee*, p. 243.

4. Woodruff, *With the Light Guns*, p. 39.

5. *OR: Armies*, ser. 1, vol. 3, p. 96; Phillips, *Damned Yankee*, pp. 247–250.

6. Bearss, *Wilson's Creek*, pp. 51–52; Robert E. Denney, *Civil War Medicine* (New York, N.Y.: Sterling Publishing Co., Inc., 1995), p. 39. Comments by Havilah Mowry Sprague, Asst. Surg., U.S. Army.

Samuel Davis Sturgis, Pa., USMA 1846. Bvt. 2nd Lt., 2nd Dragoons, 1846. Brig. Gen. Vols. on Aug. 10, 1861. Mustered out of the volunteer service in 1865 as Maj. Gen. Died in 1889. Heitman, *Register*, vol. 1.

7. Holcombe and Adams, *Oak Hills*, pp. 28–29.

8. Stephen Nolan's pension file. RG 15.

9. *OR: Armies*, ser. 1, vol. 3, p. 73.

10. Scott, *Four Years*, p. 2.

11. *OR: Armies*, ser. 1, vol. 3, pp. 74 and 67.

12. Mudd, *MHR*, 7:2:93.

13. Keyes', Miller's, Wallace's, Pratt's, and Immell's pension files. RG 15.

14. *OR: Armies*, ser. 1, vol. 3, p. 74.

15. Ibid., p. 74.

16. Robert Friedriech, "Reminiscences of Wilson's Creek," *National Tribune*, 7:12, pp. 1–2, Jan. 10, 1884. He was with the 1st Kans. Vol. Inf.

17. Porter's, Stiller's, Vaught's, Crosby's, Dooling's, Wrightenburg's, and C. Young's pension files. RG 15.

18. *OR: Armies*, ser. 1, vol. 3, p. 74.

19. Ibid., pp. 74–75.

20. Ibid., p. 68.

21. Ibid., pp. 68–69.

22. Denney, *Medicine*, pp. 39–40.

23. Pension files. RG 15. MRF, June–Aug. 1861 and Aug.–Oct. 1861. RG 94.

24. Mudd, *MHR*, 8:2:103.

25. Edwin C. Bearss and Willie H. Tunnard, *A Southern Record* (Dayton, Ohio: Morningside Bookshop, a facsimile, 1970), p. 79; Douglas John Cater, *As It Were* (Austin, Tex.: State House Press, 1990), p. 91.

26. Charles H. Smith, *The History of Fuller's Ohio Brigade, 1861–1865* (Cleveland, Ohio: no publisher noted, 1909), p. 39. On a visit to Wilson's Creek battlefield in 1990, we were shown by ranger and historian Richard W. Hatcher III of the National Park Service, an area where some seventy Union soldiers were believed to have been buried in a common grave.

27. MRF, June–Aug. 1861 and Aug.–Oct. 1861. RG 94.

28. *OR: Armies*, ser. 1, vol. 3, p. 70.

29. Woodruff, *Light Guns*, pp. 46–47. Some historians note that Totten and his men drilled and instructed Woodruff and the Pulaski battery, when Company F was stationed at the Little Rock Arsenal in 1860–1861. Woodruff states in the appendix of his book, p. 113: "It is a fact that Totten never 'drilled or instructed' this battery—unless upon the field." This writer interprets that to mean that Woodruff and his battery learned much "upon the field" at Wilson's Creek on August 10, 1861, not at Little Rock. Throughout his entire discourse, Woodruff speaks highly of Totten as a military man, an artillerist, and a person.

30. *OR: Armies*, ser. 1, vol. 3, p. 75.

31. Ibid., p. 93.

CHAPTER 7

1. MRF, June–Aug. 1861. The note in the muster roll merely indicates next to his name that Pvt. Robert J. Black was "wounded at Wilson's Creek, August 10, 1861."

2. *OR: Armies*, ser. 1, vol. 3, p. 67.

3. John van Duesen DuBois, "The Civil War Journal and Letters of Colonel John van Duesen DuBois: April 2, 1861 to October 16, 1862," *MHR*, 61:33–34, pt. 2 (October 1966). See also note 29, p. 34, disputing DuBois' claim that the Confederates had burned their camp.

John V. D. DuBois, N.Y., USMA 1855. Bvt. 2nd Lt. Mounted Rifles, 1855. Maj. , 1st Mo. Lt. Art., Sept. 1861. Resigned Vols., Feb. 1862. Col. aadc, Feb. 1862–Feb. 1866. Col., 1st Mo. Lt. Art., Aug.–Oct. 1862. Maj., 3rd Cav., May 1869. Retired May 1876. Died July 1879. Heitman, *Register*, vol. 1.

4. N. B. Pearce, "Arkansas Troops in the Battle of Wilson's Creek," *Battles and Leaders*, vol. 1, p. 303.

5. Editor's note, *Battles and Leaders*, bottom of p. 303.

6. Mudd, *MHR*, 7:2:103.

7. Ibid.

8. Wiley Britton, *The Civil War on the Border* (New York, N.Y.: G. P. Putnam's Sons, 1899, reprinted by Kansas Heritage Press, 1990), vol. 1, pp. 108–109.

9. Charles Monroe Chase, "A Union Band Director Views Camp Rolla, 1861," edited by Donald H. Welsh, *MHR*, 55:4:327–328 and 330–331.

10. MRF, June–Aug. 1861, and Aug.–Oct. 1861. RG 94.

11. SO No. 56, Aug. 19, 1861, Western Dept., St. Louis, Mo. "Continental Commands, 1821–1920." "Special Orders, Jan. 1858–Nov. 1861." RG 393, E. 5489, p. 337.

12. SO No. 144, Aug. 27, 1861, HQ, Dept. of Pa., Baltimore, Md. RG 391, E. 61.

    John Augustus Darling, Maine. Joined the 2nd Art. as a Lt. in Aug. 1861. In 1863, was a Maj. with the 3rd Pa. Art. Mustered out of Vols. in 1865. Remained with the artillery until retired in 1897. Died in 1912. Heitman, *Register*, vol. 1.

13. SO No. 157, Sept. 10, 1861, and SO No. 243, Sept. 22, 1861, HQ, Western Dept. St. Louis, Mo., pp. 383 and 421. RG 393, E. 5489.

14. MRF, Aug.–Oct. 1861. RG 94.

15. It is not clear at this juncture where the company was in the organization. The determination that it was part of Pope's division is based on the location of the division and the company's movements during this period. It was not until the New Madrid campaign in Feb. 1862 that the company would be equipped with six guns.

16. John C. Fremont, Maj. Gen., USA, "In Command in Missouri," *Battles and Leaders*, vol. 1, p. 278.

17. Fremont, *Battles and Leaders*, pp. 278–279.

18. Ibid., p. 288; MRF, Oct.– Dec. 1861. RG 94. Richard D. Martin, "Marching Through Missouri," *The Palimpsest*, 46:1:44 (January 1965).

19. *OR: Armies*, ser. 1, vol. 3, p. 554.

20. MRF, Oct.–Dec. 1861, and "Return for December, 1861" RG 94, M 727, R. 13. Pvt. Robert Wares was mistakenly listed as having deserted on an earlier muster. Aug.–Oct. 1861.

21. Robert Belt's, alias Richard Marsh, pension file. RG 15. West Point is shown on a map entitled "Battlefields of the Civil War," published by *National Geographic Magazine*.

22. SO No. 104, June 27, 1862, Jefferson City, Mo. RG 391, E. 61, and Vaught's pension file. RG 15.

23. "Return for December 1861." RG 94, M 727, R. 13.

24. Wallace J. Schutz, and Walter N. Trenery, *Abandoned by Lincoln: A Military Biography of General John Pope* (Urbana, Ill.: University of Illinois Press, 1990), p. 73; *OR: Armies*, ser. 1, vol. 8, pp. 38–40, 452, 528.

25. *OR: Armies*, ser. 1, vol. 8. There was a series of correspondence between Halleck and Pope. See pp. 466, 470, 512, 516, and 528. Also included on pp. 42–60 are reports of skirmishes, expeditions, and various operations along the Kansas-Missouri border. None of these reports include any activity by either section of Company F.

26. MRF, Dec. 1861–Feb. 1862. RG 94.

27. "Miscellaneous Records," Oath of Allegiance of Non-Commissioned Officers, Musicians, and Privates, Company I, 2nd Art., Jan. 19, 1862. RG 391, E. 76. In addition to its historic interest, this document provides insight into the literacy of the enlisted men in this company of regulars. Those who could not sign, affixed their marks. The marks were witnessed by 1st Lt. George H. Weeks and by Sgt. Maj. John Hunter, both from the 4th Art. Regt. Hunter, who served with Dey in Fla., transferred from the 2nd to the 4th on May 16, 1861.

28. "Name File." RG 391, E. 61.

29. George S. Nash's, William J. Williams', Owen Donnelly's pension files. RG 15. Donnelly's discharge is recorded both as May 8 at St. Louis and as Nov. 12 from Jefferson Barracks, Missouri.

30. Long, *Day by Day*, pp. 156–158.

31. Ibid., p. 164.

32. *OR: Armies*, ser. 1, vol. 8, pp. 509–510.

33. Ibid., p. 565.

34. "Return for February 1862." RG 94, M 727, R. 13. The departure of the Dey's section from Morristown and its arrival at Sedalia in one day's march is questionable. According to the scaled map on p. 263, *Battles and Leaders*, vol. 1, the two towns appear to be more than 50 miles apart. The other inconsistency in the return is that the left section which arrived in St. Louis on the nineteenth could not have joined the remainder of the company which arrived a day later on the twentieth.

35. MRF, Dec. 1861–Feb. 1862. RG 94. Also Immell's pension file. RG 15. Immell was given the Medal of Honor in 1893 for his actions at Wilson's Creek.

36. *OR: Armies*, ser. 1, vol. 8, pp. 91–95.

37. Ibid., pp. 80–82.

38. Ibid., pp. 113–115, Report No. 18 by General Plummer. Joseph Zimmer's, John Vallender's, John Erasmy's, Oscar O. Sisson's, and James Wallace's pension files. RG 15.

39. *OR: Armies*, ser. 1, vol. 8, pp. 126–127.

40. Ibid., pp. 81–83.

41. Ibid., pp. 165–168.

42. MRF, Feb.–Apr. 1862. RG 94.

43. *OR: Armies*, ser. 1, vol. 8, p. 97.

44. Ibid., p. 85.

45. Ibid., p. 87.

46. Ibid., pp. 91–94.

47. MRF, Feb.–April 1862. RG 94. William Ratchford's pension file. RG 15.

48. MRF, Feb.–April 1862. RG 94.

49. John Vallender's pension file. RG 15.

CHAPTER 8

1. Thomas Davis Maurice, N.Y., Mo. Commissioned Capt. in 1st Mo. Inf., Apr. 23, 1861. Transferred to 1st Mo. Lt. Art., Sept. 1, 1861. Promoted to Maj., Jan. 1, 1863. Mustered out of volunteer service on July 20, 1865. Joined the regular army as 2nd Lt., 2nd U.S. Art., Feb. 1866. Attained rank of Capt., Oct. 1884. Died March 18, 1895. Heitman, *Register*, vol. 1. Also RG 391, E. 62.

2. MRF, Feb.– Apr. 1862. RG 94.

3. Stanley, *Personal Memoirs*, p. 93.

4. Ibid.

5. Smith, *Fuller's Brigade*, p. 68.

6. Stanley, *Personal Memoirs*, p. 94.

7. Smith, *Fuller's Brigade*, p. 69.

8. Thomas Snead, *Battles and Leaders*, vol. 2, p. 719.

9. Ibid., pp. 717–718.

10. Herman Hattaway and Archer Jones, *How the North Won* (Urbana, Ill.: University of Illinois Press, 1991), pp. 170–171.

11. MRF, Apr.–June 1862. RG 94. RG 391, E. 61, regimental letter on Dey, May 31, 1862. RG 391, E. 68 for status on Hudson.

12. MRF, Apr.–June 1862, RG 94; *OR: Armies*, ser. 1, vol. 10, pp. 721, 805.

13. Stephen Nolan's and James Brennan's pension files. RG 15.

14. *OR: Armies*, ser. 1, vol. 10, pp. 721–722.

15. Ibid., p. 722; MRF, Apr.–June 1862. RG 94; Smith, *Fuller's Brigade*, p. 72.

16. *OR: Armies*, ser. 1, vol. 10, p. 722.

17. MRF, Apr.–June 1862. RG 94. Black's, Tippet's, Camp's, Wrightenburg's [on Campbell], and Williams' pension files. RG 15. "Return of May 1862." M 727, R. 13, and MRF, June–Aug. 1862. RG 94. Stanley, *Personal Memoirs*, pp. 99–100. This is from a report of the events of May 28, which was written from camp at Booneville, Miss., on June 5, 1862, HQ, 2nd Div., Army of the Mississippi. It is interesting that Stanley still refers to the company as Totten's (p. 100). He also mistakenly placed McGinnis in the 4th Art. Dey's heroics at Farmington were overlooked by both Stanley and Maurice. When Dey applied for a commission in Oct. 1863, then Col. John W. Fuller, commanding the Ohio Brigade, added to his endorsement of Dey that "His personal efforts saved at least one gun of his company at Farmington on May 28th." Dey's ACP file No. D505 C. B. 1865. Appointments, Commissions, and Personnel Branch. National Archives, Washington, D.C. Fuller might have mistaken Dey for McGinnis. Or Maurice and Stanley wrongly identified Dey as McGinnis. Or the two actions were mutually exclusive. Both men performed acts of bravery.

18. *OR: Armies*, ser. 1, vol. 10, p. 770.

19. Snead, *Battles and Leaders*, vol. 2, p. 720.

20. *OR: Armies*, ser. 1, vol. 10, p. 773.

21. MRF, Apr.–June 1862. RG 94. The muster was signed by Captain Maurice, and inspected and signed by D. S. Stanley, Brig. Gen.

22. *OR: Armies*, ser. 1, vol. 10, p. 668.

23. Hattaway and Jones, *How the North Won*, p. 105; Margaret Greene Rogers, *Civil War-Corinth, 1861–1865* (Corinth, Miss.: The Rankin Printery, 1989). General Henry W. Halleck earned his nickname, "Old Brains," on the Federal march from Shiloh to Corinth in Apr. and May 1862. Beginning with his stay in Corinth, he suffered then from one of the complaints common to all soldiers (dysentery) which he called the "evacuation of Corinth. After the well at the Veranda House was cleaned, the general's illness abated," p. 17.

24. William Starke Rosecrans, Ohio, USMA 1842. 2nd Lt. Engineers. Resigned in 1854. Joined the Ohio Vols. as Col. Promoted to Maj. Gen. in March 1862. Mustered out of volunteer service in 1866 to regain his commission in the regular

army. Resigned from the regular army in 1867. Appointed Brig. Gen. in 1889 and retired. Died March 11, 1898. Heitman, *Register*, vol. 1.

25. This material was digested fromHattaway and Jones, *How the North Won*, and from Margaret Greene Rogers, *Corinth, 1861–1865*, a small pamphlet written for the Northeast Mississippi Museum Association at Corinth. No date.

26. MRF, June–Aug. 1862. RG 94. "Letters Sent, Dec. 1844– Feb. 1901." Letter from Lt. Thomas Grey, Adj., dated Sept. 22, 1862. RG 391, E. 48.

27. Smith, *Fuller's Brigade*, p. 75.

28. Patrick Meehan's and James Twiname's pension files. RG 15.

29. MRF, June–Aug. 1862. RG 94. F. S. McGinnis' pension file. RG 15. Smith, *Fuller's Brigade*, p. 75, on drilling the army.

30. Smith, *Fuller's Brigade*, p. 75; Rogers, *Corinth*, p. 16.

31. "U. S. Army Generals' Reports of Civil War Service. Report by General William Rosecrans, Cincinnati, Ohio, 15 June 1865." (Hereafter "Generals' Reports") RG 94. M 1098, R. 3, vol. 4, pp. 523–553. "Information Maps." Rosecrans needed good topographical maps. By using a rapid map-making process, a skeleton map of the area was photographed. Copies were distributed to brigade and division commanders who were instructed to make additions or corrections. When these changes were incorporated, the maps were photographed again. Copies were then generally distributed. By the end of the war, this innovation became standard practice. Rogers, *Corinth*, p. 16.

32. *OR: Armies*, ser. 1, vol. 17, pt. 1, p. 120.

33. Ibid., p. 121. Also MRF, Aug.–Oct. 1862. RG 94.

34. *OR: Armies*, ser. 1, vol. 17, pt. 1, p. 65; E. B. Quines, *The Military History of Wisconsin* (Madison, Wisc.: Clark & Company, 1866), p. 529.

35. "Generals' Reports." RG 94, M 1098, R. 3.

36. Albert Castel, "The Battle Without a Victor...Iuka," *Civil War Times Illustrated*, vol. 12, no. 6. (Oct. 1972), pp. 15–16.

37. Smith, *Fuller's Brigade*, p. 76.

38. S. H. M. Byers, "The Battle of Iuka," *The Iowa Historical Record*, vol. 3, no. 4 (October 1887), pp. 545–546; *OR: Armies*, ser. 1, vol. 17, pt. 1, p. 119. Ord's Report.

39. *OR: Armies*, ser. 1, vol. 17, pt. 1, p. 67.

40. Ibid., p. 85.

41. Ibid., Union casualties, pp. 77–78, Confederate, p. 126.

42. "Generals' Reports," Sept. 20, 1862. RG 94, M 1098, R. 3. Byers, *The Iowa Historical Record*, p. 552.

43. Castel, *Civil War Times Illustrated*, p. 17.

44. "Generals' Reports," Sept. 23, 1862. RG 94, M 1098, R. 3.

45. *OR: Armies*, ser. 1, vol. 17, pt. 1, p. 377.

46. "Generals' Reports," Oct. 3, 1862. RG 94, M 1098, R. 3.

47. *OR: Armies*, ser. 1, vol. 17, pt. 1, p. 167. General Grant first shared a headquarters with Generals Buell and Sherman at the Mitchell House. When he took command of the Army of West Tenn., he moved to the Whitfield 900-acre plantation, south of Corinth. (Rogers, *Corinth*, p. 18, 20). It is probably the latter to which Rosecrans refers.

48. *OR: Armies*, ser. 1, vol. 17, pt. 1, p. 179.

49. Ibid., p. 196; MRF, Aug.–Oct. 1862. RG 94.

50. *OR: Armies,* ser. 1, vol. 17, pt. 1, p. 379; William S. Rosecrans, "The Battle of Corinth, *Battles and Leaders,* vol. 2, p. 748. The contention that Hamilton failed to support General Davies was disputed by Hamilton in "Hamilton's Division at Corinth," *Battles and Leaders,* vol. 2, pp. 757–758.

51. *OR: Armies,* ser. 1, vol. 17, pt. 1, p. 184.

52. Smith, *Fuller's Brigade,* p. 84; *OR: Armies,* ser. 1, vol. 17, pt. 1, pp. 247–249.

53. Ibid., p. 186; MRF, Aug.–Oct. 1862. RG 94.

54. Hugh Horton, "Confederate Brass," *The Battle of Corinth: 125th Anniversary Official Souvenir Program, October 3–4, 1987,* p. 10.

55. *OR: Armies,* ser. 1, vol. 17, pt. 1, p. 248.

56. Ibid., pp. 173–176, Union casualties, pp. 382–382, Confederate casualties.

57. Horton, *Souvenir Program,* p. 10.

58. Ibid., reprint of The Eagle of Corinth," *The Civil War in Song and Story,* p. 6.

59. *OR: Armies,* ser. 1, vol. 17, pt. 1, p. 170. The list was not actually appended to his official report. Rosecrans refers to a "a special paper herewith, wherein those most conspicuous, the number of 109 officers and men, are mentioned." This special paper was found in a file labeled AG War Records Office, "Union Battle Reports," Battle Report No. 216, Box 27, National Archives, Washington, D.C. RG 94. This list is included in its entirety as an appendix in this study.

60. *OR: Armies,* ser. 1, vol. 17, pt. 1, p. 196.

61. "Union Battle Report." Battle Report No. 216. RG 94.

62. Gustavus A. Dey's pension file. RG 15.

CHAPTER 9

1. "Special Orders Received," *Records of the United States Regular Army Mobile Units, 1821–1942,* Maurice to Lt. Thomas Grey, Adj., 2nd Art., Oct. 14, 1862, Corinth, Miss. RG 391, E. 58.

2. MRF, Aug.–Oct. 1862. RG 94. The memorandum about Brennan was attached to the MR. There is some confusion about the name since it is variously cited as Brannan. Also MRF, Oct.–Dec. 1862. RG 94.

3. SO No. 27, Oct. 27, 1862, HQ, Army of the Miss., Corinth. "Compiled Records of Volunteer Union Soldiers who served in Organizations from Missouri." RG 94. M 405, R. 308.

4. "Compiled Records of Volunteer Union Soldiers Who Served in Organizations from Wisconsin." RG 94.

5. Smith, *Fuller's Brigade,* p. 119. The material in Smith's book provided background on the conditions which Company F shared with the Ohioans. The company's muster rolls are, for the most part, just cryptic, formal entries and do not reflect the atmosphere under which these regulars moved and fought. Smith's book provides that insight into the army life these men shared. After the battle of Wilson's Creek, Company F was attached to the Ohio Brigade for most of the Civil War.

6. *OR: Armies,* ser. 1, vol. 17, pt. 1, pp. 466–467.

7. MRF, Oct.–Dec. 1862. RG 94. The dates and places on the march were extracted from the muster roll. The quoted material was excerpted from Smith, *Fuller's Brigade,* pp. 119–122.

8. *OR: Armies,* ser. 1, vol. 17, pt. 1, p. 503.

9. Ibid., p. 516.

10. SO No. 102, March 24, 1863. Fuller's order for turning Molinard's guns over to Tannarath. RG 391, E. 61. Molinard to Grey, 2nd U.S. Art. Fort McHenry requesting move to Carlisle. Only dated[?], March 1863. RG 391, E. 61. Summary sheet accompanying Molinard's assessment of his company (variously marked "1549 M. B. 493, 1863"; "Spec. Or. No. 62 see 2624 F. B. 255 1863."; "Rec'd N. 2 16 Army Corps 28 March/63) RG 391, E. 61. SO No. 106, Headquarters, Fuller's Brigade April 12, 1863, suspending SO No. 62. RG 391, E. 58. Fuller to Binsmore, AAG, 16th Army Corps, April 13, 1863. RG 391, E. 58.

11. Lt. Col. William W. Morris to Maj. D. F. Van Buren, Asst. Adj. Gen., October 24, 1861, from HQ, Fort McHenry, Md. RG 391, E. 58. (Marked "M80–24 Oct. 1861. Rec'd Hqrs. Dept. PA 25 Oct. 1861.") And Capt. Augustus A. Gibson to the Asst. Adj. Gen., U.S. Army, HQ, Dept. of Penn., Baltimore, Md., Aug. 7, 1861, from Fort Delaware, Del. "Letters, Orders, and Reports Received From or Relating to Members of the 2d Artillery ("Name File"). 1861–66." RG 391, E. 61.

12. RG 391, E. 58.

13. Morris to Brig. Gen. Lorenzo Thomas, Sept. 23, 1862. RG 391, E. 58.

14. Morris to Thomas, Nov. 9, 1862. "Letters Sent. Dec. 1844–Feb. 1901." RG 391, E. 48. In volume containing letters from Jan. 1, 1855 to Apr. 20, 1866.

15. Rosecrans and Grant to Thomas, Oct. 2 and Oct. 16. RG 391, E. 58.

16. MRF, Oct.–Dec. 1862. RG 94.

17. Molinard to Binsmore, AAG, 16th Army Corps, Apr. 8, 1863, from Corinth. RG 94, E. 61.

Molinard ACP File 2794 ACP 1871, Box 43. RG 94.

18. Fuller to Binsmore, Apr. 13, 1863. RG 391, E. 58.

19. Dulkewitz to Molinard, from Corinth, May 7, 1863. RG 391, E. 58.

Dulkewitz was the company clerk. He had had a checkered career with the company. He had transferred from the 3rd Art. at Fort Leavenworth in Aug. 1858 as a Sgt. He was reduced in rank, but in Nov. 1862, he was appointed farrier. Dulkewitz reenlisted for the third time on July 29, 1863. Then he deserted on Sept. 1, 1863.

20. Molinard to commanding officer, 2nd U.S. Art., May 18, 1863, addressed from 15 Franklin Street, Baltimore, Md. RG 391, E. 58.

21. Lt. Thomas Grey, Adj., 2nd U.S. Art., to Fuller, May 21, 1863. RG 391, E. 58.

22. Fuller to Binsmore, Apr. 13, 1863. RG 391, E. 58. Lieutenant Green was the only officer's name that Dey could recall when he applied for an additional pension in 1880.

Green was not admired by his colleagues in the 1st Miss. In May 1864, a year after his detail with Company F, Green was given his Capt. by the governor of Miss. Almost immediately, on May 10, four senior officers from the same regiment countersigned a letter to the governor protesting the promotion. Based on personal and official knowledge of Green's actions over a two-year period, Col. Warren Lothrop, Lt. Col. A. M. Powell, Maj. Thomas Maurice (who command Company F at Corinth), and Maj. Charles Mann were not convinced that Green was the type of officer or person with whom they cared to be associated. They contended that although he knew the regulations, in their collective opinions, they believed that "a more disagreeable, uncouth, and dishonorable man, one seldom meets." The four also felt strongly that Green's captaincy would only breed malice and discontent among other line officers serving under them. On May 18, the governor revoked Green's commission. On Dec. 22, 1864, Green was discharged from the service for worthlessness and habitual neglect of duty. "Compiled records of Volunteer Soldiers Who Served in Organizations from Missouri. RG 94, M 405, R. 303.

23. Report and Findings of the Board of Inquiry in the case of Capt. Julian Molinard, May 27, 1863, from HQ, 39th Regt. of Ohio Inf., Memphis, Tenn. RG 391, E. 61. The board formed as by Colonel Fuller per SO No. 113, May 7, 1863, consisted of Col. E. F. Noyes, 39th Ohio, Maj. M. Churchill, 27th Ohio, and Capt. George Robinson, 3rd Mich. Company, as recorder.

24. HQ, 2nd Art. To General McDowell, Aug. 1863. RG 391, E. 58.

25. Col. Edward Townsend, AAG, SO No. 444, Oct. 3, 1863, from the AGO, Washington, D.C. RG 391, E. 61.

For the memorandum summoning Lt. Col. Augustus Gibson to appear before the examining board, see Aug. 23, 1863, from the board to retired, disabled officers of the army to Colonel Gibson. "Regimental Orders Issued. Jan. 1838–1901." RG 391, E. 55.

CHAPTER 10

1. Smith, *Fuller's Brigade*, p. 131. MRF, Dec. 1862–Feb. 1863. RG 94.

   Grenville Mellen Dodge, Mass., Ia., Col., 4th Ia. Inf., July 6, 1861. Promoted to Brig. Gen., Vols., March 21, 1862; to Maj. Gen. Vols., June 7, 1864. Resigned May 30, 1866. Heitman, *Register*, vol. 1.

2. Smith, *Fuller's Brigade*, p. 132.

3. Report by Rosecrans, *OR: Armies*, ser. 1, vol. 23, p. 281.

4. *OR: Armies*, ser. 1, vol. 23, p. 281.

5. Dodge's Reports May 2 and 5, 1863, *OR: Armies*, ser. 1, vol. 23, p. 247.

6. MRF, Feb.–Apr. 1863. RG 94. Smith, *Fuller's Brigade*, pp. 132–133. Fuller to Commanding Officer, 2nd U.S. Art., Fort McHenry, May 8, 1863. Molinard No. 2794, ACP File 1871, Box 43. RG 94.

7. *OR: Armies*, ser. 1, vol. 23, pp. 246, 249.

8. B. A. Botkin, ed., *A Civil War Treasury of Tales, Legends, and Folklore* (New York, N.Y.: Promontory Press, 1988), pp. 307–308.

9. Smith, *Fuller's Brigade*, p. 133; MRF, Apr.–June 1863. RG 94.

10. Lothrop's lukewarm recommendation merely cited that Dunnigan was a veteran of 14 years' service in the regular army. There was no way of verifying if Dunnigan received a commission. He was discharged on May 29, per GO No. 96. HQ, 16th Army Corps. RG 391, E. 61, Lothrop's letter. MRF June–Aug. 1863 for the citation regarding Dunnigan's discharge. RG 94.

11. Smith, *Fuller's Brigade*, pp. 133–134. Murray to Lt. Grey, Adj. 2nd U.S. Art., June 17, 1863. RG 391, E. 58.

12. MRF, June–Aug. 1863. RG 94. The men were officially transferred by SO No. 21, HQ of the Army, AGO, Washington, D.C., January 14, 1864. RG 391, E. 58. See MacMurray's testimony in Charles Akehurst's pension file. John Kelly's testimony in John Fisher's pension file. And Auld's, Emery's, Englebert's, and Zimmer's pension files. RG 15.

13. MRF, June–Aug. 1863. RG 94. Lt. A. M. Murray "assigned to Lt. Company F, 2d Arty, SO# 16, Hqs., 2d US Arty, June 17, 1863. Commanding since July 28, 1863."

    Albert Morse Murray, born 1840, Canandaigua, N.Y. His parents were Albert Guthrie Murray, postmaster at Canandaigua from 1861 to 1878, and Emily Morse Murray. Appointed the USMA from N.Y., July 1, 1858. Graduated June 17, 1862, ranking twenty-fourth in a class of 28. Was assigned and served with the 5th

U.S. Arty., Army of the Potomac. Participated in the Va. Peninsular campaign, and Md. campaign. Brevetted Capt., Sept. 21, 1862, for gallant and meritorious service at the Battle of Antietam.

Transferred to 2nd Art. and was at Falmouth and in the battle of Fredericksburg, and in operations about Suffolk, Va. Commanding Company F since July 28, 1863. On the march to Chattanooga from Oct. 18, 1863 to May 4, 1864. Promoted to 1st Lt. on Mar. 30, 1864. Was in the invasion of Ga. Engaged in battles of Resaca, Dallas, Kenesaw Mt., Ruff's Station, and Atlanta. Brevetted Maj., July 22, 1864 for gallant and meritorious conduct before Atlanta. Captured there on July 22. Was prisoner of war at Macon, Ga., from July 22 to August 12, when he died from typhoid pneumonia. He had also suffered a head wound. He was 24 years old. Brevet Maj. Gen. George W. Cullum, *Biographical Register of the Officers and Graduates, U.S. Military Academy* (Boston, Mass., and New York, N.Y.: Houghton Mifflin and Company, 1891), third edition, vol. 2, 1990.

GAR Post No. 162 was named after Maj. Albert M. Murray. His brother, Henry R. served with Company G, 148th N.Y. Vol. Regt.

14. Murray to Binsmore, AAG, 16th AC from HQ, Company F, Camp near Memphis, Aug. 7, 1863. RG 391, E. 61. MRF, June–Aug. 1863. RG 94. The request, which appears to have been written by Dey, also mentioned that he be granted the furlough in place of that previously granted to Pvt. Owen Owens, who was confined on general charges on July 27. There is no record of an Owen Owens on the company's roster. Dey may have mistaken this name for that of Owen Dillon, who had recently transferred from Company M, 1st Miss. Art.

15. MRF, Aug.–Oct. 1863. RG 94.

16. Company F. Return for September 1863. M 727, R. 13.

17. Peter Cozzens, *This Terrible Sound: The Battle of Chickamauga* (Urbana, Ill.: University of Illinois Press, 1992), p. 524.

18. William Tecumseh Sherman, *Sherman: Memoirs of General W. T. Sherman* (New York, N.Y.: The Library of America edition. Two vols. in one, 1990), second printing, pp. 375–376.

19. Gustav Dey, ACP File No. D. 505. C. B. 1865. RG 94.

20. Found in Dey's ACP File. RG 94. Murray did not mention his newness to the command. He did add, below his signature his title and position as "Comdg Company," the comment ("Since Aug. 1st 1863").

21. Fuller, 27th Ohio, Commanding, from HQ, 3d Brig., 5th Div., to HQ, XVI Corps, Sept. 25, 1863. Dey, ACP File. RG 94.

22. The discussion of the mileage and route of Company F and Fuller's Brigade comes from the Company's MRF, Aug.–Oct. 1863, and Oct.–Dec. 1863, and from the company's return for October 1863. M 727, R. 13. RG 94. The commentaries both quoted and paraphrased are from Smith, *Fuller's Brigade*, pp. 135–136. The orders from General Dodge to Colonel Fuller are found on p. 136.

A recent edition of Rand McNally's *Road Atlas* shows two Prospects in Tennessee. Fuller was ordered to that which is located approximately 15 miles southeast of Pulaski on or near the Elk River.

23. Botkin, *Civil War Treasury*, pp. 339–342. There is a statue honoring Sam Davis in Pulaski, Tenn. It is also the birthplace of the Ku Klux Klan, founded on Christmas Eve, 1865. *The Washington Post*, January 26, 1993, p. A31.

24. Smith, *Fuller's Brigade*, p. 136.

25. MRF, Oct.–Dec. 1863. RG 94. Dey ACP File, letter to Gen. Lorenzo Thomas, sent from Prospect Station, Tenn., Nov. 29, 1863. As so often happened in his own

accounts, Dey invariably misstated his age. He was born in 1828. He would have been 35, not 30, when he acknowledged his commission. It is also interesting that after ten years of absence, he still claimed N.Y. as his residence. There is no evidence, throughout his entire military career, of his having visited N.Y., although he still had friends there. On his 20-day furlough while stationed at Memphis, it is doubtful if he made a trip from there to N.Y.

26. William Borrowe, N.Y., N.Y., 2nd Lt., 2d Art., Nov. 15, 1861. 1st Lt., Aug. 1, 1863. Capt., Company H, Pa. Art., April 1863. Dismissed from volunteers in March 1865. Reinstated as 1st Lt., 2d Art., July 1865. Honorably mustered out on Jan. 1, 1871. Heitman, *Register*, vol. 1. Pratt's and Sisson's pension files. RG 15.

27. SO No. 175, Fuller's Brigade, Dec. 7, 1863. Cited in MRF, Oct–Dec. 1863. RG 94.

28. *OR: Armies*, ser. 1, vol. 31, p. 567.

29. MRF, Dec. 1863–Feb. 1864. RG 94.

CHAPTER 11

1. Muster Roll, Company E (MRE) Dec. 1863–Feb. 1864. SO No. 18, HQ, Left Wing, 16th Army Corps, Pulaski, Tenn. RG 94

2. *Battles and Leaders*, vol. 4, p. 103.

3. Margaret Leach, *Reveille in Washington* (New York, N.Y.: Harper & Brothers, 1941), p. 319.

4. MRE, Feb.–Apr. 1864. RG 94. *OR: Armies*, ser. 1, vol. 36, p. 905. Report No. 219 by Burnside.

5. MRE, Apr.–June 1864. RG 94. Benjamin Franklin Cooling III and Walton H. Owen II, *Mr. Lincoln's Forts: A Guide to the Civil War Defenses of Washington* (Shippensburg, Pa.: White Mane, 1988), p. 124.

6. Charles H. Peirce, Mass. Army. Pvt., artificer, and Sgt., Army Engineers, June 1846 to Mar. 1849, and from June 1849 to Mar. 1861. Made 2nd Lt., 2nd Art., Mar. 1861. Capt. June 1864. Mustered out Dec. 1870.

   James Samuel Dudley, Vt., 2nd Lt., 2nd Art., Oct. 1861. Bvt. Lt. June 1862 for gallantry and distinguished service at Malvern Hill. 1st Lt. May 1863. Maj. 1865 for gallantry and meritorious service during the war. Honorably discharged on Oct. 1, 1870, at his own request.

   Samuel Bates McIntire, Mass., Minn., USMA Sept. 1858. 2nd Lt., 5th Art., June 1862. To 2nd Art., Oct. 1862. 1st Lt., Mar. 1864. Bvt. 1st Lt. for gallant and meritorious service at 2nd Bull Run; and Capt. Sept. 1864 for gallant and meritorious service at battle of Winchester, Va. Honorably discharged Oct. 1870 at his own request. All from Heitman, *Register*, vol. 1.

   Dey's promotion is noted in the "Regimental Descriptive Book. 1860-78." RG 391, E. 67, p. 68; and "Regimental Descriptive Book for Batteries A-M. 1861-64." RG 391, E. 68, line 38.

7. "Records of the US Army Commands (Army Posts). 1863-65." And "Returns from U. S. Military Posts. 1800-1916." M. 617. And "Historical Information Relating to Military Posts and Other Installations. *ca.* 1700-1900." M. 661. RG 94.

8. MRF June–Aug. 1864. RG 94. Company F "Return for July 1864." M. 727, R. 13. RG 94. *OR: Armies*, ser. 1, vol. 38, pt. 3. The events relative to Company F's misfortunes on July 22 at Atlanta were reported by General Dodge, General Fuller, and Lt. Lemuel Smith, among others. Smith took over command when Murray and Breckinridge were taken prisoner. Other references in the same volume can be found in the index: "Union Troops—Artillery, Light,—Regiments, 2d (Batteries) F."

General Dodge also wrote about Company F in "U. S. Army Generals' Reports of Civil War Service. 1864-1887." M 1098, R. 5, p. 373. Other accounts mention a Federal artillery company but fail to identify the company specifically.

Joseph Cabell Breckinridge, Md., Ky. 1st Lt. Aide-de-camp Vols., Aug. 1861– June 1862. 2nd Lt., 2nd Art., Apr. 1862. 1st Lt., Aug. 1863. Capt., June 1874. Maj. Asst. Insp. Gen., Jan. 1881. Lt. Col., Feb. 1885. Col., Sept. 1885. Brig. Gen., Insp. Gen. 1889. Maj. Gen. of Vols., 1898. Maj. Gen., U.S. Army, Apr. 1903. Bvt. Capt. for gallant and meritorious service in battle before Atlanta, July 22, 1864. Maj. Mar. 1865 for gallant and meritorious service during the war. Retired Apr. 1903, the day after receiving his promotion to Maj. Gen. Heitman, *Register*, vol. 1.

Rezin Gist Howell, Ky., USMA 1864. 2nd Lt., 2nd Art., June 1864. 1st Lt., Mar. 1865. Capt. 1882. Died May 1887. Heitman, *Register*, vol. 1. He served with the company at Atlanta and at Nashville, Dec. 1864. MRF, Aug.–Oct. 1864.

On Aug. 13, the 41 enlisted men who were not captured, wounded or killed were assigned to Company H, 1st Mo. Lt. Art., to work a siege gun in position about a mile from Atlanta. They fired nearly 1,300 rounds into the city. On August 26, the company was ordered across the Chattahoochie River near the railroad bridge and stayed in position until the end of the campaign for Atlanta, August 31. "Return for August 1861." M 727, R. 13. RG 94.

The company's last engagement was in the battle of Nashville, Tenn., on December 15, 1864. It returned east to join the regiment in Aug. 1865, prior to sailing for California. It did not take part in the Grand Review for Sherman's army.

Lieutenant Murray was memorialized on the front page of the *Ontario County* [NY] *Times*, vol. 14, no. 23, Wednesday, October 25, 1864:

Poetry

From the N.Y. Independent

ATLANTA

By Caroline Chesbrko

Out from the mountain-mist we sped.
The river bore us to the sea.
What heavenly splendor overhead!
But brighter looked the earth to me.

For, as we sailed, all East and West
Gave to the day a sacred sign.
I thought, were ever eyes so blest
As those overflowing eyes of mine!

If one dared shut his eyes and doubt,
As yesterday, the humblest craft
That sailed the river found him out,
And every flag and pennon laughed.

We smiled and said, the city's ours?
Atlanta is brought back. We lost
Perhaps, some men, but treason cowers,
Redemption's work, we know, must cost.

But now, in crowded streets, I think
Where is the gain to us, who paid
In dark defeat, a man. I sink
Amid the glooms of doubt afraid.

> Afraid in the great fight of Faith!
> Lord God preserve me from that shame!
> He's gone—one another saith,
> Then let me sing his saintly fame.
>
> The duty constant as the sun,
> Enduring hardness, patient, brave,
> Victorious in the race he run—
> Write this o'er Albert Murray's grave.
>
> Repulsed with slaughter. Company lost;
> *His* company—and unwon the town.
> A prisoner—sick—*defeat* has cost!
> But –from Heaven's battlements looking down?
>
> Yea—ere we flung the banners out,
> And cried, Thank God! Our hero heard
> Through Salem's streets a joyful shout,
> And VICTORY was the wondrous word!
>
> With strong amen we will respond,
> We welcome back the city lost,
> But Heaven a conquering son. Beyond
> The price we pay did Salem cost.
>
> And by our love to Him who made
> Of chaos Union fair, complete,
> We know what offering shall be laid
> By rebel hands at Victor' feet.

Piedmont, Sept. 1864.

9. MRF, June–Aug. 1864. RG 94. Immell's, Lowry's, Pratt's, Twiname's, Dewey's (and his testimony in Twiname's file), Hennessy's, Gibbins', Armstrong's, Fisher's, Havens', Noll's, Murray's, Barry's, Beck's, Steele's, Meehan's and Miller's pension files. RG 15.

10. Miller's and Meehan's pension files. RG 15.

11. SO No. 279, AGO, Washington, D.C., Aug. 24, 1864. RG 391, E. 58.

During the period at Camp Barry, the War Dept. issued other orders about Dey. SO No. 394, Nov. 11, 1864, he was relieved from duty in the Dept. of the East and "will proceed, without delay, to join his company in the Dept. of Washington." SO No. 411, Nov. 22, rescinded the previous order. RG 391, E. 58.

MRE, Oct.–Dec. 1864, showed that "Gustave Dey, 1st Lt. Transferred to Co. C, 2d U.S. Arty by promotion to 1st Lt. SO No. 394. War Dept. AGO, November 11, 1864." RG 391, E. 58.

Muster Roll, Company C (MRC), Oct.–Dec. 1864. RG 94.

12. MRC, Dec. 1864–Feb. 1865. RG 94.

13. GO No. 1, HQ, Insp. of Art., WDC, Jan. 21, 1865, for the charges against Dey. And SO No. 138, HQ, Insp. of Art., WDC, Dec. 24, 1864, for the charges against the enlisted men. RG 391, E. 61.

14. "Charges and Specifications preferred against Private George DeForest of Company 'C', 2nd U.S. Artillery," Camp Barry, D.C. Mar. 18, 1865. RG 391, E. 61.

15. Report of arrest of Dey for drunkenness, June 6, 1865. RG 391, E. 61. The same file contains the order to the Officer of the Guard, Central Guard House, "You will receive and confine in the prison under your charge the person of Lieut. Gustave Day [sic] 2d U.S. Artillery." HQ, Military District of Washington, Provost Marshal's Office, June 6, 1865.

16. McGowan to Ingraham, June 7, 1865. RG 391, E. 61.

17. Long, *The Civil War Day by Day*, p. 694; MRC, Apr.–June 1865. RG 94.

18. MRC, June–Aug. 1865. RG 94.

19. Memorandum Dodge to Col. W. W. Morris, July 31, 1865. And official notice Aug. 4. Dey's ACP file.

    Henry C. Dodge, N.Y., USMA July 1862. 2nd Lt., 2nd Art., June 1863. 1st Lt., June 1864. Bvt. Capt., Mar. 1865 for gallantry and meritorious service at the battle of Cold Harbor, Va. Died Jan. 23, 1873, lost at sea in Alaska. Heitman, *Register*, vol. 1.

20. 2nd U.S. Art. HQ, Fort McHenry, Aug. 12, 1865. RG 391, E. 61. Garry's, Halteman's, Flynn's, Boker's, and Fallbright's pension files. RG 15.

21. MRC, June–Aug. 1865. RG 94. Request to Panama RR from CO. 2nd Regt. aboard the steamer, *Ben Deford*, Aspinwall Harbor, Panama, Aug. 31, 1865. RG 391, E. 61.

22. AGO, War Dept. WDC. Dey's ACP file.

23. Obviously Dey never saw this official paper. A copy has been framed and is hanging in his great granddaughter's study in Va.

24. SO No. 529, AGO, WDC, Oct. 6, 1865, par. 8. RG 391, E. 58.

25. Leach, *Reveille in Washington*, p. 321.

26. The affidavits are located in the Gustavus A. Dey's pension file, "Soldier's Certificate No. S.C. 186876. These were consolidated with his widow's file, No. 321934. RG 15. Dey's file was used to reconstruct his life from mid-Sept. 1865 to his death on Feb. 14, 1882. An index of these affidavits is attached to the widow's pension claim, rejected on Aug. 12, 1886. Victoria's claim was filed on Dec. 11, 1884. N. H. Hill, Victoria's friend, wrote the letter of appeal to the AGO on July 18, 1890. The AGO responded on July 25, 1890. Hill's initial inquiry about the charge of desertion was sent as early as Oct. 1886. See also Dey's ACP file.

27. *The Fredonia Censor*, Wednesday, Feb. 15, 1882. The law was the Arrears Act of 1879 which provided that "veterans and widows who have already established claims to persons or _who established new claims prior to July 1, 1880_ were to receive payment effective from the date of the soldier's original discharge. Thus a veteran discharged in 1865 who had not been granted a pension until 1871 could collect all the money that would have been paid him had the claim been approved in 1865." Stuart McConnell, *Glorious Contentment: The Grand Army of the Republic, 1865-1900*. (Chapel Hill, N.C.: The University of North Carolina Press, 1992), p. 146.

28. Forest Hill Cemetery Association, "Registry of Interments," Lot 15, Section E, Fredonia, New York.

    Heitman, *Register*, vol. 1, incorrectly cites Dey's date of death as Apr. 23, 1884.

CHAPTER 12

1. The personal accounts for this chapter were abstracted from the pension files of the named individuals. RG 15, National Archives, Washington, D.C.

Bibliography

Official Sources:

Record Group 15: *Records of the Veterans Administration.*
"General Index to Pension Files, 1861–1934." Microfilm T 288, 544 rolls. And files of individuals who served in Battery F, 2nd U.S. Artillery.

"Organization Index to Pension Files of Veterans Who Served Between 1861 and 1900." Microfilm T 289. Roll 714, Battery F, 2nd U.S. Artillery.

Record Group 94: *Records of the Adjutant General's Office, 1780–1917.*
"Muster Rolls. Regular Army Artillery Regiments. 1854–1865." 2nd U.S. Artillery, Companies I, F, E, and C.

"Returns from Regular Army Artillery Regiments. June 1821–Jan. 1901." Microfilm [hereafter M + number] [M] 727, Rolls 12 and 13.

"Register of Enlistments in the U.S. Army. 1789–1914." M 233, Rolls 23, 24, 25, 26.

"Returns from U.S. Military Post. 1800–1916." M 617.

"Historical Information Relating to Military Posts and Other Installations. *ca.* 1700–1900." M 661.

"Letters Received by the Commission Branch of the Adjutant General's Office. 1863–1870." M 1064.

"General Orders and Circulars of the War Department and Headquarters of the Army. 1809–1860." M 1094.

"U.S. Army General's Report of Civil War Service. 1864–1887." M 1098.

"Names and Subject Index to the Letters Received by the Appointment, Commission, and Personal Branch [ACP] of the Adjutant General's Office. 1871–1894." Dey's ACP File No. D. 505. C. B. 1865. M 1125.

"Union Battle Reports." Battle Report No. 216, Box 27.

"Indexes to Letters Received by the Office of the Adjutant General (Main Series). 1846, 1861–1889." M 725.

"Register of Letters Received, Office of the Adjutant General. 1812–1889." M 711.

"Letters Received by the Office of the Adjutant General (Main Series). 1822–1860." M 567.

"Letters Received by the Office of the Adjutant General (Main Series). 1861–1870." M 619.

"Letters Sent by the Office of the Adjutant General (Main Series). 1800–1890." M 565.

"Carded Medical Records." Entry 534.

"Index to Compiled Service Records of Volunteer Union Soldiers Who Served in Organizations from the State of Missouri." M 390.

"Index to Compiled Service Records of Volunteers Union Soldiers Who Served in Organizations from the State of Wisconsin." M 559.

Record Group 108: *Records of the Headquarters of the Army.*

"Letters Sent by the Headquarters of the Army (Main Series). 1828–1903." M 857.

Record Group 110: *Records of the Provost Marshal General's Bureau.*

"Reports and Decisions of the Provost Marshal General. 1863–1866." M 621.

Record Group 153: *Records of the Office of the Judge Advocate General (Army).*

"Register of the Records of the Proceeding of the U.S. Army General Courts-Martial. 1809–1890." M 1105.

Record Group 391: *Records of the United States Regular Army Mobile Units, 1821–1942.*

"Letters Sent. Dec. 1844–Feb. 1901." Entry 48 [hereafter E. + number].

"Endorsements Sent. Aug. 1851–Dec. 1888." E. 49.

"Register of Letters Received. July 1851–Feb. 1901." E. 52.

"Letters Received. 1846–1901." E. 53.

"Regimental Orders Issued. Jan. 1838–Feb. 1901." E. 55.

"Special Orders Received. 1853–65." E. 58.

"Letters, Orders, and Reports Received From or Relating to Members of the 2d Artillery ("Name File"). 1861–66." E. 61.

"Register of Regimental Officers. 1812–1899." E. 62.

"Records Relating to Regimental History. 1832–93." E. 64.

"Monthly Regimental Returns. 1835–1901." E. 65.

"Regimental Descriptive Books. 1860–78." E. 67.

"Descriptive Books for Batteries A–M. 1841–64." E. 68.

"List of Locations of Headquarters and Batteries. 1821–1900." E. 70.

"Proceedings of Regimental Court-Martial. Jan. 1830–Sept. 1833 and Dec. 1870–July 1879." E. 71.

"Descriptive Books of Recruits. Jan. 1847–Mar. 1856." E. 72.

"Recruiting Returns. 1853–98." E. 73.

"Recruiting Accounts, Descriptive Lists, and Accounts of Pay and Clothing. 1857, 1861–68, and 1895–1903." E. 74.

"Miscellaneous Records. 1860–1900." E. 76.

Record Group 393: *Records of the United States Continental Command, 1821–1920.*

"Letters Sent, Register of Letters Received, and Letters Received by Headquarters, Troops in Florida, and Headquarters, Department of Florida. 1850–1858." M 1084.

"Memoir of Reconnaissance With Maps During the Florida Campaign. Apr. 1854–Feb. 1858." M 1090.

"Brief Histories of the U.S. Army Commands (Army Posts) and Descriptions of Their Records." M T912.

"Letters Sent and Orders Issued. Nov. 1853–Jan. 1856." Department of Florida. E. 1639.

"Orders and Special Orders Issued. June 1855–Apr. 1858." Department of Florida. Part I. E. 1642.

"Miscellaneous Lists and Registers Relating to Artillery. n. d." Department of Missouri. E. 2718.

"Orders Issued by Gen. James Totten, Camp Harney, St. Louis. May–June 1861." Department of Missouri. E. 2868.

"Letters Sent by General Totten. Dec. 1861." E. 2869.

"Part I Register of Communications Pertaining to General Courts-Martial Received and Forwarded. Dec. 1862–Mar. 1869." Department of Washington. E. 5436.

"Orders and Special Orders. Dec. 1853–Dec. 1857." Department of Missouri. E. 5487.

"General Orders. Jan. 1858–Nov. 1861." Department of Missouri. E. 5488.

"Special Orders. Jan. 1858–Nov. 1861." Department of Missouri. E. 5489.

"General and Special Orders Received From Troops Serving in Kansas. May 1857–May 1858." Department of Missouri. E. 5490.

"Field and Post Returns. 1858–60." Department of Missouri. E. 5493.

"Letters Sent by Troops Serving in Kansas. May 1857–May 1858." Department of Missouri. E. 5506.

"General and Special Orders Issued by Troops Serving in Kansas. May 1857–May 1858." Department of Missouri. E. 5508.

"Orders Issued. May–June 1861." Department of Missouri. E. 5509.

"Letters Sent and General and Special Orders Issued. June–Aug. 1861." Department of Missouri. E. 5511.

"Part I Register of Proceedings of Garrison and Regimental Courts-Martial Received by the Acting Judge Advocate. Jan.–Nov. 1853." Also contains Army of the West, April 1857–January 1858. E. 5581.

"Letters Sent. Oct. 1862–July 1864." Department of Mississippi. E. 986.

"General Orders. 1862." Department of Mississippi. E. 992.

"General Orders. Jan. 1863–July 1864." Department of Mississippi. E. 993.

"Letters Sent. July 1862–March 1864. Special Orders Issued. Nov. 1863." Island No. 10. E. 594.

"Letters Sent. June–Sept. 1862." Corinth, Mississippi. E. 287.

"Letters Received. Aug.–Nov. 1862." Corinth. Mississippi. E. 289.

"Special Orders Issued. Sept. 1862." Corinth, Mississippi. E. 293.

"General Orders. Oct. 1863–Aug. 1866." Corinth, Mississippi. E. 2489.

"Special Orders. Oct. 1863–Aug. 1866." Corinth, Mississippi. E. 2491.

"Letters Received and Sent. Oct. 1863–July 1865." Camp Barry, Washington, D.C. E. 6656.

"General Orders. Oct. 1863–July 1865." Camp Barry, Washington, D.C. E. 6659.

"Special Orders. Oct. 1863–July 1865." Camp Barry, Washington, D.C. E. 6660.

"Roster of Officers. 1863–1865." Camp Barry, Washington, D.C. E. 6661.

"Letters Received. 1863–1865." Camp Barry, Washington, D.C. E. 91, Part 4.

"General Reports. Apr.–June 1865." Camp Barry, Washington, D.C. E. 92, Part 4.

"Letters Sent. Feb. 1863–May 1865." 6th Army Corps [AC], Artillery Brigade [AB]. E. 4448.

"Letters Received. Feb. 1863–Nov. 1864." 6th AC, AB. E. 4450.

"Register of Letters Received. Feb.–May 1865." 6th AC, AB. E. 4451.

"General Orders and Special Orders. May 1863–Sept. 1864." 6th AC, AB. E. 4454.

"Special Orders and Circulars. Oct. 1864–May 1865." 6th AC, AB. E. 4455.

"Roster of Officers." 6th AC, AB. E. 4457.

"Register of Leaves, etc. May 1863–Aug. 1864." 6th AC, AB. E. 4458.

"Furloughs. May 1863–Mar. 1864." 6th AC, AB. E. 4459.

Robert N. Scott, et al., ed. *The War of the Rebellion: A Compilation of the Official Records of the Union and Confederate Armies.* 70 vols. in 128 books. Washington, D.C.: U.S. Congress. 1881–1901. [Hereafter *OR: Armies*]

Annual Report of the Adjutant General of Missouri, Year Ending 31 December 1865. "1st and 2nd Missouri Light Artillery," State Historical Society: Columbia, Missouri, 399–417.

Adams, F. G., ed. "Governor Denver's Administration." *Transactions of the Kansas State Historical Society, 1889–'96* 5 (December 1857–September 1858), 464–559.

Reports of the Special Committee on the Troubles in Kansas. U.S. House of Representatives. Report No. 200, 34th Congress, 1st Session. 1856.

Death Records, Ontario County [NY]: *1803–1880.*

Federal Census Records (Ontario County Only), 1840, 1850.

George R. Smith Papers, "A 20-page Summary of Brigadier General James Totten's Court Martial, c. 1870." Item no. 1028, Western Historical Manuscript Collection, University of Missouri, Columbia, Missouri.

Other Sources:

Newspapers:

"Arrears of Pensions." Editorial. *The Fredonia* [NY] *Censor,* February 15, 1882.

"A Soldier's Account of the Battle of Boonville." *Chariton Courier,* August 8, 1824.

"Federal General John Pope Establishes Base of Operations Against Island No. 10." *Arkansas Gazette,* April 8, 1862.

Obituary Lieutenant Albert M. Murray. *Ontario County Times*, Sept. 14, Sept. 21 and Oct. 5, 1864.

"75th Anniversary of the Battle of Boonville, Missouri." *Boonville Daily News*, June 23, 1936.

"75th Anniversary of the Battle of Boonville, Missouri." *Boonville Advertiser*, June 26, 1936.

"75th Anniversary of the Battle of Boonville, Missouri." *Kansas City Times*, June 17, 1936.

Walden, Colonel C. J. "The Battle of Boonville." *Kansas City Times*, June 21, 1929.

Wilkie, Franc. "The Iowa First [Regiment] Letters from the War." *The Dubuque Herald*, April 24, 1861 to August 10, 1861.

Articles and Periodicals:

Adams, George R. "The Caloosahatchee Massacre: Its Significance in the Second Seminole War." *Florida Historical Quarterly* 48, no. 4 (April 1970), 371. Map only.

"Atlanta: Special Campaign Issue." *Civil Times Illustrated* 3, no. 4 (July 1964), 8–17.

Barry, Louise. "The Fort Leavenworth-Fort Gibson Military Road and the Founding of Fort Scott." *Kansas Historical Quarterly* 11, no. 1 (February 1942), 115–129.

Bock, Lynn N. "Confederate Occupation and Union Siege and Capture of New Madrid, Missouri and Island No. 10 on the Mississippi River: August 1861 to April 1862." Monograph. New Madrid Historical Museum.

Broadhead, Lt. Col. James O. 3rd Cavalry, Missouri State Militia, USV. "Early Events of the War in Missouri." *War Papers and Personal Reminiscences, 1861–1865. Military Order of the Loyal Legions of the United States* [*MOLLUS*] vol. 1, St. Louis, (1892), 1–28.

Brown, Dee. "Wilson's Creek." *Civil War Times Illustrated* 11, no. 1, (April 1972), 8–18.

Byers, S. H. M. "The Battle of Iuka." *The Iowa Historical Record* 3, no. 4 (October 1887), 543–552.

Cannon, M. Hamlin. "Winfield Scott and the Utah Expedition." *Military History* 4 (1941), 208–210.

Castel, Albert. "Battle Without a Victor...Iuka." *Civil War Times Illustrated* 11, no. 6 (October 1972), 12–18.

Chase, Charles Monroe. "A Union Band Director Views Camp Rolla." *Missouri Historical Review* 55, no. 4 (July 1961), 307–343.

Cheever, L. "100 Days to Glory." *The Palimpest* 53 (November 1972), 469–498.

Covington, James W. "The Camp Jackson Affair: 1861." *Missouri Historical Review* 55, no. 3 (April 1961), 197–212.

———. "An Episode in the Third Seminole War." *Florida Historical Quarterly* 45, no. 1 (July 1966), 45–49.

Davis, Major General Jefferson C. "Campaigning in Missouri: Civil War Memoir of General Jefferson C. Davis." James P. Jones, ed. *Missouri Historical Review* 54, no. 1 (October 1959), 39–45.

DuBois, John van Deusen. "The Civil War Journals and Letters of Colonel John Deusen DuBois: April 12, 1861 to October 16, 1862." Jared C. Lobdell, ed. *Missouri Historical Review,* pt. 1, vol. 60 (July 1966), 436–459; pt. 2, vol. 61 (October 1966), 21–50.

Eckhardt, C. P. "A Problem of Rank." *Civil War Times Illustrated* 29, no. 6 (January–February 1991), 52–54.

Friederich, Robert. "Reminiscences of Wilson's Creek." *National Tribune* (January 10, 1884), 7: col. 1–2.

Fuller, John Wallace. "Our Kirby Smith." *Ohio Commandery, MOLLUS.* Cincinnati: H. C. Sherrick and Company. Paper read March 2, 1887.

Gallaher, Ruth A. "With Sword." *The Palimpest* 13, no. 11 (November 1932), 429–440.

Garnett, Carroll M. "A Special Response." [a letter about CSA Generals Richard Brooke A., and Robert Selden Garnett]. *Blue and Gray* 4, no. 6 (June–July 1987), 4–7.

Guttman, John. " 'Old Abe' Goes to War." *America's Civil War* (November 1990), 26–33.

Horton, Hugh. "Confederate Brass." *The Battle of Corinth: 125th Anniversary Official Souvenir Program.* Sponsored by the Northeast Mississippi Museum Association, Inc. (October 1–4, 1987), 8–10.

Humphrey, James. "The Country West of Topeka Prior to 1865." *Transactions of the Kansas State Historical Society: 1886–1888,* Compiled by F. G. Adams, 392–407.

Kennedy, Gerald. "U.S. Army Hospital, Keokuk, 1862–1865." *Annals of Iowa.* Third Series. 40, no. 2 (Fall 1969), 118–136.

Kirkpatrick, Arthur Roy. "Missouri in the Early Months of the Civil War." *Missouri Historical Review* 55, no. 3 (April 1961), 235–266.

Longacre, Edward G. "All Is Fair in Love and War." *Civil War Times Illustrated* 8, no. 3 (June 1969), 235–266.

———. "A General Vanquished in the West." *Civil War Times Illustrated* 24, no. 6 (October 1985), 16 ff.

Mahon, John K., ed. "Letters from the Second Seminole War." *Florida Historical Quarterly* 36, no. 4 (April 1958), 353. Map only.

Martin, George W. "The Territorial and Military Combine at Fort Riley." *Transactions of the Kansas State Historical Society* 7, 361–390. Address delivered September 21, 1901.

Martin, Richard. "First Regiment of Iowa Volunteers." *The Palimpest* 46, no. 1 (January 1965), 1–60.

McKenzie, John D. "Showdown in the West: Grant-Rosecrans." *Civil War* 11, no. 2, issue 40 (March–April 1993).

McLain, David. "The Story of Old Abe." *The Wisconsin Magazine of History* 8, no. 4 (June 1925), 407–414.

Merk, Frederick. "The Story of Old Abe." *The Wisconsin Magazine of History* 2 (September 1918), 82–84.

Moore, Frank. "The Eagle of Corinth." *The Civil War in Song and Poetry.* [no place given]; P. E. Collier, 1889. Reprinted in the *Battle of Corinth: 125th Anniversary Official Souvenir Program.* Sponsored by the Northeast Mississippi Museum Association, Inc. (October 1–4, 1987), 6.

Mudd, Joseph. "What I Saw at Wilson's Creek." *Missouri Historical Review* 7, no. 2 (January 1913), 91–105.

Nash, Howard P. "The Story of Island No. 10." *Civil War Times Illustrated* 5, no. 8 (December 1966), 42–47.

New Madrid [Mo.] Historical Museum. "The Siege of New Madrid" and "The Battle of Island No. 10." Monographs prepared by the museum. n.d.

Nesbit, Philander H. "Eight Months in Missouri." Norman Stewart, ed. *Missouri Historical Review* 75, no. 3 (April 1981), 261–284.

Nicolay, John G., and John Hay. "Abraham Lincoln: A History." *The Century Magazine,* vol. 34; New series, vol. 12 (May 1887 to October 1887), 82–110; 203–219; 369–396; 509 ff; 658–684; 819–850.

Nye, Colonel W. S. "How CW Artillery Was Aimed." *Civil War Times Illustrated* 3, no. 5 (August 1964), 22–25.

———. "Implements for Loading and Fuzing CW Artillery." *Civil War Times Illustrated* 3, no. 6 (October 1964), 32–35.

O'Connor, Henry. "With the First Iowa Infantry." *The Palimpest* 3, no. 2 (February 1922), 53–61.

———. "An Extract from Henry O'Connor History of the First Regiment of Iowa Volunteer Infantry." *Annals of Iowa* 1, no. 3 (July 1863), 135–139.

Oates, Stephen B. "A Personality Profile of Nathaniel Lyon." *Civil War Times Illustrated* 6, no. 10 (February 1968), 15–25.

Parkhurst, Clint. "The Attack on Corinth." *The Palimpest* 3, no. 6 (June 1922), 169–191.

———. "The Siege of Corinth." *The Palimpest* 4, no. 1 (January 1923), 1–13.

Poll, Richard D., and Ralph W. Hansen. "Buchanan's Blunder: The Utah War. 1857–1858." *Military Affairs* 25 (1961–1962), 121–131.

Robbins, Peggy. "The Battle of Camp Jackson." *Civil War Times Illustrated* 20, no. 3 (June 1981), 34–43.

Rogers, Margaret Greene. "Corinth, 1861–65." Publication A-0002. Rev. May 4, 1990. Corinth, Miss.: Northeast Mississippi Museum, n.d.

———. "Chronological Order of Events—Battle of Corinth." Publication A-0003. Rev. May 4, 1990. Corinth, Miss.: Northeast Mississippi Museum, n.d.

Rogge, Robert E. "Devil at the Crossroads." *America's Civil War* (September 1990), 42–49.

Scassellati, Robert R., Jr. "First Shots at Fort Barrancas." *Civil War Times Illustrated* 11, no. 9 (January 1973), 38–43.

Simpson, Lieutenant W. A., Adjutant, 2nd U.S. Artillery. "The Second Regiment of Artillery." *Journal of the Military Service Institution of the U.S.* 14 (1893), 905–920.

Small, Lieutenant Colonel William E. "Letter of Lieut. Col. Wm. E. Small—HQs 10th Iowa Camp Near Corinth, Miss. October 28, 1862." *Annals of Iowa* 1, no. 2 (April 1863), 87. Letter to governor of Iowa sending him their regimental flag for depositing it with the State Historical Society.

Smith, Donald. "Boonville [Miss.]—Where Sheridan Won a Battle and His General's Star." *Civil War Times Illustrated* 1, no. 6 (October 1962), 32–34.

Stimson, Byron. "Battle of Tupelo [Miss.]." *Civil War Times Illustrated* 11, no. 4 (July 1972), 4.

Suhr, Robert Collins. "Attack Written Deep and Crimson." *America's Civil War* (September 1991), 46–52.

Sullivan, Brigadier General Jeremiah C. "Corinth." *Annals of Iowa* 1, no. 3 (July 1863), 140. Letter transmitting a stand "of rebel colors" to the governor of the state.

Taylor, Hawkins. "General [Samuel R.] Curtis." *The Iowa Historical Record* 3, no. 4 (October 1887), 561–567.

Thompson, William Candace. "From Shiloh to Port Gibson." *Civil War Times Illustrated* 3, no. 6 (October 1964), 20–25.

Tracy, Albert. "Missouri in Crisis: The Journal of Captain Albert Tracy." Ray W. Irwin, ed. *Missouri Historical Review* pt. 1, 51, no. 1 (October 1956), 8–21; pt. 2, 5, no. 2 (January 1957), 151–164; pt. 3, 51, no. 3 (April 1957), 270–283.

Trimble, Tony L. "Death Struggle for Missouri." *Civil War* 11, no. 3, issue 41 (May–June 1993).

Unnerstall, Jay. "Unprovoked Tragicomedy in St. Louis." *America's Civil War*, (May 1991), 30–36.

Walsh, Edward. "Birthplace of the Ku Klux Klan." *The Washington Post*, (January 26, 1993), A 3.

Watkins, Raymond W. "A Partial List of Confederate Deaths at Island No. 10, Tennessee and Nearby Madrid Bend, Tennessee." Compiled from Record Group 109, *War Department Collection of Confederate Records*. National Archives, Washington, D.C.

Welty, Raymond. "Supplying the Frontier Military Posts." *Kansas Historical Quarterly* 7 (1938), 154–169.

"Roster of Wisconsin Volunteers." *Wisconsin: War of the Rebellion 1861– 1865*. Vol. 1. Compiled by Authority of the Legislature Under the Direction of Jeremiah M. Rash, Governor, and Chandler P. Chapman, Adjutant General. Madison, Wisc.: Legislature, 1886.

Books:

Anders, Leslie. *The Twenty-First Missouri: From Home Guard to Union Regiment*. Westport: Greenwood Press, 1975.

Andrews, J. Cutter. *The North Reports the War*. Pittsburgh: University of Pittsburgh Press, 1955.

Anderson, Ephraim McD., and Edwin C. Bearss. *Memoirs: Historical and Personal of the First Missouri Confederate Brigade*. Saint Louis: Times Printing Co., 1868. Second edition with notes by Bearss. Dayton: Morningside Bookshop, 1988.

A Standard History of Portage County, Wisconsin. Vol. 1. Chicago: The Lewis Publishing Company, 1919.

Averall, William Woods. *Ten Years in the Saddle*. Edward K. Eckert and Nicholas J. Amato, eds. San Raphael: Presidio Press, 1978.

Bartels, Carolyn M. *The Civil War in Missouri: Day by Day: 1861–1865*. Shawnee: Two Trails Genealogical Society, distributor, 1992.

Battles and Leaders. Secaucus, N.J.: Castle, 1887. Four volumes.

Bearss, Edwin C. *The Battle of Wilson's Creek*. Third edition. Republic: Wilson's Creek National Battlefield Foundation, 1988.

Bearss, Edwin C., and Arrell M. Gibson. *Fort Smith: Little Gibraltar on the Arkansas.* Second edition. Norman: Oklahoma University Press, 1979.

Bergeron, Arthur W., Jr. *Guide to Louisiana Confederate Military Units, 1861–1865.* Baton Rouge: Louisiana State University Press, 1989.

Billings, John D. *Hardtack and Coffee.* Bowie, Md.: Heritage Books, 1990.

Birkhimer, William W. *The Artillery, United States Army, Historical Sketch of the Organization, Administration, Materiel and Tactics.* Originally published by James J. Chapman, 1884. Reprint. New York: Greenwood Press, 1968.

Boatner, Mark Mayo, III. *The Civil War Dictionary.* New York: David McKay Company, 1959.

Botkin, B. A., ed. *A Civil War Treasury of Tales, Legends, and Folklore.* New York: Promontory Press, 1988.

Bradley, James. *Confederate Mail Carrier.* Mexico, Mo.: James Bradley, 1894. Reprint. Bowie, Md.: Heritage Books, 1990.

Britton, Wiley. *The Civil War on the Border.* Third edition. New York: G. P. Putnam's Sons, 1899. Reprint. Two volumes. Kansas Heritage Press, 1990.

———. *Memoirs of the Rebellion on the Border, 1863.* Chicago: Thomas Cushing Company, 1882. Reprint. Inland Printer, Ltd., 1986.

Burns, William S. *Recollections of the 4th Missouri Artillery.* Frank Allen Dennis, ed. Dayton: Morningside Bookshop, 1988.

Byers, S. H. M. *With Fire and Sword.* New York: The Neale Publishing Company, 1911. Reprint. Iowa City: Camp Pope Bookshop, 1992.

Canandaigua Roll of Honor: 1871. Unpublished, handwritten manuscript. Ontario County Historical Society, Canandaigua, New York.

Carley, Kenneth. *Minnesota in the Civil War.* Minneapolis: Ross and Haines, 1961.

Castel, Albert. *A Frontier State at War, 1861–1865.* Lawrence: Kansas Heritage Press, 1992.

———. *Decision in the West: The Atlanta Campaign of 1864.* Lawrence: University Press of Kansas, 1992.

———. *General Sterling Price, and the War in the West.* Baton Rouge: Louisiana State Press, 1968.

Cater, Douglas John. *As It Was: Reminiscences of a Soldier of the Third Texas Cavalry and the Nineteenth Louisiana Infantry.* Austin: State House Press, 1990.

Catton, Bruce. *The Coming Fury.* Garden City: Doubleday, 1961.

———. *Terrible Swift Sword.* Garden City: Doubleday, 1963.

Cockrell, Monroe, F., ed. *The Lost Account of the Battle of Corinth and the Court Martial of General van Dorn*. Wilmington, N.C.: Broadfoot Publishing Company, 1987.

Coffman, Edward M. *The Old Army: A Portrait of the American Army in Peacetime, 1784–1898*. New York: Oxford University Press, 1986.

Conover, George S., ed., and Lewis Cass Aldrich, compiler. *History of Ontario County, New York*. Syracuse: D. Mason and Co., 1893.

Cooke, Donald E. *For Conspicuous Gallantry*. Maplewood, N.J.: Hammond and Young, 1966.

Cooling, Benjamin Franklin, III, and Walton H. Owen, II. *Mr. Lincoln's Forts*. Shippensburg: White Mane Publishing Company, 1988.

Covington, James W. *The Seminoles of Florida*. Gainesville: University Press of Florida, 1993.

Cozzens, Peter. *This Terrible Sound: The Battle of Chickamauga*. Urbana: University of Illinois Press, 1992.

Cullom, George W., Bvt. Maj. Gen. *Biographical Register of the Officers and Graduates of the U.S. Military Academy*. Third edition, vol. 2. Boston and New York: Houghton, Mifflin and Company, 1891.

Davies, Wallace Evans. *Patriotism on Parade*. Cambridge: Harvard University Press, 1955.

Denney, Robert E. *Civil War Medicine*. New York: Sterling Publishing Co., Inc., 1995.

Dial, Marshall. *The Bootheel Swamp Struggle*. Lilbourn, Mo.: Lloyd Publications, 1961.

Dornbusch, Charles E. *Military Bibliography of the Civil War*. Three volumes. New York: The New York Public Library, 1961–1972.

Downey, Fairfax. *Sound of the Guns*. New York: David McKay Co., Inc., 1955.

Dyer, Frederick H. *A Compendium of the War of the Rebellion*. Three volumes. New York: Thomas Yoseloff, 1908.

Eakin, Joanne Chiles. *Battle at Blackwater River*. Independence, Mo.: Print America, 1995.

Eisenschimal, Otto, and Ralph Newman. *An American Iliad*. Indianapolis: Bobbs-Merrill, 1947.

Force, M. F. *Fort Henry to Corinth*. New York: Charles Scribner and Sons, 1881. Reprint. Wilmington, N.C.: Broadfoot Publishing Company, 1989.

Freehling, William W. *The Road to Disunion*. New York: Oxford University Press, 1990.

Gentry, Claude. *The Battle of Corinth.* Baldwyn, Miss.: Magnolia Publishers, 1976.

Gonzalez, Thomas. *The Caloosahatchee.* 1932. A facsimile reproduction by the Southwest Florida Historical Society. Fort Myers Beach: The Island Press, 1982.

Gorgas, Colonel J. *The Ordnance Manual, for the Use of the Officers of the Confederate Army.* Charleston, S.C.: Evans and Cogswell, 1863. Reprint. Dayton: Morningside Bookshop, 1976.

Grebner, Constantine. *We Were the Ninth: A History of the Ninth Ohio Volunteer Infantry: April 17, 1861 to June 7, 1864.* Frederic Trautman, ed. and trans. Kent: The Kent State University Press, 1987.

Grismer. Karl H. *The Story of Fort Myers.* 1949. Facsimile reproduction. Fort Myers Beach: The Island Press, 1982.

Guernsey, Alfred H., and Henry M. Alden. *Harper's Pictorial History of the Civil War.* Facsimile reproduction of the 1866 edition. New York: The Fairfax Press, n.d.

Hanna, Alfred Jackson, and Kathryn Abbey Hanna. *Lake Okeechobee.* New York: Bobbs-Merrill, 1948.

Hatcher, Richard W., and William G. Piston, eds. *Kansans at Wilson's Creek: Soldier's Letters from the Campaign for Southwest Missouri.* Springfield, Mo.: Wilson's Creek National Battlefield Foundation, 1993.

Hattaway, Herman, and Archer Jones. *How the North Won.* Urbana: Illinois University Press, paperback edition, 1991.

Haythornthwaite, Philip J. *Invincible Generals.* Bloomington: Indiana University Press, 1992.

Heitman, Francis B. *Historical Record and Dictionary of the United States Army.* Two volumes. Washington: Government Printing Office, 1903. Reprint. Gaithersburg, Md.: Olde Soldier Books, Inc., Second edition, 1988.

Hesseltine, William B., ed. *Civil War Prisons.* Kent: The Kent State University Press, 1992.

Hicken, Victor. *Illinois in the Civil War.* Second edition. Urbana: University of Illinois Press, 1991.

Hinton, Richard Josiah. *Rebel Invasion of Missouri and Kansas, and the Campaign of the Army of the Border Against General Sterling Price.* Chicago: Church and Goodman, 1865.

Holcombe, Return I., and W. S. Adams. *An Account of the Battle of Wilson's Creek or Oak Hills.* Springfield: Dow and Adams, 1883. Reprint. The Greene County [Mo.] Historical Society, 1985.

Imholte, J. Q. *The First Volunteers: History of the First Minnesota Volunteer Regiment, 1861–1865*. Minneapolis: Ross and Haines, 1963.

Ingenthron, Elmo. *Borderland Rebellion*. Branson, Mo.: The Ozark Mountaineer, 1980.

Jackman, John S. *Diary of a Confederate Soldier*. William C. Davis, ed. Columbia: University of South Carolina Press, 1990.

Jones, Archer. *Confederate Strategy from Shiloh to Vicksburg*. Baton Rouge: Louisiana State University Press, 1991.

Krick, Robert K. *Lee's Colonels*. Dayton: Morningside Bookshop, 1979.

Lamcas, William, M. *The Edge of Glory: A Biography of General William S. Rosecrans*. New York: Harcourt Brace and World, 1961.

Leach, Margaret. *Reveille in Washington*. New York: Harpers, 1941.

Long, E. B. *The Civil War Day by Day*. New York: Doubleday, 1971.

Longacre, Edward G. *The Man Behind the Guns*. New York: A. S. Barnes and Company, 1977.

Lossing, Benson, J. *Harper's Popular Encyclopedia of the United States History to 1876*. Two volumes. New York: Harpers, 1881.

———. *Harper's Encyclopedia of United States History 458 A. D. to 1905*. 10 volumes. New York: Harpers, 1906.

———. *Matthew Brady's Illustrated History of the Civil War*. New York: The Fairfax Press, n.d.

Lowe, Percival G. *Five Years a Dragoon*. Norman: University of Oklahoma Press, 1965.

McClellan, Phyllis I. *The Artillerymen of Historic Fort Monroe, Virginia*. Bowie, Md.: Heritage Books, 1991.

McConnell, Stuart. *Glorious Contentment: The Grand Army of the Republic*. Chapel Hill: The University of North Carolina Press, 1992.

McPherson, James M. *Battle Cry of Freedom*. New York: Oxford University Press, 1988.

Meyer, Steve. *Iowa Valor*. Garrison, Ia.: Meyer Publishing, 1994.

Miles, Jim. *Field of Glory*. Nashville: Rutledge Hill Press, 1989.

Milliken, Charles F. *History of Ontario County, New York and Its People*. Two volumes. New York: Historical Publishing Company, 1911.

Monaghan, Jay. *Civil War on the Western Border, 1854–1865*. Lincoln: University of Nebraska Press, 1955.

Morgan, James A., III. *Always Ready, Always Willing*. Gaithersburg, Md.: Olde Soldier Books, Inc., n.d.

Morrison, James L., Sr. *The Best School in the World*. Kent: The Kent State University Press, 1986.

Mudd, Joseph A. *With Porter in Missouri.* Washington, D.C.: National Publishing Company, 1909. Reprint. Iowa City: Camp Pope Book Shop, 1991.

Munden, Kenneth W., and Henry Putney Beers. *The Union: A Guide to Federal Archives Relating to the Civil War.* Washington: National Archives and Records Administration, 1986.

Ness, George T., Jr. *The Regular Army on the Eve of the Civil War.* Baltimore: Toomey Press, 1990.

Official Roster of the Soldiers of the State of Ohio in the War of the Rebellion, 1861–1865. Vol. 3, 21st–36th Regiments-Infantry. Cincinnati: The Ohio Valley Publishing and Manufacturing Company, 1886.

Phillips, Christopher. *Damned Yankee: The Life of General Nathaniel Lyon.* Columbia: University of Missouri Press, 1990.

Price, Captain Richard Scott. *Nathaniel Lyon: Harbinger from Kansas.* Springfield: The Wilson's Creek National Battlefield Foundation, 1990.

Prucha, Francis Paul. *A Guide to the Military Posts of the United States, 1789–1895.* Madison: The State Historical Society of Wisconsin, 1964.

Quines, E. B. *The Military History of Wisconsin.* Two volumes. Madison: Clark and Company, 1866.

Reese, Timothy J. *Sykes' Regular Infantry Division, 1861–1864.* Jefferson, N.C.: McFarland and Company, Inc., 1990.

Reid, Whitelaw. *Ohio in the War.* Two volumes. Columbus: Electric Publishing Company, 1893.

Rogers, Margaret Greene. *Civil War: Corinth, 1861–1865.* Corinth: Rankin Printery, 1989 edition.

Rowell, John W. *Yankee Artillerymen.* Knoxville: University of Tennessee Press, 1973.

Ruby, James S., ed. *Blue and Gray: Georgetown University and the Civil War.* Washington, D.C.: Georgetown University Alumni Association, 1961.

Sauers, Richard A. *"To Care for Him Who Has Borne the Battle": Research Guide to Civil War Material in the National Tribune.* Jackson, Ky.: History Shop Press, 1995.

Schutz, Wallace J., and Walter N. Trenery. *Abandoned by Lincoln: A Military Biography of General John Pope.* Urbana: University of Illinois Press, 1990.

Scott, Joe M. *Four Years' Service in the Southern Army.* Mulberry, Ark.: Leader Office Print Company, 1897. Second reprint. Fayetteville, Ark.: Washington County Historical Society, 1992.

Sherman, William T. *Sherman: Memoirs of General W. T. Sherman.* Two volumes in one. New York: Literary Classics, 1990.

Smith, Charles H. *The History of Fuller's Ohio Brigade, 1861–1865.* Cleveland: no publisher noted, 1909.

Smith, Page. *Trial by Fire.* New York: McGraw-Hill, 1982.

Snead, Thomas L. *The Fight for Missouri from the Election of Lincoln to the Death of Lyon.* New York: Charles Scribner's Sons, 1886.

Soldiers Buried at Union Cemetery, Kansas City, Mo. 1988. Union Cemetery Historical Society, 227 East 28th Street, Kansas City, Mo. 64108.

Stampp, Kenneth M. *America in 1857: A Nation on the Brink.* New York: Oxford University Press, 1990.

Stanley, David S. *Personal Memoirs of Major General David S. Stanley.* Cambridge: Harvard University Press, 1917. Reprint. Gaithersburg, Md.: Olde Soldier Books, Inc., 1987.

Stanton, Donald J., Goodwin F. Berquist, and Paul C. Bowers, eds. *The Civil War Reminiscences of General M. Jeff Thompson.* Dayton: Morningside Bookshop, 1988.

Strayer, Larry M., and Richard A. Baumgartner, eds. *Echoes of Battle: The Atlanta Campaign.* Huntington, W.Va.: Blue Acorn Press, 1991.

Thian, Raphael B. *Notes Illustrating the Military Geography of the United States, 1813–1880.* John M. Carroll, ed. Austin: University of Texas Press, 1979.

Thomas, Dean S. *Cannons.* Gettysburg: Thomas Publications, 1990.

Trudeau, Noah Andre. *Bloody Roads South: The Wilderness to Cold Harbor, May–June 1864.* Boston: Little, Brown and Company, 1989.

Tucker, Phillip Thomas. *Westerners in Gray: The Men and Missions of the Elite Fifth Missouri Infantry Regiment.* Jefferson, N.C.: McFarland and Company, 1995.

Tunnard, Willie H., and Edwin C. Bearss. *A Southern Record: The Story of the Third Louisiana Infantry, CSA.* Baton Rouge: Printed for the Author, 1866. Facsimile reprint. Dayton: Morningside Bookshop, 1970.

Utley, Robert M. *Frontiersmen in Blue.* Lincoln: University of Nebraska Press, 1981.

———. *Frontier Regulars.* Lincoln: University of Nebraska Press, 1984.

———. *The Indian Frontier.* Albuquerque: University of New Mexico Press, 1984.

Ware, E. F. *The Lyon Campaign: Being a History of the First Iowa Infantry.* Topeka: Crane and Company, 1907. Reprint. Iowa City: Camp Pope Bookshop, 1991.

Warner, Ezra J. *Generals in Blue*. Baton Rouge: Louisiana University Press, 1964.

———. *Generals in Gray*. Baton Rouge: Louisiana State University Press, 1953.

Watson, William. *Life in the Confederate Army*. London: Chapman and Hall, 1887. Reprint. Baton Rouge: University of Louisiana Press, 1995.

Weighley, Russell F. *History of the United States Army*. New York: Macmillan Publishing Co., Inc., 1967.

Weinert, Richard P. Jr., and Robert Arthur, Colonel. *Defender of the Chesapeake: The Story of Fort Monroe*. Third edition. Shippensburg: White Mane Publishing Company, Inc., 1989.

Wiley, Bell I. *The Common Soldier in the Civil War*. New York: Grosset and Dunlop, n.d.

Wilkenson, Warren. *Mother, May You Never See the Sights I Have Seen*. New York: Harper and Row, 1990.

Woodruff, W. E. *With the Light Guns in '61–'65*. Little Rock: Central Printing Company, 1903. Facsimile reprint. Little Rock: Eagle Press of Little Rock, n.d.

Woodworth, Steven E. *Jefferson Davis and His Generals*. Lawrence: University Press of Kansas, 1990.

Wright, Sister Catherine. *Port O' Bladensburg*. Bladensburg, Md.: Printed by Friends of Sister Catherine Wright, 1977.

Index